Germaine de Staël,
George Sand,

AND THE

Victorian Woman
Artist

Germaine de Staël, George Sand,

AND THE

Victorian Woman Artist

LINDA M. LEWIS

University of Missouri Press   Columbia and London

Copyright © 2003 by
The Curators of the University of Missouri
University of Missouri Press, Columbia, Missouri 65201
Printed and bound in the United States of America
All rights reserved
5 4 3 2 1   07 06 05 04 03

Library of Congress Cataloging-in-Publication Data

Lewis, Linda M., 1942–
    Germaine de Staël, George Sand, and the Victorian woman
artist / Linda M. Lewis.
        p. cm.
    Includes bibliographical references and index.
    ISBN 0-8262-1455-X (alk. paper)
    1. English literature—Women authors—History and criti-
cism.   2. Women artists in literature.   3. Women and literature—Great Britain—History—19th century.   4. Art and
literature—Great Britain—History—19th century.   5. English
literature—19th century—History and criticism.   6. Staël,
Madame de (Anne-Louise-Germaine), 1766–1817. Corinne.
7. Sand, George, 1804–1876. Consuelo.   8. English literature—
French influences.   I. Title.
PR468.W6 L49   2003
809.3'93527—dc21

                                                    2002044410

    ⊚™ This paper meets the requirements of the
    American National Standard for Permanence of Paper
        for Printed Library Materials, Z39.48, 1984.

            Designer: Kristie Lee
    Typesetter: The Composing Room of Michigan, Inc.
Printer and binder: The Maple-Vail Book Manufacturing Group
    Typefaces: Adobe Garamond and Decoration Pi One

        This book has been published with the generous
        assistance of a contribution from the Burmeister
        grant of Bethany College, Lindsborg, Kansas.

In memory of
Margaret H. Mountcastle

CONTENTS

ACKNOWLEDGMENTS

TRUDY LEWIS AND DIANE LONG HOEVELER read various pieces of this manuscript and offered helpful insights; to both I express my gratitude. I also thank J. David Arnott, whose musical knowledge I exploited, and Marguerite Dorsch, whose French skills augmented my deficiencies. Conversations with Philip Coleman-Hull helped me clarify certain aesthetic notions, and I gratefully acknowledge such rich colloquy. Bethany College librarian Elaine Bean provided invaluable assistance in locating obscure literary texts; I am grateful to her and to Denise Carson, library director. I am especially indebted to two perceptive readers selected by the University of Missouri Press. Their identities are unknown to me, but their thoughtful and detailed commentary was of enormous value as I revised. A thousand thanks to both.

Institutions deserving acknowledgment include Bethany College for the 2000–2001 sabbatical leave in which I wrote the initial draft of the book, the libraries of the University of Wisconsin–Madison and the University of Kansas, the New York City Public Library, and especially the University of Missouri Press. The professionalism of Editor-in-Chief Beverly Jarrett and her excellent staff merits all the thankfulness I can express. Clair Willcox, Jane Lago, and Julianna Schroeder of the press have been invariably patient and generous.

I am grateful to my husband, Frank Lewis, who lived with me as I lived within this book. His forbearance and good humor sustain me. In addition I enjoy the love and faith of a wonderful family: Terry, Trudy, Mike, Tom, Sylvia, Cliff, Lauren, Madeline, Nicholas, Edward, and Jude—my children and grandchildren.

This book owes much to the late Margaret H. Mountcastle, whose generous gift funds the Mountcastle Distinguished Chair of Humanities at Bethany College. When I was appointed as Mountcastle Professor, my patron and I embarked on an epistolary friendship, and her enthusiastic support of this project ceased only with her death in 2002. The book is fondly dedicated to her memory.

ABBREVIATIONS

Elizabeth Barrett Browning

AL	*Aurora Leigh (Ohio University Press, 1992)*
BC	*The Brownings' Correspondence*
CWEBB	*The Complete Works of Elizabeth Barrett Browning*

George Eliot

A	*Armgart*
AB	*Adam Bede*
DD	*Daniel Deronda*
FH	*Felix Holt*
GEL	*The Yale Edition of the George Eliot Letters*
M	*Middlemarch*
MF	*The Mill on the Floss*
R	*Romola*
SCL	*Scenes from Clerical Life*
WGE	*The Writings of George Eliot Together with the Life by J. W. Cross*

Geraldine Jewsbury

HS	*The Half Sisters*

George Sand

CCR	*Consuelo,* and *La Comtesse de Rudolstadt*
LGS	*The Letters of George Sand*

Germaine de Staël

C   *Corinne*

Mrs. Humphry (Mary Augusta) Ward

DG   *The History of David Grieve*
MB   *Miss Bretherton*
RE   *Robert Elsmere*
WR   *A Writer's Recollections*

Germaine de Staël,
George Sand,

AND THE

Victorian Woman
Artist

INTRODUCTION

IN THE NINETEENTH CENTURY increasing numbers of women aspired to become poets, painters, actresses, and musicians, as well as novelists who painted fictional portraits of woman-as-artist. Among female Victorian artists paternal power was everywhere apparent. Charlotte Yonge was required to submit her novels for the approval of her father and the Anglican priest John Keble. Frances Julia Wedgwood, of the Wedgwood pottery dynasty, wrote her first novel in secret but had to subject the second to paternal censorship. There was no third Wedgwood novel. The father of poet Elizabeth Barrett criticized her poems, received her dedications, and, most famously, forbade her marriage—an edict she defied when, at age thirty-nine, she eloped with her muse Robert Browning. But the power of patriarchy extended beyond the biological fathers, for the patriarchs of culture published and criticized literature, organized and promoted art exhibitions, and mounted and directed theatrical events.

As the fathers were sponsors and patrons, the sons were the artists. Victorian poet Gerard Manly Hopkins and Impressionist painter Auguste Renoir suggest that the *manly* appendage symbolizes creativity—the pen or paintbrush ejaculating beauty and truth upon the canvas or the page. Honoré de Balzac, of like mind, conferred metaphorical male gonads upon his "comrade" George Sand, whom he considered a great artist, *ergo* a man.[1] Long before Virginia Woolf's painter Lily Briscoe heard the insidious mantra "Women can't write. Women can't paint," the little French girl Aurore Lucile Dupin must have gotten the

1. Criticizing the artists Frederick Walker and Edward Burne-Jones, Hopkins says, "Now this is the artist's most essential quality, masterly execution: it is a kind of male gift and especially marks off men from women, the begetting one's thought on paper, on verse, or whatever the matter is. . . ." (*The Correspondence of Gerard Manley Hopkins and Richard Watson Dixon*, 133). Whitney Chadwick quotes Renoir's comment "I paint with my prick" in *Women, Art, and Society* (266), but the painter's misogyny was well known; in an 1891 issue of *Mercure de France*, Albert Aurier commented upon Renoir's vacuous women as rosy, plump dolls without souls or intellect (Dijkstra, *Idols of Perversity: Fantasies of Feminine Evil in Fin-de-Siècle Culture*, 181). Of George Sand, Balzac says, "She is masculine . . . she is an artist . . . she has the noble characteristics of a man, *ergo* she is not a woman" (Naginski, *George Sand: Writing for Her Life*, 1).

word. So Aurore donned trousers, was metamorphosed into George Sand, and inspired a proliferation of English Georges: Three Brontë sisters published under the masculine pseudonyms Currer, Acton, and Ellis Bell; Elizabeth Robins used the pen name C. E. Raimond; Geraldine Jewsbury considered changing her name to Gerald; Mary Ann (or Marian) Evans became George Eliot; Emily Simonds published as George Paston; and Mary Bright wrote as George Egerton. In the words of a male character commenting upon the actress/protagonist in Jewsbury's novel *The Half Sisters,* woman had "unsexed herself."[2] Aspiring to artistry was considered both unnatural and unwomanly. Did woman not realize that, as the heroine of many a Victorian novel is told, she is supposed to inspire poetry, not write it? Or, as Dorothea is complimented by a male admirer in George Eliot's *Middlemarch,* you *are* a poem. French poet Charles-Pierre Baudelaire agrees, saying that woman is the dazzling, enchanting—albeit sometimes empty-headed—idol "for whom . . . artists and poets compose their most delicate jewels"; she is "a divinity, a star, that presides over all the conceptions of the male brain. . . ." And naturally if woman is not herself the artist who produces the text of her life but only the muse for a man's art, she likely descends from her ivory tower of art to become a wife, as Nathaniel Hawthorne's painter Hilda in *The Marble Faun* becomes "enshrined and worshipped as a household saint, in the light of her husband's fireside."[3]

The interdiction against woman as creator exists from Western mythology to Judeo-Christian iconography to psychoanalytic theory. Man was created in the image of the gods; woman was created, Aristotle says, as an incomplete man, her genitals truncated—and in Western theology, her soul as well. In myth Adam named, Eve was named; Pygmalion was sculptor, Galatea, sculpted. He was the signifier; she the signified. In the long ages of Western art man as creator has found, modified, and created metaphor and myth to endorse his creativity. The artist is Icarus, soaring upward toward the very heavens. The artist is Faust, making a pact with the forces of darkness in exchange for *the gift.* The artist is Prometheus, stealing the fire of creation reserved for the gods alone. Woman, however, lacked a major myth to establish her as creator/maker/heaven-stormer: Pandora and Eve only let loose evil in the world, and the wisdom goddess Athena, while patron of artisans, represented the patriarchy in war and the civic state— enterprises that excluded earthly females. Further, woman's anatomy, unlike

2. The comment that a female artist is "unsexed" or "unwomaned" is repeated in several nineteenth-century *Künstlerromane,* for example of the actress Bianca in *The Half Sisters* (216), of women painters in Louisa May Alcott's *Diana and Persis* (74), and of the singer Armgart in George Eliot's *Armgart* (*WGE,* 19:69).

3. Baudelaire, "The Painter of Modern Life," 423; Hawthorne, *The Marble Faun; or, The Romance of Monte Beni,* 461.

man's, provided no metaphor. Even though she gave birth, for centuries she was considered as merely passive agent, a receptacle who incubated man's creation. Furthermore, in Freudian thought, the womb does not represent woman's claim to (pro)creative properties, but instead her envious desire to possess, that is, to grow her own penis in the form of the infant gestating inside her. As Simone de Beauvoir notes, woman is, like Nature, always the Other, always subject to the naming Logos.[4]

In Lacanian application of classical Freudian theory, the penis is enviable by woman because it is the locus of creative power. Man is still signifier, woman signified. She has being only as she is named in his rhetoric. Roland Barthes, on the topic of making novels and making babies, effectively deprives the woman artist of the birth metaphor as figure for her artistry when he separates (and ranks) biology and creativity:

> Love, work, write, be business-women or women of letters, but always remember that man exists, and that you are not made like him; your own order is free on condition that it depends on his; your freedom is a luxury, it is possible only if you first acknowledge the obligations of your nature. Write, if you want to . . . but don't forget on the other hand to produce children, for that is your destiny. A Jesuitic morality: adapt the moral rule of your condition, but never compromise about the dogma on which it rests.[5]

In all phallocentric thought the phallus must be envied, but never the womb; man does not require woman to create art, while woman cannot possibly become a true artist.

In this book I undertake an analysis of nineteenth-century literary figures who began seriously to question such assumptions by means of their fictional portraits of brilliant female artists: Germaine de Staël and George Sand and their English disciples Geraldine Jewsbury, Elizabeth Barrett Browning, George Eliot, and Mrs. Humphry (Mary) Ward. The French novelists Staël and Sand created the female myth that was to become the counterpart of Romanticism's Prometheus/ Icarus myth of artistic manhood. It is a fair question to ask, Why these particular Victorian writers? My answer would be that all four were serious artists who consciously adapted the Corinne/Consuelo myth of Staël and Sand to embody English women's artistic endeavors—chiefly of course their own literary endeavors—and that they deliberately invoked their esteemed artistic foremothers in creating these fictional portraits. Barrett Browning and George Eliot require no justification as subject material, provided the study sheds new light on their lit-

4. Beauvoir, *The Second Sex*, 78.
5. Barthes, *Mythologies*, 51–52.

erary portraits of artists. As for Jewsbury, the publication of a paperback edition of her finest novel, *The Half Sisters* (1994), has made this *Künstlerroman* available for the attention it deserves. Mary Ward might at first glance seem an odd choice, inasmuch as her later novels were decidedly weak and because the modernists chose to undermine her as a literary icon of belated Victorianism—a sabotage undertaken overtly by the likes of Virginia Woolf and covertly by Ward's nephew Aldous Huxley. Yet Mrs. Humphry Ward (as she insisted upon being known) was the most popular female author of her time, and her early novels were conceived by the novelist herself as falling in the George Eliot/George Sand tradition. Not only were the Ward novels runaway successes in the publishing field, but also, and to a greater extent than other "New Woman" novels of the 1890s, they allude to the literary matriarchs whom I include in this study. My purpose is to trace the female *Künstlerroman* as developing parallel to but separate from its male counterpart and to illustrate that literary matriarchy proved to be nurturing— not an anxiety of influence—to literary daughters creating their own fictions of female genius. Adrienne Rich comments, "Until a strong line of love, confirmation, and example stretches from mother to daughter, from woman to woman across the generations, women will still be wandering in the wilderness."[6] Such a line was being formed in nineteenth-century literary portraits of the female artist.

Female Genius and Feminist Commentary

Feminists have for a quarter of a century discussed female artistry and its locus. French feminist theorists have deconstructed the difference between male and female art, male and female personhood and sexuality, male and female language, and—given that language is the property of man—proposed some new, female language to "jam the machinery" of phallocentricism. Some claim the multiple erogenous zones of the female body as locus for female creation, as Luce Irigaray does in *This Sex That Is Not One.* Hèléne Cixous warns against a metaphor of generativity as power source: since woman's libido is cosmic, rather than localized, she is altogether liberated both from the birthing metaphor and from penis envy. Fearless of castration, she writes through the body as more than a subversive act: "It is volcanic," Cixous says in "The Laugh of the Medusa." Therefore an *écriture féminine* makes the female the "true mistress of the Signifier."[7] The challenge to write out of her own body has prompted such woman/body concepts as gaze theory and the female body as metaphor in menstruation, desire, pregnancy, menopause, eating disorders, rape, and incest.

6. Rich, *Of Woman Born: Motherhood as Experience and Institution,* 246.
7. Cixous, "The Laugh of the Medusa," 263, 258–59.

Other feminists note that woman as creator has lacked a myth for her own subjectivity—one that will do for woman's art what the Faustian or Promethean myth has done for man's. Grace Stewart says that the female writer has subverted the male myths of creativity, such as the Faust myth.[8] But the female writer has also revisited traditional myth as basis for her creativity and subjectivity. The Demeter/Persephone myth of mother/daughter has been appropriated to depict the daughter writing her way back to her mother. Or the Arachne myth to illustrate the female artist spinning her own story. Or the Ariadne myth to untangle the skeins of experience and exit into the light, as well as to penetrate the labyrinth and discover her own unconscious, her own subjectivity. Elaine Showalter, in her revised edition of A Literature of Their Own, says the critical paradigms themselves are so influential that they now influence female literary texts:

> Madwomen in the attic, female body imagery, mother-daughter relationships, father-daughter incest, lyric écriture féminine, the mother tongue, lesbian affiliations and romances, concentric form, embroidery and patchwork, jewelry and clothing, cooking and eating, anorexia nervosa, and the female masquerade are part of the literary repertoire of every first-time writer.[9]

As for the coming-of-age fictions of creative women, the genre that I study in this book, the twentieth century produced a wealth of novels and criticism. Nina Baym defines the female Bildungsroman as the story of a young woman deprived of expected support and faced with the necessity of winning her way in the world. Elizabeth Abel, Marianne Hirsch, and Elizabeth Langland note, however, that the genre itself embodies male norms and that "female fictions of development" are "more conflicted, less direct" than those of their male counterparts. Susan J. Rosowski, taking her cue from the title of Kate Chopin's most famous novel, refers to the "novel of awakening" and characterizes its protagonist as moving inward to a self-knowledge that is actually an "awakening to limitations."[10]

Creating is a bold act, for the artist of either gender focuses attention on the self as the creator. As George Sand puts it in a letter to her fellow artist Gustave Flaubert, "Artists are spoiled children and the best are great egoists."[11] The male

8. Stewart, A New Mythos: The Novel of the Artist as Heroine, 1877–1977, 39.

9. Showalter, "Laughing Medusa," in A Literature of Their Own: British Women Novelists from Brontë to Lessing, 321.

10. Baym, Woman's Fiction: A Guide to Novels by and about Women in America, 1820–1870, 11; Abel, Hirsch, and Langland, The Voyage In: Fictions of Female Development, 11. These authors deal with the narrative pattern of the apprenticeship but note that in the female developmental plot there is often tension between a surface plot that affirms social conventions and a submerged plot that encodes rebellion (12). Rosowski, "The Novel of Awakening," 313.

11. Sand, The George Sand–Gustave Flaubert Letters, 109.

artist, though, need not apologize for his egocentricity: It is a given. Female narcissism, on the other hand, is a different matter. Cixous says men have made for
women an antinarcissism, which "loves itself only to be loved for what women
haven't got!"—an "infamous logic of antilove." Patricia Meyer Spacks, in *The Female Imagination,* admits that creating art is a narcissistic act and that there is for
female writers and female artists a "clash between the artist's narcissism, its need
for power satisfied by creation, and the woman's need to attract others by her very
nature"—that is, a nature culturally defined by limitations. Spacks notes that
narcissism in women's writing may be more acceptable if it be that of a fictional
artist, not overtly the artist/writer herself.[12] I agree with Spacks that creativity
springs out of narcissism and that nineteenth-century women writers softened
the sharp edges of their own ambition when they projected it in thinly veiled self-
portraits of actresses, singers, poets, and painters. Yet many of them (Sand, Jewsbury, Barrett Browning, and Eliot, for example) insist that the great artist—like
the great woman—evolves out of her narcissism.

In some criticism, though, there is a mistaken notion that—aside, perhaps,
from Staël—there was a dearth of nineteenth-century predecessors of the female
Künstlerroman, that women writers studiously avoided the narcissistic act of projecting their own ambition into the fictional lives of women of genius. Linda Huf,
for example, says

> It is hardly any wonder, then, that women have frequently balked at portraying
> themselves in literature as would-be writers—or as painters, composers, or ac-
> tresses, who, as self-portraits of their creators, are invariably surrogate authors.
> Unlike men, women have rarely written artist novels; that is, autobiographical
> novels depicting their struggles to become creative artists—to become, as the
> Romantics had it, as gods.[13]

Hirsch notes that in the nineteenth-century *Künstlerroman* the male hero finds
salvation in art, a solution "virtually unavailable to the young woman in the
nineteenth-century novel," and that the female spiritual Bildung is the story of
the potential artist who "fails to make it."[14] Huf and Hirsch are not quite accurate: both Germaine de Staël's Corinne and George Sand's Consuelo, as well as
many of their successors, do "make it"—at least in the sense of artists who are
brilliant and ambitious, fascinating and famous. Granted, some female artists
fail, some retire early (usually upon their marriage), and some are peripheral characters instead of protagonists, but many "awaken" to stardom within texts that are

12. Cixous, "Laugh of the Medusa," 248; Spacks, *The Female Imagination,* 167.
13. Huf, *A Portrait of the Artist as a Young Woman: The Writer as Heroine in American Literature,* 1.
14. Hirsch, "Spiritual Bildung: The Beautiful Soul as Paradigm," 28.

their own histories. Among nineteenth-century fictional artists are not only Staël's Corinne and Sand's Consuelo, but also Staël's Mirza and Sapho; Sand's Thérèse, Daniella, Diane Florchardet, Lucrezia Floriani, and Laure de Larnac; Maria Jewsbury's Julia Osborne; Geraldine Jewsbury's Bianca Pazzi; Barrett Browning's Aurora Leigh; Felicia Hemans's Properzia Rossi; Letitia Landon's Erinna and unnamed "Improvisatrice"; Dinah Craik's Olive Rothesay and Rachel Armstrong; Fanny Fern's Gertrude Dean and Ruth Hall; Anne Brontë's Helen Huntingdon; Charlotte Brontë's Vashti; Annie Edwards's Celeste, Fridoline, and Rose; Augusta Evans's Edna Earll; George Eliot's Caterina Sarti, Armgart, Mirah Lapidoth, and Princess Halm-Eberstein; Louisa Alcott's Diana, Persis, Miss Cassal, and March sisters Jo and Amy; E. D. E. N. Southworth's Theodora Shelley; Ella Hepworth Dixon's Mary Erle; Mona Caird's Hadria Fullerton; Mary Hallock Foote's Madeline Hendrie; Mary Ward's Isabel Bretherton, Rose Leyburn, and Elise Delaunay; Sarah Grand's Beth Maclure; George Paston's Cosima; Mary Cholmondeley's Hester; Edith Johnstone's Gaspardine; Mrs. Everard Cotes's Elfride; Elizabeth Stuart Phelps's Avis; Marie Corelli's Mavis Clare and the unnamed narrator, "Mademoiselle," of *A Romance of Two Worlds;* and Chopin's Edna Pontellier.[15]

Two Frenchwomen and Four English

Germaine de Staël wrote at the height of European Romanticism, when the artist—no doubt for the first time in history—consciously created a persona of himself as misunderstood loner and as a brooding, tormented soul, dramatic and damned. Examples of such posings and portraits are Goethe's Wilhelm Meister and Werther, the latter mirrored throughout Europe by would-be Werthers in yellow vests; the Byronic hero as Lara, the Giaour, Childe Harold, Manfred, or Don Juan, and Byron himself posing in the dashing turban and robe of Epirus and dying dramatically in the war between Greeks and Turks; Beethoven as the godlike composer storming the gates of heaven; Coleridge as the Aeolian harp; Shelley as soaring skylark, the wild west wind, and the Titan Prometheus. The male Romantic soul—turbulent and troubled, proud and noble, isolated and outcast—created multiple versions of himself and speculated about his calling, whether the poet may defy the creed of ordinary mortals or whether he is the un-

---

15. In this litany are painters, poets, actresses, singers, musicians, novelists, a pianist/composer, and a dancer. From Staël's *improvisatrice* Corinne onward, most succeed in their careers, but as I note in the concluding chapter, fictional women artists of the 1890 decade tend to fail. Perhaps their failures prompted some critics of early modernism to assume, incorrectly, that the female *Künstlerroman* is a rarity and the success of its protagonist still more rare.

acknowledged legislator of the world. The myth of male genius was endlessly echoed as fire thief, sun god, and morning star.

At the very time that the male artist was casting himself as Faustian, Promethean, Luceriferan, and Apollonian, Madame de Staël was creating a portrait of her artistic self in the person of Corinne, a gifted and fascinating Italian poet, musician, actress, singer, and *improvisatrice*. When Madelyn Gutwirth says that Corinne is the Byronic equivalent for women, she could just as well say that Childe Harold is the Corinne for men, for Staël, Byron's senior in life and literature, influenced the English poet—not the other way around.[16] After the publication of her novel, Germaine de Staël was inseparable from her self-created myth; she was called "Corinne" and reportedly responded, "I am not Corinne but I can be her." Thereupon she repeatedly posed as Corinne: in a Grecian gown and with lyre in hand for a painting by Élisabeth Vigée-Lebrun and as *Corinne au cap Misène* (also with lyre) for François Gérard. Both portraits reveal that the author-as-artist became a self-created myth and serve as parallel to the famous 1813 Thomas Phillips painting of *Lord Byron in Arnaout Costume*. In the Gérard painting, Corinne/Germaine's adoring audience is set in shadow, the *improvisatrice* in radiant light. In both Corinne paintings Staël gazes upward to the skies, as the Sibyl does in the Domenichino painting to which Staël compares Corinne. The novel invents a new myth—the "Corinne myth" as Ellen Moers calls it, a "heroinism" of the "inspired priestess dedicated to the cult of genius."[17] Using a complex pattern of interrelated allusions to the Madonna, Dante's Beatrice, Virgil's Sibyl, and Apollo's Pythoness, Staël creates a new goddess—her name is Corinne, and she is inseparable from Germaine de Staël.

Similarly George Sand creates mythic womanhood. Specifically she writes versions of herself in several novels: the mistreated wife in Indiana, the dramatic Lélia who is the female counterpart of Goethe's Werther or Byron's Manfred, the industrious painter Thérèse, the orphan Fanchon who like Sand nurses a dying grandmother, the rustic prophetess Jeanne who like Sand attends a dying mother, and the actress Lucrezia who like Sand flouts marriage conventions and fiercely mothers her children and lovers. For Sand's English readership, however, it is Consuelo who serves as the larger-than-life version of the artist-as-woman. Gentle and gifted Consuelo, the opera singer who charms Venice, Vienna, and Berlin in *Consuelo* and its sequel *La Comtesse de Rudolstadt*, serves as Sand's consummate example of female genius—the angel/woman on whom the divine spirit of God has breathed. To establish Consuelo's grandeur as artist, Sand invokes the myth

16. Gutwirth, *Madame de Staël, Novelist: The Emergence of the Artist as Woman*, 282. For a study of Staël's influence on Byron's poetry, politics, and aesthetics, and especially *Childe Harold IV* as response to *Corinne*, see Joanne Wilkes's *Lord Byron and Madame de Staël: Born for Opposition*.

17. Moers, *Literary Women*, 181.

of Orpheus and Eurydice, Eros and Psyche, and the Pythian prophetess. Like Orpheus and Psyche, Consuelo braves the underworld so that she can emerge as the Sibyl/Sophia of Wisdom, her larger-than-life persona becoming, like Corinne, a myth to animate a generation. Sand is well aware of the power of Corinne; rather than ignoring the influence of Staël, though, she facetiously compares Consuelo to her predecessor and in so doing pays homage to her fellow countrywoman. In other words, Sand grasped the line of love, confirmation, and example that Rich recommends as a way out of the wilderness.

Corinne and Consuelo were important to Victorian women writers because they became the literary examples to illuminate the way into fictional female artistry for two generations of British women writers whose works are replete with subtle and overt references to the French texts, which most read in the original language. In Corinne they found an artist whose source of genius is *"l'ent-housiasme"* (creativity plus vivacity) welling up from inside herself, and in Consuelo a divine goddess visited by sacred fire, *"la flamme sacrée."* Staël and Sand are important because they began to define the woman-as-artist at the very point in literary history when Romanticism was defining the hero-as-artist and when the woman writer, rapidly becoming a presence in the English publishing world, was looking for foremothers.

One might well question why English novelists and poets looked to France for these creative foremothers—especially inasmuch as the French were distrusted throughout the Regency and Napoleonic periods and well into the Victorian era. At the very least, as one historian notes, Anglo-French relations between 1815 and 1870 "swung between extremes of friendship and hostility." A partial answer, of course, is that the English, whether or not approving, were fascinated by all things French. And this goes for women as well as men: The young Wollstonecraft, for example, was as intrigued by the Revolution as was the young Wordsworth. Another clue, however, is in the enviable freedom of French women as compared to their English sisters. The Frenchwoman Flora Tristan, who visited London in 1842, corroborates Corinne's judgments of the stale life of English women. Specifically, Tristan notes that they lead "arid, monotonous, and unhappy existences," that their intellectual and moral education is abominable, and that in respect of liberty the "French women are far ahead of the English." English women were isolated and powerless; they had no equivalent of the salon. Subsequent to Wollstonecraft and prior to Harriet Martineau, no English woman's political commentary was taken as seriously in England as Germaine de Staël's was in France. The daughters of England did not wear trousers, advise an emperor, conduct open love affairs, and proclaim themselves socialists, as did George Sand. As G. M. Young comments, "Mary Wollstonecraft left, unhappily, no equal successor, and George Sand could never have grown in English soil." England was morally conservative, and the strictures usually associated with Victorianism actually predated the ascension of Victoria and included, historians agree, the entire century. From the Regency onward the "evangelical ethic had a soothing, ameliorating effect" on English life—cutting across lines of class, religion, and politics."[18] Naturally, moral conservatism precluded anything approaching gender equality in learning and the creative arts. Rather, it promoted a rigidity of gender roles and expectations—with the female enclosed in the parlor and nursery. It is small wonder, then, that English women artists looked with envy across the Channel where women seemed free to think, write, and create, where Staël and Sand exalted *"liberté."*

Still another reason for the perceived need of female mentors is that England had produced no great woman novelist since Jane Austen. Furthermore, as Edward Glover points out, the novels of Austen, and her contemporary Scott, would scarcely have offended the Victorian puritanism of Mrs. Grundy. At midcentury, then, the English woman artist lacked a network, a tradition, and a pervading myth—as Patricia Thomson says, someone to "bridge the gap between the achievement of Scott and Jane Austen and that of the Brontës and George Eliot."[19] In Germaine de Staël and George Sand, the female English writer found female artists who were liberated, flamboyant, and iconoclastic—in a word, Romantics. In Corinne and Consuelo she found a mythology that would become for the female artist what Childe Harold and Werther were for the male artist. Never mind that the "authoress" who created her was a French woman; Corinne is half-English, half-Italian, and 100 percent cosmopolitan. English women poets and novelists wished also to transcend geographic and nationalistic boundaries as their French predecessors had transcended—to make their heroines gifted, liberated, fascinating, and often a bit scandalous. Their goal was to revive woman's writing in England but also to produce mythic women more exotic than Austen's heroine of the parish.

The opening chapter of this book depicts Staël's Corinne as a secular and political Sibyl and Sand's Consuelo as divine Sophia. In Chapter 2 Geraldine Jewsbury's actress Bianca Pazzi of *The Half Sisters* is interpreted as a daughter of both Corinne and Consuelo, as well as of Maria Jewsbury's Julia, but in Geraldine Jewsbury's hands the myth is modified into a more pedestrian heroine who must toil for her success and for her bread and in so doing becomes an exemplum of

18. James, *The Rise and Fall of the British Empire,* 179; Tristan, *The London Journal of Flora Tristan, 1842,* 245, 246–48, 253; Young, *Victorian England: Portrait of an Age,* 3–4; Himmelfarb, *Victorian Minds,* 283.

19. Glover, "Victorian Ideas of Sex," 362; Thomson, *George Sand and the Victorians: Her Influence and Reputation in Nineteenth-Century England,* 8–9. Thomson posits that Sand fills this gap, while I shall argue that Staël and Sand deserve equal billing for creating the female artist as goddess.

Thomas Carlyle's "Gospel of Work." Jewsbury, herself a professional "working woman," also manages to have some fun at the expense of the posing, melodramatic, would-be Corinne whom Bianca encounters. Chapter 3 acknowledges Elizabeth Barrett Browning's debt to both Staël and Sand in her verse novel *Aurora Leigh*—a point often acknowledged in Barrett Browning criticism but not yet thoroughly studied. I argue that in her doctrine of sexual and spiritual love Barrett Browning employs the Psyche and Eros myth to draw conclusions surprisingly similar to Sand's in *La Comtesse de Rudolstadt,* which relies on the same myth to illuminate the unnatural schism between body and soul. Chapter 4 treats George Eliot's Erinna complex—the fear of female silencing. Studying the novella *Mr. Gilfil's Love-Story,* the novel *Daniel Deronda,* and the poetic drama *Armgart,* I posit that Eliot's woman of genius is influenced by Staël, Sand, and Barrett Browning and that through her six women artists and would-be artists (Caterina, Leonora, Gwendolen, Mirah, Catherine, and Armgart) Eliot treats her own ultimate nightmare as her women of genius are silenced by miscalculation, fear, loss of their gift, and premature death. Finally, in Chapter 5, three female artists of Mrs. Humphry Ward are interpreted as exemplars of the Medusa myth. Like Staël's and Sand's heroines, the actress Isabel in *Miss Bretherton,* the violinist Rose in *Robert Elsmere,* and the painter Elise in *The History of David Grieve* exert mesmerizing and potentially emasculating power over their lovers. Employing gaze theory as traced from Freud and reinterpreted by feminist critics, I argue that Ward pays homage to her literary matriarchs the two Georges, chiefly George Sand, but that she disposes of her heroines in conventional outcomes when the myth that Ward has invoked becomes too powerful for her own conservative response to the New Woman feminism of the Victorian twilight.

Not only was the nineteenth century the era in which the artist self-consciously defined himself and created his myth, but it was also apparently a period in which he struggled in the shadow of his powerful father. Harold Bloom has identified the Romantic period as the first in which poets obsessively strove, Oedipal-style, to excel beyond the progenitor and thereby to produce a text speaking to a dead man "outrageously more alive than himself." The female poets and novelists in this study consciously speak to matriarchs, but they look to their artist/mothers for sustenance and authority, to honor them, not to slay them. To say as much is not to deny that they wanted to measure themselves against the height of their literary *brothers.* Staël considered herself an intellectual equal to the male poets and political theorists in her salon; Sand, Jewsbury, and Eliot all worked for a time in the publishing trade, where they would rarely have encountered other women of their rank and profession; Sand's artistic comrades were for the most part male poets, novelists, and musicians, and she would rather have been compared to Flaubert or Turgenev than to any woman novelist; Barrett Browning wished to have been the page of Lord Byron, revisited and revised Milton and Pope, and measured herself against Tennyson and Browning; George Eliot admired Charlotte Brontë, but seemed to have considered *herself* peerless among women novelists. Nevertheless they sought literary foremothers—Barrett Browning lamenting that she found none save Sappho among the poets—and all four acknowledge in their novels, essays, and correspondence that their true literary mothers are the Frenchwomen Staël and Sand. If these women do not create— as Bloom argues for the male poet—by slaying the parent, they do, however, risk another potential threat. Nancy Chodorow, in her work on psychoanalysis and the sociology of gender, notes a non-Oedipal danger for daughters of strong mothers: the issues of intimacy and merging, the question of how one becomes herself rather than becoming the mother whom she emulates. Chodorow says, "In the face of their dependence, lack of certainty of her emotional permanence, fear of merging, and overwhelming love and attachment, a mother looms large and powerful." Among the women in my study, literary idolatry and matrophobia are indeed issues, but it could hardly be otherwise, considering the "profound matrilineal bequest" that the daughters eagerly accept.[20]

20. Bloom, *The Anxiety of Influence: A Theory of Poetry,* 78. Sandra M. Gilbert and Susan Gubar, in *The Madwoman in the Attic: The Woman Writer and the Nineteenth-Century Literary Imagination,* posit an "anxiety of authorship" to counter Bloom's anxiety of influence—that is, the fear of a woman artist that she cannot create. Thus she looks for a female precursor who "proves by example that a revolt against patriarchal literary authority is possible," rather than seeks a literary matriarch to slay (49). Chodorow, *The Reproduction of Mothering: Psychoanalysis and the Sociology of Gender,* 82. The quoted phrase is from Rich's *Of Woman Born,* 220.

I

Secular Sibyl and Divine Sophia
Staël's *Corinne* and Sand's *Consuelo*

The first reading of "Corinne" is an epoch a woman never forgets . . .
—GERALDINE JEWSBURY, *The Half Sisters*

France must turn, with the crowning due to genius, to . . . *Corinne* &
George Sand—ELIZABETH BARRETT BROWNING, correspondence

Madame de Stael's name still rises first to the lips when we are asked to
mention a woman of great intellectual power. . . . George Sand is the unapproached artist, who . . . unites the clear delineation of character and the
tragic depth of passion.—GEORGE ELIOT, "Madame de Sablé"

"You came to France to talk of . . . George Sand?" she asked him, with dancing eyes—"mon Dieu! Mon Dieu! What do you take us for?"—MRS.
HUMPHRY (MARY) WARD, *The History of David Grieve*

NOT ONLY WERE THE French artists Germaine de Staël (1766–1817) and
George Sand (1804–1876) models as women who dared to publish, but they also
inspired nineteenth-century English women writers by their personal courage,
their uniqueness and vivacity, and their commitment to *liberté* in art and politics. Furthermore, Staël's *Corinne* (1807) and Sand's *Consuelo* (1842) became the
reference points for woman-as-artist fictions of the entire second half of the century. The central questions of female art and female creativity are raised in these
groundbreaking novels, and English women writers of the artist-as-heroine motif engage these two important texts again and again, producing works intriguing for their intertextuality, their personal slant on issues already in the air that
intellectual and creative women were breathing. In the character of Corinne is
the precedent of the artist whose creativity both establishes a larger-than-life
myth of womanhood and combats, in code, the political regime of her nation.

13

In *Consuelo* is the example of a prophetess of divine love, that is, the woman artist compelled by the divine fire of inspiration to serve God and seek truth. While the pride, the genius, the suffering, the ambition and accomplishment, and the fame or shame may be similar, at core the difference between the two approaches to art is defined in the intimate conversations of women artists, and in their attempts to name the source of artistic power. Corinne defines herself in terms of the public rhetoric of Napoleonic France (ostensibly of Italy) and defines her inspiration as a force, *l'enthousiasme,* coming from within herself; Consuelo receives divine fire, which like Pentecostal tongues bids her speak, as Promethean fire inflames her creativity.

This is, of course, a fine distinction, because in creating the genre of the female *Künstlerroman,* Staël and Sand create memorable artists who share many risks and rewards. Both Corinne and Consuelo are Vestal Virgins of art, and both accept that God is the source of their gift. Both artists, as well as their many successors in English poetry and fiction, deal with prejudice and presuppositions about woman's "place," and both confront the physical, psychological, and biological facts of being a woman. One of them, Corinne, loves a man who requires that the artist abandon her career; the other, Consuelo, risks seduction and rape as the price of artistic endeavor. Both are tempted to a domesticity that threatens to cripple art; both are orphans longing for love; both tout the necessity of freedom for the artist; both are beloved by an appreciative public; and both suffer and speculate whether suffering is necessary to produce real art. They wonder whether, as the saying goes, the artist must drink deep at the sacred fount of experience, and—if one might modify the metaphor—must risk coming away from the well thirsty, drenched, or poisoned. Furthermore, both their creators were highly political individuals; therefore to separate them into the secular and divine would seem somewhat arbitrary; nevertheless the central figure of the *Künstlerroman* of each is different. In labeling Corinne a "political Sibyl," I assert a specificity in Staël's work that is lacking in the *Consuelo* novels, in which Sand opts for universal, transcendent qualities not directly applicable to domestic French politics. Eve Sourian makes a similar distinction, noting that Sand tends to "follow her emotions" while Staël "has a genuinely political mind, interested in more immediate pragmatic solutions." Madelyn Gutwirth says that both international novels embrace vast territories but that Corinne "affirms the distinctions among the peoples," Consuelo their "primal unity."[1]

Germaine de Staël was born the daughter of Jacques Necker, minister of finance to Louis XVI, and of Suzanne Curchod, a brilliant woman and acquain-

---

1. Sourian, "Madame de Staël and George Sand," 125; Gutwirth, "*Corinne* and *Consuelo* as Fantasies of Immanence," 21.

tance of both Rousseau and Voltaire. Mme. Necker founded a salon in which young Anne Louise Germaine, a precocious only child, early became a participant and earned the titles of muse and "Apollo's priestess"—the same title that she bestows upon Corinne when, early in the novel, the poet is crowned at the Roman capitol. Apparently the mythological allusion to the Pythoness followed Germaine de Staël throughout her adult life; in 1789 when the American Gouverneur Morris visited her salon, he called her house a "kind of temple of Apollo."[2] As George Sand was to do, Germaine Necker received a personalized education of the type Rousseau promoted (for male children only) in *Emile*. She married Eric-Magnus, baron de Staël-Holstein, the Swedish ambassador, but indulged in famous liaisons with the diplomat Talleyrand, Count Narbonne, and the political thinker Benjamin Constant, among others. She became the patroness of her own salon, indulged in behind-the-scenes political activity in France, wrote a defense of Queen Marie Antoinette, helped friends escape the Reign of Terror, and for a time lived abroad for the sake of her own safety. Her international literary and political associates included Condorcet, Chateaubriand, Schiller, Goethe, Godwin, and Lord Byron, among others. Rejecting tyranny and demagoguery wherever it appeared—both in the ancien régime and in the Republic—she advocated moderation and reason as avenues to gradual political change and came to favor for France a kind of republic informed by a broader class basis than that which had precipitated the Revolution, although, she says in her posthumously published memoir, *Dix années d'exil*, she still believed the French prefer a monarchy. She was a believer in the perfectibility of human institutions but no proponent of the cataclysmic Revolution, which after all toppled her father as well as the monarchy and initially presented dire risks to Necker and his family. She became a bitter enemy of Napoleon, who exiled her from Paris in 1795 after she wrote pamphlets advocating a stable and peaceful state—including the cessation of Napoleonic aggression in Europe. In exile she spent time in Germany, Russia, and England, returning near the end of her life when Napoleon himself was an exile. For the sake of *Corinne*, which is in part an extensive accolade to Italy's past glory, it is significant that these travels took Staël for the grand tour of Italy.

Corinne was in the early decades of the nineteenth century the coming-of-age novel for many young women in England, including Jane Austen, Mary Godwin Shelley, Fanny Burney, Hannah More, Maria Edgeworth, Felicia Hemans, Maria and Geraldine Jewsbury, and Elizabeth Barrett Browning, who says that the "immortal book" deserves to be read three score times and ten (*BC*, 3:25). Barbara

2. Folkenflik, introduction to Staël, *An Extraordinary Woman: Selected Writings of Germaine de Staël*, 5; Berger, introduction to Staël, *Madame de Staël on Politics, Literature, and National Character*, 29.

Dennis notes, "Elizabeth Barrett read it over and over in Herefordshire, George Eliot devoured it in the Midlands, George Sand read it in France, Fanny Kemble in London, and Mary Godwin on her travels; and Harriet Beecher and Margaret Fuller and many others brooded over it in America." Felicia Hemans, Letitia Landon (L. E. L.), and Mary Hewitt wrote poems inspired by Corinne, and Landon translated the improvisations of the fictional Corinne. Ellen Moers notes that in America Margaret Fuller was to become the "Yankee Corinna," Kate Chopin the St. Louis Corinne, and Sarah Orne Jewett the New England Corinne, and that Corinne was for literary women of the nineteenth century the "female Childe Harold."[3] Or, as Elizabeth Barrett Browning suggests, Byron's "Harold has often spoken with the voice of Corinne, & often when he has spoken with the most passion & eloquence" (BC, 3:25). The influence of Corinne was not, however, limited to Staël's young female readership. Maurice Beebe, in his well-known Ivory Towers and Sacred Founts, credits Corinne as one of the first of the "art novels" to achieve wide recognition and serve as model for the Künstlerroman as genre.[4]

George Sand's influence on Victorian England has also been well established, notably in Patricia Thomson's George Sand and the Victorians: Her Influence and Reputation in Nineteenth-Century England and Paul G. Blount's George Sand and the Victorian World. Amantine Aurore Lucile Dupin was, on her father's side, descended from royalty (the illegitimate line) and on the side of her mother, Antoinette Sophie Victoire Delaborde, from the common people. Like Staël, she married young and unhappily, took numerous sexual partners, including the artists Sandeau, Musset, Marceau, and, most famously, Chopin. Simone de Beauvoir says Sand preferred "effeminate" men.[5] Certainly she preferred gifted and artistic men. Also like Staël, Sand was keenly interested in the politics of France. Sand was a socialist, a supporter of the Lyons radicals brought to mass trial for conspiracy in 1836, a writer for the Bulletin de la République, and after the partial and temporary revolution of 1848 she became, as Joseph Barry notes, the "Muse of the Revolution." In England Elizabeth Barrett Browning, student of the same socialist and communist thought but of more conservative bent, called Sand's followers a "Society of the ragged Red diluted with the lower theatrical."[6] Sand was not only a spokesperson for the exploited classes, but also an antagonist of any form of political, religious, or economic tyranny, and everywhere in Europe people listened when she spoke—against the Catholic church and the institution of

3. Dennis, Elizabeth Barrett Browning: The Hope End Years, 49; Moers, Literary Women, 177, 176.
4. Beebe, Ivory Towers and Sacred Founts: The Artist Hero in Fiction from Goethe to Joyce, 71.
5. Beauvoir, Second Sex, 458.
6. Barry, Infamous Woman: The Life of George Sand, 287; Browning, The Letters of Elizabeth Barrett Browning, 2:68.

marriage, or for the unification of the proletariat. As she writes in her controversial anticlerical novel *La Daniella* (1856–1857), which expresses her grief when newly republican Italy was handed back into Papal control, everywhere in Europe there seems to be conflict between dreams of fabulous prosperity for the few and the terrors of universal cataclysm. Sand had long before 1857 become one of the most celebrated and notorious women of Europe. In France aspiring poets sent her copies of their verse; Socialist editor Louis Blanc (who was, briefly, a lover) requested her journalistic collaboration; she counted the pianist and composer Franz Liszt and the painter Delacroix among her close friends; Prince Louis Napoleon even consulted with her on his essay on pauperism in France and, after she requested and received an audience with him, granted a pardon for her fellow conspirators.[7]

Sand's political novels were influential and controversial, and her literary influence was widely acknowledged. She was, in fact, a popular and important literary figure not only in France and England but also on the world stage—influencing the Russians Turgenev and Dostoyevsky, the French writer Flaubert, and the Americans Walt Whitman and Henry James. Blount notes that among the English Victorians Matthew Arnold, George Eliot, Jane Carlyle, Charlotte Brontë, and Elizabeth Barrett Browning praised Sand in their correspondence, that Ruskin, the Carlyles, Leslie Stephen, Oscar Wilde, and Thomas Hardy discussed her, and that Henry F. Chorley, Margaret Busk, Frances Trollope, William Thackeray, and Wilson Coker, among others, reviewed her. Elizabeth Barrett's letters to her literary friend Mary Russell Mitford and Geraldine Jewsbury's to Jane Welsh Carlyle are filled with references to Sand—anticipating, reading, lending, and borrowing this or that Sand novel—and, in Jewsbury's letters, repeated references to the term "George Sandism" apparently employed by Jane's famous husband as a none-too-flattering reference to women he considered bold and unfeminine. George Sand was an early topic of conversation also in the epistolary courtship of Robert Browning and Elizabeth Browning—he rejecting any inclination toward George Sandism, she avidly acknowledging her discipleship. Sand was praised and staunchly defended by the influential arbiter of taste George Lewes, companion of George Eliot, and by Italian nationalist Giuseppe Mazzini while he was exiled in England and assumed a role as a culture critic on the English literary scene. Sand was to Victorian women of independent mind a "compelling symbol, champion of the rights of two of England's more depressed groups: women and the working class."[8] Thomson offers a more complete summary of the Sandian criticism in England, including Charles Kingsley's positive

7. Sand, *Letters of George Sand,* 1:358, 361; Sand, *La Daniella,* 2:176.
8. Blount, *George Sand and the Victorian World,* 5–14, 6.

response to her democratic appeal and an unnamed reviewer's ranking of Sand as "undoubtedly the most gifted and most original female writer of her country and times." George Lewes's 1852 essay on the achievement of English "lady-novelists" uses Sand's works as a point of departure and an example of the greatness of which women are capable. Lewes's remarkable conclusion is that, "For eloquence, and depth of feeling, no man approaches George Sand." The argument of Thomson's book is not only that Sand was read, reviewed, and admired in England in the 1830s and 1840s, but also that she was a talking point in middle-class drawing rooms. Blount concurs, noting that "It is not an exaggeration to say that a cult of George Sand existed in Victorian England."[9]

The French Sibyl

The iconography of woman as Wisdom was tremendously important among the English writers who grew up with the *improvisatrice* Corinne and the *zingarelle* Consuelo as the imaginary companions of their formative years. The female Wisdom figure was variously called Minerva, Pallas Athena, Sophia, the Pythian (or Pythoness), the Sibyl, Io/Isis, and Cassandra. This Lady Wisdom had her source in both the Judeo-Christian religion and the Greek-Roman classical past. In Greek tradition the goddess of wisdom is gray-eyed Athena, who in Hesiod's *Theogony* sprang fully grown from the head of Zeus after he engorged her mother Metis, wisest among gods and mortals. Throughout the Mediterranean world, temples and shrines were dedicated to Athena's honor. As George Sand reminds us, one of her titles was "Minerva Artisana" because she was a weaver and the patron of artisans (and, Sand also notes, there is but a fine line between artisans and artists) (*LGS*, 2:252). Furthermore women who served as priestesses of the sun god, Apollo, were also associated with insight, prophecy, and wisdom. They prophesied the future, solved questions of truth and accuracy, even assigned tasks as expiation or as service to Apollo. According to Pausanias, Apollo's shrine of chief importance was the rich temple at Delphi—also known as Pytho or Pythia, and hence source of the name "Pythian" for his priestess. This Pythian, or Delphic oracle, was also a poet who composed her prophecies in hexameters and performed them in song, and is known as the Sibyl.[10]

Borrowing Athena from the Greek pantheon, the Romans made Minerva their sacred deity of wisdom and reason, but also retained the Sibylline prophetesses

9. Thomson, *George Sand and the Victorians*, 26, 12; Lewes, "The Lady Novelists," 135; Blount, *George Sand and the Victorian World*, 7.

10. Hesiod, *Theogony, Works and Days, Shield,* lines 886–94, 924–27, 35–36; Herodotus, *The History of Herodotus*, 227–28; Pausanias, *Guide to Greece* 1:416, 430.

as Wisdom figures. In Virgil's *Aeneid* Virgil supplies his epic hero Aeneas with the "divine" and "sacred" Sibyl of Cumæ. The Cumæan Sibyl is, like the Pythian, a priestess of Apollo, but she has also been made special priestess of Queen Proserpine's nightly reign in Hades. The Sibyl provides Aeneas with a guided tour of the Underworld, showing to him the secrets of the afterlife and assuring him of triumph and empire in Rome. Sibyl worship, in fact, did not die out early in the Empire, Marina Warner notes, but the books of Sibylline prophecies were kept on the Capitol in Rome (where Staël's modern Sibyl, Corinne, is crowned), guarded by a "a select number of the Republic's great and good," and periodically opened to ascertain diagnosis and remedies.[11]

In Christianity, Sophia, the Old Testament Wisdom of Proverbs and the Book of Wisdom, is conflated with the New Testament Virgin Mary. As mother of Jesus the Logos (the Word and Wisdom of God), Mary partakes of his divine spirit. In early Christianity, mythic characters and stories were retained if they could be employed to suggest some spiritual truth or doctrinal message. According to the fifth-century Christian Fulgentius, for example, Minerva was Divine Wisdom who aided Divine Foresight (Prometheus) in providing metaphorical fire and light to humans. Furthermore, some of the early gnostic Christians considered God as androgynous, "a dyad of opposites existing in harmony in one being," and the divine female principle of the dyad was Sophia, a Greek translation of the Hebrew *hokhmah,* or Wisdom. Also, the wise treatises of alchemy were often attributed to women: Isis, Mary, Moses's sister, Miriam, Cleopatra, or Theosobia. Looking backward at the *Eclogues* of Virgil, Christians interpreted the Sibyl's prophecy of a divine child/savior in the fourth Eclogue as a Messianic prophecy, notes St. Augustine in *City of God.* Therefore Virgil and the Sibyl were venerated by Christianity as God's messengers, the Sibyl even prophesying the apocalypse. Augustine quotes at some length the poems of Erythraean Sibyl on the final judgment, the abyss of Tartaros, and the reckoning of human monarchs before the bar of God. He also adds that some believe the Cumæan Sibyl, who opposes the worship of fabricated gods, belongs to the City of God.[12] In Michelangelo's Sistine painting, the female Sibyls parallel the male Old Testament prophets in the revealing of the divine relationship between God and human, as Staël's modern Sibyl Corinne notes (*C,* 265).

In spite of the misogyny of Western Christianity, vestiges of Sophia/Minerva survive and appear in the veneration of the Virgin (particularly as displayed in

---

11. Warner, *From the Beast to the Blonde: On Fairy Tales and Their Tellers,* 67, 68; Warner credits Lactantius, *The Divine Institutions.*

12. Fulgentius, *Mythographies,* 2.6, in *Fulgentius the Mythographer,* 71–72; Merchant, *The Death of Nature: Women, Ecology, and the Scientific Revolution,* 17, 18. (Theosobia was sister of a fourth-century alchemist, Zosimus.) Augustine, *City of God against the Pagans,* 10.27 in 3:375, 18.23 in 5:441.

European paintings). Nineteenth-century art historian Anna Jameson docu-
ments a number of altarpieces in which the Virgin reads the Book of Wisdom,
noting, "She is here the *Spousa Dei,* and the *Virgo Sapientissima,* the most wise
Virgin."[13] Holy Sophia as the wisdom of God appears too in texts as diverse as
Christine de Pizan's *Book of the City of Ladies,* Boethius's *Consolation of Philosophy,* and, most famously, as Beatrice in Dante's *Commedia* and the lady of his
Convivio. Recall that Dante also enthrones the Virgin as the "Mystic Rose" of his
Paradiso—thus his iconography of the divine female is associated with God's
grace, love, and wisdom, and as wife and mother of the Godhead.

When Germaine de Staël was developing her art and her politics, French culture was especially ripe with goddess allegory and iconography. Throughout the
1790s the classical female form, usually bare-breasted or wearing the thinnest of
gauze chiton, represented such qualities as Nature, Equality, Modesty, Truth, or
Law, but most frequently she is Liberty.[14] Although the literal women of France
had little power outside the salon and were valued more for passivity than for action (though Staël repeatedly notes that they enjoyed greater influence than did
women elsewhere in Europe), in the propagandist art of the period the aggres-
sive female goddess was idealized—especially if she were Lady Liberty. Gutwirth
notes the particular importance of the mythology of the goddess in Staël's youth
as an outgrowth of the Revolution and credits Staël with creating her own myth
of the goddess:

> The fall of the ancien régime momentarily toppled all institutions, includ-
> ing the Church. Into the breach caused by the abolition of the forms of faith,
> the Revolution, without recking what it did, threw goddess worship, as figures
> of Reason and Demeter replaced the dying God upon the altars. . . . Staël seized
> the occasion to posit a counter-patriarchal, feminine cult of transcendence
> through art. This is the revolutionary aspect of *Corinne.*[15]

13. Jameson, *Legends of the Madonna as Represented in the Fine Arts,* 102–3. Jameson notes that when
the Virgin is depicted without the infant Jesus (as in works of the Van Eycks, Cosimo Rosselli, and Cam-
era della Segnatura), she often holds an open book, which is to be interpreted as the Book of Wisdom,
and the seven doves around her head "characterize her as personified Wisdom—the Mater Sapientiæ"
(58).

14. See Madelyn Gutwirth's *The Twilight of the Goddesses: Women and Representation in the French Revolutionary Era,* 252–84, which includes reprints of paintings, drawings, friezes, and prints. The icon is
usually depicted in repose with a gaze upward and outward (like the Sibyl portraits of Staël), but *Liberty Triumphant, or the Cowardly Run Aground,* makes Lady Liberty a Nike of the Revolution, a sky goddess smiting her enemies who tumble head over heels (the iconography recalling Jove's roust of the Ti-
tans and Michael pursuing the rebel angels). In Prud'hon's *Liberty,* the goddess has slain the Hydra of
Tyranny, and her stance is similar to that of Donatello's David after he has slain Goliath. The icon of
goddess in reflective repose versus goddess as warrior is especially interesting for Staël's texts, in that her
political writings deal with passivity/activity of woman as myth and as influence on national character.

15. Gutwirth, "Seeing *Corinne* Afresh," 31.

One might well add that the revolutionary purpose of *Corinne* is to establish that the female *artist* is a political figure, that the wisdom of this political Sibyl can guide the nation in peace and war—another way of saying that the poet (the artist) is legislator of the world.

Especially when the Sibyl or Sophia is merged with Romantic idealism and radicalism at the end of the century and into the early nineteenth century, it serves women writers as a more radical figure of power. Marie-Jacques Hoog insists that the revival of the Woman-as-Wisdom figure predates the midcentury British phenomenon—that it is a product of European Romanticism.

> Such is the figure of the Romantic Sibyl—a prophetess holding a scroll, inspired sister of Sophia, the other face of the Virgin Mary; she, too, is filled with the sacred breath, the virgin mother of Logos. Noble poet, wearing a turbaned diadem, she reigns gravely, a book in hand. Sublime priestess, her eyes raised to the skies, mouth half-opened, she sees and foresees. She proclaims, she speaks, she is the patron saint of the creative feminine word.[16]

The idealized female as Sibyl/Sophia was also familiar to writers in mid-nineteenth-century England and America. Athena was seemingly as popular with Victorians as Liberty had been to the French Revolutionaries. The American Margaret Fuller remarks that from ancient times idealized images of woman/goddess (Egyptian Isis, Athena/Minerva, Cassandra, and the Sibylline priestesses) had represented wisdom and that the images retained power for Fuller's century. Florence Nightingale, when she penned her thoughts on religion, philosophy, work, and woman's place, called her spiritual autobiography *Cassandra.* John Ruskin says that the figure of Athena, in particular, represents to his age the attributes of art, literature, and national virtue; she is secular/political Wisdom because she teaches morality and industry to the citizens of the state, and she is aesthetic Wisdom because she guides art and literature to morality, subtlety, and higher truth.[17] At the height of the Victorian period, woman as Wisdom was incorporated into the works of Elizabeth and Robert Browning, Tennyson, Dickens, Charles Kingsley, Harriet Martineau, and George Eliot. Marina Warner argues that this Athena/Minerva/Sophia figure of Victoria's reign in England is associated with patriarchy, nationalism, and Christian authoritarianism, not radical feminism. But Barbara Taylor notes that the female figure of Wisdom was emerging in the late eighteenth and early nineteenth centuries, which would in-

---

16. Hoog, "George Sand and the Romantic Sibyl," 95.

17. Fuller, *Woman in the Nineteenth Century and Kindred Papers Relating to the Sphere, Condition and Duties, of Woman,* 51, 47, 55, 115; Ruskin, *Of Queens' Gardens,* in *Sesame and Lilies,* 133; Ruskin, *The Queen of the Air, Being a Study of the Greek Myths of Cloud and Storm,* 61, 117–18, 123.

clude the formative years of Staël and George Sand, because of the influence of several radical thinkers and socialist and religious sects—including the Saint-Simonian movement that influenced Sand (especially with its opposition to the contemporary marriage code).[18]

I posit that the myth of woman as Wisdom proved especially appealing to Staël and Sand because of Romanticism's preoccupation with myth, as well as the male artist's penchant for creating and projecting himself in the form of a mythic icon. Just as Goethe, Shelley, Beethoven, and Byron saw themselves as Prometheans, Staël and Sand appropriated the Cumæan Sibyl or Pythian priestess to depict the inspired woman artist. Admittedly there is something of the female Promethean in Staël's and Sand's heroines as well, Staël's Sapho and Sand's Lélia, for example, specifically calling themselves Prometheus, but the Pythian figure predominates. Both Corinne and Consuelo represent the Sibyl/Sophia type, but Corinne represents Sibylline devotion to the nation or state while Consuelo represents the divine love for humankind that she has learned to be the purest form of wisdom. Hence she becomes, in the Sandian canon, a modern equivalent to the divine Sophia. Both Staël and Sand are daughters of Romanticism—the former being a transitional figure whose fiction is influenced by the likes of Richardson and Goethe, the latter reaching her potential as the novel was developing under the influence of Dumas, Stendahl, Balzac, Hugo, and Sir Walter Scott. As representatives of the two generations of Romantic art, they consciously and carefully brought mythic properties to their female heroes, and each connected the Wisdom myth to herself. Both mythologize their artist/heroines by connecting them to the Sibyl/Minerva/Sophia traditions and to the radical empowerment of humanity inherent in the Prometheus myth. Myth created Corinne and Consuelo; then in England Corinne and Consuelo became the mythology for British women artists of the remainder of the century.

Corinne as Woman and Artist

Staël's Corinne sings, plays, dances, composes, acts, paints, writes poetry, interprets, and converses; she is a consummate woman and artist—as well as perfect *salonnière*. Staël believes that enthusiasm is the key element in art as in patriotism; therefore she makes Corinne's vivacity, *"l'enthousiasme,"* the key to all her endeavors—from playing the lyre or acting on the stage to lecturing on Ro-

18. Warner, *Monuments and Maidens: The Allegory of the Female Form,* 125–26; Taylor, *Eve and the New Jerusalem: Socialism and Feminism in the Nineteenth Century,* 161–82. For a more detailed commentary on the icon of female Wisdom in Victorian literature, see Lewis, *Elizabeth Barrett Browning's Spiritual Progress: Face to Face with God,* 171–211.

man architecture or quoting the poets of the Italian Renaissance. Corinne's forte, however, is the impromptu recitation of poetry created on the spot, the art of the *improvisatrice,* in Italy at the time a legitimate art form and highly valued. Wealthy, single, and twenty-six, Corinne lives as a free and independent woman in Rome: that is, independent from the necessity of earning her livelihood as George Sand's Consuelo must, independent from family (her Italian mother and English father both being dead), and independent from the male sex in that she does not require marriage—although she does seem to require men's adoration. In fact she does not invite women to her salon, and her dances and dramatizations are deliberately performed to attract the male gaze. Corinne's freedom of lifestyle is emphasized by Staël in that the artist is survivor of two love affairs, one with a German nobleman who proved to be a dullard, the other with an Italian prince who was mentally lethargic—traits which Corinne could least tolerate. As Oswald Nelvil notices, "Sa fortune . . . est tout-à-fait indépandante et son ame encore plus" (her fortune is totally independent, and her mind still more so [*C,* 169]), and as the narrator notes, perfect freedom of thought and habit had lent her charms ("une indépandance parfaite d'idées et d'habitudes donnait beaucoup de charmes à son existence" [*C,* 282]). As Ellen Moers notes, and as Elizabeth Barrett noted over a century earlier, Corinne was the female Childe Harold for literary women, the "perilous stuff" of female Byronism.[19]

The plot complication begins when Nelvil, a British military officer, comes, sees, and conquers Corinne. Conquers not in the sense that the vivacious *improvisatrice* becomes timid and demure as an English woman ought. Quite the contrary, she still expresses her opinions on art, life, religion, history, and politics; she still performs before her adoring public. Most notably, she plays Shakespeare's Juliet and dances a tarantella—thus arousing Nelvil's jealousy because in the fiery folk dance she presents herself to the admiring gaze of other males and in erotic interaction with her dance partner, Prince Amalfi. But she *is* conquered in that she gives her heart frankly and entirely to her English lover, no strings attached—in spite of the warnings of the worldly wise Frenchman d'Erfeuil. The bond of marriage can unite Corinne and Nelvil only if the two parties love equally, only if she can bear to be separated from her beloved Italy to keep house as an English wife while Nelvil participates in fox hunt or political debate. But her acquaintances, the readers of the novel, and sometimes even Corinne herself realize that such an outcome can never happen. Furthermore, for such a marriage to

---

19. Moers, *Literary Women,* 176–77. Joanne Wilkes points out that Byron's echoes of *Corinne* in *Childe Harold* include the suffering of great artists that fail to reach their potential; the celebration of dead Italian patriots; Italy's "past, present, future"; and political commentary on tyranny (*Lord Byron and Madame de Staël,* 114, 60–61, 103, 100, 120). Wilkes concludes that—despite Staël's doctrine of "perfectibility"—Byron is more optimistic than she (130).

succeed he must overcome his father's aversion to foreign-born women (Nelvil at twenty-one having gotten himself into an embarrassing predicament with a conniving French widow, and his late father having secured Nelvil's future with an English maiden quite dissimilar to Madame d'Arbigny). Corinne puts her case before Nelvil quite candidly: If he destroys the heart that she has freely given him, then she must die. She says that in losing him she will lose poetry, and art will no longer have the power to comfort her soul (*C*, 213–14). Then, when her English hero deserts her, she proves her prophecy true by writing no more poetry in her final half decade of life and—like Richardson's Clarissa—by willing the death she has prophesied.

Briefly told, the thwarted romance leads to disaster. During his romantic sojourn in Italy with the fascinating Corinne, Nelvil is recalled by his regiment for service in the West Indies; he returns to England, where he meets the perfect candidate for an "English" wife (angelic, dutiful, devout, reserved, domestic, timid), and this newly discovered treasure is quite the opposite of Corinne (angelic and religious, true enough, but also sophisticated, assertive, opinionated, extroverted, and brilliant). The narrow and undereducated Lucile Edgermond proves just deserts for Nelvil, who believes the highest human achievement for either man or woman is not in enthusiasm and imagination but in tending to domestic duties (*C*, 343). *Duty* is in fact Nelvil's watchword in all things—duty being a patriot's relationship to his nation, a Christian's obligation to his God, a son's sacred trust to his father. As fate would have it, the first time he meets Lucile, he hears her pray for strength to carry out her duty to her dying mother (*C*, 455)— a commitment that contrasts Nelvil's failure to have done the same for his late father, whom this same Lucile attended in his final days.

Lucile is Correggio's Madonna (*C*, 558) and Corinne, Domenichino's Sibyl (*C*, 52); Lucile the fair-haired blonde, Corinne the dangerous dark lady. Corinne is more fascinating, Lucile more safe. It happens that Lucile Edgermond is also the girl that Nelvil's deceased father had chosen for him over the "wild" Corinne, whom the elder Edgermond had years ago dismissed from consideration because of her vivacity and craving for attention. Lucile is also, irony upon irony, Corinne's half-sister. The late Edgermond had married an Italian, fathered Corinne, become a widower, returned to England, married a rigidly upright and dutiful English woman, fathered Lucile, and arranged with Lord Nelvil that their two English children would one day marry. After her father's death Corinne had been at liberty to flee the ennui of life in cold England, to depart the rigid English drawing rooms where nice girls do not in mixed company quote poetry in which the word "love" appears, and to return to her beloved Italy where she has been free to learn, travel, perform, converse, and receive the poet's laurel from an adoring Roman public. At the height of her public acclaim, then, on the day of her crowning at the Capitol, the Italian goddess mesmerizes the visiting Englishman Oswald, Lord Nelvil.

As Edgermond had done in the previous generation, Nelvil loves an Italian woman, then marries an English wife and becomes the father of an English daughter. Like Staël's Delphine (in *Delphine,* her other novel), the mythical prophetess Corinne is cursed with the inability to find a man worthy of herself. In Delphine's case, Léonce de Mondoville cares too much for honor and reputation; in Corinne's, Nelvil proves to need English ease, order, wealth, industry, and dignified manhood, as well as the attributes of an English family, which Staël believes to be at the core of English life and the English national character. Because Nelvil cannot simultaneously fulfill all his "duties" to his dead father, to the Italian woman whom he has loved, and to the fatherless English girl whose mother suffers from a terminal illness, his choice of Lucile over Corinne does not exactly fill his English home with happiness—but rather with remorse, guilt, and the melancholy that has marked his character from the outset. When Oswald's wife, Lucile, and his daughter, little Juliette, meet the dying Corinne in Florence, she "forgives" Nelvil and begins teaching music to the child Juliette, who much resembles the dark-haired aunt who has played Juliet on the stage. Corinne is thus molding the girl into the potential Corinne of the next generation and creating a legacy that British reserve and propriety may not circumvent. Then Corinne prepares her heart and mind for her death as an observant Catholic. While some take this religious peace at face value, Gutwirth notes that Corinne dies vengefully and that her shaping both her sister, Lucile, and niece, Juliette, into versions of herself is a bittersweet revenge on the man who deserted her.[20] Corinne wants to make sure that for the remainder of his life, every time Nelvil looks at his wife or daughter, he sees Corinne.

Like Consuelo's, Corinne's is a most public kind of art. Granted, she reads, composes, and paints in private, but she makes a splash as actress and performer. Staël attempts to convey modesty with Corinne's pride, naturalness with her magnificence, but the grandiose Corinne outshines the private, intimate woman— the performer for whom "la passion et la timidité tour à tour entraînent ou retiennent, inspirent trop d'amertume ou trop de soumission" (passion and modesty from time to time impelled or restrained her, inciting pride or forcing its submission [*C,* 198]). Yet Corinne as actress, dancer, singer, and declaimer of her verse hungers for attention (primarily Nelvil's); always she is either performing or posing, sometimes the performance being a demonstration of her enlightened opinions. More than once in their romance, Nelvil comments that he cannot take her away from her adoring public, that she cannot live without the bravos of her

20. Gutwirth, "Mme de Staël's Debt to *Phèdre: Corinne,*" 173–74.

fans. And Staël makes obvious that without her art, Corinne will wither and die. Even her acclaim, like her performances, is very much a public display—the most dramatic instance being the antique chariot drawn by white horses and carrying her to the Capitol where she is crowned. She is a national treasure, Apollo's Pythian, Sappho's daughter, and "l'image de notre belle Italie" (*C*, 57).

So Corinne is the personification of fair Italy. Each throb of her very heart ("chaque battement de mon cœur" [*C*, 385]), she says, is a call to her smiling country. From the fount of inspiration that is her soul, she personifies, symbolizes, and represents Italy. Staël depicts her artist as transported by the passion and "enthusiasm" that come from *within*, in Corinne "vivacité de l'esprit" (*C*, 55). In conceptualizing genius, Staël would agree with Shelley, who describes the phenomenon as a "power [that] arises from within, like the colour of a flower which fades and changes as it is developed, and the conscious portions of our natures are unprophetic either of its approach or its departure." It is, in fact, liveliness and spontaneity overflowing from within that mark the character of both Staël and her heroines; in *Delphine* the protagonist's lover, Léonce, being attracted by her "enthousiasme, une élévation d'âme." In the drama *Sapho* it is enthusiasm of nature and love of the beautiful that qualify one as a priest of Apollo. In *De l'Allemagne* Staël defines enthusiasm as the love of the beautiful, the elevation of soul, the enjoyment of pure devotion, and universal harmony. She adds that, with the Greeks, she accepts "l'enthousiasme signifie *Dieu en nous*" (enthusiasm signifies God in us). As Claire L. Dehon notes, imagination and enthusiasm dominate other qualities of intellectualism and creativity in *Corinne*, and both are produced by divine inspiration.[21]

Enthusiasm is the divine gift, the Promethean fire, and metaphorically speaking, Staël centers creative inspiration within the heart of Corinne. In conceptualizing the source of genius, Staël plays upon the term *cœur*, or heart, and its connection to the heroine's name. After Edgermond's death, his widow had asked her stepdaughter to conceal her connection to the Edgermond name, and Corinne had complied, taking as her pseudonym the name of the Greek poet Corinna, who had rivaled Pindar. It is, however, a fortunate coincidence that the first syllable of the chosen name sounds like the French word for "heart." Repeatedly, then, Staël focuses upon *le cœur de Corinne*. Prince Castel-Forte says she is the ideal female image clad in the hues of her own heart (*C*, 55). In referring to the sublime beauty of the Italian landscape, Corinne herself says she has found in nature and in her own heart ("dans mon propre cœur" [*C*, 85]) the audacious truths she speaks. The

21. Shelley, *A Defence of Poetry*, in *The Complete Works of Percy Bysshe Shelley*, 7:135; Staël, *Delphine*, in *Œuvres complètes de Madame la Baronne de Staël-Holstein*, 1:375; *Sapho*, 1:1 in *Œuvres posthumes de Madame la Baronne de Staël-Holstein*, 492; *De L'Allemagne*, in *Œuvres complètes*, 2:250; Dehon, "*Corinne: Une artiste heroine de Roman*," 2.

heart is the means of interpreting suffering as prophecy, Corinne tells Nelvil: "dans les passions profondes, le cœur est tout à coup doué d'un instinct miraculeux, et les souffrances sont des oracles" (in profound passions, the heart is suddenly gifted with miraculous instincts, and its own sufferings become oracles [*C*, 401]).

In a discussion with Oswald about religion, she affirms that religion consists of something deeper than morality and duty, that if it were only that, it would not be superior to philosophy and reason. She goes on to query what piety humans could truly feel, if the principal end of religion were to stifle all the feelings of the heart (*C*, 271). When she and Nelvil visit the Monks' Garden of Villa Melini with its picturesque setting and the Apennines in the background, Corinne makes a very democratic claim for all people this same spirit in all human hearts (*C*, 141)—Staël believing that the artistic perfectibility of a nation and its people depends to a large degree upon its political freedom or tyranny. Thus the forms and shapes of institutions may stifle the enthusiasm of the heart, as they may suppress individuality, responsibility, and love of liberty. From art Corinne has learned, she says, that an eternal and divine spark exists within all people—not hers alone—and that the artist fans the flame in his own breast to light the fire within others (*C*, 111–12). In her improvisation at Naples, Corinne again returns to the theme that all human hearts are creative and that the artist/prophetess discovers the truth of her own soul to speak to the collective souls of those who observe:

> Mais la prêtresse qui rendait les oracles, se sentait agitée par une puissance rendait les oracles, se sentait agitée par une puissance cruelle. Je ne sais quelle force involontaire précipite le génie dans le malheur: il entend le bruit des sphères que les organes mortels ne sont pas faits pour saisir; il pénètre des mystères du sentiment inconnus aux autres hommes, et son ame recèle un Dieu qu'elle ne peut contenir!" (*C*, 354)

> But she, the priestess of the oracle,
> Shook with the presence of the cruel power.
> I know not what the involuntary force
> That plunges Genius into misery.
> Genius doth catch the music of the spheres,
> Which mortal ear was never meant to know.
> Genius can penetrate the mysteries
> Of feeling, all unknown to other hearts;
> A power hath entered in the inmost soul,
> Whose presence may not be contained.[22]

22. The translation is by British poet Letitia Landon (L. E. L.) in the English edition of *Corinne* edited by Isabel Hill, 225.

The Promethean aspect of Corinne's art, and of Staël's, is that the female Prometheus not only bears the sacred flame (or, in the Pythian context, hears the music of the spheres) but also willingly confers it upon the hearts of those inclined to hear and understand—as Prometheus bestowed the benefits of fire upon the human race. In her recitation at Rome (*C*, 60), Corinne uses Promethean fire to suggest the genius of Dante, Petrarch, and other Italian artists, the implication being that Corinne herself is the new Promethean. In *Sapho*, however, the great poet of Lesbos notes too that the penalty for Promethean woman is perpetual suffering—the vulture of Zeus feeding upon her heart.[23]

In addition to the concern about the source and operation of genius, Staël, Sand, and their English disciples were invariably interested in romantic love and whether it is detrimental to art. Naturally, the province of the novel being sexual romance, the question has to arise. Staël's previous novel, *Delphine*, ostensibly sets out to prove—in the words of several female characters, including Delphine herself—that happiness for woman depends on marriage to the man she loves. But the novel is a set-up, Staël having demonstrated in *De l'influence des passions sur le bonheur des individus et des nations* that happiness is a commodity that, although all humans seek, they are unlikely to find. In *Delphine*, women who love face societal disapproval (as Elise does), guilt followed by death-in-life in a convent (Thérèse), marriage to a man who does not return her love, followed by death in childbirth (Matilde), disinheritance and poverty (Mme de Belmont), or misery and suicide (Delphine).

Both Staël and Sand acknowledge that women of genius, like ordinary women, seek happiness in marital domesticity or sexual bliss. As Sand's Consuelo proclaims she would abandon the stage for a great and abiding love, so does Corinne proclaim love greater than fame. In recalling her failures with the German nobleman and Italian prince, Corinne confesses to Nelvil, "Je me crus destinée à ne jamais aimer de toute la puissance de mon ame; quelquefois cette idée m'était pénible, plus souvent je m'applaudissais d'être libre . . ." (I believed myself destined never to love with all the power of my soul; sometimes this idea saddened me; more often I applauded my freedom . . ." [*C*, 388]). Deciding that Nelvil is the one great love for whom she would abandon her artistic life, though, Corinne frequently pledges to become his wife, even his slave, because love's demands are greater than art's. When, for example, he tells her that he is about to be recalled by his nation to go war with France, she entreats that he take her with him as wife or as slave: "emmenez-moi comme épouse, comme esclave" (*C*, 214). Bidding farewell to beloved Rome, she says that she loves Nelvil more than she loves the independence that the holy city has afforded her. No doubt in the passion

23. Staël, *Sapho*, 2.5 in *Œuvres posthumes*, 500.

and terror of the moment, Corinne believes that she is capable of marital domestic servitude, yet her plea seems more a melodramatic display rather than a
considered decision for a practicable future. She has allowed her enthusiasm to
prevail over her reason. In her repeated vows to become Nelvil's slave, she should
recall that servitude is not her style and that freedom has heretofore meant more
than love. Naturally Staël's passionate, vivacious, brilliant artist—like the artist
Staël herself—desires complete liberty, public adulation, and passionate love. But
in *Corinne* Staël illustrates to herself, and to the reader, that the woman as artist
cannot have it all.

Taking the traditional view of feminine purpose and fulfillment, the Romantic poet Felicia Hemans, an English disciple of Staël, suggests in "Corinne at the
Capitol" that Corinne would have been happier and perhaps better with the romantic love of one good man than with the love of all Rome.

> Radiant daughter of the sun!
> Now thy living wreath is won.
> Crowned of Rome!—Oh! Art thou not
> Happy in that glorious lot?—
> Happier, happier far than thou,
> With the laurel on thy brow,
> She that makes the humblest hearth
> Lovely but to one on earth![24]

It would appear that—although Staël was certainly a feminist of her own day—
both she and Hemans fail to measure up to contemporary feminism because they
hold that a woman should forsake all for love.

In Corinne, Staël has created a woman artist who values love and liberty above
all things, but who finds that society and fate oppose the woman who desires autonomy, adulation, and artistic freedom—even if she has become the woman
who, like Corinne, lays her considerable glory at the feet of her lover. This is the
case not only with Corinne and Delphine, but also with Pauline and the poet
Mirza, female heroes of novellas by Staël. Corinne's enthusiasm and imagination,
as well as her unquestioning love for her country, qualify her as spokesperson for
Italy. But her narcissism and her passion—together with the fate of loving the
wrong man—prevent her from fulfilling all her needs. Indeed, they prevent her
survival and cause her suffering of the type that Staël apparently believes will befall the creative, outspoken woman. At least she writes in *Dix années d'exil* that
under the emperor's persecutions, her *own* suffering was so severe that she lost all
hope, all happiness, and all faith in Providence.[25] But in Staël, in fact, it seems

24. Hemans, "Corinne at the Capitol," in *Mrs. Felicia Hemans*, 615.
25. Staël, *Dix années d'exil*, in *Œuvres posthumes*, 112.

to be a given that all artists, male and female, will suffer. The vulture of Jove is impartial in regard to gender. Repeatedly Corinne refers to the suffering of artists—the exile of Dante and Monti, for example, and Tasso's confinement as a madman. Yet, for Tasso as for Corinne, Staël speculates that without suffering, one is no true prophet (*C,* 419), for the poet draws his power from loving and from suffering (*C,* 354). Nevertheless Staël realizes that the suffering must be parsed by reason and reflection; debilitating heartbreak is the foe to creativity because it produces a gloomy agitation and mental confusion—as reflected by Corinne's meandering fragments on love once Nelvil has married Lucile and Corinne is dying. To her grief, Corinne discovers that although she says she was made for happiness, she also has, as every great artist must have, a great capacity for suffering. She also discovers that passionate love does not guarantee happiness and that talent requires internal freedom, which true love destroys (*C,* 430). Liberty is an absolute necessity for the female artist, but an artist in love can never be absolutely free.

The Corinne Myth

To establish that Corinne is fascinating and alluring, Staël brings to bear upon her characterization a number of mythic and classical allusions. In so doing she creates in Corinne a mythical character intriguing to generations of women writers. Gutwirth says that Staël "willed her Corinne to be a myth-making novel."[26] Corinne, for instance, is inheritor of the female genius of Sappho and Corinna, as she is inheritor of the patriotic womanhood of Agrappina, Cornelia, and Portia—women loved by heroes. In beauty and allure she is implicitly compared to Italy's artistic depictions of Aphrodites, Naiads, and various nymphs of beauty, particularly to the Venus di Medici, a painting she owns. She is also the Diana who restored Hippolytus to life. Oddly, Corinne is both seductress and Madonna—the Virgin being, as noted above, a manifestation of Wisdom.[27] The intoxicated Nelvil calls her a sorceress—the "magicienne" who has cast a spell over him (*C,* 158); he succumbs as Odysseus to the Siren, the crusader to seductive Armida, Aeneas to Dido, Antony to Cleopatra, Adam to Eve (Rome and Naples constituting a temporary Eden). Corinne enacts, by means of Staël's allusions, many of the most famous sexual sorceresses of Western myth. In decadent Venice she

26. Gutwirth, *Madame de Staël, Novelist,* 204. In addition to the myths I note, Gutwirth also suggests that Corinne is Persephone to mother Italy as Demeter (211) and Iseult the Dark to Lucile's Iseult the Fair (227).

27. For the observation on Corinne's connection to the Virgin, I am indebted to Marie-Claire Vallois, who notes that the blue and white of Domenichino's Sibyl are also colors of the Virgin Mary. (*Fictions féminines: Mme de Staël et les voix de la Sibylle,* 138).

performs the role of the sorceress Semiramis, in *La Fille de l'air*. The Assyrian queen of Ninevah, whom Dante in his *Inferno* places in the sphere of the lustful, is—as Corinne plays her—coquettish, enchanting, savage, courageous, ambitious, cunning, imperious (*C*, 434). The smitten Nelvil speculates whether Corinne is Armida or Sappho (*C*, 77), and the answer is that she is both—and many other mythic characters as well. In Semiramis, for example, Corinne casts herself as the seductress—a vivid contrast to casting herself as the doomed and innocent Juliet in Shakespeare's tragedy of young love.

As for the Madonna allusions, on one occasion Nelvil gazes upon the face of Corinne reflected in the Virgin Spring ("l'eau virginale" [*C*, 125]). In addition, the face of the Virgin Mary (along with that of Nelvil) dominates Corinne's room. This trait could be accounted for by her devout Catholicism, for Staël notes that peoples of the South are especially drawn to the Virgin, and Corinne claims Mary as her special intercessor. In Corinne's personal mythology, however, she mixes religion and art; they are the same—both based upon passion and enthusiasm, rather than submission and duty, as Nelvil's Anglicanism is. The Madonna, therefore, contains meaning in the narcissistic self-image of Corinne, just as do the images of seductive women, patriotic women, and doomed women. Further, Corinne feels herself a second mother to her much younger half-sister, Lucile, whom she had nestled to her breast as an infant, then taught Italian and drawing. When she returns to Florence after having lost her lover to Lucile, Corinne reflects upon Niobe crying for her dead daughter (*C*, 518–19). Thus Corinne is a childless Niobe and Madonna.

Among the works of Corinne's gallery are various spurned women, further establishing the mythic dimensions of Corinne and foreshadowing the outcome of the love affair with Nelvil; these include Phaedra and Dido, as well as the dying Clorinda pardoning Tancred, a tableau that Corinne reenacts in her own death at Florence. Although she dies claiming that she wants only repose, Corinne's revengeful death and her refusal to allow Nelvil to visit her deathbed recall the discarded queen Dido and her snub of Aeneas in the Underworld—a scene depicted in Corinne's art collection (*C*, 234). But the connection is also specifically stated by the narrator (*C*, 581).

Not only is Corinne the seductress, the great beauty, the doomed lover, the Madonna, and the divinely gifted artist, she is also—and especially—the modern Sappho and Cumæan Sibyl to Nelvil's heroic Aeneas. Jean DeJean notes that Napoleon's sister Caroline had recently been named the "Sappho" of France, hence embodying in a female mythic personhood the ideals of French imperialism, and that Staël is consciously and deliberately upstaging the Empire's Sappho with her own Sappho/Corinna, whose improvisations expose Napoleon's annihilation of Republican values. Corinne represents the Sappho of French Republicanism.[28] As a political Sibyl, Corinne must garner respect. Although a priestess of Apollo—like Cassandra, the prophetess cursed by Apollo—is usually considered merely the vessel of divinity, that is, the frenzied, possessed, or hysterical female through whom the god speaks, the Cumæan Sibyl is depicted as wise, self-possessed, and purposeful in her speech and actions. Staël wishes to make Corinne regal, independent, and self-aware; therefore she opts for this particular figure rather than, say, a Cassandra. In *Corinne* the mythical allusions to the Sibyl of Cumæ abound. For instance, Corinne's villa is located on the cascade of Teverone, facing the Sibyl's temple. As previously noted, on the day of her honor at the Capitol she is attired like Domenichino's Sibyl—an Indian shawl twined into her hair, a blue drapery over her robe of virgin white (*C,* 52). Always she speaks authoritatively, as a prophetess of Apollo would speak. Well over half of the novel consists of Corinne as tour guide through Italy, paralleling the Sibyl's guidance through the Underworld, with Corinne justifying, arguing, and explaining Italian art, history, landscapes, politics, and national character. In leading Nelvil/ Aeneas to various sights and shrines of Italy, she not only initiates him into the mysteries of passionate love, but also recalls—by means of Corinne's collection of favorite drawings—the wisdom and patriotism of Cumæan Sibyl (*C,* 234).

In Virgil's *Aeneid* the Trojan Aeneas, future founder of the Roman dynasty, stops off on the Cumæan coast and—desirous to meet the spirit of his recently deceased father and learn a propitious sign for his success—seeks out the Sibyl of Apollo deep in her cave. The Sibyl foretells his adventure and success, then leads him to the land of the dead, where he hears from the lips of his father, Anchises—whose patriarchal wisdom augments the female wisdom of the Sibyl—exactly what greatness Rome shall bestow on the world. Ceding to others the excellence in arts, sculpture, rhetoric, and philosophy, Anchises reserves to Rome the talent of governing: "But, Rome! 'Tis thine alone, with awful sway, / To rule mankind, and make the world obey / Disposing peace and war thy own majestic way." Like Aeneas, or a latter-day melancholy Hamlet "seeking his noble father in the dust," Nelvil seeks patriarchal wisdom as well. As Gutwirth rightly notes, *Corinne* is a novel of the patriarchs as *Delphine* (1802) is of the matriarchs.[29] Although Corinne claims that the Virgin is her intercessor, both she and Lucile pray to the spirit of the dead Edgermond to intercede with the deity, Lucile asking a blessing for her love, Corinne asking for an easeful death.

Nelvil believes that his own father's wishes will decide merely whether he does or does not marry Corinne, but when he encounters the dead patriarch's words

---

28. DeJean, "Portrait of the Artist as Sappho," 125–31.
29. Virgil, *The Aeneid* 6, in *The Works of Virgil,* 168; Gutwirth, *Madame de Staël, Novelist,* 157.

in the form of a letter, the elder Nelvil not only forbids Oswald the fascinating Corinne, but also, like an Anchises, speaks from the other world on matters of patriotism. That is, an Englishman is called to duty, honor, and public action, he says, for such is the national character and his personal destiny. And this is a destiny he cannot fulfill with a Sibyl whose allegiance is to Italy instead of England. Italy is a land of past glory and future promise and Corinne herself is a relic of the past, prophetess of the future [*C,* 57], but England is *the* nation of the present era—acknowledged by Staël for its free press and political candor; its prosperity, commerce, and industry; its liberty and public spirit; its common sense, tolerance, justice, and security; its energy; and the engagement of its citizens in carrying on the ideals of the nation-state.[30] Although the reader of *Corinne* is likely to consider Nelvil a moral weakling because he abandons Corinne, Staël does not object to him on the grounds of his patriotism and political activity; indeed she recognizes it as part and parcel of the English national character. It is ironic that—while the Cumæan Sibyl leads Aeneas *to* Anchises, Nelvil finds his dead father when he flees *from* Corinne, who becomes to the imagination of the English lord not a wise Sibyl, but a foreign Dido luring him from patriotic duty to a Carthage of erotic self-indulgence. Nelvil leaves the wisdom of his Sibyl— that is, the wisdom of the heart, of enthusiasm, imagination, and passion—for the duty and service that his English nature demands of him, and as Nelvil says when Corinne lies dying, "La Sibylle ne rend plus d'oracles; son génie . . . est fini" (The Sibyl utters no more oracles; her genius . . . is over [*C,* 562]).

Not only is Corinne a version of Virgil's Sibyl, she is more importantly Dante's Beatrice, a Wisdom figure central to both Italian identity and Christian iconography. Both Dante and Staël wrote extensively on politics and political theory, bringing down upon their heads the disfavor of the powers of Florence and France respectively; both were exiled; and both the *Commedia* and *Corinne* are— among other things—political art. In the months prior to writing *Corinne,* Staël read Dante's *Commedia*—an important influence on her iconography and encoded politics. The connection between the *Aeneid* and Dante's "comedy" is important, as is *Corinne's* connection to both predecessors. Virgil is to Dante, "lo mio maestro e 'l mio autore," the master who taught him, by example, the noble art of the epic.[31] Virgil leads Dante through the Inferno and Purgatorio as Virgil's Sibyl leads Aeneas. Dante critics universally accept that Virgil is Human Reason to Beatrice's Divine Grace, but Virgil as a patriotic poet of the Roman

---

30. Staël, *Considérations sur les principaux événements de la Révolution Française* in *Œuvres posthumes,* 289–321. In *Delphine,* Henri de Lebensei, who serves as Staël's political spokesman on such issues as liberty, the Revolution, and rights to divorce, comments that he admires England as a nation moral, religious, and free (*Œuvres complètes,* 1:532).

31. Alghieri, *Inferno,* 1:85.

Empire also represents chauvinism and imperialism, an aspect of the Italian epic important to both Dante and Staël. Further, Dante's political doctrines include the belief in self-destiny through the exercise of Right Reason and Free Will—an equivalent to Staël's God-given *liberté*.[32]

Dante advocates a Roman empire as the most acceptable form of government because the emperor, controlling the world, would not resort to tyranny and because the unity of one nation-state most nearly approximates the unity that is in the holy Trinity—the oneness to which, Dante believed, all things rightly aspire. Naturally Dante would *not* cede his right to his own opinions—a stance he adopted on the basis that it would be a perversion of his God-given Reason and Free Will to subscribe to papal or political pronouncements that violate his intellect and freedom of thought. Staël believed that the great experiment of freedom, once bathed in blood, should be permitted to run its course—too great a price having been paid for the nation to turn back—but like Dante she objected to empire-as-tyranny and insisted upon individual freedom. In her improvisation at the Capitol and elsewhere, Corinne recalls the lines of Dante who, she says, was republican, bard, and warrior, and whose poetry was divination revealing the human heart. Staël finds in Dante's love of Florence a parallel of her love for France, and in his pain of exile she finds an analogue for her own:

> Le Dante espérait de son poëme la fin de son exil; il comptait sur la renommée pour médiateur; mais il mourut trop tôt pour recueillir les palmes de la patrie."
> (*C*, 62)

> Methinks that Dante, banish'd his own soil,
> Bore to imagined worlds his actual grief,
> Ever his shades inquire the things of life,
> And ask'd the poet of his native land;
> And from his exile did he paint a hell.[33]

This statement prepares Staël's readers that her novel is to be read as representing her own nation and people, just as Dante's Hell, Purgatory, and Heaven are populated with citizens of Tuscany, and just as his great work is a faithful political history of his Florence. As a Dante or a Petrarch is "le poëte valeureux de l'indépendance italienne" (*C*, 62),[34] Staël serves as valorous poet

---

32. In her book on the French revolution, though, Staël comments that the "free will" of man is, under the regime of Napoleon, a metaphysical question completely pointless to consider (*Considérations* in *Œuvres posthumes*, 221).

33. Translation by L. E. L., in Isabel Hill's translation, *Corinne*, 26.

34. Vallois notes that the excursion to Naples and beyond is the descent to Hell and Purgatory (*Fictions féminines*, 144.)

of French independence and liberty, and as an enemy to Napoleon's dynastic tyranny.

Several parallels in the novel *Corinne* recall Dante's epic. Staël repeatedly quotes or paraphrases Dante's poetry or refers to his patriotism, his love of liberty, his influence on Italian art, his mixing of pagan and classic sources, and the esteem in which he is held in the minds of Florentines. Among the many allusions to Dante in the story line are that Edgermond in England wore the leaden cowl of Dante's hypocrites (in canto 23 of *Inferno*), and the frozen landscape that Nelvil and Lucile cross reminds them of the sheet of ice of Dante's Cocytus (in canto 32); streams are like the Styx, landscapes like the Elysian Fields. Nelvil represents not only the questing Aeneas but also the questing Dante. The allegorical dark wood where Dante encounters Virgil is, among other things, the sin of Despair—certainly the condition of the British hero Nelvil as well as of Dante in his pilgrimage midway though life. As Dante is guided by Virgil to the point where the master turns his pupil over to the instruction of Beatrice, so Lord Nelvil is guided by Count d'Erfeuil, who first accompanies Nelvil to Italy (all the while instructing him to forswear his melancholy), then takes him to the residence of Corinne, whom Nelvil is meant to interpret as his Sibyl and Beatrice. As is the case for Virgil, d'Erfeuil relinquishes the tutorials for Nelvil once the Englishman is in the capable hands of the female Wisdom. Several scenes that Nelvil encounters in his quest are hellish, for example the lunatic asylum of Ancoma, from which he liberates the prisoners when flames destroy the city, and the airborne disease of malaria, with which Corinne falls dangerously ill. Nowhere are the imagery of hell and the parallel of Corinne with Beatrice more blatant than when the lovers visit the volcano Vesuvius, where the literal inferno of crater, lava, flames, and ash are described in Dantean analogy of whirlwind, pitch, and sulphur, and the narrator remarks that the phenomenon inspires all poetic depictions of hell (*C,* 338). Their paid guides being far behind the lovers, Corinne proves herself a Beatrice by literally guiding Nelvil from Vesuvius, which reminds him that he is a Sisyphus struggling against the boulder of fate and misery. Beatrice-like, she then directs his sight upward to mountains nearer heaven, to remind humans of the terrestrial life as substitute for our hellish existence (*C,* 339).

No doubt Staël was drawn to Dante in part because he is a rarity among poets in that his female paragon is not only lovely, she is also the Grace, Love, and Wisdom of God himself. When Nelvil meets Corinne, drawn in her chariot to receive the crown at Rome, Nelvil reenacts Dante's receiving Beatrice in the closing cantos of *Purgatorio.* Beatrice arrives carried in a triumphal chariot drawn by the celestial griffin and accompanied by seven maidens—holy virgins who represent the cardinal and theological virtues. She wears on her head a wreath of olive leaves—the olive representing "wise Minerva's leaves." The eyes of Beatrice fix Dante, entering his soul and piercing him through and through. They are the eyes of Grace.[35] Corinne also arrives at the capital in a cloud of glory and a triumphal chariot—hers drawn by four spotless horses but also accompanied by a band of maidens arrayed in white. Exquisite music accompanies the procession in each case, and flowers are lavished upon Corinne as they are upon Beatrice (*C*, 51–52). Corinne loses the crown of bays and myrtle with which the senator had crowned her, and Nelvil pushes forward to retrieve it; when he does, Corinne's eyes meet his and she looks back repeatedly to gaze at him. Nelvil follows her— as Dante follows at Beatrice's bidding to enter Paradise—or at least Nelvil follows his Beatrice until duty and patriarchy intervene. The Dantean woman to whom Staël alludes in her creation of Corinne is no mere frenzy-possessed Pythian, but rather Sophia, the Wisdom and Word of God. As Paul A. Olson notes in reference to Dante's recurring female Wisdom figure:

> . . . this Wisdom and the Logos are one and draw all things to themselves. Dante's eternal Wisdom is a holistic source of the reforming motive, sending down flamelets of fire to her earthly lover in the form of right desire culminating in right acts. She becomes thereby the author of natural law and right love among people . . . and informs both the contemplative and the pragmatic active life. She is the Beatrice of the *Commedia*.[36]

As previously noted, at the end of the *Purgatorio*, Virgil relinquishes the guidance of Dante to the beloved Beatrice, who teaches Dante true repentance and humility and prepares his soul to enter Paradise. Staël here implies that were Nelvil to follow suit, he could learn enthusiasm, passion, and the meaning of life from his divine Sibyl/Sophia. In *Corinne* there is, however, no progression from an inferno to a paradise precisely because Nelvil does not follow his Beatrice; midway through his pilgrimage, he turns from her in betrothal to her sister, a Matilda/ Lucile of English patriotism and civic and family life—Matilda in *Purgatorio* being usually interpreted as an allegory for the active life as Beatrice is for the Contemplative. As Matilda baptizes Dante in the River Lethe after he has learned true repentance, traditional marriage to an English Matilda permits Nelvil to atone for his affairs with the French woman Mme d'Arbigny and the Italian woman Corinne—both of them representing to the English sense of duty a self-indulgent sensuality. After his marriage Nelvil lives the Active Life of English citizenship: He goes to war, thrills to the tumult of battle, exposes his life heroically, and earns the devotion of his soldiers, and he ends the novel living an exemplary—albeit unhappy—domestic life. Unlike Dante, he cannot serve two

35. Alghieri, *Purgatorio*, 30:68, 65–66, 121; 31:133.
36. Olson, *The Journey to Wisdom: Self-Education in Patristic and Medieval Literature*, 158.

masters; he cannot enjoy the love of Matilda and the love of Corinne. Following the mythic construction of Corinne as Beatrice, in the minds of Staël's readers, whether or not they make the conscious connection, it is all the more to the discredit of Nelvil that he does not follow such a paragon as Corinne—for, as Olson notes, Beatrice perfectly embodies the joys of active life and spiritual contemplation. In sacrificing Wisdom for duty, Nelvil forsakes the greater for the lesser good.

The Political Corinne

Corinne is, then, the spiritual reincarnation of the Cumæan Sibyl and the divine Beatrice, as well as "l'image de notre faire Italie." And as a political Sibyl she certainly represents liberty, intelligence, devotion, and both individual achievement and national promise. Doris Y. Kadish suggests that there is in fact still one more mythic and allegorical importance of the Domenichino Sibyl that Corinne at the Capitol is said to resemble—and this one is specifically political, connecting Corinne to the goddess allegory of Lady Liberty that was prominent in French political art. Kadish notes that the tricolors of the Republic are symbolized by virginal white tunic and blue drapery, together with the scarlet hanging in windows that form the backdrop. Corinne in this early scene in Rome is, Kadish says, "associated with the positive, moderate, non-Jacobin side of revolution and with the lofty goals and aspirations that Staël conceived after 1793 for a Republic controlled by the emerging middle class."[37] As such, she is the Liberty and Nike of Revolution-era French art and iconography. She also represents the Romantic ideal most memorably expressed in Shelley's comment that the poet is legislator of the world. Corinne, as well as Staël, is a political Sibyl, employing her genius to save the nation.

Germaine de Staël was an intensely political writer. Yet in *Corinne* she posits that writers can do nothing for their nation because they double back upon themselves without advancing even one step (*C*, 176). Staël was fascinated with the history of civilizations and intrigued with the notions of national character; she opposed Napoleon's despotism while endorsing in principle the traditional French monarchy as the form of government that best suited her nation. Staël saw modern history as having evolved in three stages: feudalism marked by inroads of the bourgeoisie, the modern-era despotisms, and the representative forms of government that she found in England and the United States (although she admitted that the latter system was still evolving). Further, Staël believed in

---

37. Kadish, "Narrating the French Revolution: The Example of *Corinne*," 116.

the perfectibility of humankind—a belief that she traces to Condorcet. Not that humans will arrive at perfection, but rather that human institutions, as well as human artistic endeavors, have throughout history been moving along a continuum of progress—although sometimes the progress has been in fits and starts rather than in some organized and orderly movement. In *Corinne,* in fact, the chronology of Italian art, Etruscan through Renaissance, reflects the progress of the human mind (*C,* 136), while political chaos and miasma are the by-products of tyranny. In Staël's contemporary political realm, the despotism of Jacobins and of Napoleon represent atavism, retarding human progress toward freedom and representative government, throwing the populace backward into earlier stages of the human condition, and negating the process that, elsewhere, the world has attained. Thus all human institutions either assist in movement toward perfection or impede the progress toward perfection and happiness, which Staël defines as the Good without its opposite Evil—hope without fear, liberty without license, rivalry without factionalism, and so on. Although the human passions of enthusiasm and ardent devotion produce creativity in all fields of artistic and civic endeavor, the human passions of avarice, pride, ambition, and pettiness undermine the perfectibility to which human political institutions tend. They are the great obstacle to political happiness; they steal from individual citizens the independence of free will that Dante valued and that is essential, Staël says, for any kind of individual happiness. Only in free states, she asserts in *De la littérature,* can both genius of action and of reflection be united; or, one might say, only in a free system can the Matilda and Beatrice aspects of life be attained.[38] Under despotism, however, even art makes no progress, because the artist serves the state—unless, of course, the artist is a "brave warrior/republican" like Dante or Germaine de Staël.

Because different countries have evolved under different political systems and in different social and religious climates, Staël posits that different national characters result. As noted in delineating Nelvil's conscience, the English character is open, patriotic, engaged—although aloof, rigid, and narrow-minded in its attitude toward women. Under a monarchy and in the milieu of the Court, the French developed wit, urbanity, mental finesse, and sophistication—but unfortunately even eloquence declined in France during the Revolution. Americans expect political equality because only they have enjoyed it. German and English poetry and philosophy are more "scientific" and objective, and those of the French are more intuitive, based upon enthusiasm. In the novel, Corinne explains that Italians are without pride, ceremony, fashion, hypocrisy, and as a peo-

---

38. Staël, *Considérations,* in *Œuvres posthumes,* 179; *De l'influence des passions sur le bonheur des individus et des nations,* in *Œuvres complètes,* 2:108; *De la littérature,* in *Œuvres complètes,* 2:288–300.

ple they value genius first among all gifts. Theirs is a national character that inspires a woman with greater enthusiasm. Even the various cities and regions have their own "national" character: The Piedmontese are more warlike, the Florentines are more well-educated because of their history of more liberal rulers, the Venetians and Genoese are more political because they have enjoyed the benefits of a republican aristocracy, and the Neapolitans are more rebellious because of their repressive government (*C,* 160–62). Using the concept of national character, *Corinne* illustrates the results of tyranny and promotes the concept of republic.

Staël began *Corinne* in 1805, immediately after Napoleon named himself king of Italy, and it was published in 1807, but the setting is 1794—the mid-1790s when the Reign of Terror had done its worst. In *Considérations,* Staël compares the Terror to Dante's Hell, each circle of torment being worse than the one that preceded it. First the nobles, then the priests, then talent, then all beauty and goodness were destroyed, she says. By 1793, she adds, there were no more possible revolutions, everything having been overturned. With the Terror came Napoleon, who committed more acts of arbitrary insolence every day of his life than any monarch of Europe would commit in a whole year.[39] That the plight of France is always in the background of the literal plot and action Staël keeps in the reader's mind by means of Nelvil's personal and military career. As a foreigner, he had to leave his French mistress in 1791; the following year, the Reign of Terror took the life of his friend Count Raimond in the massacre at the Tuileries; and after 1796 when he thinks of returning to Italy to comfort the abandoned Corinne, he is prevented from doing so because Rome and Florence are now occupied by French troops. While Nelvil's career brings to mind the chronology of the Revolution, the condition of Italy represents simultaneously both itself and the condition of the Napoleonic empire. Reflecting upon the Italian national character, Corinne reminds Oswald that Italy's great achievements, its great artists and poets, were of the past, and that currently Italy is ruled by despotism. Castel-Forte corroborates that if his nation were freed from ignorance, envy, discord, and sloth, it would be great again (*C,* 57). Corinne also laments the current lack of liberty in Italy as well as the decadence of the age in which self-interest, not national pride, seems to be the ruling principle (*C,* 71). Corinne, as relic/ spokeswoman of Italy's great history, praises the achievement of Rome's classic past, saying that while they mourned for liberty, the Romans strewed the world with wonders (*C,* 66)—a statement that would indeed be accurate but was also a coded criticism that Napoleon rightly read as pointed toward contemporary France, which "mourned for liberty" under the Napoleonic code. Because the rep-

---

39. Staël, *Considérations,* in *Œuvres posthumes,* 178; *Dix années d'exil,* in *Œuvres posthumes,* 363.

resentative republics of Europe and the New World are free (that is, have attained the third stage of human destiny), they are nations of the present; because France and Italy are under a despot, they are frozen in the second stage—their glory dead, their future in doubt.

When Corinne and Nelvil arrive in Naples, they find the worst shambles of government that they have yet seen. The people are indolent and unmotivated, sluggish and unambitious. While Nelvil, as representative of a nation in which the individual [male] citizen actively serves the nation, remarks that the people have the government they deserve, Corinne responds that rather the government has determined the character of the people—a viewpoint that more closely matches Staël's. Since the Neapolitan government behaves as a potentate or sultan and the citizens experience all the confinements of women in a seraglio, then what can one expect other than to have the citizens behave like so many odalisques. On the one hand, Staël notes that the code of Napoleon is a retrogression to despotism, not a move forward toward a representative government, and therefore the French citizens will be expected to behave as the Neapolitans, not with the energetic, active commitment to the state that Staël finds in representative republics. No wonder Bonaparte disliked Staël, and she returned the favor.

Finally, while *Corinne* is a statement on political repression, it also serves Staël as gender politics. For example, because the English system is open and free, English men like Nelvil feel called to duty without compulsion; at the same time— as she repeatedly notes in *Corinne*—English women are prohibited from public attention. English men have dignity; English women, only modesty (*C,* 447). When Corinne notes that according to Propertius, Roman women *do* have dignity (*C,* 131), Staël calls attention to the influence and dignity, not so much of the Roman woman of the final decades of the first century B.C. as of late-eighteenth-century French women of the salon—a condition that, Staël insists, is a distinct part of the French national character. On the other hand, Staël suggests that in places where the national conventions deny respect to women, females too behave like odalisques rather than Corinnes. As the salon of Mme Necker permitted Germaine to become Apollo's priestess, mother Italy allowed Corinne to develop into a secular Sibyl and divine Beatrice. Although Staël is often considered no feminist in that she did not advocate anything approaching political equality for women, she is certainly progressive in that she sees the condition of woman as one telltale sign of the progress of nations on their road to perfection. Here again Napoleon fails to measure up. This woman, whom Napoleon exiled, charges that he hates women and retains the Jacobin antipathy to brilliant women. Thus the Corsican outsider could never appreciate the wit of Parisian society and the power of the salon, both part of the French national character developed by centuries of monarchy, aristocracy, and intellectual skepticism.

As Beatrice educates Dante for Paradise, Corinne tries but fails to enlighten Nelvil—who, after all, sees his duty as going to war with France. When she lies dying, Corinne's last song repeats the nationalistic fervor of her art, reminds Nelvil of what he has lost, and needles Napoleon for having banished such a paragon as this modern-day Beatrice/Sybil, Germaine de Staël: "Dès les premiers jours de ma jeunesse, je promis d'honorer ce nom de Romaine qui fait encore tressaillir le cœur. Vous m'avez permis la gloire, oh! vous, nation libérale, qui ne bannissez point les femmes de son temple . . ." (*C,* 582).

> From my first days of youth, my inward hope
> Was to do honor to the Roman name;
> that name at which the startled heart yet beats.
> Ye have allow'd me fame, O generous land!
> Ye banished not a woman from your shrine![40]

Both *Delphine* and *Corinne* are political novels, the former set in France and dealing more specifically with the events of the Revolution, the latter encoding a condemnation of Napoleonic empire, while pleading for freedom and dignity for women, affirming the possibility of human political progress, and longing for a future of enlightened, united, energetic, and independent people—as opposed to either the dead ancien régime or the empire of Bonaparte. Kadish posits that, in this novel, gender is a code for class and that the novelist suggests the new republic should be based upon the middle class, rather than the aristocracy—that is, admitting women to the political mix. She sees the crowning of Corinne at the Capitol as a proposed alternative to Napoleon as king of France because Corinne represents simplicity, equality, and republican values.[41] Perhaps that is so, but more powerful than the suggested code that gender means class is the epic literary tradition of Virgil and Dante that Staël invokes. The mythic status of Corinne combines the Pythian and Aeneas's Sibyl, together with the Christian iconography of the Virgin Mary and Dante's Beatrice. For most of the English writers who knew and admired Staël, Corinne remains a figure for the artist as divinity.

George Sand's *Consuelo*

George Sand wrote the rise and fall of numerous artists. Among them are the questing painter Jean Valreg (who in *La Daniella* recalls Nelvil's pilgrimage through

---

40. Translation by L. E. L. in Isabel Hill's translation, *Corinne,* 378.
41. Kadish, "Narrating the French Revolution," 118–19.

Italy), the poet Sténio (in *Lélia*), the musicians Consuelo, Porpora, Joseph Haydn, Corilla, Anzoleto, Albert, Caffariello, and Umberti Porporino, among others (in the *Consuelo* novels), the fascinating actor Lélio and the actress/playwright Lucrezia Floriani (in *La Marquise* and *Lucrezia Floriani*, respectively), the tenor d'Argères, the artist Descombes, the musician Laure de Larnac, and the poet Baron de West (in *Adriani*), the bagpiper Joseph Picot (in *Les maîtres sonneurs*), the painters Thérèse Jacques and Laurent de Fauvel (who are also lovers in *Elle et lui*), the Italian musicians Favilla and Anselme (father and son in the play *Maître Favilla*), and the painters Flochardet and Diane (father and daughter in the short story "Le Château de Pictordu"). Also in Sand's works are a number of female characters who, though not literally musicians, painters, poets, singers, or actresses, are nevertheless artists under Sand's broad definition of the artist as one who feels and thinks most intensely, who is inspired and in love with beauty and truth. Among them are the healer Fanchon (in *La petite Fadette*), the "druidesse" and prophetess Jeanne (in *Jeanne*), the doomed aristocrat Valentine, who renounces her class for a pastoral life (in *Valentine*), and the fascinating and sublime muse/prophetess Lélia (in *Lélia*).

Consuelo, however, is perhaps George Sand's finest novel; certainly it has been the most admired of her seventy or so works of fiction—both in France and elsewhere. According to an 1877 essay by Matthew Arnold, it remained the most popular literary work in England more than three decades after its 1842 publication.[42] In *Consuelo* and its sequel, *La Comtesse de Rudolstadt* (1843), Sand pulls out all the stops, and she pours into the singer Consuelo much of her own soul and many parallels to her own life. Also, as the narrator frequently comments directly to the presumed female reader, Sand provides an intimate understanding of how much Consuelo forsakes for her art. *Consuelo* and *La Comtesse* are populated with artists: professional and amateur, lazy and diligent, inspired and insipid, some who sing for the glory of God and others who are ruled by the lust for glory, some who prostitute their art and others who honor the divine afflatus as a gift of the divinity.

Like a five-movement symphony or a five-act drama, *Consuelo* is a pentagonal construction, each side of the figure mirrored by a parallel section in *La Comtesse de Rudolstadt*. The five-part structure not only involves much suspense and many twists and turns of plot, but also permits the novelist to display her virtuoso performance in various modes, tones, and styles—from gothic to comic to tragic. Sand is here rather like a great performing soloist exercising the various trills and modulations of her art. The first movement of *Consuelo* is a *Künstlerroman* in miniature set in Venice, the second a Gothic mystery at the Rudolstadt Château

42. Blount, *George Sand and the Victorian World*, 8.

des Géants in Bohemia, the third a picaresque with travelers Consuelo and Joseph Haydn moving across the Bœhmer-Wald en route to Vienna, the fourth an exposé of intrigue and deception backstage at Vienna and at the royal court of Austria, and the fifth a dramatic resolution of the love story with Consuelo's marriage to the dying Albert, Count of Rudolstadt. In *La Comtesse,* the first movement is Consuelo's initiation in Berlin's music halls, which mirrors the Venice section of the previous novel; in the second, the Gothic prison at Spandaw mirrors the Gothic Rudolstadt Chateau; in the third, Consuelo is again on the run as in the *picaro* section of *Consuelo;* in the fourth (in which the mirroring is less obvious and the similarity appears only to be the stasis in each), she is in quiet confinement, preparing her for a final reunion with Albert; and in the fifth she and Albert are reunited as they were at the conclusion of *Consuelo.*

In the first act of *Consuelo,* Sand introduces the unaffected, naive, "gypsy" girl, Consuelo, as the illegitimate daughter of an exotic Spanish mother, the most promising of the adolescent pupils of the renowned Maestro Porpora, and the betrothed of the Venetian singer Anzoleto, who is, the narrator says, handsome as Apollo. During her apprenticeship as *cantatrice,* Consuelo loses her mother to death and Anzoleto to the embraces of her musical rival, Corilla, whom Sand introduces to contrast laziness, vanity, and beauty to Consuelo's hard work, humility, and plainness. Physical beauty or the lack thereof interests George Sand (as it was to interest many British women writers for whom it was an important decision whether to create their fictional artists as beautiful or ordinary). Sand herself comments in *Histoire de ma vie* that although she had two beautiful parents, she herself was plain. Maxime Prévost notes that, prior to the publication of Sand's *Consuelo* and Marceline Desbordes-Valmore's *Domenica,* musical reviews in France featured elaborate tributes to the singer's eyes, figure, grace, and sometimes coquetry before ever getting around to criticism of her talent. Prévost says Sand insists that Consuelo later becomes beautiful *because* she is an artist, while Corilla represents the spoiled, superficial beauty long on looks and short on talent that was the ideal of the French theatergoing public and some of Sand's male friends.[43] Rounding out the first movement of the novel, Consuelo survives the loss of Anzoleto, avoids the advances of the lecherous Count Zustiniani, and becomes the rising star of the San Samuel Theatre, but leaves Venice as Porpora's device to protect his favorite pupil from entanglements that might damage her.

The second movement is the beginning of Consuelo's spiritual journey to wisdom and at the same time Sand's treatment, sometimes tongue-in-cheek, of the Gothic genre. At the Château des Géants, Consuelo serves as companion and

---

43. Sand, *My Life,* 25; Prévost, "Portrait de la femme auteur en cantatrice: George Sand et Marceline Desbordes-Valmore," 124–26, 128, 134. Prévost notes that the character of Consuelo is based upon Pauline Garcia, who specialized in the Rossini canon, and Corilla upon Garcia's rival, Giulia Grisi.

voice instructor to the young Rudolstadt heiress, Amelia, but is almost immediately claimed by Count Albert de Rudolstadt, who believes that Consuelo, whom he calls "Consuelo de mi alma," is destined in this incarnation to be his wife. Albert, who believes his own previous incarnation was as a follower of the Protestant martyr Jan Hus, is given to trances, visions, somnambulation, and mysterious absences that cause dismay for his family and possible danger to himself. Performing the role of the Sybil leading Aeneas through the Underworld or—as several critics have noted—that of the musician Orpheus searching out Hades for his lost Eurydice to restore her to life again,[44] Consuelo tosses a cake to the Cerberus-like Zdenko, who is Albert's would-be protector; she braves subterranean passages, secret doors, hidden vaults, and a grotto; nearly drowns in an underground cistern; and survives being interred alive—adventures worthy of the female Gothic adventure, although Sand modestly proclaims that she is no Anne Radcliffe. Later (in *La Comtesse*) when Consuelo performs *Ariadne Abandonnée* in Berlin, Sand calls forth still another myth, and the reader recalls that Consuelo, as a clever and resourceful Ariadne, has led her Theseus through dark labyrinths and that in dying he has abandoned her to the dangers of the political intrigue of Prussia. Consuelo as Sibyl/Orpheus regains and restores her Aeneas/Eurydice—Eurydice, in that he is led out of death by the strength of love, and Aeneas, in that he is a searcher—not for father Anchises as Staël's Nelvil is, but for his mother, Wanda.

Significantly, Albert is a self-taught musician—music serving in the *Consuelo* novels as holy calling, divine gift, and voice of God. Albert has placed his Stradivarius on the "altar" of his grotto church, but he accidentally drops it, and before Consuelo leads him out of the Underworld, she insists that he retrieve it and bring it up with him, symbolically suggesting what Consuelo does not yet consciously know—that divine art/divine wisdom must be put to heavenly service in the present world. Consuelo, however, is not ready for marriage, not ready to forget her adolescent first love, Anzoleto, or her musical aspirations, and certainly not ready for the ennui of life in the Rudolstadt castle. Nor is she spiritually sanctified for the service Albert requires of her—although he has no objection to Consuelo's career, for he realizes that music is divine, that "[a] l'aurore des religions . . . le théâtre et le temple sont un même sanctuaire" (in the dawn of religion, the theater and temple were the same sanctuary), and that, since music and poetry were the highest expressions of faith, "la femme douée de génie et de beauté est prêtresse, sibylle et initiatrice" (the woman endowed with genius and

44. See, for example, Naginski's *George Sand: Writing for her Life*, 205–7. Sand revisits the Orpheus and Eurydice motif again in *La Daniella* (1:130), in which the artist (a painter but also musician) Valreg rescues the beautiful English heiress Medora, but when the painter finds his true muse in Daniella, the myth is changed to biblical Eden and the petulant, fickle Medora plays the serpent role.

beauty is priestess, sibyl, and leader).[45] When Anzoleto shows up at the Château des Géants to vex and embarrass her, though, Consuelo flees once more—this time fleeing both Anzoleto and Albert, Anzoleto representing to Consuelo the love of the beautiful, and Albert, the thirst for the ideal.

The adventure-filled picaresque that makes up the middle section of the novel features Consuelo and Joseph Haydn, the as-yet-unknown singer from St. Stephen's of Vienna, whom Consuelo chances to meet on her path. The two young people form a platonic bond—Consuelo traveling unimpeded by disguising her gender with masculine clothing, as George Sand did, for greater freedom of movement and protection from unwanted sexual propositions. For safety's sake they pretend to be what they indeed are—itinerant and indigent musicians. Among their adventures, "Beppo" (Haydn) and "Bertoni" (Consuelo) are kidnaped to be impressed as piper and trumpeter for the Prussian army, are taken in by a canon at whose home they assist in the delivery of Anzoleto and Corilla's illegitimate child, and suffer other misadventures with blackguards, heroes, and patriots whom Consuelo is destined to meet again. Northrop Frye has famously noted that all myth is really about the return to Eden,[46] and if this is the case, one could also make an argument that Consuelo desires to regain the childhood she is losing, for in the narrative Sand frequently returns her to a succession of gardens—the first of them in the picaresque section of *Consuelo*. Nature is lush and maternal, and Consuelo is happy—remarking to Joseph, after they have scaled the walls and trespassed in the canon's garden, that it is a "jardin enchanté, au milieu de fruits dignes de la terre promise" (an enchanted garden, where the fruit is worthy of the promised land [*CCR*, 2:119–20]). Consuelo is of course seeking to recapture the first Eden of infantile acceptance, not the post-lapsarian paradise of enlightened salvation of Milton's Eden "happier far," and much later she recognizes the narcissism and immaturity of her initial search. When she later finds herself in the intrigues of the Austrian court, she recalls even the Château des Géants as a lost Paradise—although at the time of entering the Rudolstadt estate she had looked upon the event as Dante entering Hades and the occupants of that castle as "Shades"—an allusion that calls to mind, in her retrieving Albert from Hades, Beatrice's salvational role for Dante, as well as Psyche's mission to the Underworld on behalf of Eros and Orpheus's mission to regain Eurydice. The allusions mark a basis of kinship between *Consuelo* and *Corinne*.

---

45. Sand, *Consuelo, La Comtesse de Rudolstadt,* ed. Simone Vierne and René Bourgeois, 1:388. All future references to either novel will be cited as *CCR* from this edition, a publication of the two novels as a single three-volume work.

46. Frye, *Anatomy of Criticism: Four Essays,* 136, 141–58. Frye's theory of myth is the construction of Paradise versus the city of destruction, the apocalyptic versus the demonic world, innocence versus experience.

In the fourth movement, Consuelo and Haydn are with Porpora in Vienna and also in the middle of professional and political intrigue, fawning and bootlicking, treachery and backstabbing. Here Sand is permitted, by means of the rhetoric of Consuelo's surrogate father, Porpora, to make an analogy between the pseudo-royalty of the crowned heads of Europe (the Austrian queen Marie-Thérèse making a cameo appearance as Frederick of Prussia does in *La Comtesse*) and the true royalty of talent—although unfortunately the system of patronage permits the "actors" playing the roles of political royalty to stymie the careers of the true royalty like Consuelo. Believing that it would be a crime to bring a divine goddess with a voice like Consuelo's off the stage and into marriage with the Bohemian count, Porpora intercepts and destroys letters between the two lovers and thwarts Albert's hope for Consuelo as the Austrian queen and Consuelo's jealous enemies thwart Consuelo's career.

Finally, in the last movement of *Consuelo,* Sand brings hilarity and, in the coda, pathos—the humor when Consuelo rehearses a performance at the Moravian estate of Count Hoditz and the heightened emotion when she is wed to the dying Albert, who had been led by Porpora's deception to believe that Consuelo has abandoned him. In Prague Consuelo learns of Albert de Rudolstadt's grave illness, but she arrives at the Château des Géants just in time to marry and mourn Albert. As a young widow, Consuelo laments that she has never loved Albert as he deserves and, not yet understanding the necessity that he die married to his soul mate in order to be resurrected free of the atrocities of his ancestors that had always tormented his sensitive soul, she sets off with Porpora to uphold a contract for performance in Berlin. In reference to the recurring travels of the *Consuelo* novels, Robert Godwin-Jones notes that they "become signposts in [Consuelo's] development . . . from egotism toward a commitment to work for others."[47] One might also comment that Consuelo's travels back and forth across the borders of many nations, as well as the international identity of her birthright and the gypsylike wanderings in childhood, indicate that—unlike Corinne's— her prophecy transcends political boundaries.

In *La Comtesse de Rudolstadt,* the characters, situations, and myths of *Consuelo* reappear. Again, as in *Consuelo,* there are intrigues and mysteries, masks and disguises, and mythical gardens of Eden. The recurring myth of the Sibyl/Sophia is employed in *La Comtesse* as Consuelo finishes her journey of spiritual development, the "sibylle" of the novel who leads and teaches Consuelo being Wanda de Prachalitz, the mother of Albert and high priestess of the Invisibles (the underground quasi-religious, quasi-political utopianists whose rituals are loosely based on Freemasonry and whose goal is liberty, equality, and fraternity).

47. Godwin-Jones, "Consuelo's Travels: The German Connection," 108.

"Vive la liberté" is, throughout the *Consuelo* novels, the cry of the artist, but in *La Comtesse* Consuelo is perpetually imprisoned, first by evil and later by good. Forcibly separated from Maître Porpora, she is in the first movement a virtual prisoner of Frederick of Prussia, who houses her in a private residence that he can visit at will, demands that she perform on cue, and is rumored to be involved in a "mésalliance de cœur" with the young singer. Her operatic performances as the "pearl" of Frederick's theater are flawless, but are uninspired and therefore uninspiring. Dead as priestess of art, she occupies a metaphorical purgatory of confinement, despair, and the danger of being lured into a coup d'état planned by the king's household and underground agents of the Invisibles. Although neither the reader nor Consuelo is yet aware of the fact, Albert de Rudolstadt has not died. In a sort of suspended animation, he was spirited from the tomb by his mother and the Invisibles, and in a series of disguises Albert now takes his turn as Orpheus to rescue Consuelo/Eurydice from court and prison—Sand once more upending the gender identities of rescuer and rescued in the original myth and thereby moving both Consuelo and Albert toward androgyny.

In the second setting of *La Comtesse,* Sand again revisits the Gothic motif, in this instance the moat, tower, and esplanades of the prison at Spandaw recalling Radcliffe's *Castle of Otranto* even more closely than the Rudolstadt castle does. When Frederick confines Consuelo in the fortress, she finds herself in yet another hell, the role of Cerberus this time played by the wife of the Swartz family, devilish keepers of the prison who even own a cat named Beelzebub. Interestingly it is in this prison of suffering that Consuelo begins composing music; her singing voice matures, becoming less conventional and more pure. Albert is a fellow prisoner at Spandaw and—his identity disguised by a mask—he pulls off a daring rescue and escape. At one level Sand treats the reader to the titillating Gothic aspects of the irresistible masked hero and the Galatea-like Consuelo awakening to mature sexual passion—a motif replayed from Radcliffe to formula-Gothic Harlequin Romances and the Gothic-kitsch *Phantom of the Opera.* In the third movement, Consuelo's dramatic flight with Albert recalls the picaresque travels across Bœhmer-Wald with Beppo in the third movement of *Consuelo*—down to the detail of the Prussian army deserter Karl recurring as fellow traveler, this time as Albert's accomplice. The next abode/prison of Consuelo is the one to which Albert—known to Consuelo only as the Chevalier Liverani—delivers her; it is a palace of art and wisdom (with a well-stocked library of the world's great philosophers) surrounded by a garden that recalls to Consuelo the canon's garden of paradise. Here she waits, studies, walks in the garden, exchanges letters with Liverani, grows restless, and again is irked by confinement.

The fifth and final movement of *La Comtesse* returns Consuelo to the Underworld, the secret location of the underground order of the Invisibles. In their occult ceremonies the Invisibles incorporate the insignia and ceremonial rites of Judaism, Christianity, Egypt, and various cabalistic signs and hieroglyphics. A faith militant, they have spies in major European capitals and oppose cruelty everywhere—whether the discipline of cane and lash in the Prussian military, the knout that governs Russian serfs, or the brutal treatment of slaves in America. Consuelo is brought before the tribunal of the Invisibles, catechized, and given lessons and lectures on the tyranny, cruelty, suffering, and martyrdom undertaken in human history in the name of God and country. She is taught the philosophy of a socialism and communist system of government that would level the opulence and poverty among classes, a political belief to which Sand subscribed.[48] She accepts the doctrine of a faith beyond Christianity, declaring as George Sand herself believed that Christ is simply a great prophet (*LGS*, 2:317, 333, 339–40), but that Christianity is an evolving faith, ever open to new wisdom (*CCR*, 3:311, 378).

Consuelo as Mythic Heroine

In *La Comtesse,* Sand incorporates a number of legends and myths as Staël does in *Corinne,* the effect in each case being to create a new goddess myth by combining elements of various classic, religious, and mythical figures. Sand also toys with the Corinne myth, facetiously trumping Corinne in that while Staël's Sibyl is carried to her coronation in an antique carriage pulled by four spotless steeds and is crowned with bay and myrtles, King Frederick tells his guards to be respectful of their talented prisoner because—were she in Rome—she would have deserved the triumph of a carriage with *eight* horses and crowns of *oak* (*CCR*, 3:131), the oak being the sacred tree of Zeus himself. George Sand is of course perfectly aware of Corinne's mythic status, and—if she cannot out-trope Staël—she risks the facetious remark to acknowledge that Consuelo is born in Corinne's shadow and that Sand would prefer to have her own heroine the greater luminary. George Sand apparently feels both the obligation to honor Staël and the need to differentiate herself from the great matriarch.

As Corinne is many myths merged into one, Sand's divine *cantatrice* is also an Ariadne, Galatea, Cinderella, and Psyche. The Galatea and Cinderella myths are used to suggest her metamorphosis from ugly duckling to a desirable beauty. In

48. George Sand herself endorses the principles of both socialism and communism (*LGS*, 137, 157, 198–201). As I interpret her commentary on politics, however, she does not endorse a single world order, or a one-Europe doctrine, as the Invisibles promote, and she insists that even in French socialism there are twenty or thirty versions and it is never safe to oversimplify. Since this book is about Sand's aesthetics, rather than her politics, her pronouncements "I am a socialist" and "I am a communist" must suffice.

Consuelo the myth of Orpheus is invoked in Consuelo's rescue of Albert from his first mysterious absence in the labyrinths of the mountain cavern and echoed in his rescue of her life from the abyss of the grave when he dismisses the medical man, bleeds her, then nurses her back to life. The narrator remarks that like the hero of fable Consuelo "était descendue dans le Tartare pour en tirer son ami" (had descended into Tartaros to rescue her lover [*CCR*, 1:373]). From that point the rescuer and rescued roles of Orpheus and Eurydice are several times reversed in the *Consuelo* novels. She comes again to his rescue when she gives him her hand in marriage; in *La Comtesse* he penetrates the Spandaw prison and leads her out again into the light. When she is tempted to unmask this rescuer whom she knows only as Liverani, she is "comme la curieuse Psyché" (*CCR*, 3:303); and like Psyche with her "petite lamp" (*CCR*, 3:383) she looks for her Eros/Liverani in the underworld of the Invisibles' initiation rite. Like Orpheus she is cautioned not to look back as a shadowy figure of Eurydice (Liverani/Albert) follows her though the darkness. The symbolism of this underworld adventure recalls and reenacts not only Psyche and Eros, Orpheus and Eurydice, but also Aeneas and the Sibyl and Beatrice and Dante. Once more Sand tips her chapeau to Staël. Unlike Psyche, Consuelo does not spill her lamp and burn Liverani; unlike Orpheus she does not look back and lose her Albert—although by the end of *Consuelo* she had both injured and abandoned him. At the conclusion of the sequel, though, she has finally attained wisdom, and because she has, she is worthy to become the wife of Albert and member of the utopian order. True to his pledge, Albert does not prevent Consuelo from performing, and she, at the same time, becomes the Muse for his Promethean political agenda of igniting the entire world with the flames of freedom.

Consuelo as Goddess among Artists

Throughout *Consuelo* and *La Comtesse de Rudolstadt,* Sand entertains the questions of art and the artist previously asked by Staël and subsequently asked in some form by most of the women writers included in this study. These questions include: Who is the artist, and what is the source of genius; what contribution should one make to the world by means of her art; are freedom and suffering necessary for the artist's development; and is the artist superior to the codes and rules of common, everyday humanity?

The question of who is the artist George Sand answers numerous times and in multiple ways. Her portrait of angelic Consuelo is idealized, and Sand knows this. But she is elevating Consuelo to the level of myth as Staël had done with Corinne, and realism must in such instances play second fiddle to grandiosity. In her preface to the 1855 play *Maître Favilla,* Sand remarks that she has been considered an absurd Don Quixote in making her characters—here the violinist Favilla—"trop aimants, trop dévoués, trop vertueux" (too loving, too unselfish, too virtuous).[49] Yet if art is to be the divine calling, the true artist must be above reproach and must be impassioned for art. He or she is willing to make great sacrifices for art—a trait seen in the youthful apprenticeship of both Haydn and Consuelo. Another example is the painter Jean Valreg, who in *La Daniella* voluntarily opts for poverty and love above fortune and glory. In *Consuelo* Sand defines the artist as one who feels life with "intensité effrayante" (frightful intensity [*CCR*, 1:54]), one endowed with the romantic spirit of adventure, freedom, and vitality. In her correspondence Sand defines an artist as a man of impulse (*LGS*, 3:2), a lover of the ideal (*LGS*, 2:261), an explorer who should allow nothing to daunt him from the business of ascertaining the state of health of his own soul (*LGS*, 3:8), one who seeks the beautiful and the good (*LGS*, 3:242), one who sees beyond his contemporaries and beyond his own times (*LGS*, 3:220), one who has faith that a good work will stir the heartstrings of humanity, and one who struggles against the darkness of the world (*LGS*, 2:304).

In the preface to *La petite Fadette* (1851), Sand acknowledges the Dantean genius that "writes with his tears" when the nation suffers, but she has suffered through the 1848 Revolution for which she had such high hopes and now, as the heartbroken patriot, "the less virile artist" than Dante, she has chosen to write what some critics condemn as escapist pastorals.[50] In so doing, she argues that although it is certainly noble to exhort the nation (to serve as a secular Sibyl), it is also an acceptable role of the devastated and suffering artist merely to bring pleasure to others who suffer from the political malady of the age. Resorting to the classical definition by Horace, one could note that, for Sand, the twin purposes of art are to instruct or to delight. Consuelo in fact also acknowledges that the artist's purpose is, in part, to dispense pleasure. For instance, when she and Joseph Haydn encounter the poor, she suggests that the love of art and beauty would lighten their load: "l'amour de l'art pour poétiser la souffrance et embellir la misère . . ." (the love of art is to make suffering poetic and misery beautiful [*CCR*, 2:42]). It is because Consuelo combines Sand's litany of idealized attributes, not merely the qualities of talent and ambition, that she evolves into Sand's divine Wisdom.

Consuelo and her admirers speak of her gift as more than talent; everywhere it is referred to as a divine gift and a sacred trust, and the young woman who possesses the fire of genius is sent on a divine mission to serve God in the world. In *La Daniella,* the protagonist realizes that "le feu sacré" is not to be extinguished

---

49. Sand, *Théatre complet de George Sand,* 2:226.
50. Sand, preface to *La petite Fadette,* 1:15–16.

but respected. This fire of inspiration, the narrator warns in *Elle et lui,* is potentially dangerous, though, because it overflows for public enjoyment and pleasure
and consumes the artist.[51] When Consuelo sings before Count Zustiniani in
Venice, Sand notes the sacred quality of her art:

> Un feu divin monta à ses joues, et la flamme sacrée jaillit de ses grands yeux
> noirs, lorsqu'elle remplit la voûte de cette voix sans égale et de cet accent victo-
> rieux, pur, vraiment grandiose, qui ne peut sortir que d'une grande intelligence
> jointe à un grand cœur.

> A divine glow spread over her features, and the sacred flame of genius darted
> from her large black eyes, as the vaulted roof rang with that unequaled voice
> and with those lofty accents that can proceed only from an elevated intelligence,
> joined to a great heart. (*CCR,* 1:100)

And upon hearing Consuelo, the count pronounces her a Saint Cecilia, Saint
Teresa, "Saint" Consuelo. In the narrator's description and Zustiniani's attribu-
tions, it is obvious that Consuelo, favored of God, has been endowed with both
a great talent and a great passion. She is a Pythian priestess bearing the Delphic
fire, and she is a female Promethean.

But there is the opposite kind of artist as well, one who lives for fame, who
takes shortcuts, who is unoriginal, narrow, or self-absorbed. This is the failed
artist: no matter how famous or self-satisfied, she or he has prostituted the divine gift. In Sand's story "Le Château de Pictordu," the successful painter Flochardet unfortunately has perfected only one style—a rather bland and idealized
feminine image. Although he modifies a ringlet or a ribbon, the type is invariably the same—as identical, the narrator notes, as statuary of Renaissance goddesses endlessly reproduced. The result is not artistic honesty, but flattery. Nevertheless Flochardet has been handsomely rewarded for being a frivolous artist,
for he lives in an age of frivolity—of knickknacks and shameless distortions. In
Elle et lui the painter Laurent is given to posing and melodramatic "suffering,"
and in *Lélia* the poet Sténio petulantly blames his writer's block on the woman
who has loved him.

In the *Consuelo* novels Sand draws portraits of a number of frivolous, vain
artists who are prodigal with their talent, and she has no patience with them.
Consuelo's childhood friend, Anzoleto, for example, relies on his handsome good
looks to carry him in the heroic roles rather than rehearsing as he should. The
singer-actress Corilla conducts one backstage intrigue after another while at the
same time spreading rumors about Consuelo's lack of sexual purity; she snipes

---

51. Sand, *La Daniella,* 2:155; *Elle et lui,* 83.

pettishly when Consuelo receives the accolades due her. When Anzoleto and Corilla's illegitimate baby is born, the new mother hands over the infant, takes a stiff drink, and runs through a few trills to make sure that labor and delivery have not adversely affected her voice—a prime example of what Sand as an artist and mother saw as having her priorities reversed.[52] Caffariello, who believes himself the world's foremost singer, thinks that heaven has bestowed genius on poets and composers only to enable him to perform. He is quite miffed that Louis XV bestowed upon him only a miserable gold and diamond snuffbox as a memento of his royal debut.

In *Consuelo* connoisseurs of the arts come in for their share of the satire as well. Count Zustiniani judges his sopranos based on their good looks and declares that it is a curse for a great voice to be attached to a homely face. Count Hoditz "teaches" singing to students whose talent and training exceed his own, and he is too blind in taste and discretion even to notice. Further, the setting of the great performance and fête at the estate of the count is a hilarious satire on the *dilettanti* of the fine arts—including Hoditz's artificial and tasteless "decor" and architecture, his stage sets that constitute a tacky Enlightenment-era theme park, and his badly written opera that successfully plagiarizes the worst musical compositions of his age.

In Sand's 1833 novel *Lélia* (greatly modified and republished in 1839), she treats the flawed and failed artist more seriously than she does in the satiric scenes of *Consuelo*. In *Lélia* the self-dramatizing Sténio is the stereotypical Romantic poet, celebrating youth, passion, self-realization, and nature's sublimity. He is adolescent in behavior and idealistic in art, philosophy, love, and religion. He needs Lélia as sister, mother, lover, muse (as Laurent in *Elle et lui* needs Thérèse, repeatedly calling her his Sister of Charity, because she repeatedly saves him). Sténio passionately desires Lélia, but she is weary of passion and at a masquerade she engineers his passionate embrace with the disguised courtesan Pulchérie, Lélia's sister, to "cure" him of his sensuality. He also longs for God, but Lélia has robbed him of faith, he says, by her atheism. Sténio next abandons himself to debauchery and debasement in tavern and brothel. Without God, without love, without hope, and without Lélia, he despairs and takes his own life. In Sténio George Sand has created a poet/artist who believes in the divine spark of art but who is too weak to fan it into flames, who would rather blame a woman for quenching to a final spark "le feu sacré" within himself.[53]

Above all, Sand has only contempt for the artist who poses and flaunts his

52. Sand's correspondence reveals her devotion to her children, as does her continued legal battle to gain parental custody. Her parenting was perhaps not wholly satisfying and successful; at any rate relations with her adult daughter were strained.

53. Sand, *Léila*, 1:98.

artistry, who is jealous of the more talented or inspired artist, and who covets all attention for himself. In her letters she admits that this spoiled infant of an artist is all too common: "The *jealous artiste,* that is to say the wicked and unfortunate artist, is nearly synonymous with artiste" (*LGS,* 2:280). Sand tends to reserve the most wicked denigrations of artists for the voices of those fictional characters who, like Sand herself, are members of the profession, and hence ought to know whereof they speak. Two examples serve to make the point—those of Maître Favilla and Maître Porpora. The conflict of the play *Maître Favilla* arises when the star-crossed offspring of two families fall in love. The bourgeois German father, Keller, is much at a loss to understand the eccentric and artistic Italian family into which his son proposes to marry. Not surprisingly, misunderstandings result and feathers are ruffled. Favilla, the bride's father, tries to rub ointment on all wounds and assures Keller that a rich, successful German merchant is in no way inferior to a titled but poor Italian musician, and besides, all artists, including Favilla himself, are temperamental and vain.[54] In *Consuelo* Porpora, having had his fill of spoiled and pampered artists, says, "Mais les artistes! tous lâches, tous ingrats, tous traîtres et menteurs" (But artists! All cowards, all ingrates, all traitors and liars [*CCR,* 2:162]). Vienna is, in fact, a hothouse of vanity and competition among singers, composers, and musicians. But then so are Venice and Berlin. Thus Sand suggests that the temperamental artist is a universal type and that self-promotion is a universal temptation. This fact, of course, illustrates all the more that the guileless Consuelo is a paragon among artists when, for example, she saves Corilla's career by keeping her guilty secret. In fact her goodness inspires Corilla to return the favor by sharing a dressing room and sacrificing the prima donna role to her former rival—although bribery to keep the secret could well be Corilla's motive.

　　Whether the pure artist can survive and prosper is, in Sand's works, by no means a given. While Staël's creative heroines Corinne, Delphine, and Mirza die after much suffering, Sand's heroes and heroines sometimes suffer and sometimes prosper. Sténio takes his own life, and both Lélia and Joseph Picot, the "stargazer," are murdered. In the 1853 *paysannerie* (peasant tale) *Les maîtres sonneurs,* the bagpiper *(sonneur)* Joseph, modeled upon the dreamer of the same name in the Old Testament, expects his fellow pipers to bow down and admit his superiority, as the biblical Joseph dreams his brothers eventually will. For his art Joseph gives up his family and his beloved Brulette, whom he has adored from childhood, to become an exile in a strange land, reminiscent of the biblical Joseph when he is sold into Egyptian slavery by his brothers. It is rumored that, in exchange for his gift, Joseph has sold his soul to the devil, who tears the bagpipes

54. Sand, *Maître Favilla,* 2.2, in *Théâtre complet de George Sand,* 2:259.

from the hands of the *sonneur* and breaks them on his back. Laurent, in *Elle et lui,* uses the metaphor of childbirth to depict his struggles; Sténio uses the analogy of barrenness to depict his writer's block. Both suffer and both wallow masochistically in their suffering.

Yet Sand's generous, worthy artists who are kindly disposed to others, who devote work to their craft, and who humbly accept poverty and anonymity while lesser artists gain wealth and notoriety, often prosper. Examples include Adriana and Jean Valreg, who, unlike Joseph Picot, marry their respective muses and live happily; Diane, who also marries happily, sells her art, and founds a school for girls; Thérèse, who is fortunate to lose the faithless Laurent and find her long-lost son; and Consuelo, whose marriage with Albert is as normal as marriage can be to a political radical whose goal is to remodel the world. If Joseph Haydn evolves into a great musician and Anzoleto is forgotten, one senses that, in a Sandian world, each has to some extent willed or deserved his own success or failure. Consuelo, however, does not ask fate or God to supply her with happiness. Rather, she asks for love and liberty—although at different points in the novel the balance between the two shifts from one to the other.

Porpora teaches Consuelo that liberty is the only happiness, the only necessary attribute for the artist to flourish. Elsewhere in Sand's fiction, other artists affirm this necessity; for instance the female characters Thérèse and Lélia (in *Elle et lui* and *Lélia* respectively) live in Paris with supreme indifference to bourgeois domesticity, just as Staël's Corinne does in Rome. Naturally Porpora defines freedom for Consuelo as the single life, informing her that when she gives herself away, she loses her divinity—suggesting of course that she must be a *virgin* Pythian and that the female role as wife and mother would render her unfit for the divine music. The well-meaning Hayden, too, advises Consuelo not to marry. Hayden himself intends to take a wife, but as a man he admits that he can enjoy both a domestic life and devotion to his work, while Consuelo cannot. Unless she is performing in a role requiring elaborate costuming, Consuelo affects a nunlike simplicity of garment, and once, at a masquerade in Berlin, she actually appears in a habit. This device serves to suggest not only that Consuelo is virtuous and virginal, but also that she prefers simplicity to ostentation. And it suggests that she lives as a sanctified high priestess of art.

On the other hand, there is no doubt that Consuelo loves freedom and grows restless when confined. She relishes the freedom of platonic relationships with men—from childhood, when she and Anzoleto wander about the streets of Venice with no one to complain that her reputation would be damaged, to her trek across Bœhmer-Wald with Haydn. She also wants freedom to study, to rehearse, to sing, and to accept or reject musical engagements. Most of all, she wants the freedom to be an artist. "Liberty" is her watchword, and in prison at

Spandaw Consuelo composes songs of sadness in solitary confinement and sings Almirena's tribute to freedom in Handel's *Rinaldo:*

> Lascia ch'io piango
> La dura sorte,
> E ch'io sospiri
> La libertà.

> Ah, let me weep
> My cruel fate;
> And let me sigh
> For liberty. (*CCR*, 3:260)

George Sand herself insisted upon freedom of association, fiscal independence, a legal separation from her husband, Dudevant, her rights as mother, and freedom to come and go at will and keep whatever hours she liked. Small wonder that she expresses such sympathy for Consuelo's repeated confinements and repeated complaints. One aspect of *Consuelo* as *Künstlerroman* is this struggle to find one's place as artist and woman, and to decide whether freedom for art requires a vow of withdrawal from the world. As previously noted, Corinne struggles with the same issue; her becoming Nelvil's slave undermines her artistry, for an artist must have a free heart, Staël says, in order to make art. Similar conflicts were also to be replayed again and again by English poets and novelists as their fictional artists consider the inevitable conflict between art and love. In *Consuelo* the sentiments come in the form of the prayer:

> Si je suis née pour pratiquer le dévouement, Dieu veuille donc ôter de ma tête l'amour de l'art, la poésie, et l'instinct de la liberté, qui font de mes dévouements un supplice et une agonie; si je suis née pour l'art et pour la liberté, qu'il ôte donc de mon cœur la pitié l'amitié, la sollicitude et la crainte de faire souffrir, qui empoisonneront toujours mes triomphes et entraveront ma carrière!

> If I am born for devotion, God blot from my mind the love of art and poetry and the desire for liberty, which are a torment and agony; if I am born for art and for liberty, may He take away then from my heart the pity, devotion, anxiety, and fear of giving offense, which will always poison my triumphs and hinder my career. (*CCR*, 2:192–93)

Consuelo declares that if she were to love one man truly and passionately, she would sacrifice even sacred art for him (prompting some to label George Sand as no true feminist), but it is not until the end of the sequel that she finds a near-perfect liberty in art and love, and the *Consuelo* novels document her quest.

Elsewhere Sand considers the confinement of the artist as imposed by class—yet another type of restriction that Aurore Dudevant would understand, because she, too, was born into the titled aristocracy. The novel *Adriani* (1853) is a *Künstlerroman* about a French Italian tenor, Adrien d'Argères, whose professional name is Adriani. He is surrounded in the text by other artists of varying degrees of talent, as well as varying degrees of success: the Baron, who spends an unsuccessful lifetime seeking fame for poetry or his projected libretto; the painter, Descombes, who, like Sténio, dies a suicide; and the grieving widow, Laure, whose vocal duets with d'Argères foreshadow their union in a happy marriage. Written in an experimental three-pronged approach made up of narrative, epistles, and entries from the diary of Adriani's *valet de chambre,* Comtois, the novel permits many comments about art and artists—some of them amusing, several of them woefully biased. Comtois, for example, is aghast to discover that his employer, whom he assumed to be only a gentleman, is an artist as well, for Comtois assumes that all artists are either fools or scoundrels ("ou des toqués ou des canailles"), or both. The aristocratic mother-in-law of Laure snobbishly affirms that no artist is a gentleman, and no gentleman an artist, and she threatens that should the name of Adriani ever appear on an opera poster, she will sever all ties with Laure. Here Laure's *belle-mère* behaves much like Corinne's. While Consuelo is not prohibited from performing on stage after she marries a gentleman, this very situation faces several women artists in English fiction—for example, in novels of Geraldine Jewsbury and Mrs. Humphry Ward. Obviously the class assumption that artists are a certain "type" and "class" proves intriguing to Victorian women writers, for whom social and class standing was based upon the husband's status. In Sand's novel even d'Argères himself is smugly secure in the knowledge that he need never place his self-respect or his financial well-being in the hands of a fickle public; he can sing for the pure love of his art. As the artist who is free, he has never received "le baptême de l'esclavgage" (the baptism of slavery). He has tempted fate, however, and when fiscal disaster occurs at the climax of the novel, Adriani sacrifices his dream of a future with Laure when he makes his stage debut, receiving acclaim and instant popularity and accepting the "seal of slavery" as a paid musician. To his surprise and Laure's credit, his twice-revived Galatea is reborn as wife and mother, as well as muse for Adriani's operatic career.[55] In fact Laure proves as understanding and affirming for d'Argères as Albert is for Consuelo, while Laure is, like Galatea and also like Consuelo, awakened to female sexuality.

At the beginning of *Consuelo* the child Consuelo is comparatively free as a Venetian street urchin of *no* class,[56] and she longs throughout her spiritual odyssey

55. Sand, *Adriani,* 206, 252, 254.
56. Gutwirth notes that the gypsy Consuelo, although receiving acclaim for her magnificent art, re-

to indulge herself again in that freedom of childhood; at the conclusion of *La Comtesse,* however, Consuelo has learned that being great involves servitude to a cause greater than oneself. Certainly this is not freedom in the sense of license. On the other hand, Sand illustrates through Consuelo that the great artist is not free to live for pleasure and fame, to please herself, or to devote herself to ephemeral goals. From whom much is given, much is expected.

The Divine Consuelo

At the end of *Consuelo,* Sand's heroine has not yet attained the position of divine Sophia, but at the end of the sequel, *La Comtesse,* she has become Sand's divinity among artists. Because she is suddenly silenced by the loss of her voice, however, one can only guess what her future will hold. Discounting Consuelo's destiny beyond the final page of the sequel, Sand has created a mythic, larger-than-life star who is ready to attain wisdom because she has suffered, and because she resolves to reconstruct her priorities with the needs of family and the service to humankind outranking her own career—the choice that, according to her correspondence, Sand endorsed. Throughout the novels Consuelo has been considered a saint, a divinity, the "Bride of Heaven" and an "angel" to almost everyone who meets her. Sand repeatedly connects her to a divinity, for example:

> Mais quelle miraculeuse transformation s'était opérée dans cette jeune fille. . . . Son large front semblait nager dans un fluide céleste, une molle langueur baignait encore les plans doux et nobles de sa figure sereine et généreuse. . . . Il y avait en elle quelque chose de grave, de mystérieux et de profond, qui commandait le respect et l'attendrissement.

> But some marvelous transformation had occurred in this young girl. . . . Her lofty brow seemed to be dampened in a celestial fluid, while a gentle languor diffused the noble and subdued outline of her form. . . . There was something about her, solemn, mysterious, and profound—commanding respect and fascination. (*CCR,* 1:100)

Indeed, Consuelo has the divine spark of greatness, but she must cultivate wisdom—that is, divine greatness and generosity of heart, the willingness to sacrifice herself for others, to put the higher good ahead of the lesser and universal human suffering ahead of her own personal satisfaction and fame. At this point in her life, however, she is—as she notes in retrospect—only a high priestess of art, not a prophetess of truth:

---

tains her "proletarian character as the poor, chaste and obedient woman" ("*Corinne* and *Consuelo* as Fantasies of Immanence," 22).

> Et artiste à jamais! . . . c'est-à-dire indépendante, vierge, et morte à tout senti-
> ment d'amour, telle enfin que le Porpora me représentait sans cesse le type idéal
> de la prêtresse des Muses!

> And an artist forever! . . . that is to say, independent, virginal, and dead to all
> feelings of love, such Porpora has always represented as the ideal type of the
> priestess of the muses! (*CCR,* 3:75)

Others attest to Consuelo's potential for wisdom. For example, the *chanoinesse,*
Albert's aunt, says, "la Porporina est brave commme un lion, et sage comme un
docteur" (*CCR,* 1:297). In various charitable acts, such as forgiving the cad
Anzoleto, saving his and Corilla's baby girl, sponsoring Haydn's apprenticeship
with Porpora, and befriending Albert and all the members of the family, she
proves that she desires wisdom and goodness. In *La Comtesse* she recognizes that
she has been infantile in her understanding of art and divinity, and in her narcissism; in her interrogation before the Invisibles she characterizes herself:
"Femme et artiste, c'est-à-dire enfant!" (Woman and artist, which is to say an infant! [*CCR,* 3:265]). She has become a searcher for truth, however, and when she
discusses truth with the Invisibles, she inspires a comment on her sagacity and
bravery: "C'est là répondre avec sagesse et courage" (*CCR,* 3:316).

Especially in the latter half of *La Comtesse de Rudolstadt,* then, Sand makes obvious that Consuelo has not yet arrived at wisdom. She must achieve wisdom by
maturing from girl to woman, by finding the lost mother/muse; she may become
an apprentice sibyl only by sitting at the feet of the Sibyl, who sends Consuelo
to perform deeds worthy of her son, Albert, as Aphrodite does Psyche in Apuleius's *Metamorphoses.*[57] As Porpora is her surrogate father, Wanda becomes Consuelo's surrogate mother. Because the lessons she has learned from the patriarch
are but half-truths, the wisdom of Porpora, that an artist/woman must live for
art alone, is to be supplanted by the wisdom of the divine Sibyl/Sophia, that love
of art must be secondary to love of truth. This higher wisdom will permit the liberty and art that Porpora preaches and the pity and devotion for which Consuelo's heart has also yearned. In the final movement of *La Comtesse,* Consuelo becomes an apprentice sibyl; repeatedly she is termed the "néophyte," and her
mother-in-law, Wanda, once unmasked as one of the male judges of the tribunal,
is "la sibylle inspirée" (*CCR,* 3:410) or, most frequently, "la sibylle." According to
cultural historian Marina Warner, the sibyls of the classical world included prophetesses of various ages—from extreme youth to wise old age.[58] Sand's Wanda is

57. In Chapter 3, Sand's use of the Eros/Psyche myth is traced as influence on Elizabeth Barrett Browning's *Aurora Leigh.*
58. Warner, *From the Beast to the Blonde,* 81–88. According to Warner, Christian iconography supplied
a sibyl in the form of Saint Anne, the mother of the Virgin, conflated with Anna, the prophetess who

such a figure, the older matriarch/prophetess/crone who has attained wisdom through experience, solitude, and contemplation.

When Consuelo is given the spotless robe of neophyte, Wanda tells her that it will become the devouring tunic of Dejanira if she is not worthy. And if she is unworthy, the sibyl Wanda, as Consuelo's confessor, examiner, and judge, will know. Wanda, as Consuelo's mother-in-law, will become the lost mother figure for whom Consuelo has sought since her own mother's death. As the "infant" Consuelo has labored to get back to Eden, she has also tried to return to the arms of her mother, whose womb and breast represent infancy and innocence in the human family *and* in the myth of human genesis. Both longings suggest the same narcissism and spiritual infancy. The loss of mother/muse is a recurring motif in nineteenth-century fiction—in which many heroines, artists or not, are motherless—as it also has been an interest of post-Chodorow criticism. In Consuelo's case, she recalls that her mother was devout, and she often asks herself what her mother would have wanted for her. When she gives Liverani/Albert a filigree cross that had belonged to her mother and that she had carried throughout her long odyssey, she wonders at herself for giving it away. Yet at an unconscious level she is acknowledging that her mother would have endorsed this passionate love. This scene recalls that Albert had, years ago, given her mother a guitar; thus the symbolic connection between Consuelo's mother and both aspects of Albert— the passionate utopianist and the passionate musician and lover. But that first mother exists no more as a Sophia figure in Consuelo's life; the attempt to return to her is *retrogression,* while Wanda must lead in Consuelo's spiritual *progression.* Wanda, like Albert, has been "dead" and resurrected to wisdom; Consuelo will, like Wanda, become a sibyl in her own right as she is resurrected to serve a more expansive vision than art alone.

In "Le Château de Pictordu," a fairy tale written for her granddaughter Aurore in 1873, Sand again explores this need for the female artist to reclaim the mother. The protagonist of "Le Château" is a female artist—the painter Flochardet's young daughter, Diane. This born artist finds herself in the clutches of a greedy stepmother who squanders Flochardet's earnings and tortures the motherless artist/daughter by outfitting her in froufrous and fripperies, no doubt like those adorning the vacuous beauties whom Diane's father paints in seemingly endless succession. Diane falls under the tutelage of Monsieur Féron, her mentor as Porpora is to Consuelo, and when the public taste changes to a more natural style, her star rises as her father's falls. The central motif, however, is not the mentorartist relationship but the muse-artist relationship—that is, the matriarch/muse

---

endorsed the infant Jesus brought to the Temple for the rite of circumcision; in Western art the Saint Anne/Priestess Anna figure is sometimes depicted as a wise Sibyl.

who teaches her the beautiful and the true. Diane, obsessed by the veiled lady she once encountered at the magic Castle of Pictordu, paints the face of the beautiful woman who has obsessed her and discovers: "C'était bien la même figure qu'elle avait dessinée; c'était la muse, c'était le camée, c'était le rêve, et c'était pourtant sa mère; c'était la réalité trouvée à travers la poésie, le sentiment et l'imagination." (It was indeed the same face she had drawn; it was the muse, cameo, dream, and it was her mother; it was the reality found through poetry, sentiment and imagination.) Like Diane, Consuelo has irretrievably lost her mother in the literal sense, although both reclaim the mother through memory, dreams, and art. Sand illustrates through both Consuelo and Diane that a woman can have family and profession, love and beauty, as Sand herself apparently did, although she testifies that it was at great cost. She asserts that "[l]es grands cœurs aiment le sacrifice, cela est bien heureux pour les cœurs étroits" (Noble hearts love sacrifice, which is fortunate for narrow natures).[59] The artist Diane marries well, secures fame, forgives her stepmother, befriends her father, and founds a school for girls.[60] In this little story, however, the real crone/Sibyl is the grandmother who wrote the story for little Aurore after having qualified herself to serve as high priestess of art, beauty, and truth. Or rather, grandmother Aurore casts herself— in place of the child's mother—as the beautiful muse. Like Wanda she is the prophetess/crone/Sibyl.

"I Am Not Madame de Staël."

In 1852 George Sand wrote, "I am not Madame de Staël. I possess neither her genius nor the pride with which she struggled against the twofold might of genius and power" (*LGS*, 1:146). It is a statement of remarkable humility of the kind that Sand admires in her Consuelo, who is invariably surrounded by outsized egos. Yet Sand often questions her genius and suspects that as an artist she will not endure the ages. Given the elaborately drawn portrait of Consuelo, however, and given that Consuelo might as well be Corinne's younger sister in her mythological status, her courageous longing for wisdom, and her guidance of her lover through the Underworld as a Sibyl, Psyche, and Orpheus, it is obvious that this particular literary "lady doth protest too much." George Sand struggled to individuate herself, to establish that her monumental women are not Corinne.

59. Sand, "Le Château de Pictordu," in *Contes d'une grand-mère*, 1:89, 1:112.
60. The basis for the story may well be the history of Rosa Bonheur, France's most celebrated woman artist of the century. Like Diane, Bonheur was the daughter of an artist, lost her mother in death, acquired a stepmother, eclipsed her father, and ran a drawing school for girls (Yeldham, *Women Artists in Nineteenth-Century France and England*, 1:337–41). Establishing a school seems to have been a noble course for a woman artist, once married and retired; Jewsbury's Bianca of *The Half Sisters* follows this career path, as noted in Chapter 2.

Yet aspects of Staël's myth appear not only in Consuelo but also in Daniella, Jeanne, and Lélia.

Like Staël's Delphine and Corinne, Sand's protagonists in *Consuelo, Valentine, Indiana, Lélia,* and *Jeanne* become figures seeking wisdom, and together they establish a composite of the Sand feminine myth. *Jeanne,* published only one year after *La Comtesse de Rudolstadt,* is a transitional work between the woman-as-Sibyl novel and the pastoral novel (novels of Sand's "green period," as Naginski refers to them)[61]—incorporating elements of both, as well as of classical and national myth. Jeanne, a cowherd and child of nature, is a spiritual reincarnation of the druidess Valléda. Because of her innocence, other characters, female and male, refer to her as an angel (a trait that she has in common with both Consuelo and Fanchon of *La petite Fadette*), and her regal beauty reminds them of several goddesses: She is "[p]uissante comme Junon ou Pallas, fraîche comme Hébé, gracieuse comme Isis, la messagère des dieux" (mighty as Juno or Pallas, fresh as Hebe, gracious as Isis, the messenger of the gods"). Jeanne's blend of paganism, superstition, and Catholicism seems quaint and uninformed, but she demonstrates absolute incorruptible adherence to virtue. In fact Jeanne is, like several of Staël's and Sand's females, a paragon so idealized that she can be accepted more easily as myth than as human female. As Consuelo dresses in the simplicity of a nun, Jeanne makes and keeps a nun's vows of chastity, poverty, and humility. Gislinde Seybert says that the holy grail Consuelo has been seeking is found when Consuelo becomes "la déesse de la pauvreté" (the goddess of poverty),[62] a lesson that the male artist Jean Valreg of *La Daniella* learns and that Jeanne recites throughout Sand's "druidesse" novel. Because of Jeanne's poverty and her single-minded will to follow her own sense of right, she recalls her namesake, the French heroine Jeanne d'Arc.[63] In addition to the name, the valor and devotion of Sand's heroine, and the symbolism of fire, establish the connection to Jeanne d'Arc. When Jeanne enters a burning cottage to rescue the corpse of her dead mother, she emerges from the flames "belle et terrible comme une druidesse dans cet acte de piété farouche et sublime" (beautiful and inspiring as a druidess in an act of piety fierce and sublime), just as when she deposits the body on the ancient druid slab of Ep-Nell, she is a modern version of an ancient priestess.[64] The comparison to the Maid of Orleans is a powerful sign—and an appropriate one—be-

61. Naginski, *George Sand: Writing for Her Life,* 7. Naginski refers to Sand's nihilism of the 1830s as her "blue and black period," the movement to affirmation in the 1840s as the "white period," and the life-affirming pastorals as the "green period."

62. Seybert, "George Sand, *Consuelo, La Comtesse de Rudolstadt:* A Woman on the Road between Violence and Desire," 118.

63. Consuelo is also compared to Jeanne d'Arc; the narrator of *Consuelo* says that Consuelo dreamed of the pilgrimage to save Albert as Jeanne dreamed of the pilgrimage to save France (*CCR,* 1:268).

64. Sand, *Jeanne,* 210, 104; see also 188, 233 (references to the druidess), 199, 201, 216 (references to Jeanne d'Arc), and 169 (additional reference to Isis).

cause both Jeannes are virgins, both receive visions or voices, both rejoice in poverty, and both are single-mindedly devoted to God and truth. Furthermore, in recalling Jeanne d'Arc, George Sand deliberately invokes the national French myth of woman as hero, as virtue and unflagging patriotism, merging her with the classical mythic female Wisdom—and in fact paralleling the Nike goddess of the Revolution to which Staël alludes in her *Corinne*.

Lélia is a more complex and more learned woman than Jeanne or Consuelo, but she shares with them the passion for truth. As they take on mythological properties, so Lélia in her black velvet robe looks the part of a goddess/priestess. Like both Jeanne and Consuelo, she also contains aspects of George Sand. For example, we see Lélia dressing in men's clothing as Consuelo does on the road and Sand does in the theaters of Paris. Like Sand she exhorts and encourages young poets. She seeks God but temporarily loses sight of him, as did Sand. Also like Sand, she rejects sensuality as the meaning of life, driving herself to seek answers to the toughest questions that plague her.

Lélia is "one of Corinne's most illustrious descendants,"[65] an independent woman artist around whom men congregate as disciples and slaves; they celebrate her eyes "brillaient d'un feu sacré" (burning with sacred fire) and worship at her palace of art. She asserts, ". . . moi femme, moi artist, il me faut un palais; je n'y serai point heureuse, mais du moins je n'y mourrais pas . . ." (a woman, an artist, I need a palace, not where I will be happy, but where I will not die).[66] Lélia's particular artistry is neither as public performer nor as private creator, but rather as an imaginative conversationalist and penetrating philosopher—a talent she shares with Corinne. She is androgynous, nihilistic, chaste. While rejecting God, she fears that there is no God to suffer her rejection. She abandons the Christian religion, then the worship of art, sex, beauty, and philosophy, to become exclusively herself. A would-be muse to several men, she drives one, the poet Sténio, to suicide and another, the monk Magnus, to murder.[67] To the poet Sténio she is a female Christ. To the Byronic Trenmor she is Pygmalion's Galatea, the poetic lover Romeo, the ascetic visionary Hamlet, the heartbroken Juliet, the mute and mysterious Lara, the young Raphael contemplating the virginal ideal, and the dying Corinne hearing her last poem performed—another of Sand's outright acknowledgments of the influence of Staël.[68]

George Sand also employs in her depiction of the prophetess Lélia the central

65. Isabelle Naginski makes this observation in her study of the influence of *Corinne* on the 1839 revised *Lélia*. She says that the new Lélia is an *improvisatrice* and that her last oral improvisation is a "Sandian version of Corinne's poetic declamation on the Cap Misène" ("Germaine de Staël among the Romantics," 183).

66. Sand, *Léila* 1:63, 1:93.

67. Or so Sténio charges before he drowns himself and Magnus claims when he strangles Lélia with his rosary in the 1833 version of the novel.

68. Sand, *Léila* 1:89.

myth of Romantic consciousness. For Lélia is also a female Prometheus as Sapho is for Staël. The fire-thief was repeatedly employed by European Romantic artists to suggest secular heroism (Napoleon having been a prominent example), iconoclasm and alienation (for example, the Byronic or Shelleyan hero), and the creative artist (as the Prometheus who shaped mortals in Beethoven's *Creatures of Prometheus*). By the end of the novel, Lélia—formerly a reluctant agnostic—has become an abbess. She finally loves God and accepts the Promethean suffering of Christ. In fact she dies as a Promethean martyr. Sand says in her letters that Lélia has "plunged" her into skepticism; hence the rewritten 1839 edition squares the author with God, and it also reinforces the Romantic mythological status of Lélia beyond what Sand had attempted in the 1833 *Lélia*. More than even Trenmor enchained as prisoner on his island, Lélia embodies the Prometheus myth: the suffering of both Christ and Prometheus, and the mythical, expansive love on behalf of human creatures—the love that the "sibylle inspirée" teaches Consuelo. Lélia in her dying words to Trenmor compares *herself* to the "sibylle désolée"—another similarity to Staël's Corinne—and to the Prometheus who would fain have liberated man from the chains of mortality and suffering. As Hoog notes, it is through the Prometheus and Don Juan myths that the "marginal Lélia finally enters the realm of the mythic: Léila on her rock. . . . [S]he is calm and accomplished, as Christ is accomplished, when on the last page she finally calls herself by her real name, the *Sibylle désolée*, the mute Pythia."[69]

Like Germaine de Staël, George Sand uses the recurring Woman-as-Wisdom myth, creates women who are bold Protheans, and establishes the larger-than-life goddess of art that was to influence Victorian women writers. Like Staël, Sand is outspoken in political ideology, but her Consuelo, unlike Staël's Corinne, is not a political prophetess. Naomi Schor says that *Consuelo* and *La Comtesse de Rudolstadt* are not political novels because they "lack the paradoxical underpinning necessary to Sand's political fiction."[70] Corinne is indeed motherland and patriotism, as well as Virgil's Cumæan Sibyl, Apollo's Pythian, Dante's Beatrice, the Madonna of Wisdom, the model for female genius. Sand realized her indebtedness to Staël and—knowing that Consuelo would be compared to Corinne—initiates the comparison within her own text. Invoking the Corinne myth and all the mythology it entails, as well as the myths of Orpheus and Eurydice and Eros and Psyche, Sand intends to differentiate herself from her literary foremother. Also—because Consuelo is a divine Sophia rather than a political Sibyl—Sand insists that her own female artist is on a holy mission from God as well as a quest for beauty and truth. Consuelo evolves into a goddess of poverty, humility, and liberation as well as a high priestess of art.

69. Sand, *Léila* 1:88, 2:158; Hoog, "George Sand and the Romantic Sibyl," 103.
70. Schor, *George Sand and Idealism*, 100.

2

Geraldine Jewsbury
Art and Work as Vocation

IN GEORGE SAND's *Consuelo,* the magnificent young singer is saint and angel, goddess and empress, but she is also a consummate professional. Often she is seen in study, rehearsal, and practice or heard lecturing Anzoleto or Joseph Haydn on the necessity of discipline in their musical craft. At the end of the novel, when the newly widowed Consuelo is given the family jewels, she declines them, both from her distaste for ostentation and her unwillingness to accept a life of ease that she could afford were she to accept and sell the jewels. She tells the aunt who proffers the gift that she has simple tastes and a love of labor. Indeed, one of Sand's many issues in *Consuelo* is the distinction between the artist who squanders the divine afflatus by sloth and profligacy and the one who nourishes it by sacrifice and discipline. The genius comes unbidden, but she on whom it falls must prove worthy of the gift. For art is not only Consuelo's gift, it is also her vocation, her calling. Consuelo's art becomes her raison d'être, consoles her for life's losses, and provides her with challenge and exhilaration, meaning and identity. In brief, it is her profession—both in the archaic sense of that which she "professes" as faith or religion and in the more mundane sense of the means by which she earns her livelihood.

The necessity of earning one's way in the world was important to Consuelo's creator even before she became George Sand. In her autobiography Sand says that, although as Madame Dudevant she was ostensibly an heiress, the family estate at Nohant was under the control of her husband and she needed money for her incompetent half brother and his frail wife, as well as to remove herself and her children from the "baneful influence" of pleading with Casimir Dudevant for an allowance. Furthermore, she was bored with inactivity and "absolutely powerless" in her dependence upon the man whose name she wore but for whom she felt neither love nor loyalty. The solution: find a pleasurable activity for which she could earn cash. Aurore first considered translations (which she rejected as too time-consuming), portrait painting (lacking in originality), millinery or dressmaking (too slow), and at first lit upon painting ornamental flowers and birds on lacquer boxes. Feeling that she had neither the well-trained talent nor the ambition to be a writer, she nevertheless became George Sand when she turned her "slight genius" into success by means of long hours, tough self-discipline, and hard work.[1] One of the most famous verbal sketches of Sand comes from the testimony of a lover who, after a night of exhausting amour, was annoyed to awake and find Sand in her wrapper, scratching away with her pen—practicing the vocation that gave her fame, power, and independence. Like Sand herself, the Sandian female artists are invariably workers. Consuelo slaves away at rehearsals, Thérèse (of *Elle et lui*) at her painting—not only creating her own original works but also producing copies of famous paintings to earn a livelihood for herself and her lover. Thérèse's work as copyist serves, some would suggest, as a useful analogue to Sand's own prolific writing to pay the bills—together with the suggestion that the Sand canon would be of higher quality if Sand had not needed the money so desperately.

The English "Working" Woman

Earning an income as means of survival was also a necessity for many middle-class English novelists and poets of the nineteenth century. In her famous 1856 essay "Silly Novels by Lady Novelists," Marian Evans, who was soon to become the novelist George Eliot, belittles sentimentality and stereotypes in popular novels by women, and in so doing she attacks the notion that "[e]mpty writing" could be justified by "empty stomachs," insisting that most "lady" novelists "write in elegant boudoirs, with violet-coloured ink and a ruby pen," and their only poverty is the "poverty of brains." One wonders why Eliot, who was about to embark on her career as fiction writer, perhaps in part because she too needed cash, would so callously overlook the financial hardship of many of her contemporaries, as well as of the female writers who had been shaping the female-as-artist tradition of her century. Among the more remarkable examples of writers who were workers for necessity's sake are the poet Felicia Hemans, who supported herself and five children after her husband abandoned them; novelist Dinah Mulock Craik, who supported herself and two younger brothers after her mother died and her father was incarcerated in an insane asylum; novelist Amelia Barr, who fed herself and her surviving daughters after her husband immigrated to Ameri-

1. Sand, *My Life,* 196, 197–99.

ca and died; actress/novelist Mary Elizabeth Braddon, who was principal bread-winner for her mother, husband, and six children; novelist Margaret Oliphant, who was the sole supporter of her children and nephews; and composer/poet Caroline Norton, whose sheet music and collections of ballads, glees, and duets paid the bills when her husband deserted her. Even Mrs. Humphry Ward, the final novelist whose female artists are studied in this volume, apparently worked rapidly to produce one novel after another because of pressure to support her son's parliamentary career and pay his gambling debts, make up the difference for her husband's money-losing investments in art, and support the Wards in the style to which a literary success and her entourage were expected to live. Among the British women who worked in the professions at midcentury were also some of the most gifted and self-consciously professional writers of the century—the literary editor Marian Evans, the teacher Charlotte Brontë, the art critic and historian Anna Jameson, and the poet Letitia Landon. Moreover, a number of visible and vocal women were labeling their works as professions—whether or not they received pay. Such women were the politician Beatrice Webb and the nurse Florence Nightingale, for whom work became a religion. Nightingale, who dedicates her autobiography to the artisans of England and "fellow-searchers" after moral truth, says that work is God's purpose for mortals and the only source of human happiness.[2]

Harriet Martineau, an unmarried Victorian woman who earned her own livelihood as journalist, political writer, and novelist, estimates that at the middle of the nineteenth century one-third of English females over the age of twenty were supporting themselves and their households. Gertrude Himmelfarb posits that throughout most of the century, one-quarter of English women worked outside the home or at home for pay, most of them working-class women. Deborah Gorham says, however, that no middle-class woman could raise her status through effort in the world of work because earning meant, for her, a loss of caste—her status, such as it was, always gained or lost by her connection with a man. John Sutherland notes that of the 312 Victorian female novelists, 280 were married women or "spinsters" with no other vocational attribution—a fact that does not negate that some creative wives and spinsters were "self-employed" as writers earning their livelihood from their art, just as the French writer George Sand was earning hers. Elaine Showalter estimates that until 1780 most women writers were

2. Eliot, "Silly Novels by Lady Novelists," in *Essays of George Eliot*, 393–94; Sutherland, *The Stanford Companion to Victorian Fiction*, 156, 46, 80, 477. Weliver notes Norton's work as composer in the 1840s (*Women Musicians in Victorian England, 1860–1900: Representations of Music, Science, and Gender in the Leisured Home*, 43–45); Sutherland, *Mrs. Humphry Ward: Eminent Victorian, Pre-eminent Edwardian*, 307–8, 324–28, 335–36; Nightingale, *"Cassandra" and Other Selections from "Suggestions for Thought,"* 150.

married, by 1790 a good many spinsters were writing as well, and that about half of those born between 1800 and 1900 were married.[3]

A litany of self-supporting professional women writers must include Geraldine Endsor Jewsbury, whose finest novel, *The Half Sisters,* adapts the Corinne/Consuelo artists of French Romanticism to a more down-to-earth, middle-class depiction of art as profession and the actress as professional woman. Specifically, Jewsbury adapts the Carlylean Gospel of Work to show that an "inspired sibyl" (*HS,* 155) owes something real and serious to the profession that sustains her life—that art cannot be taken up for a lark, then put aside when it has served its purpose. Rather, art requires the passion and commitment of the artist, female as well as male. Jewsbury's contribution to the discussion of female genius and female art is her depiction of the steady labor of artists as "professional women," a term that she repeatedly uses for "authoresses, actresses, and what not" (*HS,* 221). Through the gifted actress Bianca Pazzi in *The Half Sisters* she treats the topic of the actress as artist, as well as her dignity and professionalism in face of the vicissitudes and disrespect that women of her profession received in Victorian England. Jewsbury's treatment of the subject of woman as artist takes the approach that the author never saw a goddess go; her artist treads upon the ground. More deliberately than her many English contemporaries who were adapting *Corinne* and *Consuelo,* Geraldine Jewsbury revises the portrait of the female artist to represent the "Gospel" of work and professionalism.

Jewsbury as Professional

A professional journalist/reviewer/novelist, Geraldine Jewsbury wrote six novels and two children's stories, edited and partially wrote Lady Morgan's *Memoirs,* and produced over sixteen hundred reviews for the *Athenaeum,* as well as pieces for *Westminster Review, Douglas Jerrold's Shilling Magazine,* and Dickens's *Household Words.* Geraldine was, in fact, only one of the Jewsbury novelists; her older sister, Maria Jane, had served as chief reviewer for the *Athenaeum* and published works of fiction and poetry before dying young in 1833, a dozen years before Geraldine published a first novel. As for the younger Jewsbury sister, she is characterized by her biographer as an emotional, fast-talking, diminutive, boyish sylph of a woman with a taste for the metaphysical, a curious and "masculine" mind, a "wild and wayward spirit," and a passion for Shelley and George Sand.[4]

3. Foster, *Victorian Women's Fiction: Marriage, Freedom, and the Individual,* 7 (Foster's source for the Martineau claim is an 1851 *Edinburgh Review*); Himmelfarb, *The De-moralization of Society: From Victorian Virtues to Modern Values,* 106; Gorham, *The Victorian Girl and the Feminine Ideal,* 8; Sutherland, "The Underread," xxii; Showalter, *Literature of Their Own,* 47.

4. Howe, *Geraldine Jewsbury: Her Life and Errors,* 12, 23.

She was a seriously professional woman, a woman who claimed she had no "vocation" for propriety, but a decidedly strong vocation for work.

Jewsbury may well have been bisexual in inclination. At the very least she was, in her words, "born to drive theories and rules to distraction." Her passionate female friendships included the American actress Charlotte Cushman, the German novelist Fanny Lewald, and the famously unhappy literary wife Jane Welsh Carlyle. Jewsbury's remarkable letters to Jane Carlyle are sprinkled with appellations such as "my darling" and "my dear love." Furthermore she confesses to Jane, ". . . I feel towards you much more like a lover than a female friend!" On one occasion Geraldine was furious because Jane was "making love before my very face to *another man!*" and Jane in turn comments on Geraldine's "mad, *lover-like* jealousy." Annie E. Ireland, who knew Jewsbury and edited her letters to Jane Carlyle, delicately comments that if their love did not "pass the love of woman," it "certainly reached the boundary of which that sacred 'relationship of the spirit' is capable." Norma Clarke believes, however, that what Geraldine wanted in her older friend was the intimacy of a mother surrogate to replace the mother and older sister, both of whom had died young, leaving Geraldine the only woman in a family of men.[5] No doubt the two women were drawn to one another in part because both were restless and brilliant and both suffered periods of intense depression. An additional attraction for Jewsbury, however, was that of Jane's husband: She was drawn to Carlyle's philosophy and to his wife's personality and perspicacious critical insights—especially those pertaining to Jewsbury's works in progress.

In regard to men and marriage—that most expected occupation for a proper Victorian woman—Jewsbury grumbles that she does not see how women can "sell their souls for the sake of furniture and respectability." Somewhat androgynous in behavior, Jewsbury enjoyed considerable freedom in her career as a publisher's reader, used rough language, liked a good smoke, and hoped the day would come when individuals of the two genders could sit down for conversation and a companionable cigar without the barrier of flirtation to remind them that they were of "opposite" sexes. She was the more assertive partner in her romantic relationships, and she apparently proposed marriage to three men—one of whom she approached when she was writing *The Half Sisters,* and none of whom took her seriously. At times she wished for "a good husband and a dozen children" but realized few men would be up to the challenge of marriage to Geraldine Jewsbury:

5. Jewsbury, *Selections from the Letters of Geraldine Endsor Jewsbury to Jane Welsh Carlyle,* 191; Howe, *Geraldine Jewsbury: Her Life and Errors,* 53; Woolf, "Geraldine and Jane," 1; Ireland, introduction to *Selections from the Letters,* vi; Clarke, *Ambitious Heights: Writing, Friendship, Love: The Jewsbury Sisters, Felicia Hemans, and Jane Welsh Carlyle,* 183.

Only the difficulty is that "women of genius" require very special husbands—men of noble character, not intellect, but of a character and nature large enough, and strong enough, and wise enough to take in them and their genius too, without cutting it down to suit their own crotchets, or reprobating half their qualities because they don't understand what to do with them, or what they are intended for. And so, as I shall never meet with the special man who could manage me wisely, it is lucky I have met with no one who has claimed to do so.[6]

A number of women in Jewsbury's novels suffer Jewsbury's "lucky" fate of finding no special man to marry and "manage" them; numerous others, unluckily and unwisely, sell themselves for furniture and respectability—and much misery in the bargain.

Jewsbury refused to join the most advanced feminists on the "Woman's Question," taking exception, Susanne Howe says, to their methods and their demands that women should have sole right to all their earnings. Nevertheless she advocated the expansion of women's education and careerism, believing somewhat naively that with open opportunity for women in these areas, full equality before the law was not a necessity. She balked, for example, at the idea of women as soldiers, barristers, and members of Parliament—or at least Lord Melton, her spokesman for women's rights, does so in *The Half Sisters*. Although "dependency" seems to be a most horrible fate for her female characters and although she relished her own independence, she often suggests that women require a strong guiding hand if they are to become contented, productive, and whole. She laments, as Mary Wollstonecraft had done in the previous century, that English women, instead, are educated as if for a harem—that is, merely in the accomplishments that ornament a middle-class household. Her rhetoric of moral equality for the two sexes is exactly that of Wollstonecraft, who insists that nature has made no difference between male and female in regard to moral duty, that moral inequality of the sexes is a "pernicious" doctrine, and that "chastity, modesty, public spirit, and all the noble train of virtues, on which . . . happiness is built, should be cultivated by all mankind, or they will be cultivated to little effect." In *The Half Sisters* Melton echoes Wollstonecraft's statement right out of *A Vindication of the Rights of Woman:* "Women . . . must not have their moral sense palled and tampered with by *conserves* of morality, or a gospel according to *gracefulness;* there is only ONE law of what is really right, for men or for women, and no second motive, no sense of decorum, will stand either man or woman in stead in the hour of trial" (*HS*, 222). Monica Fryckstedt insists that Jewsbury was in the forefront of the feminist movement in England because in the 1840s she was ahead of her

6. Jewsbury, *Selections from the Letters*, 57, 369.

contemporaries in advocating love as the prerequisite for marriage (which Fryck-stedt attributed in part to her "George Sand gospel of passion") and in her criticism of the social evils of England in the essays she wrote for *Douglas Jerrold's Shilling Magazine*—issues of class, gender, exploitation, and workers and employers—although Fryckstedt issues the caveat that Jewsbury has more faith in the "republicanism of trade" than did her more famous contemporary also from Manchester, Elizabeth Gaskell.[7] Jewsbury's less-than-wholehearted support for feminism is surprising, given that she was an independent, self-supporting professional; her viewpoint is also troubling for some contemporary readers who suspect that Jewsbury would not entitle all women to the freedom that she and her fictional actress Bianca enjoy.

Criticism of Jewsbury's works either takes her at her word on the statement that a young woman needs someone strong to control her or cites as proof of this viewpoint a few choice examples from the novels.[8] Jewsbury's view that a woman needs guidance does seem at first blush quite insulting, especially when Jewsbury, somewhat as Jane Austen does with Emma and Mr. Knightly, accommodates a fictional woman's needs by marrying her off to a much older, wiser man with considerable gravitas in the world—as she does both Bianca in *The Half Sisters* and the heroine of the novel *Marian Withers*. In regard to Bianca's half sister, Alice, in *The Half Sisters,* however, the narrator's comment that "wise guidance is precisely the blessing that seldomest falls to a woman's lot" (*HS,* 41) refers to failures of women *and* men—of Alice's mother, sister-in-law, and husband, who are all older and presumably much wiser than she. In reference to Bianca, her future husband, Lord Melton, says the same thing: "[W]ise guidance and government is what [all women] yearn after" (*HS,* 219). In fairness to Jewsbury, however, it must be acknowledged that many of the older and "wiser" husbands utterly fail to lead, teach, and educate their young wives. Prominent examples of such failure are Gifford, the husband of the protagonist, Zoe, in the 1845 *Zoe: The History of Two Lives,* and Bryant, husband of Alice in *The Half Sisters.* Furthermore, in some Jewsbury novels, the wisdom and education required for a young woman are provided by an older, wiser *female* mentor or mother surrogate, for example, Aunt Margaret in *Constance Herbert,* Lady Southend in *The Sorrows of Gentility,* Miss Airlie in *The History of an Adopted Child,* and Aunt Alice in *Marian Withers.* As a matter of fact, Jewsbury nowhere in the fiction insists that a woman requires a

7. Howe, *Geraldine Jewsbury: Her Life and Errors,* 104–5; Wollstonecraft, *A Vindication of the Rights of Woman with Strictures on Political and Moral Subjects,* 245. Melton/Jewsbury also agrees with Wollstonecraft that "blind propriety," in place of reason, is an inadequate basis for woman's virtue and that a woman, like a man, requires either a family or a profession, idleness being, for both men and women, a major source of moral decadence; see Fryckstedt, "Geraldine Jewsbury and *Douglas Jerrold's Schilling Magazine,*" 334, 336.

8. See, for example, Calder, *Women and Marriage in Victorian Fiction,* 58.

man to control and educate her, but rather that a young, inexperienced woman—whether a professional or not—needs an older, wiser, more experienced *person* to check her proclivities. She laments to Jane Carlyle that if only Maria Jane had not died, she herself would have enjoyed such a mentor to curb her dilettantism and assist her to become more practical in business and professionalism. As previously noted, Jewsbury may have wished Jane to become such a guide.[9]

It is also worth mentioning in Jewsbury's defense that not only do young *women* in Jewsbury's fiction need mentors; so do young *men*. In the novel *Zoe*, for example, the doubting young priest Everhard, for example, earnestly seeks clerical mentors. But since Jewsbury concerns herself with women's issues, women characters, and the lack of adequate education for girls, one sees many more instances of lost, confused, and misguided young women than young men—who were, after all, granted a superior education, greater freedom, and access to the networks of their professions.

Zoe and the Failed Search for Profession

Geraldine Jewsbury's first novel, *Zoe: The History of Two Lives,* is in some ways a rehearsal for *The Half Sisters* in that the fascinating, exotic woman for whom the novel is named is, like Bianca, creative and artistic, but like Bianca's half sister, Alice, intellectually starved. Also, as she was to do in *The Half Sisters,* Jewsbury in *Zoe* contrasts women who find a satisfying vocation and with those who do not. In a Parisian salon one brilliant woman in the novel laments:

> Out of the million of women who are flattered by being told they possess genius, not one ever achieves a work that endures, or that obtains higher praise than of being something very wonderful for a woman. . . . Whenever a woman attempts to throw herself into the *mêlé* of action, and to contend with men on a footing of equality, she is always seen in the end, to commit either some grave fault, or some signal folly. No woman has ever succeeded in gaining lasting fame, but many have lost their reputation in the attempt.

In her more pessimistic moments, Jewsbury agrees. For example she writes to Jane Carlyle that "every woman who does as I have done—[who] make their lot contrary to custom, are always broken in the attempt."[10]

Published in 1845, *Zoe* was controversial because of its depiction of illicit love between a married woman and a priest. No doubt it was this aspect of the book,

9. Jewsbury, *Selections from the Letters,* 203–4.
10. Jewsbury, *Zoe: The History of Two Lives,* 1:67–68; Jewsbury, *Selections from the Letters,* 29.

together with its exposure of hypocritical pastors and priests, that caused a reviewer to comment it was "tabooed by the orthodox" and had disturbed the
"Dorcases of provincial rule." Zoe is, like Staël's Corinne and like Bianca Pazzi
in the Jewsbury novel that was to follow, a beautiful, exotic woman of mixed-
national ancestry—in Zoe's case, half-English, half-Greek. Given the intensity
and frustration of her passion, Zoe's "George Sandism" is most like that in *Indiana*—although her elderly husband sympathizes with Zoe's intellectual hunger
and is not like the domestic tyrant whom Indiana despises. Like Indiana, Zoe
marries a man much older than herself, then is awakened as a passionate, sensual woman; like Indiana, she experiences passion for two men who are not her husband; also like Indiana, she becomes a young widow—though in Zoe's case much
earlier in the novel's plot, and the widowed Zoe does not as consequence of her
widowhood end the novel in the arms of a strong man like Indiana's Sir Ralph.
Jewsbury would not be the least bit taken aback by comparisons between herself
and George Sand: She generously admitted the influence, for example, in a conversation and letter to Giuseppe Mazzini.[11]

In *Zoe,* Jewsbury sets out to prove her theory that a woman of intelligence and
energy requires interesting and productive work—else she will make herself and
those around her miserable. Zoe "has the soul of an artist," but in art she is a
dilettante—a talented musician who plays the harpsichord, a dancer, and an om-
nivorous reader of scandalous French novels like *Les liaisons dangereuses* and *La
nouvelle Héloïse.* As a bored, frustrated wife, she conquers the heart of the agnostic priest Everhard; as a coquette and woman of passion, she narrowly escapes
a love affair with the French *roué* Mirabeau. Clarke comments that Zoe's simul-
taneous love for Everhard and passion for Count Mirabeau, like the choice between femininity and genius, illustrates the "strength bought by evasion"—the
inability to reconcile intellect, passion, and femininity.[12]

Throughout the novel, Jewsbury provides both unacceptable and acceptable
answers to the question of what a talented woman is to do with her life: Zoe's relative Marian Gifford spends her days making jellies and carpets (which Zoe finds
silly because the cook can make jelly and pretty carpets can be bought retail). Zoe
and her friend Lady Clara de Mandeville, as two rich, merry widows, spend an
inordinate amount of time and energy flitting about Vanity Fair with its intrigues, foibles, and fashions, but the widowed Adéle, the mother of Everhard,
has a natural aptitude for business, runs the family investments, rides daily with
the bailiff at five in the morning to inspect the estate. Zoe's stepdaughter,
Clotilde, devotes her life to God and becomes the mother superior of a convent,

11. Chorley, *The Athenaeum*, Feb. 1, 1845; "Letters to and from Geraldine Jewsbury" (appendix in
Howe's *Geraldine Jewsbury: Her Life and Errors,* 205).
12. Jewsbury, *Zoe,* 1:182; Clarke, *Ambitious Heights,* 173.

a position in which she enjoys the double challenge of being both a matriarch and administrator—with a fair number of a "daughters" and "employees" to supervise and manage. She teaches Zoe that "all . . . gifts must seem wasted unless they are dedicated to the highest uses, not to our own glory." Clotilde, like Everhard, has experienced a life-changing love for an unattainable and unworthy object of love, and both have been made better for their suffering. This emphasis on love as salvation is an overriding theme of all Jewsbury's novels. In reference to the priest's life of service after Zoe, the narrator comments:

> Love, rightly conceived in its highest manifestations, ceases to be a mere passion; it becomes a worship, a religion; it regenerates the whole soul; till a man has found an object to love, his faculties are not developed; they lie curled round himself, crude and dwarfed; he may have the capability of becoming great and noble, but he *is* neither, until the divine fire is kindled within, burning up all worldliness, selfishness, and the dross of sensuality, that eat like cankerworms into the beauty of man.[13]

The pathetic waste of Zoe's life is that she never finds a profession, a calling, a love of equals that can be equally reciprocated, or even a worthwhile hobby in which she can invest all that energy, passion, sensitivity, and talent that Jewsbury has generously bestowed upon her. Such waste of female creativity and female genius it was Geraldine Jewsbury's lifelong mission to lament and criticize.

Professional Women, Professional Star

Given that many Victorian women had to earn their own livelihoods and that the novelists did so by means of their art, it is not surprising that several woman-as-artist novels depict middle-class women who use extraordinary talent as painters, actresses, or singers to provide bread for the table, a roof above the head. In this, art mimics life, and fictional characters work as professionals—from the governess in a domestic space to an actress on a public stage—where they can be, like their creators, to varying degrees independent, challenged, and creative. Thus Jane Eyre and Lucy Snowe make money as educators, while Anne Brontë's Helen Huntingdon of *The Tenant of Wildfell Hall* maintains herself and her small son by painting, Craik's Olive Rothesay in *Olive* also paints to pay off her father's debts and support her mother, and George Eliot's Mirah Lapidoth in *Daniel Deronda* employs her lovely singing voice as the sole source of income for the singer and her father. In addition to *Corinne* and *Consuelo*, numerous fictional

---

13. Jewsbury, *Zoe*, 3:257, 2:260–61.

artists perform on the stages of Europe, for example, in Sand's 1846 *Lucrezia Floriani,* and in the English novels *The Actress of the Present Day,* by an unknown author, *The Morals of May Fair* by Annie Edwards, and *Pomfret* by H. F. Chorley. Following the publication of Jewsbury's novel, actresses are depicted in *Florence Sackville* by Mrs. E. J. Burbury, *The Head of the Family* by Dinah Mulock Craik, *Villette* by Charlotte Brontë, and *Pendennis* by Thackeray, as well as the long poem *Armgart* by George Eliot, and, at the end of the century, the novels *Miss Bretherton* by Mrs. Humphry Ward and *The Tragic Muse* by Henry James. In Jewsbury's *The Half Sisters,* there are three gifted female artists—Bianca, Clara Broughton, and the Fornasari—all of them stage performers.

On the surface, acting was a rather bohemian career of glamour and excitement; yet behind the scenes were the drudgery of rehearsals, the insecurity of being unemployed and hence strapped for cash between productions or, in the case of illness, innuendos about the actress's character, sexual advances from fellow professionals and fans, and the "coarse, gaudy, glaring, accessories" (*HS,* 145) of costuming and stage effects that Jewsbury's Bianca—like Sand's Consuelo—dislikes, but realizes to be a necessary aspect of her art. In George Sand's *Lucrezia Floriani,* the retired actress Lucrezia says that, although art is a demanding profession for either sex, the female performer pays the higher price; wearing provocative clothes and showing herself on the boards, she is either figuratively or literally searching for "clients" to whom she can prostitute herself in order to meet the demands that her needy relatives impose upon her.[14] Sand's countryman Baudelaire agrees; in his 1859–1860 essay on modern art he notes, "These reflections about the courtesan may, to a certain extent, be applied to the actress; for she too is a creature of show, an object of public pleasure." Conrad Percy, the man beloved by both half sisters of Jewsbury's novel, remarks that actresses "play with the passions of men to some degree like courtesans" (*HS,* 216). On nineteenth-century actresses, Tracy Davis says that the profession was for attractive young women an alternative to the "drudgery, exploitation, and hazards of needle and domestic trades, teaching and retailing, or industrial and manufacturing jobs"—needlework and clerking being the very professions that a Catholic priest recommends to Bianca, but which she refuses. As Tracy remarks and as Jewsbury's Conrad comments in the novel, when a Victorian woman violated the terms of her womanliness by exchanging the private for the "public sphere"—and nothing could be more public than displaying herself on a stage—she invited public conversation about her personal life, and speculation about her morality. In *Villette* Charlotte Brontë illustrates that an actress's talent is, in the male gaze, of

14. Jewsbury probably knew the Sand novel when she wrote *The Half Sisters;* in her correspondence she mentions lending out her copy of the novel in 1849, the year after her own actress novel was published (*Selections from the Letters,* 292.)

less interest than her person—either the person she is offstage, or the pose she presents onstage, or a composite of both. In that novel when Lucy Snowe and Dr. John attend the theater to behold the "Pythian inspiration" of the actress Vashti, the critical, clinical "[c]ool young Briton" Dr. John "judged her as a woman, not an artist: it was a branding judgment."[15]

Bianca initially works as a performer to feed herself and her ailing mother. Judith Rosen suggests that in introducing Bianca as a girl of "conventional female virtue" inside the private sphere of family, Jewsbury avoids provoking the distaste that would be attached to the actress if she had been motivated initially—instead of secondarily—by ambition, the desire for freedom, and "passion" for her art. There is, nevertheless, no denying that Bianca loves her profession and that she is ambitious. She says, "The stage is to me a *passion*, as well as a profession; I can work in no other direction; I should become worthless and miserable; all my faculties would prey upon myself, and I should even be wicked and mischievous, and God knows how bad, if I were placed in any other position" (*HS*, 134). In other words, she could have been Zoe. That Bianca passionately loves performing and that her career sustains her emotionally through the death of a mother and abandonment of a lover—while similar suffering destroys her half sister Alice—constitute for some readers a valid concern with the novel. Namely, whether Jewsbury's issue is that women seek employment from fiscal necessity or for personal fulfillment. As J. M. Hartley sees it, Jewsbury "blurs the issues at stake in the employment question, issues which centered not upon the necessity of work for middle-class women but their need for something worthwhile to do."[16]

Granted, it would be for a Victorian readership less unseemly to present a needy actress (furthermore one who prudently leaves the stage, as Bianca does, when she marries a wealthy English aristocrat), but it is also an accurate reference to the lives of numerous Victorian women artists who must live by their craft, if Martineau is even close in her estimate about the one-third of mid-Victorian women who were earning income for themselves or their families. Furthermore, one could respond to Hartley's argument that the novel attempts to parallel different kinds of female needs—aspects of the general need to be productive, independent, and worthwhile, as pertains to both the impoverished orphan Bianca and the well-married, well-do-do half sister, Alice. The passion for one's work, as well as the way one defines herself by work, is a central theme in the novel as it was in Jewsbury's life. Jewsbury held that just as a man becomes himself by the

15. Baudelaire, "The Painter of Modern Life," 431; Davis, *Actresses as Working Women: Their Social Identity in Victorian Culture*, 35, 69; Brontë, *Villette*, 2:10.

16. Rosen, "At Home upon a Stage: Domesticity and Genius in Geraldine Jewsbury's *The Half Sisters* (1848)," 27; Hartley, "Geraldine Jewsbury and the Problems of the Woman Novelist," 146.

professional choice he takes and the way he conducts himself in that profession, a woman also should evolve into her womanhood by the work she does, although that work can include philanthropy or public service and does not have to be remunerated employment. In fact, again and again in the Jewsbury canon are brilliant, creative women whose souls are cursed because they are stifled by ignorance, class, family circumstances, prejudice, or their own timidity. One might well conclude that if Bianca Pazzi, the woman of genius in *The Half Sisters,* had not been fated to the right combination of necessity, talent, opportunity, courage, desperation, and devotion to her mother, she might not have become an actress after all. Yet, as Jewsbury writes in a letter to Jane Carlyle, ". . . if women have chance to have genius, they have it, and must do something with it. . . ."[17] That Bianca, like Sand's Consuelo, finds the career fit for her temperament and extraordinary gift becomes her salvation. Consuelo and Bianca (as well as Sand and Jewsbury) have in common that they can say, "I have had work to do, and I have done it" (*HS,* 250).

Departure from the Myth

In reference to the dichotomy of the female artist as secular sibyl or divine Sophia that I propose in Chapter 1, it should be noted that Jewsbury's *The Half Sisters* is a more pedestrian, realistic novel than either *Corinne* or *Consuelo.* Nor is Jewsbury as political a writer as either of her French predecessors. Nevertheless she was profoundly influenced by both writers, especially Sand. Because *The Half Sisters* is not a product of Romanticism, though, there are no treks to the mouths of volcanoes or imprisonments in romantic Spandaw-like castles. In fact when Bianca's half sister, the impressionable Alice, first reads *Corinne,* she is seated upon the "Romantic Rocks"—a mimicry of the Romantic sublime with skeletal frame and tangled shrubs (*HS,* 60), highly suggestive because Alice has temporarily escaped the ordinary to indulge briefly in romantic escapism and because she is about to receive a wedding proposal from the most prosaic of men. Rather un-Corinne-like, the half sisters live and struggle in a more recognizably middle-class environment. Bianca is more than once given titles like "inspired sibyl" (*HS,* 154) or "priestess" of art (*HS,* 162), but there is no elaborate mythological structure for Bianca's art as there is for Corinne's or Consuelo's—although there are deliberate and telling allusions to Staël's and Sand's heroines and plots.

Furthermore, Jewsbury was, during the 1840s, somewhat of a religious skeptic and hence unlikely to think in terms of the artist being sent on a divine mission for God, although both Bianca and the esteemed actor who becomes her

17. Jewsbury, *Selections from the Letters,* 368.

mentor acknowledge that hers is a God-given genius. As Jewsbury's mentor Thomas Carlyle notes, we attribute to the work of the artist—based, as it is, on inspiration rather than deduction—"the gift of a divinity." All of Jewsbury's characters, though, are busy working out their own salvation or failing in the attempt, and not questioning whether the divine breath of God has bestowed upon them a mission to remodel the world, as Consuelo comes to understand the mission of art.[18] It is Bianca's more scaled-down mission to remodel her profession, but initially even she performs to give pleasure and for the exhilarated buzz of having turned in a compelling performance. More like their creator, Jewsbury's women are trying to find meaning and fulfillment, stave off ennui and depression, and get through life without doing major damage to those around them. Invariably the Jewsbury novels ask, in one form or another, the following questions: (1) What is happiness, and why do we think we deserve it or will attain it; (2) does love—in whatever form—make us better people or cheapen us; and (3) for what meaningful work or profession are we intended?

Specifically, in *The Half Sisters,* Jewsbury makes her unique contribution to the question of female genius and professionalism by means of the elaborate and provocative parallel between art and love. One must work to make love a success, and the artist must work to perfect her professional skills. If men and women consider love an amusement, Jewsbury says, then they fail at love. Selfishly they miss out on giving and receiving happiness, on allowing love to elevate them morally and spiritually—as it is love's inclination to do. In all of Jewsbury's novels there are women and men who "take up [love] lightly," when they should treat love as a "weighty responsibility" (*HS,* 166). Similarly, if artists create their works—their performances, writings, paintings—merely to amuse themselves, to make money, or to provide diversion for other people, then they have failed. They have prostituted the genius that has been given them. To discharge the responsibility, they must neither exploit divine talent in feeding their human ego nor pander to the lowest common denominator of contemporary public taste; rather, they must elevate literature, the theater, or the visual arts. In capsule this is Jewsbury's version of the Victorian Gospel of Work and its application to female genius.

18. Carlyle, *Characteristics,* in *The Works of Thomas Carlyle in Thirty Volumes,* 28:5. In the 1840s Jewsbury underwent a crisis of faith, which she chronicles in *Zoe,* a novel about religious hypocrisy. To Jane Carlyle, Jewsbury wrote, "I neither know anything nor believe in anything" (*Selections from the Letters,* 63). In *The Half Sisters,* a judgmental priest considers Bianca a fallen Mary Magdalene, nuns live in "placid negation" and "moral suicide" (*HS,* 302, 303), and Conrad's conversion is "pure fanaticism" (*HS,* 330). Zoe is agnostic; Alice Bryant has but a "vague, poetical sense of religion" (*HS,* 187); and Bianca is but a nominal Catholic.

An English *Corinne*

Jewsbury invites readers to compare *The Half Sisters* to Staël's famous novel: She boldly announces her indebtedness to *Corinne* when the "English" sister, an allusion to Staël's Lucile, reads Staël's *Corinne* and the narrator remarks that a young girl's first reading of *Corinne* is an epoch a woman never forgets (*HS*, 60). Not only is Staël's novel an important source for Jewsbury's more mundane depiction of a stage performer, but also two other texts are much in evidence in the shaping of *The Half Sisters*—Sand's *Consuelo* and Maria Jane Jewsbury's 1831 novella, *The Enthusiast*. Analysis of the intertextuality of Jewsbury's novel reveals it to be more complex and more insightful than it might otherwise seem and shows how it sharpens her commentary on art as work and profession.

In Jewsbury's novel, the role of Corinne is taken by the actress Bianca Pazzi, who, like Staël's character, is half-English, half-Italian. But Corinne is an heiress, and Bianca is illegitimate; Corinne *is* Italy ("l'image de notre belle Italie"), and Bianca is without a country. Long before the opening of Staël's novel, the elder Nelvil had married first an Italian, then a British wife, each marriage producing one daughter, and Jewsbury's novel follows the same pattern. Years earlier, Bianca's father, Philip Helmsby, had an affair with a beautiful Italian, then returned to England where he married a staid, rigid English girl—heiress in the iron business where Helmsby prospers. When the novel opens, Helmsby has died, leaving two daughters now in their early teens and totally ignorant of the existence of each other. When the suffering Italian mother and her daughter immigrate to England, the half-Italian, half-English Bianca—unlike the wealthy Corinne—turns professional to support her dying mother. Meanwhile the younger half sister, Alice, like Staël's Lucile, grows up in a proper and altogether boring home much like that which Corinne despises and where life is made up of "petty interests and trivial rivalries" (*HS*, 42). Jewsbury's most astonishing reversal of Staël's novel is that the Lucile-like character dies, and the Corinne-like character survives and prospers.

One of Jewsbury's secondary purposes in the novel is to refute the stereotype that a "professional" woman is at risk of bad associations "or worse," while a girl once safely married has irrefutably accomplished her purpose in life. In *The Half Sisters*, though, it is Bianca who withstands the temptations not only of the director's couch but also of the passionate romantic love for a young English equivalent of Nelvil, Conrad Percy, whose abandonment does *not* slay her, as Nelvil's defection does Corinne. Ironically—and shockingly—this same young Percy later tempts Alice to abandon the home of her husband, the well-to-do businessman Bryant, and to become his mistress—an outcome averted only because Alice dies in the process of eloping. That Bianca suffers, but is resilient and scrupulously moral, is not surprising. After all, the fascinating and gifted actress is based in part on Geraldine Jewsbury, who considered herself not only a free and independent professional but also an upstanding and responsible woman. The gifted and miserable Alice, on the other hand, may be a fictionalized portrait of her dearest friend, the gifted and miserable housewife Jane Carlyle, to whom the novel is dedicated.[19] Whereas professional women (whom Jewsbury's characters group together as the infamous three *As*—artists, actresses, and authoresses) are subject to temptations arising from their comparative freedom, Jewsbury demonstrates that wives too are vulnerable. Lisa Surridge comments that in *The Half Sisters,* the domestic space, more than the theater, is locus of female artifice—the actress is natural, the domestic woman artificial.[20] And this wife falls, while the symbolically named heroine boasts a soul white and spotless, whether or not her reputation is.

There is, however, an English precedent for the reversal that Jewsbury plays here, although it is uncertain whether Jewsbury was familiar with the 1817 novel *The Actress of the Present Day.* In that earlier novel, a young actress, Mary Irwin, although plagued by the "unwarrantable addresses of one sex, and the marked object of envy and detraction in the other," nevertheless maintains her virtue, while her judgmental sister, Hester, loses hers and then dies in childbirth, leaving to Mary the motherless infant and the attendant reputation of being a fallen woman who takes her "bastard" on the road for her theater engagements.[21] Like *The Actress of the Present Day,* Jewsbury's novel illustrates that morality resides in persons, not professions. The outcome reverses *Corinne* and—whether or not Jewsbury knew the 1817 novel—cleverly questions the assumptions about the public and private spheres.

The English half sister, Alice (almost an anagram for Lucile), marries young and marries well, but she suffers stagnation of soul and intellect. Instead of taking his impressionable young bride to Mount Blanc for the honeymoon, as promised, Bryant takes her along on a business trip to the mining district of Wales; instead of sharing decisions with her, he insists that his place is the business sphere, hers is the domestic. In her marriage Alice is more than bored; she is burdened with what Jewsbury elsewhere calls the "nothings [that] make the sum of female life!"[22] The aborted artistry of her soul is revealed in that she has tried to paint, but produced only "blurred and patched daubs" (*HS,* 265). With

19. Clarke, *Ambitious Heights,* 178, 185. Lisa Surridge suggests that Bianca is also a tribute to the American actress Charlotte Cushman, a Jewsbury friend who played the role of "Bianca" in an 1845 production of Milman's *Fazio* ("Madame de Staël Meets Mrs. Ellis: Geraldine Jewsbury's *The Half Sisters,*" 86–87).

20. Surridge, "Madame de Staël Meets Mrs. Ellis: Geraldine Jewsbury's *The Half Sisters,*" 88.

21. *The Actress of the Present Day,* 2:55.

22. Jewsbury, *Selections from the Letters,* 100.

no children, no profession, no friends, and no challenges, she suffers ennui that amounts to severe depression—the affliction of Zoe Gifford in Jewsbury's previ- ous novel. Enter Conrad Percy, on the rebound after his romance with Bianca and an affair with a young opera singer and soured with "French-novel style of women" (*HS,* 178), no doubt of the Staël and Sand type. As Nelvil wins both Corinne and Lucile, Conrad makes both the Helmsby sisters his conquests. When Conrad reads Wordsworth to her, Alice responds with the passionate, breathless fervor that Bianca feels when she first sees and hears a renowned Shake- spearean actor perform *King Lear,* and that later in the novel Bianca's protégée, the singer Clara, experiences when she first hears Mozart's *Don Giovanni.* This fervent, palpitating response to art is in fact a trademark of Jewsbury's creative heroines whose souls have been starved for beauty. Marian Withers, on first hear- ing the same opera, feels "as if the spirit of the music had entered into and pos- sessed her," and in *Constance Herbert* the heroine responds similarly to *The Mar- riage of Figaro.*[23] In this detail Jewsbury's characters are similar to Consuelo, whose features are overspread with a divine glow when she is transported by the passion of music. But Consuelo and Bianca are sustained by the passion; Alice is destroyed in her search for it.

Early in the novel Conrad Percy becomes Bianca's Nelvil—her other passion. Conrad is the novel's prime example of a character who "takes up love lightly" for his own amusement; though a stereotype, he is not a villain. He appears like a guardian angel and introduces the needy Bianca to Simpson, the circus man who becomes her first employer—although she certainly is no Sissy Jupe in equestrian skills. She leaves the circus to become a "sixth-rate actress in a provin- cial town" (*HS,* 154), plays bit parts, escapes the clutches of a stage villain, and nurses, then buries, her mother. She dedicates her performances and her profes- sional career to Conrad, laying her tributes at his feet as Corinne does at Nelvil's. And he is in fact enchanted; when he attends her performance as Juliet in Shake- speare's tragedy, he is as mesmerized as Nelvil was upon seeing Corinne appear in the same role. But Bianca declines to marry Conrad for three years so that she can prove herself worthy. Her unselfish renunciation of love is prompted by Conrad's father, who first proposes to his son that the two young lovers simply have an affair until Conrad has sown his "wild oats," tires of his actress, and aban- dons her—as, ironically, Bianca's English father had done with the Italian beau- ty whose love he had "taken up lightly." But the devotion to an English father becomes even more similar to *Corinne* when the senior Percy dies and when the erring son Conrad is faced with obeying a voice from the grave, as Nelvil does. Naively Bianca believes she will become good enough for the Percys when her

23. Jewsbury, *Marian Withers,* 1:132; Jewsbury, *Constance Herbert,* 2:77.

great genius will have made her famous and rich; Corinne, older and more worldly-wise, knows that she will never measure up.

Midway through the novel Bianca meets Lord Maurice Melton, a sophisticate and feminist whose ideas are about as classless and liberal as would have been possible for an aristocrat of the day. Melton is as enlightened as Conrad and Nelvil are provincial. It is one annoying facet of Jewsbury's rhetoric, however, that her most advanced ideas on education and careerism for women are voiced by Melton, as if they are more weighty when spoken by a male character than they would be coming from a female. Melton falls in love with Bianca, but at the time she still carries a torch for the worthless Conrad. Impatient with her misplaced affections, Melton goes abroad for several years, and his adventures in Italy mirror some of those of Staël's Nelvil. Meanwhile, Bianca has taken on the responsibility of educating Clara, a young student in the boarding school of Melton's sister, Lady Vernon, and is supervising Clara's preparation as a great opera diva of the future. Thus she is "elevating the profession" as her own mentor, the old actor (now deceased), had told her she has been called to do. During Melton's absence Bianca decides that she loves Melton more than she loves her career. He returns to England, the inevitable marriage follows, and Bianca gives up the stage, leaving Clara as her legacy, as Corinne leaves little Juliette. She does so in part because Lady Vernon has a distaste for actresses—especially, it is assumed, actresses who are related to her.[24] One cannot help wincing to see Bianca next crocheting a cushion for Lady Vernon, but, not to worry, Jewsbury says, "[i]t is a great mistake to suppose that genius is shown in one special mode of manifestation alone;—it inspires its possessor, and enables him to feel equal to all situations" (*HS,* 391). As Staël's heroine is equally gifted as poet, dancer, singer, actress, and *improvisatrice,* Bianca proves herself talented at acting, costuming, domesticity, philanthropy, and crochet.

Although the histories of the half sisters parallel Staël's novelistic situation, it is significant that Alice perishes simply because she is undereducated, docile, and married—attributes that guarantee the survival of Staël's Lucile; Bianca flourishes because she is independent, fascinating, gifted, and free—and these traits fail to save Corinne. By Jewsbury's logic the deciding difference is that Alice has no meaningful work; Bianca has a vocation that gives her life and purpose. Not

24. According to Tracy C. Davis, actresses had greater access to the male elite than did other women of their class, and enough of them married nobility to prompt a *Punch* joke about actresses revitalizing the gene pool with strength, vitality, and good looks (*Actresses as Working Women,* 76). Davis omits the date of the *Punch* reference, but in *The History of an Adopted Child* (1852) Jewsbury points out that the myth of actresses becoming "peeresses" has turned the heads of young girls aspiring to careers on the stage. Jewsbury's starstruck Clarissa Donnelly is told by the director that the actresses who marry peers can be counted on his fingers, while "hundreds and thousands . . . have drudged for years upon the stage, and retired in their old age to poverty and a garret" (271).

only is the "professional authoress" Jewsbury making a point about working women in her own time and nation; she is also giving her heroine a secular version of a sacred trust: Bianca as divine prophetess is to raise the estimation of her art. So long as theater is considered as a diversion, mere entertainment and escapism, theater people will be considered as trivial, and actresses in particular will be subject to snide remarks and disdain for their work. Jewsbury repeatedly makes the point that Bianca is born to act and that, because she is, she must serve the profession, leaving it on a higher level than she found it. That charge too is part of what Jewsbury means about "profession"; it is part of her work. The attention to Corinne is both deference to Staël for her remarkable influence on female art and a point of departure so that Jewsbury can make a detailed argument on a very practical, unromantic aspect of the issue of female creativity and professional responsibility.

A Tribute to Maria Jane

Jewsbury's *The Half Sisters* also recalls the artist novel of her older sister, reversing the outcome from the genius and fame that produce misery for Maria Jane's poet, Julia. Bianca both enjoys and endures similar stardom, sadness, and loneliness, but she emerges triumphant. It is as if Geraldine is responding that if Julia were only to hang on and remain engaged in her professional and creative life, a turning point might come as compensation for her sorrowful labor. In *The Enthusiast,* a short work in a triptych of stories published as *Three Histories,* precocious and passionate Julia Osborne reads Goethe, Schiller, Petrarch, Shelley, and predictably, Madame de Staël. This female "enthusiast" is a combination of "Italian passion, English thought, and French vivacity" and possesses extraordinary intelligence. Ellen Peel and Nanora Sweet contend that Julia is created to prove it is impossible for an English woman to live with Romantic sensibility and that her name "Julia" recalls Rousseau's Julie (who influenced Staël), and the Juliette who is Corinne's niece, her spiritual reincarnation. Peel and Sweet further suggest that the characterization of Julia is based upon Maria Jane herself and her friend, the poet Felicia Hemans.[25]

In the novella, Julia's grandmamma, "tolerably resigned to the affliction of genius" in the girl, allows her to study with their neighbor, the parson, whose other pupil is Cecil Percy, whom Julia loves for her lifetime. Here Geraldine even goes so far as to follow Maria Jane's lead in choosing a name, Cecil Percy be-

25. Maria Jane Jewsbury, *The Enthusiast,*in *The Three Histories: The History of an Enthusiast, The History of a Nonchalant, The History of a Realist,* 79; Peel and Sweet, "*Corinne* and the Woman as Poet in England: Hemans, Jewsbury, and Barrett Browning," 213, 212.

coming Conrad Percy in *The Half Sisters*. Julia publishes a first book, becomes the puppet of a London socialite who promotes her as a literary "lioness," discovers "adulation as the opiate of life," and forgets her upbringing and former friends. She proves in her life what Geraldine Jewsbury's Conrad charges of actresses and authoresses: that they are "too much accustomed to admiration to be able to do without it" (*HS*, 214). Incidentally, it is the same objection that Lord Nelvil's father makes in regard to Corinne. When her grandmamma dies, Julia sells the family estate and cuts her ties with the past. But she discovers that society is a "Moloch," genius and fame a curse:

> Ah, what is genius to woman, but a splendid misfortune! What is fame to a woman, but a dazzling degradation! She is exposed to the pitiless gaze of admiration; but little respect. . . . However much . . . she may have gained in name, rank, and fortune, she has suffered as a woman; in the history of letters she may be associated with a man, but her own sweet life is lost. . . . She is . . . a splendid exotic, nurtured for display. . . .[26]

The ultimate devastation for Julia is that once she realizes she has sealed herself within a coffin of living death, Cecil inadvertently nails down the lid when he reveals to her what the author already knows, that a man may worship a goddess but he marries a human on his own level. Cecil is dispatched to service in the East Indies, and Julia is left to contemplate herself as bleeding upon the thorns of life—as in Shelley's "Ode to the West Wind." This is an ironic contrast to Julia's childhood friend Annette Mortimer, who is the skylark, the rose, and the maiden in Shelley's "To a Skylark," which Annette's husband fondly recites to her, proving that men believe beautiful women should inspire poetry, not create it—as Baudelaire says, she is the divinity that presides over the conceptions of the male brain.

That Geraldine's response to her dead sister's work is deliberate, not accidental, is obvious on even a superficial reading of the separate texts. Not only is the Percy name an obvious clue, but also are the repeated references to Shakespeare's *Othello* as allusion for love gone bad. Julia is Desdemona, Cecil, a "white-faced Othello" in jealousy; Geraldine's Bryant is an experienced, traveled Othello, and Alice listens with "Desdemona-like avidity" [*HS*, 68] to the fascinating adventures he recounts. More pertinent, however, is the fact that Maria Jane's novel contrasts the lives of two young girls growing into womanhood in separate paths: Annette, who desires the private sphere and who is to all appearances blissful as the wife of an adoring man, and Julia, the "Pythoness," or an English version of

26. Maria Jane Jewsbury, *Enthusiast*, 49, 85, 113.

Corinne.[27] But Maria Jane's Corinne character is devastated, with the major departure from the Corinne myth being the promise of interminable life—whether or not Julia makes much of it as artist and woman—rather than melodramatic death. In *The Half Sisters,* Geraldine's response to and reversal of both works, the Lucile/Annette character is cursed in marriage, while the Corinne/Julia character has strength to survive the death of her mother, the drudgery of her work, the defection of Conrad, the wiles of a seducer, and the professional pettiness and jealousies of her theater company, all because her profession gives her life. Her work and art, and in a sense her religion, are one.

The Consuelo Factor

Jewsbury's *The Half Sisters* also consciously parallels George Sand's *Consuelo.* George Henry Lewes, noting Sand's influence on Jewsbury in his 1852 essay "The Lady Novelists," comments that the style of *Zoe* is heavily influenced by Sand, but that the "style is toned down to a more truthful pitch" in Jewsbury's second novel. If the style is less derivative, the plot and the human relationships are at least as much influenced by the *Consuelo* novels as *Zoe* is by *Indiana.* In the absolute commitment to serve the profession and to work at her art, Bianca is more like Consuelo than she is similar to either Corinne or Julia Osborne. As noted in the previous chapter, Jewsbury's letters to Jane Carlyle are peppered with allusions to Sand and "George Sandism"—a term of the Carlyles that seemed to refer to the free, independent, and androgynous lifestyle that Sand enjoyed in Paris but also to the dramatic, flamboyant, and passionate lives of Sand's heroines. Thomas Carlyle disliked "George Sandism" in women; Jewsbury was attracted both to Sand's androgyny and to her heroines; Jane referred to Geraldine as "my Consuelo."[28]

As she does with Staël's *Corinne,* Jewsbury immediately invites comparison and a revisiting—as well as, it turns out, a reenvisioning—of the themes of the French predecessor. For one thing, Consuelo, as an illegitimate only child, nurses her dying mother, a former beauty who was in her youth exotic and musically talented. Likewise, fatherless Bianca supports and nurses her dying mother, who was in youth passionate, beautiful, and fascinating. Both mothers die early in the respective plots, leaving the daughters to negotiate their way in professions filled with risk, jealousy, and treachery. Second, the sexual predator is similarly portrayed. In *Consuelo* Count Zustiniani, a patron of the opera who has an eye for beautiful young singers, represents a sexual threat to Consuelo, and Montague

27. Ibid., 80, 126.
28. Lewes, "The Lady Novelists," 140; Howe, *Geraldine Jewsbury: Her Life and Errors,* 178.

St. Leger fulfills a similar role in *The Half Sisters*. He is the director who seduces his future leading ladies, promotes them, then discards them when he sees younger, prettier conquests waiting in the wings. In Sand's novel, Zustiniani tries to maneuver young Consuelo into his gondola and thereby into his lecherous embrace; St. Leger invites Bianca for a private meeting in his office, where he attempts to ply her with wine, which she refuses, then openly propositions her: In exchange for sexual favors, she can bid farewell to bit parts and be awarded the lead in the company's upcoming production. Jewsbury even goes so far as to create a parallel for Corilla, the rival of Consuelo who becomes the mistress of both Zustiniani and Consuelo's beloved Anzoleto. In *The Half Sisters*, this role is played by Harriet Douglas, the actress whom St. Leger has easily taken up, then abandoned. As Consuelo befriends Corilla, Bianca persuades Miss Douglas not to commit suicide, takes her home and feeds her, then finds employment for her with the circus, where Bianca had first begun her professional life.[29]

The famous thespian who is Bianca's mentor echoes Maître Porpora, a central figure in Sand's *Consuelo*. As Consuelo's musical patriarch, Porpora, is a musical genius absorbed in Consuelo's perfecting of her divine gift, Bianca finds such a teacher in the "old actor" whose name is never given, but who is merely identified as the most distinguished Shakespearean in England during the day, roughly the 1830s. Bianca obviously yearns for a father—finding temporary ones in the circus manager, the prompter at her first real theater, and finally the distinguished actor who masterminds her three-year apprenticeship in Bath, times her London debut, tutors her on the professional aspects of her craft, and becomes the source of her wealth in bequeathing her his London home. Both Porpora and the actor are venerable practitioners of their respective arts, and both treat the profession with reverence and see their respective young protégées as divine prophetesses of a sacred calling. As Porpora teaches Consuelo to reach for ever higher goals and to make herself worthy of the sacred flame, the old actor teaches Bianca never to be ashamed of her professional aspirations, for they are "the voice of God" (*HS,* 100).

Since Jewsbury believes that impressionable young women need an older, wiser patriarch or matriarch to teach them about life and values, she provides both of the orphaned half sisters with different outcomes, and the sister who is saved both personally and professionally is the one who has been found by a worthy

29. The actress as "fallen" woman is admittedly a recurring figure as well: in Annie Edwards's *The Morals of May Fair,* for example, the dancer/actress Rose Elmslie falls first as the mistress of a count, then ends as a gin-swilling beggar and prostitute in Haymarket; in Dinah Craik's *The Head of the Family,* the actress Rachel Armstrong takes revenge upon her seducer and harms others in her path. George Eliot and Mrs. Humphry Ward also depict various actresses as morally suspect, as will be noted in Chapters 4 and 5.

teacher—the teachings of Alice's mother that women are made for "good wives," not the "silly romantic notion[s]" found in novels having ill served romantic Alice (*HS*, 47, 46). While Maestro Porpora is the ideal teacher for Consuelo, he is not the perfect father. He advises, even orders, her never to accept romantic love, and he deceives her by hiding Albert's letters. The true reality, he says, is in music and on the stage; everything else is pretense—the actors in the boxes, not the performers on stage, being the true frauds. As noted in the previous chapter, the interfering master misreads the affection of Consuelo's heart, bullies her, and makes several miscalculations all designed to keep Consuelo sanctified for her calling. In introducing the old actor as Bianca's mentor, Jewsbury recalls Porpora but turns the tables in that the actor's advice is right for Bianca, while Porpora's does not answer the needs in Consuelo's heart. Specifically, Porpora's veto of the Albert affair is echoed in the actor's advice to Bianca that Conrad Percy is unworthy of her, that she is destined to have her heart broken by him. Of course Conrad proves him right.

The old actor's great lesson, however, is the mission of leaving the profession better than she has found it—a concept that Bianca initially cannot accept because she can understand only that motivation that comes from within herself—that is, if she does not have a mother to support or a lover to worship and to lay her genius at his feet, she sees no possible goal beyond pleasing herself. Norma Clarke takes this injunction to mean that Bianca is to become a "Clotilde of the theater," purifying it of sensualism and turning it into a nunnery. Judith Rosen comments that the old actor's advice, rather than focusing on her self-creative powers and developing the genius that animates Bianca's being, merely extends the domestic injunction that a woman is to beautify her world by "bringing to the stage the ideals of Home," another form of self-abdication for the creative genius.[30] If this is what the old actor has in mind, then his concern is purely morality, certainly not art. I disagree with Rosen.

Granted, a Victorian woman was to "ornament" her home by displaying the lovely—albeit superficial—graces of hospitality, decorating, and entertaining, along with enough "ornamental" accomplishments to snare a husband in the first place. In Jewsbury's *Zoe* the protagonist is dismissed as a "fashionable" ornament—as opposed to unfashionable women who are practical and useful, and for example, make vestments and ornaments for the church, rather than for themselves.[31] It is precisely this term, *ornament,* that the old actor uses to *discredit* the status of the contemporary stage, not what he recommends. If the fine arts are considered by the public as "merely amusing, or at best ornamental," he

---

30. Clarke, *Ambitious Heights,* 196; Rosen, "At Home upon a Stage," 28.
31. Jewsbury, *Zoe,* 2:55.

says (*HS*, 161), they will continue to be a diversion, an entertainment, but they will never instruct or ennoble the public. To the degree that people take art seriously, art can become serious, and to the degree the artist is serious about her or his work, that artist continually presents to the public a higher, finer, and more serious art. This is, for Jewsbury, where genius meets professionalism. In fact, charging her to raise the level of her profession shows that the old actor takes Bianca seriously as a great artist and a true professional: He does not consider her a mere ornament of the stage. Further, in selecting her as his successor, the old man before dying presumably leaves the profession better than he has inherited it. By example he discovers raw talent and serves as mentor to the possessor of that talent, and Bianca, in doing the same for Clara, illustrates that Jewsbury has in mind an androgynous stepping out of the sexual roles—and elevating men and women as comrades, as Jewsbury would prefer. In the novel, elevating the profession and encouraging young talent who will carry on the tradition after one has left the stage is a charge that seems entirely gender neutral.

The Moral Perils of a Diva

In reiterating her point about the duty that a woman of genius owes to herself, to the profession, and to others, Jewsbury adds to the already complicated plot two additional women artists, the Fornasari and Clara—the former to illustrate the opposite image of stardom to that which Bianca exhibits, and the latter to illustrate Bianca's passing the torch to a younger artist when she herself retires from the stage, just as her old master has said she should and as, marrying and dying, Maria Jane in a sense made way for her younger sister—both at the *Athenaeum* and in fiction.

Critics of the novel have not kindly received the Fornasari, largely because she is intrusive in the novel's plot and because she seems an obvious and heavy-handed depiction of the spoiled, vain prima donna and sexual cesspool that Bianca has avoided becoming—her decadence contrasting with Bianca's upstanding life. There is no subtlety here: Jewsbury spells it out for the reader when Melton says that the Fornasari is an "odious libel" on Bianca, "both in her life and profession" (*HS*, 350). A point missing in this criticism, however, is the allusiveness of the character, for Jewsbury employs the Fornasari to represent an aspect of Corinne that the more pragmatic, realistic English working professional finds self-indulgent, and this connection is made explicit through the literary/operatic character Semiramis, played by both Corinne and the Fornasari.

When in Milan making her operatic debut, the soprano known as the Fornasari has indulged in a short-lived love affair with Conrad Percy. Conrad, lonely for Bianca, from whom he has separated to appease his father, is initially attracted to the singer because of her striking similarity in appearance to the woman he has left behind. Much later when Lord Melton, the other man to love Bianca, sees the Fornasari onstage, the resemblance startles him; the singer's "bold, insolent, defiant look" almost shakes his faith in Bianca (*HS,* 350). That the two young women are simultaneously at the outset of their careers makes obvious that Jewsbury is presenting them as two sides of the same coin, two avenues to professionalism, two responses to fame. Conrad soon learns that his mistress has been unfaithful to him, and before she is reintroduced into the novel, this "syren" has made numerous conquests, one man has died for her in a duel, and everyone knows that her genius permits her to live beyond the pale of traditional moral values. The Fornasari's luxurious, eclectic, tasteless, glitzy apartment is not like Corinne's salon, which is a place where men flock to discuss art and ideas (and, admittedly, to admire Corinne); instead, it is where men gather like Circe's swine to snatch a few morsels of her attention and to win or lose large amounts of money at the gaming tables busy there every night. The woman lives for the present, turns every professional performance—as well as every offstage act—into a celebration of herself. She is narcissism to the bizarre degree. But she is not blind; she knows her genius will never ennoble herself, her world, or her art. She says, "[m]y life is like the last scene of a pantomime, or a display of fireworks; there is a very flat and smouldering result—but the audience will have dispersed before then." In other words this "Delilah" will have shorn the public Samson before it realizes that it has been defrauded. In a frank discussion with Lord Melton, she derides the stupidity of public taste: "Genius may break its heart in the endeavour to infuse a spark of sensibility or sympathy" into the collective stupidity, which has a "leaden superiority to all my genius" (*HS,* 343, 344). Knowing her looks and voice to be ephemeral, she exploits them to bring fame, attention, and luxury to herself and her voluptuous Bower of Bliss, rather than to improve the level of European opera—as Bianca is charged to do with the English theater. Admittedly the details of this singer's promiscuity and vanity, and even the abandonment of her bastard child, recall Corilla of Sand's *Consuelo* novels, but the Semiramis allusion also recalls aspects of *Corinne.*

The Fornasari appears in Rossini's opera *Semiramide,* a performance that Lord Melton witnesses. Even though the woman's voice and acting are magnificent, Melton is repulsed by the intrusion of the actress: "Music, singing, acting, all seemed nothing but so many vehicles for the glorification of *herself*" (*HS,* 340). Rossini's adaptation of the Semiramis legend was a perpetual favorite of European sopranos of the nineteenth century because it requires "florid singing of almost insuperable difficulty," and is therefore an appropriate vehicle for the Fornasari to celebrate herself and for Jewsbury to make her point. The libretto too is rather gruesome, Semiramide being somewhat of a Babylonian Clytemnestra, with the added complication of Phaedra-like incest in the heroine's passion for her son, Arsace, who, Orestes-like, must slay her in vengeance for her murder of his father. But in the scene with Arsace, the Fornasari shows a glimmer of maternal love worth redeeming. And, fortuitously, Melton's purpose in meeting the Fornasari is to lead her to her son, from whom she has been separated and whom Melton in Trieste has rescued from drowning—an echo of Nelvil's saving an elderly Neapolitan in the same way. When the boy is restored to the Fornasari, the reader is to imagine that she is metamorphosed into something less like Semiramide and more like Jochebed because *The Half Sisters,* like all the Jewsbury fiction, repeatedly insists that love of others makes one noble and good, while love of self destroys. Both as contrast to the Fornasari's depiction as a mother and to prepare the reader for Bianca's abandoning the stage for the role of wife and mother, Jewsbury puts her into a similar situation of enacting a mother. Lord Melton, seeing this performance, comments to Bianca, "What a mother you would make!" and she acknowledges that a woman has only half her soul developed until she is a mother, that her depths of tenderness, devotion, strength, and wisdom "can only be unsealed in her for her children" (*HS,* 223). This type of rhetoric has the effect of undermining Bianca's efficacy as a literary study of the artist, but Jewsbury seems to endorse Dinah Mulock Craik's comment in the *Künstlerroman Olive:* "there scarce ever lived the woman who would not rather sit meekly by her own hearth, with her husband at her side, and her children at her knee, than be the crowned Corinne of the Capitol."[32]

The role of Semiramide is the same role that Nelvil sees Corinne perform in Venice, Staël describing the Babylonian queen Semiramis as a fascinating coquette—savage, cunning, and imperious (*C,* 434). Corinne, because she is a brilliant actress, is equal to the part, but Staël does not suggest that latent in the *improvisatrice* is a streak of malice, cruelty, or ambition on a par with that of the Babylonian queen. Indeed, Corinne is equally fetching as the innocent Juliet. In giving Bianca the Juliet role to portray and the Fornasari the decadent Semiramide, however, Jewsbury splits Staël's creation into two Corinnes and makes an interesting point about female art. In Corinne, fascinating and brilliant though she is, Jewsbury has recognized a woman who loves self-display, who uses every vehicle to showcase her multiplicity of talents, a celebration of Corinne as Narcissus. Corinne is not a professional in the way Consuelo and Bianca are; she is not subject to the whims of a "stupid" public audience, the vagaries of the theater, jealousies of the greenroom, discomforts of the nomadic life. We never see her serving an apprenticeship, seeking a mentor, or sidestepping either lechers or

32. Simon, *The Victor Book of the Opera,* 382–83 (in the original libretto, by Gaetano Rossi, the ghost of the dead king demands the slaying of Semiramide; in the revised denouement, Semiramide lives and Arsace slays instead her coconspirator, Assur); Craik, *Olive,* 126.

runaway circus horses. Rather, in each production, Corinne is producer, director, and star. Jewsbury's response seems to be that, for her own time, such a role exists only in Romantic escapism, which, delectable though it is, cannot transfer itself to the professional challenges of the real world. In contemporary art, she holds, actresses and "authoresses" must subscribe to the gospel of hard work and hard knocks, must invest long hours of backstage drudgery and rehearsal; they do not arise in the world rich, famous, and accomplished. To attempt such Corinne-like display and ostentation makes the midcentury artist a ridiculous and grotesque parody like the Fornasari. Jewsbury warns aspiring female artists to avoid reading *Corinne* on the "Romantic Rocks."

Bianca recognizes stupidity in the public taste, just as the Fornasari does, but when she is young and powerless, she can do nothing about the ridiculous scripts she receives. In her mind she can readily separate art from trash, and she knows what it is to struggle to perfect her craft, but as a young actress she cannot understand any motivation higher than dedicating her career to some person whom she loves. She does understand that one must not consider the theater as an "amusement," but she is not sure how she has the power to make it more noble. In her conversation with her mentor, she recalls the passion of a Consuelo, contrasts the Fornasari (and probably Corinne), and illustrates commitment that the art is outside and above the individual ego:

> Let *me* be nothing for ever, if I may only once give shape to those unutterable
> mysteries which at times seem as if they would cleave my very soul in sunder,
> with their dumb ineffectual strivings to become manifest. There are moments,
> when it seems as if I must become *mad*, I feel so incapable to give them shape
> and utterance; as if it needed that I, myself, should be broken to pieces like a
> jar of clay, that all which is blindly stirring within me may find way. (*HS*, 163)

In expressions such as this, Jewsbury illustrates that Bianca, almost like a pythoness, is inspired by her art. Also like a pythoness, then, she is compelled to "profess" for the theater, which has given her beauty, success, and life.

Bianca's charge as a professional is to elevate the taste of the public by selecting and patronizing the best roles from the best playwrights, and it happens that her final mission is to pass along to Clara Broughton the very favor bestowed upon her by the old Shakespearean—that of patronage. "I must repay my obligation," she says (*HS*, 358). Her love for the profession prohibits her from taking up art lightly and leaving it. Thus the thematic importance of the youngest artist, whom Bianca takes from Lady Vernon's school, which is dedicated to teaching the domestic, not the dramatic arts. In Clara's case, Lady Vernon, somewhat like Julia's grandmamma in Maria Jane Jewsbury's story, finally acquiesces that Clara may study the fine arts, because "if God is pleased to give a woman faculties, I suppose she must cultivate them" (*HS,* 356). But Clara, like Bianca, requires a mentor; she is immature, headstrong, gifted, and impressionable. Bianca can teach the young singer to work hard, to learn the fundamentals of her craft, to "[m]easure [her]self always against the highest" (*HS,* 364), and to consider herself a professional with an obligation to her art. At the end of the novel, Bianca places Clara in intellectual and aesthetic apprenticeship to a new husband—who has been her old music teacher—and he will finish the professional instruction that Bianca has begun. Critics have rightly complained that the ending is too convenient in giving Clara a ready-made protector for her pilgrimage to Italy and a musical career, that such a conclusion undermines the validity of the case of Bianca, who has toiled alone in the world. Admittedly, the conclusion is flawed in this regard; furthermore Clara is insufficiently developed as a character for the reader to have much interest in her career. Jewsbury merely includes her to illustrate that young artists need mentors and that the dictates of professionalism include giving back to the art that has given to the artist and raising the standards of that art. Now Clara is enjoined with the same trust that the old actor has given Bianca. To that end, Jewsbury closes the novel with the "supremely happy" couple in Milan, the very city where Conrad first discovered the Fornasari and where Clara, like Bianca, is to be the antidote to the spoiled, self-centered prima donna. Everyone expects that Clara, when she returns to her homeland, will "*raise the credit* of the English school" (*HS,* 396, italics mine).

Jewsbury and Carlyle

Thomas Carlyle's ideas on human happiness and the necessity and dignity of work (the "Gospel of Work") shape the philosophy in all Geraldine Jewsbury's novels, and in *The Half Sisters* it is the source of Bianca's stability and merit, placing the working actress on a moral level above that of the preening goddess like Corinne. In 1840 Geraldine Jewsbury chose Carlyle to provide for herself the spiritual guidance that she believed young people need, and that young women usually do not find. In this step, by the way, she merely followed the leadership of her sister, Maria Jane, who similarly chose William Wordsworth as her mentor. Because she read him during her spiritual crisis and found in his writings some of her own opinions on human nature and human responsibility, Jewsbury wrote Carlyle. He became interested in her and responded. When Jewsbury's brother married and she was thereby liberated from housekeeping obligations, she moved from Manchester to London to be near the Carlyles. Throughout the intense friendship with Jane Carlyle, Jewsbury remained committed to Thomas Carlyle's writings and ideas, although a careful reading of the letters suggests she did not have as much respect for him as the marital partner of her "darling" Jane as she found him a great man of letters. Some believe that Carlyle fell out of favor with her, as she with him. Certainly on the personal level he found her annoying as, frequently, did his wife. Furthermore, as Clarke points out, Jewsbury several times facetiously repeats Carlyle's idea that a wife should be a "beautiful reflex" of her husband. In *The Half Sisters,* for example, this particular Carlylean opinion on wives is spoken by the misguided Conrad. Nevertheless Jewsbury's biographer, Susanne Howe, believes that Jewsbury throughout her long life never regretted her commitment to Carlyle's philosophical ideas.[33] She found them a useful authority for her own theory on art and life; the artist must not ask for happiness but for work to do and the energy to pursue it.

Carlyle writes in *Past and Present* that his contemporary era in England lives by the "Gospel of Mammonism" and the "Gospel of Dilettantism," but Carlyle proposes instead a "Gospel of Work." Mammonism, the greed for money, has profit as its heaven and loss as its hell. Dilettantism is idleness. Whereas the gospel according to Mammon at least preaches work in order to make money, that of Dilettantism is to "Go gracefully idle in Mayfair." Furthermore Carlyle defines atheism as the worship of happiness; its prophets preach, "Thou shalt be happy; thou shalt love pleasant things, and find them." Whether through the rewards of industry, the promises of democracy, or the worship of laissez-faire, the English, Carlyle complains, have bought the same end result: the "Greatest-Happiness Principle" of utilitarian thought. He offers the challenge, "what difference is it whether thou art happy or not!" for in the Carlylean gospel, happiness is not god. Rather, in the new gospel the highest commandment is "Know thy work and do it," for all true work is religion. The "wages" of every good and honest work lie in heaven, and the truly noble worker seeks no other reward:

> For there is a perennial nobleness, and even sacredness in Work. Were he never so benighted, forgetful of his high calling, there is always hope in a man that actually and earnestly works: in Idleness alone is there perpetual despair. Work, never so Mammonish, mean, *is* in communication with Nature; the real desire to get Work done will lead one more and more to truth, to Nature's appointments and regulations, which are truth.[34]

All of Jewsbury's novels show this Carlylean thought: Her idle characters know "perpetual despair," and her working characters are led to truth. For example, Alice, Zoe, and Nancy Arl (of *Marian Withers*), suffer from ennui, but Bianca,

---

33. Clarke, *Ambitious Heights,* 190; Howe, *Geraldine Jewsbury: Her Life and Errors,* 179.
34. Carlyle, *Past and Present,* in *The Works of Thomas Carlyle in Thirty Volumes,* 10:150, 153, 154, 196, 203, 196.

Clotilde, and Adéle reap the benefits of employment. The bereaved Bryant—once preoccupied with his factory and contracts—turns away from Mammonism for philanthropic works. He becomes a patriarch to employees now destined to become his surrogate children.[35] Similarly, Bianca's husband, Lord Melton, follows Bryant's lead by ameliorating the conditions of the peasantry on his Scottish and Irish estates. Even Conrad belatedly realizes the emptiness of Mayfair Dilettantism.

Perhaps Jewsbury would have reached the same conclusions about happiness versus work had she never read *Past and Present,* but by invoking Carlyle's famous gospel, she authenticates her own stand—that which she recommends for the characters of her novels, women as well as men. In *Zoe,* Jewsbury sets out to prove that "half the wickedness committed in the world arises more from the absence of some engrossing employment than from any special depravity," and the lapsed priest Everhard tries teaching the children of a mining district in Wales and then joins a community of scholars in Germany. Having renounced the church and given up Zoe, he concludes that "the only happiness to be aspired after by man is to see clearly what lies before him to do and to set about doing it with diligence." In her anticlerical novel *Right or Wrong* (1859), another man of God learns the religion of work. Michael, head of the Petit St. Antoine of Paris, prefers the contemplative life to the active, but he is chastised by his loyal friend, Brother Paul: "That is a life for no created being. . . . Work is man's only true prayer. . . . Rest is not the condition in which any man can dwell with safety. . . ."[36]

Jewsbury's female characters are not excused from the lessons on work. In *Constance Herbert,* the aunt of the young protagonist tells Constance that we are all called to a work; we do not choose it, rather it is chosen for us. Constance's father lives a miserable, worthless life of self-pity, spite, and suffering because he believes in nothing and is one of those men "who fail to give their lives to a work." Learning from the two women who are her mentors, Constance—unlike her father—takes up "the work that fell to her lot" and as a result will achieve worth and contentment, will understand that she has erred in asking for happiness. In *Marian Withers,* the protagonist's Aunt Alice teaches the self-centered Marian, "Happiness is NOT the most precious gift bestowed upon man. It is NOT the precious metal with which virtue is rewarded." Protesting she is not "trying to do

35. Here Jewsbury supports the role of the industrialist as patriarch, a conservative political view also found in *Marian Withers.* In an essay for the *Shilling Magazine,* she classifies masters and men together as "Labour," but depends upon the "practical republicanism of trade" to do its part in educating the "lower orders"—at the same time admitting that "amateur benevolence" cannot "educate and civilise" an entire class, that government must become involved as well ("The Civilisation of the Lower Orders," *Douglas Jerrold's Shilling Magazine,* 6:448, 450, 451).

36. Jewsbury, *Zoe,* 2:40, 3:29–30; *Right or Wrong,* 1:66.

the Lady Bountiful," Marian nonetheless finds her philanthropic calling in alleviating the conditions of the factory workers—a version of the same calling that the valuable and enlightened men of the novel have espoused. In *The Sorrows of Gentility*, young Gertrude Morley suffers from a run of bad luck and bad choices in life, and she is understandably miserable. She is, however, taken in hand by a gentlewoman, Lady Southend, who essentially tells her to stop feeling sorry for herself and to find employment to support herself and her infant. Her message is, Give up trying to be happy; such narcissistic thinking puts the emphasis in the wrong place. Finally, Gertrude's daughter, Clarissa Donnelly, in *The History of an Adopted Child* says, "I do not know that it is wise to talk much about happiness, but the nearest approach to it that I can imagine, is to have work suited to our capacity, and to arise every morning with the definite duties of the day marked out before us. . . . I am convinced that half the unhappiness in life arises from an unacknowledged, obscure sense of remorse, for time left waste, and faculties unemployed, thereby tormenting their possessors, by their blind, restless, ineffectual stirrings, producing a vague feeling of undischarged responsibility lying heavily upon the soul. . . ."[37]

In *The Half Sisters* the charge of the old actor to Bianca to "become [art's] priestess" is to "give yourself with your whole soul to the work appointed you" (*HS*, 162). Later Bianca herself tells Conrad, "if one has work to do one must do it; no one worth the name of a rational being ever dreamed of living for the sake of amusing himself" (*HS*, 327). In a paean to work, Jewsbury acknowledges that Bianca's work, however wearying and lonely, is a "supreme blessing" because

> No matter how mean or trivial may be the occupations which are appointed to us,—we can work at them with courage and perseverance, so long as we do not feel condemned to them as the "be all and end all," the *realisation* of our *life*,—so long as there is a side on which we may escape from that which is seen and definite, into that which is unseen and infinite. It is the being condemned to live with those who lead mechanical lives—lives without significance—who see in the daily routine of household business, in the daily occupation of going to the mill, the counting-house . . . nothing but modes of filling up days and weeks, called in the aggregate *life*,—without an idea of looking round—much less *beyond*,—it is *this* which drives passionate souls mad; but if there be one opening through which the air from the everlasting universe of things may breathe upon us, we can feel strong and cheerful—no matter how bare of material comforts our lot may be. (*HS*, 109)

37. Jewsbury, *Constance Herbert*, 2:132, 1:189, 3:295; *Marian Withers*, 3:132, 1:65; *The Sorrows of Gentility*, 278; *History of an Adopted Child*, 328–29.

Jewsbury separates occupation from profession. To be occupied with the counting house, the mill, the household chores, even the good works of the Sisters of Mercy, which have been "drilled to rules" (*HS*, 303) and drained of free will, or even mending costumes and memorizing scripts, is merely to wear out the tedium of one's days until the end. To bring passion, energy, and creativity to one's profession is an art. Unlike the majority of women who "want an object . . . want a strong purpose . . . want an adequate employment," Bianca has "had a definite employment all my life: when I rose in the morning my work lay before me, and I had a clear, definite channel in which all my energies might flow" (*HS*, 249). She is converted to the Carlylean doctrines of the old Shakespearean, that "Labor is Life"—awakening one to knowledge, self-knowledge, and truth, and this is the gospel that she teaches her protégée, Clara.[38] Like Carlyle, Jewsbury asks the ageless philosophical question whether we are meant to be happy in life, and like Staël and Sand, she speculates whether suffering is necessary to make art. Her answer to that second question is that suffering is inevitable whether or not one is an artist, but that Work is necessary not only to create art but also to find truth and God, and to find oneself. She teaches Clara, "When people make a great fuss about 'happiness our being's end and aim,' it is a very vulgar affair, and rather impertinent to the toiling, busy world, which has plenty of its own complicated affairs to mind" (*HS*, 365).

Bianca's Work as Educator

A final objection to the novel is the new work given to Bianca by the novelist, that of operating a school. At the conclusion of the *Künstlerroman* a reader feels cheated because Bianca, born for the stage, retires when she is well married. Jewsbury attempts to supply motivation in that Bianca, like Corinne, has always held that love is greater than fame and greater than art. Loving Melton, then, Jewsbury reasons, she can leave her profession with no regrets, no recriminations, no resentments. Rachel Brownstein notes that the "marriage plot" of a novel succeeds time and again because a fictional heroine must have her uniqueness singled out from among all other women by a man; the female protagonist becomes "heroine" only when validated for her womanly role as sex and marriage object.[39] That the vivacious, independent actress, who meets men as equals and has become, as Conrad complains, "unsexed" by her shrewdness in her profession, should walk away from it all without a longing look backward is truly a lapse on Jewsbury's part, but the "authoress" who wrote *The Half Sisters* was similarly

38. Carlyle, *Past and Present*, 10:197–98.
39. Brownstein, *Becoming a Heroine: Reading about Women in Novels*, xv.

trapped by the conventions of the novel and by her inability to think outside the paradigm. Furthermore, to leave Bianca on the stage when a worthy male capable of liberated thinking about the Woman Question had singled her out for his wife, would have turned her into a Corinne who either lives with the adulation of many men or dies for the lack of love from one. Jewsbury's only justification is this: At the height of her success, Bianca is trying to live as a "priestess, cold, strong, and pure, to the utterance of the oracle confided to her" (*HS*, 355), but increasingly she finds that this is not enough. She loves Melton and worries that he has abandoned her, as Conrad did and as her father had done. At this point she takes on the Clara project; then Melton returns and she gives up the role of prophetess for that of bride. Much later, we are informed in the afterword that Lady Vernon dies, whereupon Bianca takes over the school and founds others on the same Carlylean model.

Organizing a school is, for many Victorian writers, an acceptable solution to the question of what is to be done with a creative woman. Here too there is an example in George Sand in that her painter Diane Flochardet, after marriage to a nobleman in "Le Château de Pictordeau," opens a school for girls. And Sand's disciple Jewsbury apparently considers it an appropriate profession for a talented woman. In her 1855 *Constance Herbert* are two women who find fulfillment through the management of schools. The aunt of the young protagonist fulfills her destiny first by rearing little Constance, then by putting her creative energies into her theories about the education of children. To that end, Margaret attempts to pension off the deaf and nearly blind teacher of the Dame school, whom she considers as inept as Pip describes Biddy's great-aunt in *Great Expectations,* but the locals accuse her of being a Jacobin who "wishe[s] to introduce sedition and revolution"—a controversy unsettled until the local squire and clergyman support her and she organizes her village school for both boys and girls "on her own plan." Also, Sarah Wilmont, whom Constance's own father had jilted, eventually marries and finds employment in running schools and a household—an occupation that makes her "very happy and very busy." An even more felicitous example is the case of Clotilde, who in the novel *Zoe* becomes Mother Angelique and as mother superior is chief administrator of a convent, and its school, teachers, and pupils. In *Marian Withers* the daughter of the Manchester industrialist, once she is a wife, operates a school for the females who work in the mills and conducts a singing-school class for local people one night a week.[40] In *The Half Sisters,* Lady Vernon has noticed that girls born in "the odour of gentility" but with no hope of inheriting wealth or an easy life are given only a "smattering of all sorts of knowledge" (*HS*, 237, 239). In her school these girls are taught the ba-

40. Jewsbury, *Constance Herbert*, 1:147, 1:149, 3:115; *Marian Withers*, 3:245.

sic curriculum with more thoroughness, taught the practical skills and crafts "for them to fall back on" if they must earn their own livelihoods, and most importantly taught the Gospel of Work—that work is noble and idleness frivolity. Bianca approves the teaching and philosophy of her future sister-in-law, with the single objection that the school does not accommodate the rare genius of a girl like Clara. One can assume that the Lady Melton schools will remedy this oversight.

Although most of Jewsbury's novels are historical (often set in the 1790s), for a gifted and energetic woman of Jewsbury's own era the possibility of finding rewarding employment as founder and administrator of a school was a distinct possibility—although such opportunities were more frequent and more visible later in the century. Some two decades after the publication of *The Half Sisters,* for example, Anne Jemima Clough became first principal of Newnham College, and Emily Davies founded Girton College. In fact George Eliot contributed to the founding of Girton, and her friend Barbara Bodichon, an artist and feminist leader, solicited funds for the school. But Jewsbury's assumption that brilliant women are adaptable in many departments will not do. Granted, certain qualities like energy, tenacity, and originality can be applied to various professions, but it does not follow that a woman with genius to write poetry, sing arias, or paint landscapes will be just as happy running a school. Having first insisted that Bianca's gift compels her to perform on the stage, Jewsbury does not persuade the reader that being a wife and an educator will do just as well—even though Bianca understands that a woman, like a man, must have meaningful work in the world and will teach her young female students accordingly. In choosing the new "career" of educating future generations of women, Jewsbury has sent Bianca along a path that no Victorian feminist could reject as trivial—given that, as Jewsbury everywhere reveals, women are inadequately educated for life, for professions, and for knowing themselves. Further, one can assume that the job of educator is most certainly a call to Work, in the Carlylean sense. Jewsbury successfully propagandizes the Gospel of Work, but she fails to acquit herself in the department of the inspired artist. She answers the question of what to do with a creative, gifted woman, but not the question of female genius. On that score, her novel is less courageous than Staël's *Corinne* and Sand's *Consuelo.*

When *The Half Sisters* was published in 1848, *Douglas Jerrold's Shilling Magazine* greeted it as a work of genius and praised the author for the "pungency of her style, the penetration of her observation, the nobility (we had almost said) the manliness of her sentiments. . . ." Elizabeth Barrett Browning writes to Miss Mitford, "There's a french sort of daring, half audacious power in [Jewsbury's] novels." Eighty years later, in her essay "Geraldine and Jane," however, Virginia Woolf comments that Jewsbury would not have expected to have readers in 1929;

being a competent critic of fiction, she would have said of her own novels: "They're such nonsense, my dear."[41] No literary historian seeking to revive underread Victorian fiction would classify Jewsbury's novels in the same league as those of George Eliot or Charlotte Brontë, even though the *Shilling Magazine,* which devoted only a half-page to *Jane Eyre,* granted nine pages to *The Half Sisters* (perhaps in part because Jewsbury wrote for the magazine). Nor, for that matter, is Jewsbury in the same league as fellow Manchester novelist Elizabeth Gaskell, although her finest novel is every bit as strong as Gaskell's weakest ones.

Jewsbury, however, should rate as something more than a footnote to Victorian letters. *The Half Sisters* is a fervent manifesto to the freedom and independence of the professional woman and a thought-provoking application of Carlyle's Gospel. Not that Jewsbury is the only writer whose fictional woman artist is a disciple of Carlyle. Elizabeth Barrett Browning's Aurora Leigh, for example, is also an artist and convert, as was Aurora's creator. The fictional poet Aurora says, "Get leave to work / In this world—'tis the best you get at all . . ." (*AL* 3.161–62). Additionally George Eliot's male characters like Adam Bede and Caleb Garth find meaning in work, while her creative women Dorothea Brooke and Romola vainly seek it. Nevertheless *The Half Sisters* is both coherent ideology and an intriguing reinvention of the Corinne/Consuelo myth for the working environment of midcentury England. Like the heroines of the French matriarchs, Bianca possesses rare genius that is a gift, a mystery, and a passion. Like Corinne and Consuelo, she cultivates and reveres the gift. And especially like Consuelo, she labors to perfect her art. Jewsbury's novel is a tribute both to George Sand, whom Jewsbury emulates, and Germaine de Staël, whom she refutes.

41. "The Half Sisters: A Tale," 369; Browning, *The Letters of Elizabeth Barrett Browning to Mary Russell Mitford, 1836–1854,* 3:331; Woolf, "Geraldine and Jane," 1.

3

Elizabeth Barrett Browning's
Aurora Leigh and the Labors of Psyche

IN THE FINAL PAGES OF George Sand's *La Comtesse de Rudolstadt* the opera singer Consuelo—formerly daughter of the people, then queen of patrician fêtes—is reunited in marriage with Albert Rudolstadt—formerly heir to the Bohemian castle, title, and authority of the Château des Géants. Now a member of a secret revolutionary brotherhood known as the Invisibles, Albert has sacrificed title and wealth for the cause, absolute equality being impossible so long as aristocrats hold on to inherited privilege and fortunes. It has been a tortuous and treacherous path for both Consuelo and Albert since their separation at the end of *Consuelo,* at which point the singer/actress married the dying aristocrat then resumed her career, believing Albert forever in his grave. Having affirmed at last her teacher Porpora's ceaseless admonition that she is "priestess of muses" and not meant for mortal lovers, Consuelo had lapsed into a deep melancholy—insensible to the fire of inspiration and the excitement of performing. Then when she was incarcerated by her patron, Frederick of Prussia, because she would not reveal what she knew of an alleged plot against his throne, she was rescued by a swashbuckling cavalier whose breath, kiss, and arms awakened her to a woman's passion she had never known. The rescuer is Albert in disguise, the very Albert who was, like Consuelo, a prisoner in the Spandaw fortress and whose violin playing in the night inspired her hymns to God. Forced as an initiate into the secret society to choose between two lovers, Consuelo chooses Albert over the masked cavalier Liverani, for the divine breath of Albert's soul has passed into hers, and she acknowledges the spiritual essence of her humanity to be greater than personal sexual gratification. She is a fortunate woman to receive both in the same man.

Albert and Consuelo believe that their union is a miracle, that they have perhaps loved and been separated in some previous existence, as they have in this current life, but that divine intervention has united them. He says, "C'est la main de Dieu qui nous rapproche et nous réunit comme les deux moitiés d'un seul être inséparable dans l'éternité." (It is the hand of God that brings us together and reunites us, as the two halves of a single being inseparable through eternity [*CCR*, 3:411].) The greatest of human loves, that which combines sexual passion and spiritual connection, is—like the inspiration for art—spoken of in terms of divine breath, divine flame, and divine fire in both *Consuelo* novels (*Consuelo* and its sequel, *La Comtesse*). Although a lengthy two-part *Künstlerroman* about the genius of a great prima donna of the operatic stage, Sand's "rambling female odyssey," as Elizabeth Barrett called it, is also conceived by Sand as a passionate romance so strong that the artist cannot create without loving. Art devoid of love grows lethargic and tame, for the artist herself is cold and detached, while the artist in love experiences creative exuberance and inspiration. Furthermore loving God, the good, and the divine within herself and her partner, she can give herself in service to the oppressed, downtrodden, and suffering of the world.

An English Poet's George Sandism

Elizabeth Barrett Browning's epic-novel *Aurora Leigh* (1856), *her* rambling female odyssey, is much indebted to *Consuelo* and its sequel in that the phases of Aurora's love for Romney parallel Consuelo's for Albert and in the sense that the lovers are whole and complete only when they are together. In each work the man harbors a vision of a utopian world, a dream for which he sacrifices his estate, prestige, and wealth. Romney's self-assigned mission on earth (to save the dregs of English society—the jobless, the homeless and hopeless, the battered wives and prostitutes) parallels the mission of Albert (to stamp out the remnants of feudalism, hideous abodes, savage fortresses, religious wars and persecution). In both works the man professes love and devotion to the woman artist as muse for his life's great political calling—Albert's passion expressed in the recitative "O Consuelo de mi alma!" and Romney's devotion presented first in a proposal that she become helpmate in his political agenda, then in an offer altogether too flowery for Aurora's taste: "my flower, . . . let me feel your perfume in my home / To make my sabbath after working-days. / Bloom out your youth beside me . . ." (*AL* 2.828–34).

In both instances, though, the female artist resists taming and opts for liberty and art rather than domesticity. Yet the male lover never stops loving, and when the two destined pairs of lovers, like separated halves of a perfect sphere, are reunited in mutual adoration, the union affirms both the art of the woman and the visionary politics of the man. To assert as much is not to prove an influence; indeed the romance plots of countless novels depict lovers separated then reunited in a deeper love. I argue, however, that although the adventures that befall the two questing artists are by no means similar, the spiritual growth in art and in love are similar. Further, both female artists—the raven-haired soprano and the intense poet—struggle and labor in art, fight for independence and autonomy, serve as spiritual muse to their respective lovers, become converted to the lover's political cause, and are rewarded in romantic/spiritual love that inspires art, rather than slaying it. The *Consuelo* novels and *Aurora Leigh* are centered upon the connection between love and creativity; both were for their respective times shockingly candid about female passion and sexuality, and both works explore the connection between soul and sex, the spiritual and physical dimensions of a woman artist's life. Furthermore, both Consuelo and Aurora, unlike most female artists in most fictional depictions, manage finally to have both art and love.[1] And the quest of both artists to find love is depicted in the form of the Psyche and Eros myth. Specifically both Consuelo and Aurora play the role of Psyche in search of differentiation from the mother, creative independence, and love that combines the spiritual and physical aspects—transcending the borders of both.

Corinne loses Nelvil and dies; Jewsbury's Bianca finds love but gives up the stage; George Eliot's heroines are devastated with loss of their art, a silencing that overshadows their glorious successes; and Mrs. Humphry (Mary) Ward's heroines either give up performance to marry or, like Ward herself, give up pure art to produce potboilers. Among the literary quests in this study, Sand and Barrett Browning are the exception in that they refuse to compromise art for love and insist that a great love perfects the artist's life and her works.

Like Geraldine Jewsbury and most other English female readers of her generation, Elizabeth Barrett had an advanced case of George Sandism. Barrett had looked everywhere for poetic grandmothers and found none save Sappho, but in George Sand, more than in any other female, she found a genius she could—and did—call "my sister."[2] Elizabeth Barrett herself consciously followed the career trajectory of the serious male poet, Virgil to Milton, working her way from pastoral, ballad, and sonnet, to the epic, and she considered poetry a far more serious art form than prose fiction. Novels were a pleasant distraction, but they lacked the grandeur and sublimity of poetry. For George Sand, however, she made an exception, treating Sand with the respect reserved for those writing in the more rarefied genre. Barrett called Sand the greatest female genius and greatest woman poet the world has ever known (*BC,* 8:211, 240), her style a "french *transfigured*" (*BC,* 6:234). Barrett's correspondence is sprinkled with references

1. In a postscript to *La Comtesse de Rudolstadt,* Consuelo loses her remarkable voice, but the present chapter will not deal with the silencing of the female artist (instead, see Chapter 4). For the purpose of the comparison of Consuelo's history to Aurora's, I trace their pilgrimages only to the point of the lovers' reconciliation and marriage, and their trust that the woman artist will achieve even greater heights as bride than as virgin.

2. Barrett, "To George Sand. A Recognition," line 7, *CWEBB,* 2:239.

to various Sand novels: *Consuelo* and *La Comtesse de Rudolstadt* are "full of beauty" despite the occasional heaviness (*BC*, 9:49); the sexually explicit *Lélia* is "a serpent book" for its "language-colour & soul-slime" and caused Barrett to blush to her fingertips to read it (*BC*, 6:233) because of its "disgusting tendency" of "representing the passion of love under its physical aspect!" (*BC*, 9:167); *Jeanne* is "full of beauty, of profound beauty & significance"—an "exquisite" book, although Jeanne is too "divinely idiotic" (*BC*, 10:138). Barrett Browning prefers her heroines with far more intellectual and political savvy, more like her own Lady Geraldine and Aurora Leigh. Helen Cooper suggests that Sand's passionate female novels soothed some of Barrett's "indignation" that Nature made her a woman and that Barrett's love of the Sandian canon, together with her shock at Sand's "shamelessness," made Sand in Barrett's imagination a female "Promethean usurper of the God-granted male power of language."[3]

In 1844, the same year that she recommended *Consuelo* and *Comtesse* to her correspondent Miss Mitford, Barrett published not one, but two sonnets to George Sand (in the volume *Poems, 1844*). In these poems the androgynous Sand is a "large-brained woman and large-hearted man," and a "true genius, but true woman," who before the world "burnest in a poet-fire" and whose "woman-heart beat evermore / Through the large flame." In "Desire" Barrett wishes for Sand "two pinions, white as wings of swan" and free from stain in order that she might exercise her "woman's claim / And man's" to join the host of angel spirits. There is contrast between the two sonnets, though, for in "Recognition" Sand's moral reputation is irrelevant, and Barrett prophesies to Sand that God will "unsex thee" on the heavenly shore, where seemingly Sand has now joined those who "purely" aspire. Sandra Donaldson comments that the sonnets characterize Sand as angel and genius—both androgynous creatures—and furthermore that Barrett praises Sand for having found strength in female passion, a trait that would otherwise seem to be a liability.[4]

In the epistolary courtship of Elizabeth Barrett and Robert Browning, the two English poets discuss George Sand, who failed to impress Browning. He writes, "There lies Consuelo—done with!" as if it were an onerous task to complete the long novel marked by the "customary silliness . . . styled a *woman's* book." His chief objection to Sand's artist heroine is her put-upon passivity:

> and how does Consuelo comport herself on such an emergency? Why, she
> bravely lets the uninspired people throw down one by one their dearest preju-

3. Cooper, *Elizabeth Barrett Browning, Woman and Artist*, 62–66.

4. Barrett, "To George Sand. A Desire," lines 1, 9–11; and "To George Sand. A Recognition," lines 1, 10–12, 14 (*CWEBB*, 2:239). Donaldson, "Elizabeth Barrett's Two Sonnets to George Sand," 39–40. Donaldson interprets Sand's female passion in the poem's description of her disheveled, floating hair.

dices at her feet, and then, like a very actress, picks them up, like so many flowers, returns them to the breast of the owners with a smile & a courtesy and trips
off the stage with a glance at the Pit. (*BC,* 11:29)

Further, Browning dislikes awkward contrivances in the plot, disbelieves in
Anzoleto and others because the characterization is faulty, and despises the "horrible Porpora." He does admit, though, that Sand's portraits are admirable and
the descriptions eloquent, but he still holds that Sand is too voluble—"la femme
qui parle"—and he concludes his long commentary, "So I am not George
Sand's—she teaches me nothing. I look to her for nothing . . ." (*BC,* 11:30).

One can well understand Browning's distaste for Porpora because of the old
patriarch's despotic insistence that Consuelo is never to marry. By the date of this
letter Browning was a frequent visitor to the invalid poet's room in the Wimpole
Street residence and was quite perceptive enough to know that Porpora's edict is
exactly that given by the Browning patriarch to Elizabeth and all her siblings (although not on the grounds that they are all divinities of art, as Porpora insists
about Consuelo). And as for Consuelo's acquiescence to the tyranny of Porpora
and her acceptance of all the pettiness and prejudice of everyone she meets,
Browning may well be responding to the readiness of his own artist/sibyl, the
poet Elizabeth Barrett, to gather like precious flowers the arbitrary and tyrannical opinions, edicts, and criticisms of Edward Moulton-Barrett and the Barrett
brothers.[5]

Barrett's response to Browning's disdain is to capitulate on certain points and
admit that the conclusion, with the resurrected Albert having been in a trance
and now metamorphosed into Consuelo's ideal, is somewhat contrived. Yet she
holds out for the books' greater merits:

> As to "Consuelo" I agree with nearly all that you say of it,—though George
> Sand, we are to remember, is greater than Consuelo & not to be depreciated ac-
> cording to the defects of that book, nor classified as "femme qui parle," . . she
> who is man & woman together, . . judging her by the standard of even that
> book in the nobler portions of it. For the inconsequency of much in the book,
> I admit it of course—& *you* will admit that it is the rarest of phenomena when
> men . . men of logic . . follow their own opinions into their obvious results—
> nobody, you know, ever thinks of doing such a thing: to pursue one's own in-
> ferences is to rush in where angels . . perhaps . . do *not* fear to tread, . . but

5. By the date of the letters about Sand, Browning had seen Barrett give in to pressure from her father
and/or brothers on her proposed Corn Law poem and on an anticipated winter at Torquay to relieve the
symptoms of her illness, and already she was under pressure from her father and two brothers on the
subject of her romance with Browning. See Forster, *Elizabeth Barrett Browning: The Life and Loves of a
Poet,* 149, 159, 174.

where there will not be much other company—So the want of practical logic shall be a human fault rather than a womanly one . . if you please—: & you must please also to remember that Consuelo is only "half the orange,"—& that when you complain of its not being a whole one, you overlook that hand which is holding to you the "Comtesse de Rudolstadt" in three volumes.! Not that I, who have read the whole, profess a full satisfaction about Albert & the rest—& Consuelo is made to be happy by a mere clap-trap at last: and M^{dme} Dudevant has her specialties, . . in which, other women, I fancy, have neither part nor lot, . . even *here*!—Altogether, the book is a sort of rambling Odyssey, a female Odyssey, if you like, but full of beauty & nobleness, let the faults be where they may. (*BC,* 11:31–32)

The infatuation with Sand continued. In 1851 Elizabeth Barrett Browning, vowing, "I wont die, if I can help it without seeing George Sand," arranged through a communiqué to see Sand in Paris.[6] Her plan succeeded early in the following year. Predictably she was enchanted—and just as predictably Robert Browning was not. He considered Sand patronizing, unseemly, unfeminine, and unattractive. Jubilantly in her next letters, however, Barrett Browning described every detail of Sand's dress, appearance, and manner and quoted Sand's obligatory note that followed the meeting.

Barrett Browning's Female Odyssey

By 1844, the height of her George Sandism period, Elizabeth Barrett had already conceived the idea of a novel in epic form. In one of her early letters to Browning (1845) she describes her ambition:

But my chief *intention* just now is the writing of a sort of novel-poem—a poem as completely modern as "Geraldine's Courtship," running into the midst of our conventions, & rushing into drawing rooms & the like "where angels fear to tread";—& so, meeting face to face & without mask, the Humanity of the age, & speaking the truth as I conceive of it, out plainly. That is my intention. (*BC,* 10:102–3)

Barrett had been for about a year deliberating a work that, like Sandian fiction, would intrude where even angels dare not go and would be a new genre in literature: a blank-verse epic of modern life as opposed to one that "trundles back his soul five hundred years" (*AL* 5.191) to a supposedly more glorious past. Her epic turns out to be a *Künstlerroman* about the intellectual and spiritual evolution of

6. *The Letters of Elizabeth Barrett Browning to Mary Russell Mitford,* 3:347.

a female poet; *Aurora Leigh* engages political, intellectual, and aesthetic debates of the day in Europe—chiefly Fourierism and other forms of socialism, the Tractarian movement, the Woman Question, and the issue of what constitutes poetry. It comes to life on a canvas of grand scale as a female odyssey from a Florentine childhood to dignified English country life, then to grimy reality in the "great weltering fog of London," and it circles back again to Italy, its place of origin. *Aurora Leigh* contains what Barrett Browning called "my highest convictions upon Life and Art" ("Dedication," *AL*, 161), and a dozen years were to elapse between the time she began mentioning the project in her correspondence and the date when the work was finally done.

In the interim she secretly married Robert Browning, relocated with him to Tuscany, became a mother, and produced several works on which her reputation is in large part deservedly based. Among them are "The Runaway Slave at Pilgrim's Point," about an infanticide committed by a young black slave woman in America; the famous *Sonnets from the Portuguese*, inspired by her love for Browning; and *Casa Guidi Windows*, a long work—part prophecy, part polemics—about her hope for the Risorgimento. While selections from the sonnet sequence dedicated to Robert Browning were for years the only Elizabeth Barrett Browning poetry anyone knew, quoted, or anthologized (quite a comedown for a literary reputation that upon the death of Wordsworth prompted speculation that the Laureateship was destined to be hers), in the past twenty-five years *Aurora Leigh* has received more critical attention than in the first three-quarters of the twentieth century. Feminist critics have examined the poem for its insights on matriarchy, patriarchy, sisterhood, Madonna imagery, aesthetic theory, mysticism, religion, and gender politics. At least two critics, Kathleen Blake and Glennis Stephenson in *Love and the Woman Question in Victorian Literature* and *Elizabeth Barrett Browning and the Poetry of Love* respectively, study *Aurora Leigh* as a statement on love and art—the very topic that I propose to address in this chapter.

It has become a truism that Barrett Browning's artist heroine owes much to Staël and Sand, but the effect of the English poet's allusions to her French precursors, especially in the case of Sand, has not been traced, and comparisons have been general. Beyond the acknowledgment that Aurora Leigh's name may well be a tribute to Aurore Dudevant, little attention has been paid to the conversation that Barrett Browning initiates with the "great-souled" woman George Sand on the subjects of "Life and Art," creativity and love. In fact most critics who mention the influence merely content themselves with bowing to Patricia Thomson's pronouncement that *Aurora Leigh* is more influenced by several other (unnamed) Sand books than it is a tribute to or commentary upon *Consuelo*, while other critics point to both *Consuelo* and *Corinne* in general terms but ignore *The Countess of Rudolstadt*, which influenced *Aurora Leigh* at least as much, if not more, than either *Corinne* or any of Sand's other works. I contend that the spiritual quest of Aurora echoes that of Consuelo and that the unity of physical and spiritual love and transcendence that Sand proposes is modified to fit the religion of love that was Barrett Browning's faith at the end of her life—especially the ideas on human and divine love that she encountered in Emanuel Swedenborg's *Conjugial Love.*

As a professional poet, Aurora insists upon the personal and artistic freedom of a Consuelo or George Sand. Like Barrett Browning, Aurora wishes to believe that the mind is not gendered and that her own mind is androgynous—a trait that Barrett Browning perceives in Sand. At the outset of her epistolary courtship she writes Browning, "You will find me an honest man on the whole . . ." (*BC*, 10:51). Perhaps what Barrett Browning meant to depict through her autobiographical Aurora Leigh is that—while ordinary women are in some respects weaker than males—genius visits either gender and the artist exists quite apart from gender distinctions. Like Consuelo, Aurora affirms that liberty is a necessary requisite for the artistic soul to soar. Although Aurora neither smokes a cigar, as Geraldine Jewsbury did, nor wears trousers and hobnail boots like George Sand's, she does reject the attributes that supposedly make women attractive— domesticity, passivity, timidity, and dependence. Like a liberated Aurore or Geraldine, the fictional Aurora heads for London, negotiates her way in the publishing world, humors her fans, is bemused by her critics, placates her editors, and manages to hold male friendships—for example Lord Howe and the painter Vincent Carrington—without in any way compromising her reputation as Barrett's literary sister George Sand had done in her relationships, which prevented her genius from being "sanctified from blame."[7] Aurora proudly proclaims, "No fly-blow of gossip ever speckled my life" (*AL* 9.265).

Immediately upon its publication, the critics of *Aurora Leigh* lamented the crudity of Barrett Browning's indelicate, "unfeminine" language, especially the candid acknowledgment that females do indeed have sexual urges; they also disapproved the masculine or androgynous bent of the protagonist Aurora. The *Dublin University Magazine,* for example, complained that the poet "assumes, as it were, the gait and the garb of man, but the stride and the strut betray her. She is occasionally coarse in expression and unfeminine in thought . . ." and *Blackwood's Magazine* commented, "The extreme independence of Aurora detracts from the feminine charm, and mars the interest which we otherwise might have felt in so intellectual a heroine. In fact, she is made to resemble too closely some of the female portraits of George Sand, which never were to our liking."[8] Thus Barrett Browning's George Sandism is a long-standing truism.

7. Barrett, "To George Sand. A Desire," line 12 (*CWEBB*, 2:239).
8. Quoted in the appendix of *The Complete Works of Elizabeth Barrett Browning,* ed. Porter and Clarke, 4:224, 217.

Echoes of *Corinne*

Like Jewsbury's *The Half Sisters,* Barrett Browning's *Aurora Leigh* at the obvious level echoes Germaine de Staël's *Corinne* more than it does any other single literary predecessor. Like other English women writers of the period, Elizabeth Barrett had read Staël's *Künstlerroman* not once, but several times. In 1832 when she was twenty-six (Corinne's age when she is crowned at the Capitol and meets Lord Nelvil), Barrett writes in a letter to a friend, "I have read Corinne for the third time, & admired it more than ever. It is an immortal book, & deserves to be read three score & ten times—that is, once every year in the age of man" (*BC,* 3:25).

Echoes of *Corinne* appear in several of Barrett's works prior to 1856, most notably in "Bertha in the Lane." The female speaker of the dramatic monologue has been for years a surrogate mother to her golden-haired younger sister, Bertha, watching fondly over her as Corinne does Lucile. Both sisters love the same man, Robert, who has first sworn to love the older sister as Nelvil has loved Corinne. But the speaker's hope has proved a "hasty claim" and—as the jilted and dying woman admits, "Women cannot judge for men" (*CWEBB,* 3:101, verse 16, ll. 112) The rejected speaker has "pitied my own heart" as her life withered, but nevertheless she has sewed the wedding gown for the bride, and she blesses Bertha as Corinne does Lucile. Stephenson points out that the elder sister, in the instructions for the viewing of her corpse, "arranges herself as a bride awaiting her groom"—which, one might add, is what Corinne does while awaiting Nelvil's valedictory. Also, like the dying Corinne, the dying victim of love in "Bertha in the Lane" hopes to find peace in Jesus's divine love, a substitute for the sexual love that has been denied her—in other words, a substitution of eternal love for the temporal. Cooper remarks that, among Barrett's dying heroines—and there are a great many in her various ballads—none dies so meekly as does the speaker of "Bertha in the Lane," but at the same time Cooper finds the last line "I aspire while I expire" so ludicrous and inappropriate that "we question how virtuous is the speaker's self-sacrifice."[9] Similarly there are those who doubt the sincerity and selflessness of Corinne's final hours (as noted in Chapter 1).

In reference to Barrett Browning's verse novel, several critics have noted her indebtedness to Staël's *Corinne.* Barbara Dennis says that in some places *Aurora Leigh* reads like "a versification of *Corinne.*" Cora Kaplan comments that *Aurora Leigh* "carries on an extended debate with *Corinne,*" but there is no single plot element that Barrett Browning does not change in some significant way.[10] One

---

9. Stephenson, "'Bertha in the Lane': Elizabeth Barrett Browning and the Dramatic Monologue," 5; Cooper, *Elizabeth Barrett Browning,* 73, 72.

10. Dennis, *Elizabeth Barrett Browning,* 53; Kaplan, introduction to *"Aurora Leigh" and Other Poems,* 18.

might well add that although Barrett Browning also significantly alters every major character and thematic concept, she still leaves a trail of clues back to *Corinne*. Therefore the superficial similarities between Corinne's history and Aurora's serve to dramatize the differences in philosophical values of the two writers and in their concepts of the female artist and genius.

Like Corinne, Aurora is the daughter of a stable, dutiful, "austere" Protestant English gentleman with apparently only one major character flaw—a weakness for exotic Roman Catholic women from Italy. Corinne's mother is Roman; Aurora's is a Florentine whom her father saw in a religious procession and instantly loved. A major distinction in the two deceased fathers, however, is that Edgermond bequeathed Corinne quite enough money to support herself as an independent woman, while Aurora's father left her only his favorite books, a few memories of his awkward tenderness, and his injunction to "Love, my child, love, love!" (*AL* 1.212). Thus Corinne maintains a palazzo in Rome and collects works of art, while Aurora, who rejects marriage to her rich cousin, must live in a London flat and work "with one hand for the booksellers / While working with the other for myself / And art" (*AL* 3.303–5). The needy Aurora in fact lives rather more like an Aurore Dudevant or a Geraldine Jewsbury than an Elizabeth Barrett, who was well provided financially by the Moulton-Barrett family's holdings and later by an inheritance. Angela Leighton suggests that a central revisiting and revisionist purpose of Barrett Browning's multiple references to *Corinne* is the consciousness of the power of a father—a creative woman's first "muse," especially if he is a dead father.[11] Indeed, biographers have remarked upon the unusually intense and long-lived Electra complex of both Germaine Necker and Elizabeth Barrett and that life influences art.

In addition, both daughters feel—in Aurora's words—"a mother-want about the world" (*AL* 1.40) in that both lose their Italian mothers to death, Aurora when she is but four, Corinne just before age ten. Both children, however, receive feminine nurture and maternal affection from Italian nannies, Corinne's Theresina and Aurora's Assunta. Aurora goes through childhood mesmerized by the portrait of her mother painted from the dead face—a mother who seems "[g]host, fiend, and angel, fairy, witch, and sprite" (*AL* 1.154), while a pubescent Corinne, lacking a mother, turns mother herself in rendering care to her little English half-sister, Lucile. Both daughters, having been deprived of their mothers by death, are then wrenched from the arms of mother Italy—which in both works represents fecundity, beauty, and passion—and transplanted to English soil, representing austerity, duty, and conformity. In both works the shock nearly slays the heroines. For both protagonists the transition comes at the crucial time when she

11. Leighton, *Elizabeth Barrett Browning,* 26–54.

is evolving from a girl into a woman: Corinne at fifteen to join her father and English stepmother, the orphaned Aurora at thirteen after her father's death to live with his maiden sister.

To Corinne, England is cold, dreary, damp, and devoid of the beauties of poetry and art that make life endurable. To Aurora, England's cold "frosty cliffs" (*AL* 1.251), oppressive skies, and regular, circumscribed plots of land cause her to wonder how "Shakespeare and his mates" (*AL* 1.266) could have absorbed the light here—there being no radiant color and sublime landscapes to match those of Italy. The second Lady Edgermond, whom Corinne characterizes as cold, dignified, and silent, undertakes the mission of eradicating all the vivacity and Italianate characteristics of the half-English girl, and filling her mind with trifles. There exists no interest in science, literature, or liberal thought among the English females of Lady Edgermond's acquaintance, in short nothing to compare to the French salon. The aunt of Aurora, who lives a "cage-bird life," tries to tame Aurora, the "wild bird scarcely fledged" (*AL* 1.305, 310). Upon their first meeting, the aunt examines the niece with "two grey-steel naked-bladed eyes" (*AL* 1.327), as if looking for any latent Tuscan qualities to be stamped out by an English education, which is defined as learning the collects, catechism, creeds, and Tracts; a bit of ladies' French, algebra, assorted useless facts, and music; and the female "accomplishments" of spinning glass, stuffing birds, "washing out" landscapes of nature, drawing costumes, and modeling flowers in wax—in Deirdre David's words, "hardly apt apprenticeship for building the New Jerusalem."[12]

Aurora has no younger English half-sister to befriend, educate, coddle, and lose to the one true love of her life as Corinne or Barrett's Bertha does, but in Marian Erle, a drover's daughter, Aurora much later in the action finds a "sweetest sister" in need (*AL* 7.117)—a young victim wronged, raped, misjudged, and abandoned. Aurora takes Marian into her home to make restitution for the world's, and Romney's, wrong to her. Marian does not marry Aurora's Romney as Lucile does Corinne's Nelvil, but she very nearly does. Romney twice proposes to Marian—once to atone for the wrong his class has committed against hers and a second time because he feels that her predicament as an unmarried mother and "ruined" woman has been indirectly caused by him. It is in the department of love that the two female *Künstlerromane* differ greatly. For love of the unworthy Nelvil destroys Corinne, while Aurora is almost destroyed spiritually in that she denies womanly love and a worthy lover.

There is also in each work a failed attempt to dispose of the aspiring young artist by means of marriage to a respectable English gentleman. Lady Edgermond wishes to match Corinne to an unsuspecting Mr. Maclinson, an honorable, rich,

12. David, "'Art's a Service': Social Wound, Sexual Politics, and *Aurora Leigh*," 177.

handsome, and highly born neighbor who has not the slightest doubt of a husband's right to govern his wife, nor the slightest idea of Corinne's vivacity and—as she puts it—her eccentricity. Similarly Aurora's Aunt Leigh has in mind for Aurora, now turned twenty, an honorable, rich, handsome, and highly born neighbor, Aurora's cousin Romney Leigh; the aunt insists:

> You love this man. I've watched you when he came,
> And when he went, and when we've talked of him:
> I am not old for nothing; I can tell
> The weather signs of love: you love this man. (*AL* 2.688–91)

The man in question has been destined from boyhood to be Aurora's marital partner. From his grave Romney's father had struck a deal to choose his daughter-in-law—just as Nelvil had done in choosing Lucile and forbidding Corinne. Vane Leigh had ordained that Romney marry his orphan cousin Aurora so that the estate will support future Leighs of both lines merged into one. Leigh's will is deemed by the aunt a charitable act without which Aurora, who considers her uncle's purpose as truly "vain," will be a pauper once Aunt Leigh dies. Aurora, however, thinks her cousin cold, abstract, and detached; it is only a decade later, after both have suffered and matured, that she learns he "loved me, watched me, watched his soul in mine, / Which in me grew and heightened into love" (*AL* 9.763–64). Aurora denies that she loves Romney, rejects his dream for reforming the world in a socialist utopia of his own devising, proudly rejects a proposal that she considers mere charity, and decides that—the woman's person being mere property in most marriage contracts—Romney

> might cut
> My body into coins to give away
> Among his other paupers; change my sons,
> While I stood dumb as Griseld, for black babes
> Or piteous foundlings; might unquestioned set
> My right hand teaching in the Ragged Schools,
> My left hand washing in the Public Baths . . . (*AL* 2.790–96)

It is better by far, Aurora reasons, to work with the left hand for the booksellers, the right for her poetry, for such an arrangement at least allows her to call her soul her own, and freedom tastes sweet for the aspiring artist, as it no doubt must to the "male Iphigenia" bound by a dead father's contract (*AL* 2.779).

Some eight years later Aurora is a successful poet, and another offer comes with similarly phrased rhetoric. This time her friend Lord Howe gently reminds Aurora that she is neither young nor rich and that were she to marry a certain honorable, rich, and highly born suitor, she could still have freedom to write and would be set free from worry about finances. Howe's candidate, John Eglinton, collects art and presumably artists, for when Aurora declines his proposal letter, she says that Eglinton might just as well have filled in the salutation to Anne Blythe the actress, Pauline the dancer, or Baldinacci the singer, for what he wants is a "star upon his stage of Eglinton" (*AL* 5.915). Every marital proposal to Aurora seems in fact a transaction—so much offered for so much received in goods: "With women of my class . . . / We haggle for the small change of our gold, / And so much love accord for so much love, / Rialto-prices" (*AL* 4.187–90). Corinne and Aurora similarly refuse to haggle for marriage and similarly deride as marriage material a trophy-collecting, though proper, English gentleman.

Barrett Browning's Romney is nearly entrapped by a voluptuous temptress, and herein lies another similarity to the situation in which Staël's Nelvil finds himself. After the rejected marriage proposal, the Leigh cousins go their separate ways—Romney looking down at the worms under his boot heel, Aurora looking upward to the stars. As their mutual friend, the painter Carrington, puts it, he goes to make bread, she to make poems. The wealthy young widow Lady Waldemar pretends interest in Romney's phalanstery and his paupers because she has fallen in love with him and she wants to entrap him in marriage. The Lamia-like Waldemar mirrors Staël's deceitful French widow Madame d'Arbigny, who loves Nelvil and deceives him with the fiction that she is pregnant with his child. Kathleen Hickok suggests that Lady Waldemar represents the "dilemma of the post-Regency aristocrat,"[13] and most certainly Madame d'Arbigny depicts the spoiled aristocrat of pre-Revolutionary France. Both Waldemar and d'Arbigny are in fact Duessa women, fair of face and form but spiritually deformed in the nether regions of the soul.

Lady Waldemar is no less devious than Nelvil's former mistress. A second woman to love Romney is the previously mentioned Marian Erle, the young innocent who ran away from parents who beat her, worked her, and tried to pimp for her and whom Romney, as her "angel," has rescued, found employment for, and planned to marry. Waldemar foils the marriage and arranges the disappearance of the trusting Marian, whom she has convinced that she is not good enough for such a gentleman as Romney; consequently he is left at the altar chagrined that his magnanimous offer has come to nought. Marian is spirited away to a brothel, raped, and abandoned on the human trash heap of used womanhood. At first she is nearly suicidal, until her child restores her to the living, or at least restores the mothering aspect of her womanhood if not the capacity to seek or accept sexual or marital love. Aurora departs for Italy when she hears rumors of

13. Hickok, "'New yet Orthodox': The Female Characters in *Aurora Leigh*," 137.

the impending marriage of her cousin to that "Lamia-woman" Waldemar, but on the way she stops off in Paris and finds the lost and "dead" Marian with a one-year-old son; Aurora takes the young Madonna and child home with her, where the three will live in a matriarchy, two "sisters" living as mother to a single child, with Aurora serving as the secular saint/prophetess/Athena to Marian's Mary-like matriarchy.[14]

Meanwhile Romney's utopian community fails because, he says, he has been too proud to work hand-in-hand with established institutions such as the church, and furthermore has not attempted to reform souls but merely to fill bellies. Ironically it is the father of Marian Erle who does him in; when the oppressed people that Romney has tried to save turn on him and set fire to Leigh manor, William Erle strikes the blow that injures and blinds Romney, punishing him for his Messiah complex. Romney follows Marian and Aurora to Italy and proposes to the victimized Marian that he will be her husband and the father to her little son, but she rejects him, saying that she is "dead" except as mother. He too feels dead in a sense—"mulcted" as a man because of his dependence—but Aurora, seeing that he is blind and battered, decides that she herself loves Romney, that her love is not pity merely, as he fears. Rather, the vulnerability of the contrite and wounded man prompts her sudden, dramatic realization that she truly loves the man—loves him sexually and spiritually—as all her female acquaintances (aunt, Lady Waldemar, and Marian) have known all along. She throws herself into his arms and her future into his hands in an ending that some have criticized as plagiarism of *Jane Eyre,* while others have objected that it is a demonstration of a perverted notion of womanly strength that the man must be made into an impotent cripple before she can lead him. The two Leigh cousins, united at last, vow to do God's salvational work on earth—she, as poet/prophetess/sibyl, will be their mouthpiece; he, as visionary/reformer/muse, will inspire her life-giving song. The resemblance between Barrett Browning's text and Germaine de Staël's is notable, but the contrast of the conclusions is stark. Love causes Corinne to languish and die; Aurora languishes temporarily, but when she belatedly discovers love, she is resurrected to a new art.

Aurora Leigh is also like Staël's artist Corinne and Sand's Consuelo in that she becomes a Pythian, a figure for Wisdom, a female sage. Like young Germaine Necker in her mother's salon or Aurore Lucile Dupin being tutored by the very instructor who had taught her father, Elizabeth Barrett herself enjoyed a privileged childhood—even if her Aurora does not. From the nursery to adulthood, Elizabeth became an independent scholar and an invalid who perhaps exploited

14. For a study of Marian Erle as "self-effacing" and "self-abasing" Madonna and of Barrett Browning's Mariolotry, see Patricia Murphy, "Reconceiving the Mother: Deconstructing the Madonna in *Aurora Leigh*," 21–26.

her delicate health to make space for her reading, study, translating, creating, and correspondence, for she lived in a world of texts. But she knew from childhood that she was meant to be a poet, and she aspired to genius. As a little girl she wrote a poem, "The Battle of Marathon," in which the wisdom goddess Athena leads to victory the worthy Athenians against the Persians, who serve Cytherea/Venus. At seventeen or eighteen she wrote "An Essay on Mind," which honors Pope and exalts wisdom and genius. As Marian Evans and Mary Arnold were to do, she mastered as many languages as she could, including, in Barrett's case, Hebrew, Greek, and Latin, because she wanted to read the Bible and the classics in the original tongues. She twice translated Aeschylus's *Prometheus Bound* as well as several Latin poets and Greek Christian poets.

As noted in Chapter 1, both Germaine and Aurore were precocious children who created an image of their own Pythian characteristics, then created in their female artists a mythology of woman as Wisdom and incorporating the iconography of Aeneas's Cumæan Sibyl, Apollo's Pythian, Dante's Beatrice, and the Virgin Mary. Elizabeth Barrett also was a precocious child; as an adult creator she tapped into the mythology of woman as Wisdom to enhance her depiction of Aurora as inheritor of the mantle of Corinne and Consuelo. As England's foremost woman poet, she was soon hailed in the critical community as a modern Athena and a prophetess. For instance, the *League* referred to her as a prophetess (*BC,* 9:378), the *Southern Literary Messenger* as a Minerva (*BC,* 10:383), and the *American Review* as an Athenian sibyl (*BC,* 10:335). Aletha Hayter notes,

> It is extraordinary how often both her admirers and her detractors compared her with the priestess of Delphi and other prophetesses—she was Deborah, Minerva, Alruna, the Sibyl, the Pythoness, the anointed priestess: delirious, shrieking, possessed and contorted, or clamorously earnest and inspired with a sacred passion, according to whether she was being blamed or praised, but always the Pythoness.[15]

Aurora Leigh, like her creator, yearns after wisdom and yearns too for the status of a sibyl. In comparing her to Cassandra, Mariam, and Godiva, Barrett Browning calls forth the Woman-as-Wisdom figure that evolved from the Sophia and Minerva traditions and became merged, in Victorian England, into an icon of female virtue and patriotism—Athena as Britannia. Aurora sets out to learn wisdom just as Elizabeth Barrett had done, and Lord Howe praises her as the "prophetess, / At Delphi" (*AL* 5.942–43)—another Pythian, just as Corinne is. Also, Aurora is ridiculed by Lady Waldemar as a "young prophetess." This is just

15. Hayter, *Mrs. Browning: A Poet's Work and Its Setting,* 194.

what she indeed aspires to be, but Waldemar sees her intellectual pride and tells her that such women as herself starve their hearts to develop their brains—a common opinion, but excessively insulting when used by one woman to ridicule the striving of another. In fact the two sides of woman—the goddess and the witch—that the child Elizabeth Barrett in "The Battle of Marathon" configured as goddess of venality and goddess of wisdom appear in *Aurora Leigh* in the form of Lady Waldemar and Aurora, respectively. At Lord Howe's dinner party, Waldemar appears in a low-cut gown in danger of falling off, and the men refer to her as the "Venus Meretrix" (*AL* 5.765); on that same evening, the more modestly clad Aurora is characterized by Howe as the statue of Pallas in the Vatican (*AL* 5.799).

Elsewhere Aurora is the Old Testament prophetess and singer Mariam. Like the reference to "prophetess," the allusion to Mariam is employed as both insult and praise. When Romney first proposes marriage, he also tells Aurora that women are made for work, not art; that there are Mariams among them but no Moses and no Christ. The Moses/savior figure will of course be played by Romney, who in his "diminution of typology" expects Aurora as his Mariam to compose a song, rattle the tambourine, and dance to celebrate his victory. But Mariam is a Wisdom figure in that she reprimands Moses for his foreign marriage, thereby assuming, as Alicia Holmes says, "the verbal power of sanctity by speaking the holy words of the law." Furthermore, as noted in Chapter 1, Mariam was considered in the tradition as an alchemist and therefore a scholar, as well as a singer/poet. Thus Barrett Browning retrieves the Mariam icon and employs her to suggest both poetry (via her song) and wisdom (via her sermon). Marjorie Stone, who labels *Aurora Leigh* as "sage discourse," notes that "it is Miriam's prophetic singing that creates the possibility of the new spiritual and social order that Moses envisions." And Romney finally testifies to the power of the singer's word: "My Miriam, whose sweet mouth, when nearly drowned / I still heard singing on the shore!" (*AL* 8.334–35)—and perhaps, as Cynthia Scheinberg suggests, now considers himself an Egyptian oppressor, instead of a Moses/savior.[16]

As for other paragons compared to Aurora, both Godiva and Cassandra represent wisdom. Godiva has been altered into a Wisdom figure by Leigh Hunt's "Godiva" (and to a lesser extent by Tennyson's poem of the same title). In Hunt's essay, Godiva's judgment is discerning, her politics are liberal, and her famous gesture is intelligent and principled. Cassandra is of course the Trojan princess

16. Holmes, "Elizabeth Barrett Browning: Construction of Authority in *Aurora Leigh* by Rewriting Mother, Muse, and Miriam," 599 (Holmes argues that Miriam in the temple, Aurora's mother in the procession with her face clashing "like a cymbal," and Aurora herself incarnate prophetic power and performing text); Stone, *Elizabeth Barrett Browning*, 148; Scheinberg, "Elizabeth Barrett Browning's Hebraic Conversions: Feminism and Christian Typology in *Aurora Leigh*," 312, 317.

cursed by Apollo because she will not willingly submit to his embrace, and like Mariam she is a vatic—albeit tragic—bard of her people. In short, Barrett Browning, like her French predecessors, deliberately attempts to make her artist a wisdom goddess with the voice of a poet/singer and prophet. Aurora is Io, Godiva, Athena, Pythoness, Cassandra, and Mariam, as well as a version of Corinne.[17]

The path to true love is anything but smooth, and Aurora—although she follows Corinne in independence, intelligence, vivacity, and talent—seems determined not to follow Corinne's path in love. At the outset of the love plot, Romney finds Aurora on the morn of her twentieth birthday, the dawn of her poetic career, crowning herself with ivy. She deliberately chooses no bay or myrtle, the leaves of Corinne's wreath at the coronation in Rome, because the "fates deny us if we are overbold" (*AL* 2.39). Ellen Moers rightly notes that every young English reader would smile at the allusion to *Corinne* and sense that, although Aurora might aspire to the creativity, fame, and genius of Corinne, she certainly does not desire Corinne's tragic outcome[18] any more than George Eliot's dark-tressed Maggie Tulliver, who refuses to finish reading *Corinne* in *The Mill on the Floss,* wants to see the blonde sister find love while the ebony-haired sister is left out in the cold. Besides, Aurora avoids the myrtle because it means "chiefly love; and love / Is something awful which one dares not touch / So early o' mornings" (*AL* 2.40–42). That is, in the dawn of her career this young artist intends to give her heart to no Nelvil, but instead to do God's work among the poets, the "only truth-tellers now left to God" (*AL* 1.859).

Corinne's case is, after all, instructive for Aurora as would-be artist. It will be recalled that upon the day she is crowned with bay and myrtle, the *improvisatrice* had all of Rome eating out of her hand and that she was the spirit of "fair Italy" before she gave her heart to the English nobleman. Corinne loves Nelvil in spite of herself; she knows that while she has a capacity for happiness, there is in her soul "an abyss of despair" that she can avoid only by preserving herself from love. But the vulture talons of passion seize her heart (*C,* 125) as the talons of Zeus's vulture preyed on the artist Prometheus. While love inspires her performances before the eyes of Nelvil or teaches her how to play Shakespeare's Juliet because she now knows what it is to be star-crossed and doomed, love eventually poisons her creativity and she can find no antidote. Corinne tells Nelvil that to one who requires genius to sustain life, it is a great misfortune to love as she does. Love takes away her flamboyant freedom, makes a slave of her, and reduces her to

---

17. For a detailed study of the development of Aurora Leigh's persona as Lady Wisdom, see Lewis, *Elizabeth Barrett Browning's Spiritual Progress,* 176–210.

18. Moers, *Literary Women,* 182.

sneaking about England and Scotland and spying on Nelvil and Lucile. Corinne's tragedy is three-pronged; she loses the man whom she loves with what she believes to be an extraordinary ability to love, she who has always desired fame dies believing she will be forgotten, and, perhaps worst of all, she outlives her genius. The Sibyl speaks no more oracles; in her last five years, Corinne publishes nothing. Her genius having originated from within, from "l'enthouiasme," Corinne is a silent, empty shell of her formerly vital and scintillating self.

Aurora as a poet cannot afford to be silenced. It is therefore hardly surprising that she determines not to follow Corinne in all things—not to don the myrtle of love, but rather the ivy that grows from graves, not only the grave of her patriarch, but also graves of the poetic progenitors like Dante. Thus Aurora toils alone at life and art. But loneliness is difficult for a young artist, as it would be for any other worker. Romney may have misjudged his woman in the appeal he makes to Aurora: "Work man, work woman, since there's work to do / In this beleaguered earth . . ." (AL 2.134–35). But one thing Romney does know and Aurora does not is that human workers in this world need helpmates. In his marriage proposal he pleads, "I ask for love, . . . for life in fellowship / Through bitter duties" (AL 2.353–55); she retorts that he is already married to his pet theories, and furthermore, "I too have my vocation,—work to do . . ." (AL 2.455). It is Barrett Browning's theory that a woman's art is all the better for the artist's love, and Aurora's quest is in part a matter of learning love will sustain, not undermine, her vocation.

Elizabeth Barrett, like Aurora at the beginning of the epic, discredited the likelihood of a happy outcome for lovers. She had learned from *Corinne* that love's poison may well have no antidote—therefore the woman is doomed, or the artist is slain, or the artist within the woman dies. Thus when Aurora on the dawn of her third decade decides to dispense with the myrtle, her choice announces that she intends to become no Corinne. But by the time she writes *Aurora Leigh*, though, Barrett Browning has changed her mind on love, and having found in Robert Browning the kindred spirit who complements her creative life, she rewards Aurora with a husband more like Consuelo's Albert and Elizabeth's Robert than Corinne's Nelvil.

Barrett's Aurora and Sand's Consuelo

Barrett Browning's poet Aurora and Sand's singer Consuelo have numerous similarities both as women and as artists. The English poet deliberately borrows from Sand, as she does from Staël, in order to enter into a literary dialogue on feminist aesthetics. In the case of multiple allusions to Sand, the dialogue affirms the compatibility of art and love, and the lives of the female artists demonstrate it. An obvious similarity between the two is that both Sand's and Barrett Browning's female artists are independent. Initially Consuelo meanders from Venetian street carnival to quay with her childhood sweetheart, Anzoleto; she is fearless because it never occurs to her that a daughter of the people could be in danger. Later when she parts with Anzoleto, she is devastated; she has never in her mind separated love for her art from love for her fiancé. Thus when he abandons her for the flirtation with her rival, Corilla, she tells Porpora that he is half her existence; without him she is incomplete as woman and artist (*CCR*, 1:171). Porpora, however, persuades the heartbroken Consuelo that she is meant for solitude and absolute liberty, and surprisingly, without her handsome Adonis, she does flourish as an artist. When Count Christian, the father of Albert, speaks to her of Albert's love, Consuelo responds that although she admires and loves Albert's soul, she has but one gift in life and she must have independence to pursue it. Independence once attained is fiercely protected by both Consuelo and Aurora. Barrett Browning's poet of course has no Anzoleto (so much the better for her). But she is, like Consuelo, a homeless orphan who believes that solitude and liberty are necessary to her art. Therefore when Romney speaks to Aurora of his own love, she responds that she must discover whether a "woman's soul, like man's, be wide enough / To carry the whole octave (that's to prove) / Or, if I fail, still purely for myself" (*AL* 2.1185–87). She believes that Romney needs a woman who will lose herself and "melt like white pearls in another's wine" (*AL* 5.1079) and that her own quest for artistic autonomy precludes such melting.

As professionals, both artists become adept at warding off danger and flourishing as free women. Leaving Venice, Consuelo goes first to accept employment at the Château de Géants, then to perform in Vienna, and as previously noted in Chapter 1, she travels companionably with Joseph Haydn, enjoying an easy familiarity similar to that which she and Anzoleto had enjoyed before they were old enough to consider themselves affianced lovers. Aurora goes to London, the "gathering-place of souls" (*AL* 2.1182), where, like Consuelo, she enjoys more artistic and personal freedom than the typical woman of her own day. For instance, Aurora's friend the artist Carrington shows her two nude studies and frankly tells her that the recumbent, post-coital study of Danae "indicates more passion" than the Danae whose arms and breasts strain to "burn [Jove] faster down" (*AL* 3.124)—a rather bold comment to make to an unmarried Victorian miss, illustrating that Carrington takes Aurora for an atypical woman. Another friend, Lord Howe, invites her to a soiree at his home, which she attends unescorted. Alone she goes into Margaret's Court, a poverty ghetto of London, to meet Marian Erle; alone she travels to Paris, where she rediscovers Marian. Consuelo must fend off the would-be seduction of Zustiniani in Venice and Baron Trenck in Vienna and must avoid the perils and intrigue of Frederick's court in

Berlin and the jealousy, gossip, and backbiting of the court of Marie-Thérèse in Vienna; Aurora must negotiate with the publishers and editors for whom she writes and must have the grounded confidence for separating artistic wheat from chaff, for she will not compromise on the one to have the other. In short she will not sell out to the critics, her public, or her publishers—signifying that she will not become a literary prostitute for the sake of popularity. Or perhaps, as Gail Houston suggests, she has enough savvy to laugh away the literary prostitution of her talent.[19] Even in this, Aurora parallels Consuelo, who allows herself to be managed by the maestro Porpora, and he occasionally books her for performances that she considers a waste of her genius.

In independence and courage each woman artist is a "lioness," a term that Barrett Browning also applies to George Sand in her sonnet "To George Sand. A Desire":

> Thou large-brained woman and large-hearted man,
> Self-called George Sand! Whose soul, amid the lions
> Of thy tumultuous senses, moans defiance
> And answers roar for roar, as spirits can . . . (*CWEBB*, 2:239, ll. 1–4)

When she resides at the ancestral Rudolstadt castle as companion and musical teacher for the young Amelia, Consuelo is called by her pupil the "lovely lioness" of St. Mark ("ma belle lionne de Saint-Marc!" [*CCR*, 1:205]), and later Count Albert's aunt, the Cannoness Wenceslawa, says that Consuelo has the courage of a lion (*CCR*, 1:297). Similarly Aurora considers herself a lion and her aunt the lion-keeper (*AL* 2.561); she is called a "netted lioness" by Romney who, having been refused as suitor, tells her "I do not hold the cords of such a net; / You're free from me, Aurora!" (*AL* 2.1097, 1101–02). Later she is flattered as "my lioness" by Lady Waldemar who, when she first meets Aurora, wishes to charm her into breaking up the intended wedding of Marian and Romney, to "help Androcles [Waldemar], / For all your roaring." (*AL* 3.529–30). Still later Lord Howe offers to protect her from the "lion-hunters" (*AL* 5.816) who stalk the successful poet Aurora at Howe's dinner party. The lioness image for both Consuelo and Aurora means—as it does for Sand—that they are regal, bold, fierce, and courageous.

Consuelo and Aurora are also similar in their final fortune in love. In the persons of Albert Rudolstadt and Romney Leigh, Consuelo and Aurora love men who are similar in aristocratic status, in their studies of political systems and hu-

---

19. Houston argues that the "value" of woman as prostitute and writer is played in a "good-humored" fashion by Barrett Browning, who uses words such as *debt, owe, prize,* and *trade* to refer both to the marriage market and the marketing of verse, but that she is capable of "angry augury" on the subject ("Gender Construction and the *Kunstlerroman: David Copperfield* and *Aurora Leigh*," 231).

man suffering, and in their single-minded passion to reform the world. Albert is descended from the royalty of Bohemia, but he never thinks as a nobleman; as a young boy he wanted his family to bestow all that they had upon the poor, and when the Rudolstadts restricted their Christian charity to alms that caused them no self-privation, Albert gave away his own possessions. He swooned when he saw the powerless abused and punished by the rich and powerful. As a young adult, he has traveled around Europe systematically studying the inequities and evils in the world, and when Consuelo meets him, he is considered mad by members of his own family who believe that his mind has been compromised by the melancholia of his thoughts. Only Consuelo believes that he is not a madman but a saint, that his madness is that of "vertu sublime" (*CCR*, 3:181), but at times even she has her doubts about his sanity. Indeed Albert is a divine fool; given to trances, he communicates with the spirit of his supposedly deceased mother, Wanda, thinks himself descended from John Ziska, and insists that Luther is a reincarnation of Jan Hus.[20] With his untrimmed black beard and hair, his diseased imagination, his searching for mystical reunion with a dead parent, and his seeming inability to assume the dignity of his role as prince, the handsome Albert is a modern Hamlet.

As for Romney Leigh, he too has studied the inequities in the world, but his study has tended away from the historical and religious and toward contemporary political and sociological theory. He has read Cabet, Louis Blanc, Considérant, Comte, and Fourier and has compiled statistical charts and tables that illustrate the inequitable distribution of wealth in England. His own brand of Fourierism is a Christian socialism that demands of himself that he part with the Leigh estate, converting it into a communal phalanstery in which all people will share responsibility and the fruits of labor. Like Albert he is driven by the nightmares of suffering in the world and believes that he carries a personal obligation to devote his life and his wealth to curing them; he feels the "whole world tugging at [his] skirts for help" (*AL* 8.371), and he could not, even if he would, shake them free. Also like Albert he is considered a madman by those who best know him. His own aunt, for example, believes that "the sun of youth / . . . shone too straight upon his brain . . . / And fevered him with dreams of doing good / To good-for-nothing people" (*AL* 2.643–46). The London public concludes, "He's stark,—has turned quite lunatic upon / This modern question of the poor" (*AL* 4.662–63), and Lady Waldemar says he "[w]ent mad upon them . . . madder and more mad" (*AL* 3.560). Even Lord Howe, who holds that Romney is the finest man among his fellow reformers, affirms that he is also deranged from a "sudden

---

20. The Rudolstadts are Catholic, but from his mother Albert inherited a militant Protestantism— more Husite than Lutheran—that blames Catholics, particularly the Jesuits, for repression and cruelty.

madness seizing a young man / To make earth over again" (*AL* 3.119–20) and that "he's mad, our Hamlet!" (*AL* 4.757). Only Marian Erle sees that Romney is a "real angel" driven nearly to madness by the incongruities among mortal men and women—in Consuelo's words, his seeming madness is "vertu sublime."

Not only are Consuelo and Aurora similar in the situations and in the "mad" utopians whom they ultimately love, they are also similar in the quality of their love. Both Consuelo and Aurora are acknowledged to be not only spiritual but also sexual creatures, a claim hardly surprising for Sand's fiction, given her own sexual liberation, but shocking to Victorian critics who found it in Barrett Browning's verse novel. Consuelo in a letter to her friend Beppo frankly confesses that something strange and wonderful has happened: her head burns, her heart trembles as if it would burst from her very body to be joined with another soul, and for the first time in her life she knows a love that is madness and intoxication, but she feels no shame because such passion comes as a gift from God. It is a "flamme ardente et sacrée"—as is the divine and ardent inspiration for art. (*CCR*, 3:231). Aurora also testifies to a woman's passion: The reunion at the close of the epic catalogs "hot" tears, "large explosive hearts," words "melted in the fire," a "convulsive" embrace, "deep, deep, shuddering breaths," and a kiss "[a]s long and silent as the ecstatic night" (*AL* 9.717–23). Questioning the quality of Lady Waldemar's love for Romney, Aurora passionately affirms a woman's right to such passionate sexual love:

> I love love; truth's no cleaner thing than love.
> I comprehend a love so fiery hot
> It burns its natural veil of August shame,
> And stands sublime in the nude, as chaste
> As Medicean Venus. (*AL* 3.702–6)

To Aurora, Lady Waldemar is an atheist because she separates desire from religion, while Aurora—like her creator and George Sand—interprets sexual desire as a gift from God. Susan Walsh traces Aurora's sexuality from an adolescent "green" stage through her delivery of "stillborn, embryonic poems" and to her "miscarriage" when Jove's "hot fire-seeds of creation" fail to produce artistic progeny; she argues that the overt sexuality of the protagonist serves as metaphor for her passionate desire to conceive and produce living verse.[21] In other words, having been "[p]assioned to exalt / The artist's instinct in me at the cost / Of putting down the woman's" (*AL* 9.645–47), Aurora has always acknowledged woman's sexuality, but until her reunion with Romney she has never allowed herself to em-

---

21. Walsh, "'Doing the Afra Behn': Barrett Browning's Portrait of the Artist," 165–77.

brace it, for her passion has been channeled into the making of art and—like Consuelo—she has been fearful that she cannot embrace both sex and art.

Psyche and the Female Quest

The Psyche allusion is a tie between Aurora and Consuelo in that both female artists are versions of the same myth of female desire and the female quest. The Psyche/Eros story is best known in *The Metamorphoses* of Lucius Apuleius, parts of which were translated, or "paraphrased," in 1845 by Elizabeth Barrett. Aphrodite sends her son, Eros, to smite the mortal female Psyche, whose beauty is so astounding that humans pay tribute to her rather than to the goddess. Eros is assigned to consume Psyche with passion for some vile creature, "a cruel and wild and snaky monster."[22] In obedience to the gods, Psyche's parents abandon her to her fate. But instead of the death for which she is prepared, Psyche is wafted by the wind Zephyr into a bejeweled and enchanted castle and made the bride of Eros, who is entranced by her beauty but who protects his identity by visiting her only at night. Psyche grows to treasure Eros's nocturnal visits until, goaded by her jealous sisters, who tell her she has married a loathsome dragon, she arranges to decapitate the monster. Armed with lamp and knife, she looks, loves, pricks herself with his arrow, and falls passionately in love. In Barrett's translation: "The light, the lady carried as she viewed, / Did blush for pleasure as it lighted him" and she "made her blood some dewdrops small distil, / And learnt to love Love, of her own good-will" (*CWEBB*, 6:144, 145, ll. 11–12, 48–49). But Psyche accidentally burns Eros's shoulder with liquid wax from her lamp, and he flees to the court of his mother, who—when Psyche shows up searching for her lost love—turns her over for a lashing and cuffing from her handmaids Trouble and Sadness. Aphrodite then assigns Psyche four impossible labors: to separate a huge mound of seeds by varieties (a task that insects undertake for her), to fetch golden fleece from the mountain goats (which a reed teaches her to accomplish), to bring an urn of water from the streams of Cocytus (in which she is assisted by the eagle of Jove), and to appease Aphrodite with a casket of the beauty of Persephone. Psyche descends to the halls of Orcus, tricks Cerberus, persuades her divine hostess, pays the ferryman Charon, but succumbs again to curiosity and opens the casket, finding not beauty, but sleep. She is rescued by Eros, who goes over the head of his mother and entreats Jove himself to restore his bride. Psyche is metamorphosed from mortal to goddess, all Olympus celebrates, and Psyche soon gives birth to a daughter named Pleasure. This child is mortal, not divine,

22. Apuleius, *Metamorphoses* 4.22 (1:247).

only because Psyche betrayed the secret of Eros—thereby making sexual pleasure of the body not the soul, and transient not eternal.

Erich Neumann interprets the tale of Apuleius as the individuation of the female, the Psyche principle connecting "knowledge, the growth of consciousness, and psychic development"—a "psychology of encounter" in which the female is finally elevated to the status of goddess and "experiences the redeeming logos in herself, through which she attains to illumination and deification." Her descent to Persephone signifies that she must look death in the face. And her reunion with Eros signifies her triumph over the Great Mother (in Consuelo's case, read mother-in-law) and entry into true, passionate, responsive sexuality. Carolyn Heilbrun applauds Neumann's interpretation of the "emerging female self" that disturbs the "male need for power." But Heilbrun goes on to speculate whether the Psyche myth, as well as other mythic versions of female consciousness, might just as fairly be interpreted as a woman's search for her own daemon—her own creativity—as opposed to the search for adult eroticism.[23] Elizabeth Barrett Browning's Psyche, like George Sand's, searches first for individuation and creative power, and only after having found them does she seek completion through the sexual and spiritual Other. Both Barrett Browning's Romney/Eros and George Sand's Albert/Eros are wounded by the "explosive power" of the female psychic life and passion, but both are rewarded in the end by Psyche's awakening.

Consuelo and Psyche

As noted in Chapter 1, George Sand's Consuelo is a composite of several myths—Psyche being one of the more prominent. In the first novel Consuelo searches for a wounded and endangered Albert, braving the waters of the Styx, tricking a prototypic Cerberus with a cake, and rescuing Albert from the labyrinthine cavern of the Schreckenstein. As in the myth, the burning with molten wax of the lamp is inadvertent. Like Psyche spying on Eros and finding him beautiful, Consuelo perceives that Albert is generous, handsome, and noble, but she is unable to return his love. Therefore she pursues her self-actualization as artist, learning to live for herself and her art. The wounded Albert's healing does not begin until he plays his violin in the dark Spandaw fortress, woos Consuelo from behind a black mask, and meets her in clandestine darkness. Consuelo, like Psyche, is filled with desire for a lover she cannot see; she pricks herself with the arrow of Eros.

23. Neumann, *Amor and Psyche: The Psychic Development of the Feminine. A Commentary on the Tale by Apuleius*, 90, 145; Heilbrun, *Reinventing Womanhood*, 150, 144.

In *La Comtesse* she again descends into hell to rescue Albert and to propitiate his mother—this time in the initiation rites of the brotherhood and with the myth of Psyche explicitly named by Sand. The narrator of *La Comtesse* says that even before Consuelo's trial of faith she has longed, like curious Psyche, to unmask the erotic lover Liverani, who puts his hand to his mask as if to tear it away, and "Consuelo, comme la curieuse Psyché, n'avait plus le courage de fermer les yeux . . ." (Consuelo, like a curious Psyche, no longer had the courage to close her eyes [*CCR,* 3:303]). In her trial of faith, she is given a small silver lamp ("une petite lampe d'argent") to light her way into the dark caverns in which she will witness humanity's cruelty and prove her worthiness to join the Invisibles in their militant fight against evil. When she is catechized by Albert's mother, the wise "*sibylle*" Wanda, who makes Consuelo prove her worthiness to love Albert, she is reenacting a version of the labors assigned by the protective mother, the goddess Aphrodite. Forced finally to choose (Liverani or Albert), Consuelo chooses correctly because she has been "illumined" to recognize that Albert's pure soul elicits no other response. Isabelle Naginski notes that

> Sand retains the idea of human plenitude in love, but her schema is trinary rather than binary. Consuelo is the Psychean figure in this case, but her lover is double, since Liverani, the man she desires, represents Eros, while Albert, the man she married out of compassion, is Agape. When Consuelo finally realizes that the two are the same person, the opposition of sexual and altruistic love is transcended. The dichotomy disappears and Consuelo discovers that psychic integration can take place. . . . Thus the apotheosis of both Psyche and Consuelo is underscored by a triple mark of integration—reunion with the spouse, inclusion into a privileged group of gods or initiates after a period of exile or imprisonment, and a psychic sense of inner unity—what Jung called personal integration.[24]

Throughout the *Consuelo* novels the heroine and hero have devoutly believed in the sainthood of one another; each respects the spiritual aspect of the other. Especially in Albert's comments the novelist makes clear that Consuelo is, like Psyche, Albert's soul and spiritual helpmate. For instance, he refers to Consuelo as his soul and life ("mon âme, ma vie" [*CCR,* 1:343]), and the truth of his life, who gives heavenly peace to his troubled soul (*CCR,* 1:345).

This is not to suggest that Sand's *Künstlerroman* is merely an allegory, for it is a far more complex work than such a label would allow. Consuelo is not merely Soul, Albert not merely Eros—or Eros plus Agape. Rather, she is a sensitive and gifted artist, a spiritual woman, and a religious quester who has puzzled over her

24. Naginski, *George Sand: Writing for Her Life,* 208–9.

mother's fanatic Catholicism, Amelia's rational Deism, and Porpora's jealous, absolute, demanding God and tried to decide just what she *does* believe. As a woman endowed with the spirit of love and the genius of an incomparable talent, together with a great hunger to employ that gift, she nevertheless has had the courage to pray

> Maître suprême! s'écria-t-elle dans son cœur, oubliant les formules de sa prière accoutumée, enseigne-moi ce que je dois faire. Amour suprême! enseigne-moi ce que je dois aimer. Science suprême! enseigne-moi ce que je dois croire!

> "Supreme Master," she cried in her heart, forgetting the form of her prayer, "teach me what I should do. Supreme Love! teach me what I should love. Supreme Wisdom! teach me what I should believe." (*CCR,* 1:290)

Consuelo's spiritual quest leads to an integration of the sensual and spiritual love. George Sand was reared as a Catholic; at one time in her girlhood, she had considered a religious calling, but she came to believe in a God who endorses a woman's right to a sexual dimension along with other aspects of her womanhood. As the sibyl Wanda knows and the Pythoness Consuelo learns, woman can be saint, nun, mother, lover, artist—and none of these diminishes the other aspects because she comes to any of these dimensions through the experience of love— love of the infinite God and of the finite world. Although she underplayed the influence, Sand was likely influenced by the Saint-Simonianism of her age—an influence that in France "remained one of the most potent emotional and intellectual influences in nineteenth-century society, inchoate, diffuse, but always there, penetrating into the most improbable places." At the heart of the Comte de Saint-Simon's "new" Christianity, as practiced by Sand's contemporaries, were the commitment to free love, the search for a Female Messiah to liberate her sex, and the rejection of the Christian dichotomy of body and soul—a tradition that identified woman with the flesh, man with spirit. Like the Saint-Simonians, Sand believed in freedom to love "in accordance with one's psychic nature."[25] Belinda Jack notes:

> Sand did not accept the trenchant division of love into the "purely physical" and "purely intellectual." There was never "love without a single kiss and a lover's kiss devoid of sensual pleasure." To separate the mind and body, Sand claimed, led to "convents and places of ill repute." She believed that the spiritual and the physical were constituent and inalienable facets of our fundamental humanity.[26]

25. Manuel, *The Prophets of Paris: Turgot, Condorcet, Saint-Simon, Fourier, and Comte,* 153, 155.
26. Jack, *George Sand: A Woman's Life Writ Large,* 271.

Although she herself never found a permanent union capable of nurturing both soul and spirit, Sand bestows upon her fictional artist the very happiness that she believes a spiritual and searching artist like Consuelo (or George Sand) deserves. It is only after her choice—adieu to Liverani, restoring the pledge to Albert—that she is elevated to the position of Pythoness: "Une sorte de vertige s'empara d'elle et, ainsi qu'il arrivait aux pythonisses, dans le paroxysme de leurs crises divines . . ." (*CCR*, 3:397)—she was seized by a vertigo like that of the ancient Pythonesses, who in their divine crises express their inspired song in the most thrilling and fervent of religious enthusiasm. For in Sand's philosophy, divine love and sensual love are inseparable, as now Albert and Consuelo are— vowing in the final pages to love throughout this life and into eternity.

Aurora and Psyche

In *Aurora Leigh* there are two references to Psyche: The first occurs in a litany of goddesses called to Aurora's young mind as she views the portrait of her dead mother, and the second is a Cupid/Psyche sculpture in her residence in Italy. The first allusion has received much attention by critics and has been variously interpreted to refer to Marian Erle, Aurora's mother, or Aurora herself. Haunted by the portrait, Aurora recalls

> . . . And as I grew
> In years, I mixed, confused, unconsciously,
> Whatever I last read or heard or dreamed,
> Abhorrent, admirable, beautiful,
> Pathetical, or ghastly, or grotesque,
> With still that face . . . which did not therefore change,
> But kept the mystic level of all forms
> Hates, fears, and admirations, was by turns
> Ghost, fiend, and angel, fairy, witch, and sprite,
> A dauntless Muse who eyes a dreadful Fate,
> A loving Psyche who loses sight of Love,
> A still Medusa with mild milky brows
> All curdled and all clothed about with snakes
> Whose slime falls as sweat will; or anon
> Our Lady of the Passion, stabbed with swords
> Where the Babe sucked; or Lamia in her first
> Moonlighted pallor, ere she shrunk and blinked
> And shuddering wriggled down to the unclean;
> Or my own mother, leaving her last smile
> In her last kiss . . . (*AL* 1.146–65)

Cooper makes the point that—woman's identity being created by the cultural economy—Aurora reverts to the pictures of woman that she had absorbed as a child and places every woman in some category of the wide range suggested by the haunting portrait: Lady Waldemar as the Lamia/Medusa female; Marian as the other side of the coin, the Madonna and the Psyche who loses sight of love. Dorothy Rosenblum also considers Marian to be Psyche and the restored love to be the "skyey mother and father both in one" or androgynous god. Barbara Gelpi says that the mythical female images suggest Aurora's ambivalence toward her own womanhood—that she herself cannot become both mother and artist. Joyce Zonana, however, argues that as Aurora the artist moves toward an "excruciating disembodied experience of herself," she *herself* becomes the disembodied muse/Psyche, while the English aunt is Medusa, Waldemar the Lamia, and Marian the suffering Madonna. Patricia Srebrnik interprets Aurora's categories as Zonana does, but she points out that seeing Waldemar as Lamia or Medusa, Marian as the Virgin Mary, and herself as "a Muse and a Psyche" are examples of Aurora's interpreting woman "according to conventionally misogynistic imagery."[27] I agree with Zonana and Srebrnik that Aurora is Psyche because it is she who—like Consuelo—represents the inspired artist searching first for psychic self-identity and then for the fulfillment of complete love, attaining wholeness in a union with Romney as Consuelo does with Albert. Marian Erle does not seek sexual union, but flees it; Lady Waldemar seeks only the sexual, disregarding the spiritual; and Aurora integrates both the spiritual and sexual. I do not argue that Aurora perceives herself as a searching Psyche, but that Barrett Browning considers her a Psyche.

To solidify this connection, another reference to the Psyche occurs, this in the Florentine villa where both the sibyl Aurora and the Madonna Marian make their home with the baby.

> The statuette on the console, (of young Love
> And Psyche made one marble by a kiss)
> The low couch where I leaned, the table near,
> The vase of lilies Marian pulled last night
> (Each green leaf and each white leaf ruled in black
> As if for writing some new text of fate)
> And the open letter, rested on my knee . . . (*AL* 7.666–72)

One might assume the Psyche to be Marian because the embracing Cupid and Psyche are placed near the vase of lilies she has gathered. Both here and elsewhere

27. Cooper, *Elizabeth Barrett Browning,* 156–57; Rosenblum, "Face to Face: Elizabeth Barrett Browning's *Aurora Leigh* and Nineteenth-Century Poetry," 333; Gelpi, "*Aurora Leigh:* The Vocation of the Woman Poet," 38; Zonana, "The Embodied Muse: Elizabeth Barrett Browning's *Aurora Leigh* and Feminist Poetics," 250; Srebrnik, "The Central Truth": Phallogocentrism in *Aurora Leigh,*" 10.

in the poem, the lilies of the Virgin are clearly associated with Marian, but the context reveals that to consider the Psyche as Marian would be a misinterpretation. The "open letter" Aurora holds is from the painter Vincent Carrington, and it announces that in Kate Ward, his muse/model and now wife-to-be, Carrington has found a union of sexual and spiritual love and a new art, and that he has left behind the old mythologies which, after all, the entire *Aurora Leigh* advocates abandoning for a more relevant, contemporary art. For himself, Carrington implies, Cupid and Psyche have been united, and a more nearly perfect art will come from a more nearly perfect happiness—Kate being his romantic love and soul mate, whose "whole sweet face . . . looks upon my soul / Like a face on water, to beget itself" (*AL* 7.593–94). References in the same letter leave in Aurora's mind no doubt that Romney, the man she loves, has married Lady Waldemar, no soul mate at all but a deceiver.[28] The Cupid/Psyche statuette reflects and endorses the love of Carrington and Kate but parodies the bond of Romney and Waldemar. Carrington's news is an affirmation of perfected spiritual and physical love; Romney's assumed bond is a mockery of it.

But as a matter of point the sculpture is an objet d'art belonging to Aurora herself, and it occupies in the villa an honored place next the vase of lilies. By means of the reference, Barrett Browning suggests that Aurora searches for a union of soul and spirit, sexual love and soul bliss, even though she cannot yet acknowledge it. Like Consuelo, she has escaped the surrogate patriarchs, mothered herself, and presided at the birth of her own artistic independence and fulfillment, only to find her achievement hollow. Essentially Aurora's search parallels Consuelo's—although the allusions to Psyche and Cupid are not as explicit, detailed, and elaborately drawn—and in each work the Psyche who seeks also finds. Aurora's labors have not required her to separate seeds, find golden fleece, fetch water from Cocytus, or retrieve the beauty of Persephone, but she *has* been buffeted by the handmaids Trouble and Sorrow. Her quest has taken her to London to eke out a lonely livelihood, to Paris to rescue the discarded Marian, and to Italy and her parents' graves. She is in an abyss, an underworld of loneliness and disappointment, and she hungers for a miracle. She is reunited to her Eros when Romney journeys to Italy, as Eros does to the Underworld, and rescues her from despair, resurrecting her heart and soul to love.[29]

Elizabeth Barrett was fascinated by Psyche, who possessed her creative imagination perhaps more than any other mythical character with the exception of Pro-

---

28. Stephenson suggests that Aurora distorts the nature of Lady Waldemar's "openly lusty love" because she is still trying to transform sexual passion into selfish desire, still denying woman's sexuality and trying to elevate the self-effacing womanhood represented by Marian (*Elizabeth Barrett Browning and the Poetry of Love*, 101).

29. Romney is also the Resurrection angel, as in *Sonnets from the Portuguese* the lover is the angel "unhoped for in the world!" (42.14, *CWEBB*, 3:247).

metheus. Not only did she translate sections of Apuleius's *Metamorphoses* containing the myth of Psyche, but also, in 1841, she collaborated with Richard Hengist Horne in a projected drama "on the Greek model," tentatively called *Psyche Apocalypté*. Years after the death of Barrett Browning, Horne published the correspondence and preliminary outline the two poets had shared for the proposed lyrical drama on Psyche's power (as suggested in Barrett's proposed titles "Psyche the Pursuer," "the Persecutor, or "the Terrible" [*CWEBB*, 6:329]). Notes reveal that in the drama the pursued and persecuted would have been named Medon, a man betrothed to the beautiful Evanthe, but neglecting and, indeed, vainly trying to escape his Soul or Psyche—a figure who it appears would function as the spiritual or feminine part of himself, somewhat like Blake's Emanation and Shelley's Epipsychidion. In recalling the collaboration in a May 1845 letter to Robert Browning, Barrett describes the project as the story of a man "haunted by his owl soul" but adds, however, that Psyche was to be a "separate personal Psyche, a dreadful, beautiful Psyche" (*BC*, 10:204). Mary Loeffelholz says that the problem of Psyche's agency (whether part of or separate from him) is an unresolved ambivalence of the project, a problem that Loeffelholz suggests may have been resolved for Barrett when, in the 1845 "paraphrase" of Apuleius, Barrett assigns Psyche an active agency of her own story. Loeffelholz notes

> Barrett manages to imply—against the grain of the received tale—that Psyche's own love, learning, and will set her out on her laborious quest. Both Barrett's alteration of ignorance to learning and her decision to end the first poem with Psyche's will assert Psyche's place as the active subject of the story.[30]

As Heilbrun asserts of the Psyche myth, here the explosive power of the woman's quest for selfhood endangers male authority.[31] As Barrett writes, "this was not a love story, but a Psyche one" (*CWEBB*, 6:344). The male Medon, separated from his feminine soul, is doomed. When Love in the form of Evanthe conquers Soul, the Spirits of the Island, something like the Five Senses, sing: "O Medon! Banish doubt and dole;—A lover should forget his soul!" (*CWEBB*, 6:328, 333). Love-minus-Soul survives for a time, but Psyche "haunts Love with mystic and mourn-

30. Loeffelholz, "'In Place of Strength': Elizabeth Barrett Browning's Psyche Translations," 72. In Barrett Browning's translated lines previously quoted, Psyche of her own enlightened free will chooses to love; in Apuleius, she acts in ignorance: "Sic ignara Psyche sponte in Amoris incidit amorem" (Thus without knowing it Psyche of her own accord fell in love with Love [*Metamorphoses* 5.23, 1:292–93]). Loeffelholz hints that the paraphrase of Apuleius may prefigure *Aurora Leigh* in that Aurora is a Psyche who assumes agency for her own life and loves.

31. Heilbrun, *Reinventing Womanhood*, 144. Heilbrun says that, because the male does not want a mature Psyche, she either capitulates or risks the loss of her lover to attain her destiny, hence the threat to his power over her. Newmann also acknowledges the danger when a Psyche experiences the "logos" (the masculine creative power) within herself (*Amor and Psyche*, 145).

ful voices," and Evanthe, a woman passive from deficiency of intellect and mental sympathy, dies believing she has lost Medon's love. Medon flees into Nature to escape Psyche, but he comes to realize that "Evanthe has been the victim of his condition with relation to Psyche—and that every woman would most likely be made a victim under such circumstances" (*CWEBB,* 6:342). At the funeral rites of Evanthe, the Christian iconography calms the troubled man and his troubled Soul; a vision of the Cross causes Psyche to be softened and beautified, and Medon is purified and exalted in the light of divine agony.

Because the project was never completed and because the ideas as adumbrated came from both Barrett and Horne, it would be a risky interpretation to assign allegorical traits from the Psyche project to *Aurora Leigh.*[32] Instead one can note the sensual and spiritual parallels to the drama: Romney, like Medon, desires Love; he attempts to find in one woman, Aurora, the combination of Eros and Agape—desirable woman, gentle wife, and loving humanitarian. Instead she opts for the life of the soul; therefore he settles for Evanthe, or, rather, he becomes successively involved with two separate women who combine the aspects of Evanthe: Marian Erle the passive, timid, gentle aspects, and Lady Waldemar the sensual attractiveness and "deficiency of intellect." In *Aurora Leigh* Evanthe dies in that both Marian and Waldemar are—symbolically speaking—dead women at the end of the epic. In trying to explain the devastation of her rape, the gentle Marian repeatedly uses language of death and the grave—for example, "Marian's dead," "murdered," "I'm dead, I say" (*AL* 6.813, 771, 819), and "Once killed, this ghost of Marian loves no more" (*AL* 9.389). Lady Waldemar dies, too, and refers to herself without Romney as Dido without Aeneas. She writes in a missive to Aurora

> . . . with him, I were virtuouser than you
> Without him: so I hate you from this gulf
> And hollow of my soul, which opens out
> To what, except for you, had been my heaven,
> And is, instead, a place to curse by! (*AL* 9.168–72)

Thus Romney, like Medon, is abandoned and bereft. In the proposed *Psyche Apocalypté,* however, Medon passes his life near the tomb of Evanthe, fearing Psyche no more because religion has comforted his soul. Aurora is not specifically a Psyche; she has not tormented Romney like some vengeful Fury. But she has trou-

---

32. Anne Blainey says that the ideas of "spiritual purification arising from 'a casualty relating to the body' and the superiority of emotion and imagination over utility and reason" in the abandoned project were recycled in three epics: Horne's *Orion* and *Ancient Idols* and Browning's *Aurora Leigh* (*The Farthing Poet: A Biography of Richard Hengist Horne, 1802–84, a Lesser Literary Lion,* 122).

bled him by her manifest lack of faith in his reformer's zeal, by her refusal to love him, and, surprisingly, by her poetry, which has converted him and possessed his soul. At their reunion he tells her

> . . . 'for the book is in my heart,
> Lives in me, wakes in me, and dreams in me:
> My daily bread tastes of it,—and my wine
> Which has no smack of it, I pour it out,
> It seems unnatural drinking.' (AL 8.265–69)

The doubly wounded Romney—physically blind and spiritually adrift—obviously is given metaphorical sight into his wrongheadedness and pride.[33] But that is not all he is given. As a result of his abasement and repentance, which correspond in timing to Aurora's regret that art and fame are not enough, Romney *and* Aurora are rewarded with the mutual melting of souls and bodies in the completed, perfect union that Swedenborg taught and in which Barrett Browning believed. When Romney makes his way to Aurora's portal, she is reading Boccaccio's tale of the falcon, in which Federigo, a formerly rich man who has for years faithfully (and vainly) loved the same woman, is finally accepted because the newly enlightened heroine "would liefer have a man that lacketh of riches than riches that lack of a man."[34] Although Romney counts himself as "[t]urned out of nature, mulcted as a man" (AL 9.564), Aurora has finally learned that love is all and that Romney does not "lack of a man."

As for the Psyche aspects of Aurora's own quest, she has sought to unleash the feminine power in art alone—and she has thought of artistic creation in terms of sexual metaphor. She has been like Danae trying to "burn Jove down," like Io longing for the touch of his hand, and has desired to be impregnated with Jove's "hot fire-seeds of creation" (AL 3.252). Walsh argues that Aurora's creative "eruptions," like the "orgasmic tremors" that signaled her early verse, mitigate against the view that sexual love is unnecessary to make art: "This model . . . unintentionally . . . blunts the edges of Barrett Browning's radical idea that women poets do not have to live with wronged Magdalenes, or dandle babies, or embrace sexual lovers, to produce deeply knowing art and impassioned art theory." But

---

33. Romney's blindness has prompted comment that his creator has aped Brontë's blinding of Rochester in *Jane Eyre* (an observation made, for example, by George Eliot in "Belles Lettres," for *The Westminster Review*). Susan Friedman sees it as a "symbolic castration" of patriarchal authority ("Gender and Genre Anxiety: Elizabeth Barrett Browning and H. D. as Epic Poets," 219); Stephenson argues that Romney's powerlessness "paradoxically represents his new strength" in understanding the subjective inner [female] world (*Elizabeth Barrett Browning and the Poetry of Love,* 113); Angela Leighton says that Romney's blindness is Aurora's sight (*Victorian Women Poets: Writing against the Heart,* 91).

34. Boccaccio, *The Decameron,* 449.

Blake says that in *Aurora Leigh,* as in *Consuelo,* the conflict of art versus love is more compelling than the resolution, and that if Aurora had not "analyzed, confronted, questioned, and been complicated enough to distrust love, Romney would never have come around to see that women can produce great poems, because she would not have produced one."[35] While it is true that Aurora has produced a poem that Carrington, Kate, and Romney applaud, she is dissatisfied with it. She confesses that the fault is her own because she has been

> . . . Passioned to exalt
> The artist's instinct in me at the cost
> Of putting down the woman's, I forgot
> No perfect artist is developed here
> From any imperfect woman. (*AL* 9.645–49)

Love will perfect Psyche/Aurora as woman and poet. If the Apocalyptic conclusion of Aurora Leigh reveals hope for Romney's social vision, it certainly bodes well for the vision in Aurora's yet-to-be-written poems, which, like Elizabeth Barrett Browning's, will be greater than those she wrote as a single, unloved woman.

Before the reunion with Albert and Romney, respectively, Consuelo and Aurora taste phenomenal success, followed by despair at the loss of love. Before Frédéric le Grand and the freezing indifference of Prussian audiences in the cold Berlin climate, Consuelo gives lackluster performances "avec cette méthode consciencieuse et parfaite qui ne laisse pas de prise à la critique, mais qui ne suffit pas pour exciter l'enthousiasme" (with rigid and perfect precision that leaves the critic nothing to complain of, but which does not excite enthusiasm [*CCR,* 3:7]). Similarly, Aurora is also unhappy and unfulfilled. She has ripped up her verses and found no blood on the rapier because they contained only an embryo of life (*AL* 3.246–47). She has judged her pastoral as merely "a book / Of surface-pictures—pretty, cold, and false" (*AL* 5.130–31) and has admitted "the book is weak, / The range uneven, the points of sight obscure, / The music interrupted" (*AL* 7.880–82). With Marian and the infant in Italy, she acknowledges "[s]urely I should be glad" (*AL* 7.952) and "I should certainly be glad" (*AL* 7.957). But saying so does not make her happy. Thinking Romney married to Lady Waldemar, she cannot write, read, or even think; she feels like a "passive broken lump of salt / Dropped . . . to a bowl of œnamel . . . dissolving slowly, slowly, until lost" (*AL* 7.1308–11). Thus Psyche looks death in the face and nearly despairs—Consuelo in Spandaw prison, Aurora living "tenderly" and "mournfully" in "my grave / Called life here" (*AL* 7.1150–51). But this is the very point where, in the myth,

35. Walsh, "'Doing the Aphra Behn,'" 179; Blake, *Love and the Woman Question in Victorian Literature,* 188

Eros intervenes and awakens Psyche: Albert Rudolstadt is inside the prison and waiting to liberate Consuelo; Romney comes to Aurora in Italy.

The goal of *Aurora Leigh* is to achieve a fusion of the literal with the ideal, the spiritual with the sensual, the temporal with the eternal—hence all the dichotomies that Barrett Browning explores in the text. Like George Sand, who believes that true love is simultaneously physical and spiritual, Barrett Browning also bases the unity of her Psyche and Eros upon her understanding of the nature of sexual love and the nature of God. Elizabeth Barrett was reared as a Protestant, but she did not subscribe to the tenets of any one denomination, and her "dogma" became more unorthodox as she aged. In her final decade and more she was increasingly intrigued by the writings of the Swedish prophet Emanuel Swedenborg because they purported to explain the afterlife of the soul, the nature of Divine Love and Wisdom, and the nearness of the dead to the living. Barrett Browning, who mourned her beloved dead, who always considered her own life fragile, and who no doubt felt she would soon leave her husband and son, needed to believe that only a "thin veil" separates the living and dead. Swedenborg not only corroborated this belief but also elevated marital love, including the sexual intimacy within marriage, as an outcome and symbol of the Divine Love of God. In *The Delights of Wisdom Pertaining to Conjugial Love,* he writes that eternal happiness is derived from the delights of bodily senses and the soul, the former animated by the latter. To Swedenborg, marriage is preferable to celibacy because God ordained it in Eden, because it is the state in which humans are fully themselves, and because—in Swedenborg's system of "correspondences"—the state of marriage mirrors the relation of Christ to the world with the church as bride, Christ as bridegroom. In her correspondence to Miss Mitford in 1848, Barrett Browning reveals she was reading Swedenborg's *Conjugial Love;* in her biography of the Brownings, Julia Markus says that the Brownings studied the book together shortly after they married.[36]

If Saint-Simonianism is a trickle in Sand's soul, Swedenborgianism is a wide river in Barrett Browning's. In faithfulness to the concept of spiritual and sexual love in Sand's religion, she gives Consuelo and Albert the total love that obviates brothels and convents; in Barrett Browning's insistence that the sexual bond between marriage partners is the earthly expression of the love that finds its correspondence in Divine Love, she rewards Aurora and Romney with an earthly res-

---

36. Swedenborg, *The Delights of Wisdom Pertaining to Conjugial Love,* 16, 156. Swedenborg assigns woman the inferior role, suggesting that she is incapable of seeing into the "same sphere of light, and of viewing things with the same depth . . ." (175); thus in marriage the wife is deemed as a correspondence with the physical, the husband with the spiritual or Divine Love. Browning, *Letters of Elizabeth Barrett Browning to Mary Russell Mitford,* 3:231; Markus, *Dared and Done: The Marriage of Elizabeth Barrett and Robert Browning,* 219.

urrection into a holy love that promises to transcend death. As Barrett Browning writes in the most famous of her *Sonnets from the Portuguese,* "if God choose, / I shall but love thee better after death" (*CWEBB,* 3:248, verse 43, ll. 13–14). Furthermore, Consuelo does not retire from the stage after her marriage to Albert (at least not until the loss of her voice forces her retirement); nor is Barrett Browning's questing Psyche required by love to forsake her art. Rather, love perfects art. Aurora says

> . . . Art is much, but Love is more.
> O Art, my Art, thou'rt much, but Love is more!
> Art symbolises heaven, but Love is God
> And makes heaven. (*AL* 9.656–59)

In Romney and Aurora's epithalamion, she speaks of "God's love" as the first principle; to which he smiles and adds, "And next . . . the love of wedded souls, / Which still presents that mystery's counterpart" (*AL* 9.881–83).

No doubt Barrett Browning was drawn to the *Consuelo* novels because the wedded lovers at the end of *La Comtesse* have discovered the "mystery's counterpart" and have given themselves in love to all humanity. As Madelyn Gutwirth notes, Consuelo is the "vision of a godly female immanence, informed by art but not dominated by it, prepared to fight for the world's rebirth to devotion and freedom." Art is much, but Love is more. Although Barrett Browning repeatedly denies that she is like Sand a socialist or communist, her Aurora and Romney— like Sand's Consuelo and Albert—will use art to "grow spontaneously / New churches, new œconomies, new laws / Admitting freedom, new societies / Excluding falsehood" (*AL* 9.946–49).[37] Both the French novelist and the English poet employ the Psyche/Eros myth to illustrate that the great artist is no narcissist. Made complete by human and divine love, she loves and serves humankind through her art.

---

37. Gutwirth, "*Corinne* and *Consuelo* as Fantasies of Immanence," 27. Sand referred to herself as both communist and socialist; Barrett Browning repeatedly denied that she was either because she held that socialist systems "quench individualities in the mass" (*Letters of Elizabeth Barrett Browning,* 1:363).

4

The Erinna Complex and
George Eliot's Female Artists

In the "épilogue" of George Sand's *La Comtesse de Rudolstadt*, Consuelo and Albert have been engaged for a decade in the transnational faith of the Invisibles—religion, moral science, and revolution. It is the latter of these tenets that lands Albert in a prison cell in Prague—that and charges of espionage and high treason. Consuelo, now thirty, is at the top of her career. Although she invests her energies as wife, mother, and crusader with Albert on behalf of the oppressed of Europe, her voice has never been better, and she continues to perform on the greatest stages of the musical world. To join her imprisoned husband in Prague, however, she asks of Queen Marie-Thérèse permission to assign her current role to an understudy. When her request is denied, Consuelo worries, rehearses, neglects her health, and spends her nights in prayerful vigil. When she presents herself on schedule at the theater, she has lost her voice. The crowd responds with boos and catcalls, and the *cantatrice* tries repeatedly to sing, even to speak up and explain. But she cannot utter a single word. The queen believes the sudden loss of the divine gift is a hoax on the part of the prima donna, but this proves not to be the case, for "Consuelo avait irrévocablement perdu la voix" (*CCR*, 3:434). Consuelo and Albert still have their undying love, but the Invisibles, their utopian political cause, has been damaged by persecution from without and charlatanism from within. The last we hear of the count and countess, they have renounced the Rudolstadt heritage and wealth and have sought refuge in France or England or the forests of Bohemia—no one is quite sure. It is the end of a noble dream, the death of a great talent. God has given the divine gift, and God has taken it away.

For Consuelo, the loss of the divine fire would seem to be a cruel punishment for love. Maryline Lukacher says that the loss of her gift is Consuelo's price for Albert's life. As the female Orpheus, Consuelo has never looked back. And if that is the case, she does not regret Albert, the children, the politics. Lukacher adds, though, that at the end the myth is again inverted, this time to the traditional order of gender. Albert, the musical speaker/philosopher, has become Orpheus, and the silenced Consuelo is now Eurydice dying for the second time: "Le regard d'Orphée condamne Eurydice à la mort une deuxième fois." Isabelle Naginski suggests that Sand herself had a Cyane complex—Cyane being Proserpina's nymph who witnessed the abduction by Pluto but was silenced by the god of Hades, who took away her power of speech. Thus George Sand herself was terrified of losing her own voice and drove herself to write because "silence for her was the equivalent of death."[1]

George Eliot as Erinna and Sibyl

If George Sand has a Cyane complex, George Eliot would also qualify as having a Cyane or an Erinna obsession—Erinna being the Greek maiden who perished because relegated to a woman's sphere and thus denied a voice. Or, as Letitia Landon says in the preface of her 1826 poem "Erinna," she was silenced when she died at age eighteen—a premature silencing, which Landon connects to that of Staël's Corinne.[2] Eliot's unfinished poem "Erinna" depicts this creative poet/singer who dies chained to the womanly craft of spinning and hence deprived of the preferred labor of poetry:

> She held the spindle as she sat,
> Erinna with the thick-coiled mat
> Of raven hair and deepest agate eyes,
> Gazing with a sad surprise
> At surging visions of her destiny—
> To spin the byssus drearily
> In insect-labour, while the throng
> Of gods and men wrought deeds that poets wrought in song. (*DD*, 624)

Eliot quotes this stanza of "Erinna" as epigraph for the chapter of her novel *Daniel Deronda* in which the world-renowned opera singer Alcharisi describes her own silencing; she says that when she began to sing out of tune, she "felt my greatness sinking away from me" and "could not endure the prospect of failure and decline," so married and "acted" the part of wife because "I would not wait

---

1. Lukacher, "Consuelo ou la défaite politique de la femme," 43; Naginski, *George Sand: Writing for Her Life*, 220.
2. Landon, "Erinna (Introductory Notice)," in *Selected Writings*, 87. Landon's "Erinna" was first published in *The Golden Violet*, 1826.

till men said, 'She had better go'" (*DD*, 639). Similarly Armgart, the opera star in Eliot's dramatic poem *Armgart*, loses her voice and asks, "What is my soul to me without the voice / That gave it freedom?" She answers her own question: "a Will / That, like an arm astretch and broken off, / Has nought to hurl—the torso of a soul" (*A, WGE*, 19:112, 106).

This fear of silencing or of the loss or sacrifice of genius—of being, as Armgart and Gwendolen Harleth put it, only "middling"—shadowed George Eliot throughout life, and was in fact far more terrifying in terms of personal contentment than was Sand's "Cyane complex." In youth, Marian Evans's great fear was that she would never find the route to a meaningful, extraordinary life—at the same time fearing her pride in her own extraordinariness to be a sin. Before she was metamorphosed into George Eliot, she became an intellectual with, as she herself describes it, an insatiable hunger for knowledge. Her rebirth as George Eliot coincided with her first literary work, *Scenes from Clerical Life*, not published until she was in her late thirties. As one friend commented of Miss Evans, "Large angels take a long time unfolding their wings, but when they do, soar out of sight."[3] Having left behind her Evangelicalism and puritanical ideas about art and having received international acclaim for her first novel, *Adam Bede*, she rejoices in a letter to her friend, the painter François D'Albert-Durade, "I have at last found my true vocation . . . I have turned out to be an artist—not, as you are, with the pencil and the pallet, but with words" (*GEL*, 3:186). Repeatedly she insists that art, in order to be worthwhile, must be moral, must refine the suffering of the artist into precious metal of compassion. This she had a compulsion to do, in spite of the difficulties of a life thus sanctified to the service to art. In the form of headaches, depression, and fear, Eliot suffered *for* her art.

George Eliot's terror of silencing as a novelist is legendary: She feared that each book would be her last, that the muse would desert her and that she would have nothing left to say. Writing *The Mill on the Floss*, she reports that she is a "prisoner in the Castle of Giant Despair, who growls in my ear that [*Mill*] is detestable" (*GEL*, 3:254); as for *Felix Holt*, she says, "I have no confidence that the book will ever be worthily written" (*GEL*, 4:221); after completing *Armgart*, she laments her "almost total despair of future work" (*GEL*, 5:119); on writing *Middlemarch*, she admits depression because the work is "more than usually below the mark of my desires" (*GEL*, 5:261); and midway through *Daniel Deronda*, she fears the possibility of "breaking down" or of "doing what is too poor to afflict the world with" (*GEL*, 6:113). Her consort, George Henry Lewes, repeatedly cautioned her publisher, John Blackwell, that she is "unusually sensitive" (*GEL*, 2:276), often morbidly depressed about her writing, and she "simmers and sim-

---

3. Bessie Parkes in a letter to Barbara Leigh Smith (later Bodichon), quoted as a footnote in *GEL*, 2:9.

mers, despairs and despairs, believes she can never do anything again worth doing . . ." (*GEL*, 6:11).[4]

Eliot's works also reflect her terror and morbidity in the form of creative performers whose voice is stifled, the gift lost as Consuelo's is—and as Eliot feared
her own would be. But it is also the case that most of Eliot's monumental women
are silenced or fear they will be: The singer Caterina Sarti is, like Staël's *improvisatrice* Corinne, silenced in death; the preacher Dinah Morris is forbidden a
pulpit; Maggie Tulliver is drowned before she achieves her true voice; Romola
speaks out but her voice is ignored by the powerful leader whom she tries to persuade; Dorothea Brooke is born to be Saint Theresa but becomes "foundress of
nothing"; the love-starved Mrs. Transome stoically represses her voice on the
principle that the sorrows of women "would be averted if they could repress the
speech they know to be useless" (*FH*, 117); and the singer Mirah Lapidoth has a
beautiful voice but no great ambition or desire for self-display, while in the same
novel Gwendolen Harleth has an overabundance of both qualities but must learn
that she has neither the gift, the training, nor the patience for a career as artist.

Eliot's daughters of Consuelo fear, as George Eliot did, that they do not have
the divine gift or that—possessing it—they will have it stolen away. And Eliot
herself fears that, having lost her own voice, she will continue plying her craft.
With *Daniel Deronda* still unwritten and Eliot beginning to feel the loss of physical stamina, she writes, "Some time or other, if death does not come to silence
one, there ought to be deliberate abstinence from writing—self-judgment which
decides that one has no more to say" (*GEL*, 5:451). Having begun her artistic career late in life, though, Eliot no doubt feels the intense pressure of little remaining time to have her say—as her artist Armgart puts it—to "stir" the world
"before I sink to winter" (*A, WGE*, 19:78). Eliot also fears that—like the Alcharisi—she will miss her cue, exiting too soon or too late. When her voice is stilled,
however, she will be like Armgart, whose only worth was her genius and who,
when it is gone, laments, "Oh, I had meaning once, / Like day and sweetest air.
What am I now? / The millionth woman in superfluous herds" (*A, WGE*, 19:102).
The superfluity of woman without vocation is also a recurring theme in the
George Eliot canon. Eliot's novels demonstrate that before the inevitable silencing, a great artist can rise above the level of superfluous women, but such a path
is only for the brilliant and the bold.

It has been frequently acknowledged that George Eliot coveted the image of
herself as sibyl and sage, to speak and write "invita Minerva" (*GEL*, 1:250). Fur-

---

4. Lewes even went so far as to protect George Eliot from having to encounter reviews—favorable or
otherwise—and cautions even her friends with such admonitions as this to Sara Sophia Hennell: "*never tell her anything that other people say about her books, for good or evil. . .*" (*GEL*, 4:59, emphasis Lewes's).

thermore she became first George Lewes's "Madonna" and later J. W. Cross's "Beatrice." Like Elizabeth Barrett Browning, she was intellectually gifted and a serious student of languages and literature, politics and history, philosophy and theology, but Eliot also studied social science and scientific theory. As the translator of Strauss's *Das Laban Jesu* and Feuerbach's *Essence of Christianity*, and as assistant editor of *The Westminster Review* (where, most biographers concede, she had the responsibilities, though not the title, of editor), she was already known in intellectual circles before she formed a liaison with the cultured and learned George Henry Lewes and before she wrote her first fiction. Her reputation for erudition grew with the literary fame established early in her career when *Adam Bede* became a best-seller. George Levine says that between *Scenes from Clerical Life* and *Romola* she had made herself into "an epic novelist, a sage, a figure above the ordinary experience whose significance she always preached."[5] After the publication of *Romola,* she was a world celebrity, and by the time *Middlemarch* was published, Eliot had became the "divine Sibyl" to her admirers and apostles— the "[l]ords and ladies, poets and cabinet ministers, artists and men of science" (*GEL,* 5:275)—that Lewes reports as visiting on open-house Sundays at the Leweses' Priory.

One young man, Alexander Main, who in 1872 published a volume of the "wise, witty and tender" sayings of Eliot as gleaned from her novels, "worships George Eliot as having done for the Novel what Shakespeare did for the Drama" (*GEL,* 5:206). Another, having received an audience with Eliot, writes to his wife, "[Herbert] Spencer thinks she is the greatest woman that has lived on the earth . . . and I imagine he is not *far* from right" (*GEL,* 5:465). Frederic Meyers, who met "wiser than the wise" George Eliot in 1874, notes

> her grave, majestic countenance turned toward me like a sibyl's in the gloom; it was as though she withdrew from my grasp, one by one, the two scrolls of promise, and left me the third scroll only, awful with inevitable fates. And when we stood at length and parted . . . I seemed to be gazing, like Titus at Jerusalem, on vacant seats and empty halls,—on a sanctuary with no Presence to hallow it, and heaven left lonely of a God.

Oscar Browning, a friend and later a biographer, recalls "to many souls she was a prophetess. . . . Her voice was like that of a great captain which cheers . . . those who are in the forefront of the conflict . . . [or] hear the roar of warfare from afar."[6]

5. Levine, "George Eliot's Hypothesis of Reality," 3.
6. Haight, *George Eliot: A Biography,* 464 (Haight quotes from *Century Magazine* 23 [Nov. 1881]); Browning, *Life of George Eliot,* 149.

While young men, including J. W. Cross, whom she married in 1880, paid court to the aging writer, so too did her spiritual "daughters," such as Edith Simcox. In 1870 an eighteen-year-old Mary Augusta Arnold, later the novelist who published as Mrs. Humphry Ward, met George Eliot and recalls in her memoirs, "I realised . . . that I was in the presence of a great writer" (*WR*, 1:145). Elaine Showalter notes that while Eliot's "insistent patronage" rankled with many female authors, others were effusive in their praise of the "Santa Teresa." Gillian Beer says of Eliot, "She was a 'sibyl': woman as prophet, amazingly learned, exceptional, peripheral, powerful but inactive. . . . [S]he seems in her later years to have accepted the characterization of herself as sibylline." John Holloway opens his Eliot chapter in *The Victorian Sage* with the bold statement: "George Eliot is quite plainly a novelist who is also a sage." Deirdre David concurs with the "canonized myth" and adds "Eliot becomes sibylline—obviously still female, but by virtue of her 'magnificence' ascending to an androgynous zone."[7]

Dorothea Barrett sets out to undermine the sibyl myth because to perpetuate it, she believes, elevates Eliot to a plane where the anger, bitterness, cynicism, and self-obsession of Eliot's novels are implicitly off-limits for discussion. Nevertheless Barrett accepts that

> both George Henry and Marian Lewes manufacture[d] and disseminate[d] an image of George Eliot that would be powerful, morally authoritative. . . . This can only be understood in the context of the severe disapprobation she had suffered all her life, for being plain, for being passionate, for being intellectual, and above all for being unmarried. The initial creation of the sibyl image was the means by which an embattled woman, whose character and circumstances threatened the dominant ideology, gained peace, power, and acceptance in Victorian England.[8]

Thus the artist George Eliot was a self-created sibyl/Madonna/Beatrice—an English myth to stand beside the French Corinne and Consuelo, lacking only the physical attribute of personal beauty, which she bestows upon her statuesque and stunning artists and goddesses.

Eliot is also like Barrett Browning in her belief that a true sibyl must appeal to the spiritual dimension. Eliot holds that religion should be based less upon personal consolation and more on responsibility to others (*GEL*, 5:31). From an Evangelical girlhood in which she distrusted art (even religious novels) as an af-

---

7. Showalter, "The Greening of Sister George," 293–94; Beer, *George Eliot*, 26; Holloway, *The Victorian Sage: Studies in Argument*, 111; David, *Intellectual Women and Victorian Patriarchy: Harriet Martineau, Elizabeth Browning, George Eliot*, 166–67.
8. Barrett, *Vocation and Desire: George Eliot's Heroines*, 5.

front to the Deity, she moved into a sphere of intellectuals influenced by the new science and philosophy, and while she continued to respect the beauty and power of ceremonial liturgy and symbolism, she came to believe in the divinity within humans—God as the highest, best, and most unselfish of human virtues. She says, "The will of God is the same thing as the will of other men, compelling us to work and avoid what they have seen to be harmful to the social existence." In this concept Eliot is a follower of Feuerbach, who teaches that "The divine being is nothing else than the human being, or rather, the human nature purified."[9] The "Promethean efforts" of moralists, philanthropists, politicians, and especially artists illuminate the consciousness of others. Eliot characterizes her motives for creating art:

> And the inspiring principle which alone gives me courage to write is, that of so presenting our human life as to help my readers in getting a clearer conception and a more active admiration of those vital elements which bind men together and give a higher worthiness to their existence; and also to help them in gradually dissociating these elements from the more transient forms on which an outworn teaching tends to make them dependent. (*GEL,* 4:472)

For Eliot the eternal truths are the capacity for self-sacrificing charity, the passion to give more than one receives, to suffer with and for other persons who suffer. These are the "feminine" or "motherly" qualities found in the biblical Jesus hung on a cross and on his mother, the Madonna, who is like the Comtean woman noble, gracious, and loyal to the grave and beyond. Yet it is exactly her proclivity for preaching morality that, according to Gordon Haight, cost Eliot popularity in the period of early modernism.[10]

It is no accident that in the Eliot canon the sibyl's voice is usually expressed in song. George Eliot was herself a musician; she played the piano and loved opera and oratorio. She gives her heroine Dorothea Brooke a voice like an Aeolian harp, a voice that reminds one of Handel's *Messiah* (*M,* 80, 205, 534). She says that music is inherently superior to the visual arts because, while painting and sculpture idealize our human existence, music "arches over this existence with another and a diviner" (*GEL,* 1:247). Because music was to her the purest expression of art, she expresses her own art in the metaphor of song—an aspiration to "join the choir invisible / Whose music is the gladness of the world."[11] And she expresses her Erinna complex in the fictional histories of silenced singers.

---

9. Browning, *Life of George Eliot,* 105; Feuerbach, *The Essence of Christianity,* 14.
10. Haight, preface to Eliot, *The Yale Edition of the George Eliot Letters,* 1:x.
11. Eliot, "'O May I Join the Choir Invisible,'" *WGE* 19:273.

The George Sandism of George Eliot

While there is, especially in their sibylline authority, a tenuous bond between Eliot and Madame de Staël, there is a stronger bond between Eliot and George Sand. Like Geraldine Jewsbury and Elizabeth Barrett Browning, Marian Evans practically worshiped Sand. Parallels between the two Georges have been noted by several critics, who have commented that Sand and Eliot admire and treat with dignity the rustic people of the Nohant region and of Warwickshire respectively in a series of "pastoral" novels; that both spent a devout girlhood, then underwent a crisis of personal faith and in their writings distrust established religion and monasticism; that both deal sympathetically with human suffering and passions. In Eliot's own time comparisons between the greatest living French woman novelist and her English counterpart were inevitable. One writer even compares their portraits and concludes that they look alike. In "Daniel Deronda: a Conversation," a review of Eliot's 1876 novel, *Daniel Deronda,* Henry James features a three-way discussion that—among other things—compares Eliot and Sand. In it, "Pulcheria" (no doubt based on Sand's prostitute Pulchérie in *Lélia*) finds both Georges voluble, inartistic, and addicted to moralizing; the moralizing "Theodora" insists that George Eliot is pure and George Sand impure, while the critic "Constantius" (a thinly veiled James) refers to several aspects of *Daniel Deronda* that Sand would have handled better, then adds "George Eliot is solid, and George Sand is liquid"—his metaphor implying, he explains, that Eliot's writing is the more contrived and artificial. Mathilde Blind, in an 1885 biography of Eliot, draws several parallels between Eliot and Sand but notes too the important distinction that Sand was the "greatest idealist" and Eliot the "greatest realist" of her sex, that Sand's genius is "impassioned, turbulent, revolutionary" and embodies Rousseau, while Eliot's is "contemplative, observant, instinctively conservative," and she is the sole novelist to incorporate the ideas of Comte, Mazzini, and Darwin.[12] Recent critics, including Patricia Thomson and Daniel Vitaglione, have traced the influence of certain Sand characterizations and situations upon her English successor.

In her essay on women in France, Eliot herself praises Sand as "the unapproached artist who, to Jean Jacques' eloquence and deep sense of external nature, unites the clear delineation of character and the tragic depth of passion."[13] On Sand's influence, Eliot says

12. James, "*Daniel Deronda:* A Conversation," in James, *Partial Portraits,* 73–74; Blind, *George Eliot,* 8, 10.

13. Eliot, "Woman in France: Madame de Sablé," in *Essays of George Eliot,* 55.

> I should never dream of going to [Sand's] writings as a moral code or text-book. I don't care whether I agree with her about marriage or not—whether I think the design of her plot correct or that she had no precise design at all but began to write as the spirit moved her and trusted to Providence for the catastrophe, which I think the more probable case—it is sufficient for me as a reason for bowing before her in eternal gratitude to that "great power of God" manifested in her—that I cannot read six pages of hers without feeling that it is given to her to delineate human passion and its results . . . [and] some of the moral instincts and their tendencies—with such truthfulness such nicety of discrimination such tragic power and withal such loving gentle humour that one might live a century with nothing but one's own dull faculties and not know so much as these six pages will suggest. (*GEL,* 1:277–78)

Eliot not only admires her predecessor's truthfulness, power, humor, moral instincts, and passion, but she also admires Sand's strong, larger-than-life women, such as Lélia and Consuelo. For Eliot's other great debt to Sand (and, to a lesser degree, Staël) is her monumental female characters. As Vitaglione notes, both Sand and Eliot repeatedly create strong women characters hungering for freedom and knowledge, and as Thomson says, Eliot's "beautiful, ardent, trustful, high-souled young women bear a considerable family resemblance . . . to the heroines of George Sand . . . and to Sand's own account of herself as a girl."[14] Like Sand, Eliot creates female goddesses. As Indiana, Consuelo, Lélia, Jeanne, Valentine, Lucrezia, and Daniella are regal, so are the "queenly" or "majestic" Romola, Dorothea Brooke, Dinah Morris, Maggie Tulliver, Leonora Halm-Eberstein, Gwendolen Harleth, and Mrs. Transome. When Maggie Tulliver rows alone in the flood to save her brother Tom from drowning, her singular act of lone courage is as grand and memorable as that of Sand's Jeanne carrying the corpse of her mother from a burning cottage. When Romola moves freely about the city of Florence to treat those suffering of the plague or Dinah Morris unself-consciously travels from one village to another to preach the Gospel, their self-sufficiency and natural independence match that of Consuelo moving freely about first in the city of Venice and later in the music capitals of Europe. Romola's bold confrontation of the formidable Savonarola is similar to Consuelo's of European royalty. Valentine's insistence that she will marry Benedict regardless of what her neighbors think about her stooping beneath her rank is the same proclamation that Dorothea makes in marrying Will Ladislaw. The Alcharisi in retirement bears the same regal and commanding stage presence as Sand's Lucrezia. Although the Victorian period was an era of idealized womanhood, one would look in vain for a more remarkable series of goddess/Madonna/Sophia figures with

---

14. Vitaglione, *George Eliot and George Sand,* 174–77; Thomson, *George Sand and the Victorians,* 161.

the stature of Eliot's—unless of course one looked to the French predecessors Corinne and the Sand heroine. Dickens's pure women are innocent, unassuming, and virtuous; Gaskell's heroines are patient, humble, and faithful; Charlotte Brontë's are independent, clever, brave, and resourceful (if small and drab and—with the exception of Shirley Keeldar—decidedly not on the goddess model); Emily Brontë's Catherine is a waif and tigress. But Eliot's heroines are like Sand's and Staël's—statuesque and beautiful, bold and courageous, fascinating and brilliant, curious and ambitious. Perhaps one would have to look to the fiction of Nathaniel Hawthorne to find anything near Eliot's succession of spectacular women, but among his goddess/women Hawthorne chooses incomparable models in the American heroines Margaret Fuller and Harriet Hosmer, and his artist Mariam also traces her lineage from Staël's Corinne.[15] That Eliot's magnificent models of womanhood, talent, and ambition are usually silenced is one of her most prominent recurring themes.

Dinah Morris, Preacher and Angel

George Eliot's angelic Dinah Morris *(Adam Bede),* her bewitching Maggie Tulliver *(The Mill on the Floss),* her Madonna Romola *(Romola)* and her philanthropist Dorothea Brooke *(Middlemarch)* are goddesses silenced by convention and tragedy, by life and by death. Portraits of Dinah the preacher, Maggie the ascetic, Romola the politician, and Dorothea the would-be saint are influenced by Staël and Sand—and in some instances by Barrett Browning as well—in that multiple mythic sibyls and goddesses are invoked in their creation. Furthermore they are—like the various female artists in other Eliot texts—depictions of the Erinna complex.

The heroine of Eliot's best-selling first novel, *Adam Bede* (1859), is based upon her admired aunt, Mrs. Samuel (Elizabeth) Evans, a Methodist preacher who, like Dinah Morris, accompanied to the gallows a young woman convicted of infanticide. For her male hero Eliot chooses aspects of her beloved late father, Robert Evans, who like Adam Bede was a carpenter, an honest and hardworking man but also a proud and unyielding one, and a manager for an estate.[16] Hetty Sorrel is the morally infantile Eve that Adam loves and "earns" by working for

15. Hawthorne's painter Mariam (in *The Golden Faun*) beholds herself in the same Virgin Spring in Rome where Corinne gazed on her own reflection.

16. George Eliot claimed her characters are not depictions of actual persons, that *"[t]here is not a single portrait in Adam Bede"* (*GEL,* 3:155). Yet her brother Isaac Evans recognized the characters and declared that no one other than his sister could have written *Adam Bede.* Eliot said that her aunt Elizabeth Evans *did* leave her religion to join the New Wesleyans when the group to which she belonged no longer allowed women to preach (*GEL,* 3:175).

her, as the biblical Jacob did for his Rachel, only to discover her a Leah in disguise. In Adam's case this is not a deceit perpetrated by a father who wants to dispose of his daughters as biblical Laban did; rather, Adam is victim of self-delusion—his skill in "measuring" character being incommensurate with his arithmetic exactness in measuring his carpentry projects. Finally Arthur Donnithorne, Adam's employer and Hetty's seducer, is a pampered younger member of the squirearchy who eternally banishes the latter-day Adam from his Eden of naïveté and innocent love. When Hetty is convicted of infanticide, Adam suffers in the "upper room" as a Christ-figure, learns never to be "hard" again, grieves his lost dream, and is eventually rewarded with marriage to Hetty's "cousin,"[17] the preacher Dinah Morris, who soon after the wedding is "silenced" from public proclamation when the Wesleyan convention decides that the practice of allowing women to preach is not in the best interest of the faith. Dinah is such a powerful figure that both Lewes and Blackwood, Eliot's readers of the evolving narrative, expected her to emerge as the central figure at the novel's close and to find happiness in the arms of a chastened and sadder-but-wiser Adam Bede. In that expectation Eliot's denouement did not disappoint.

Dinah is a prophetess, a Methodist sibyl, a Madonna, the resurrection angel. With her "lily-face" she recalls the iconography of the Virgin; in her plain gray or black dress she seems not only Quaker-like, but also nunlike, an image caricatured by the insubstantial "water-lily" or woodland dryad, Hetty, who in one scene at Hall Farm "poses" as Dinah for the entertainment of her relatives, the Poysers.[18] Dinah's sermon on the Hayslope village green alludes to the account of Jesus' teaching of the adulterous Samaritan woman at the well, and we first assume that it applies to "naughty" Bess Cranage, whom Dinah persuades to reject vanity in the form of fake garnet earrings. Not until the end of the novel is it apparent that Hetty, another possessor of showy earrings, is the *real* Samaritan woman whom Dinah must eventually persuade to renounce something far more horrifying than petty displays of female vanity. In place of exterior ornamentation, Dinah carries an inner peace, displays none of the feminine graces that could be interpreted as coquetry, and moves unself-consciously in all environments. When we first see Dinah, she is about to preach on the Village green, and as Eliot describes her, she

> walked as simply as if she were going to market, and seemed as unconscious of
> her outward appearance as a little boy: there was no blush, no tremulousness,

17. Dinah and Hetty are "sisters" in a figurative sense; literally, though, Hetty is the niece of Mr. Poyser, and Dinah is the niece of his wife.

18. Not only is Hetty a wood dryad, she is also an Undine-like "water-nixie" (*AB*, 243) and the "water-lily," an ersatz Madonna who dresses in Dinah's garb and is contrasted to Dinah, the pure lily.

which said, "I know you think me a pretty woman, too young to preach"; no casting up or down of the eyelids, no compression of the lips, no attitude of the arms, that said, "But you must think of me as a saint." . . . There was no keenness in the eyes; they seemed rather to be shedding love than to making observations; they had the liquid look which tells that the mind is full of what it has to give out, rather than impressed by external objects. (*AB,* 33)

Furthermore Dinah's oratorical style is compelling; she speaks with a "sincere, articulate, thrilling treble, by which she always master[s] her audience" (*AB,* 97). A true disciple of the Jesus who spoke in open, outdoor spaces, she delivers her sermon while standing in a cart under a maple tree. Also like Jesus she is an itinerant preacher and voluntarily poor. As the Jesus of Luke's gospel feels particularly attracted to the outcasts most frowned upon by society, Dinah has a special affinity for people in "hard" places, as witnessed by her preference for Stonyshire, where life is difficult, over Loamshire, where nature's fecundity might tempt her to become "soft."

Dinah is immediately recognized as extraordinary by the male characters of the novel. Adam's brother, Seth, loves Dinah, wishes to marry her, and would willingly follow the "St. Catherine in a Quaker dress" (*AB,* 71) in her itinerant preaching. Irwine, the Aeschylus-quoting Anglican clergyman, meets the young Methodist prophetess and concludes that only a "miserable prig" would lecture her on theology, given that her form of religion is, for her, as natural as trees growing in whatever shape nature has destined them. Late in the novel when the misogynist schoolmaster Bartle Massey shares sacramental bread and wine in the upper room with his friend Bede, Dinah enters to bring a report from Hetty's cell, and Bartle is "transfixed" by her (*AB,* 432); he is also reported to have said that women "wouldna ha' been a bad invention if they'd all been like Dinah" (*AB,* 494). Witnessing Dinah's warmth and compassion in Hetty's suffering, Arthur Donnithorne says, "I could worship that woman" (*AB,* 445).

While the inclination to "worship" the woman could well indicate that Dinah is a modern-day Madonna, Eliot's predominant figure for Dinah is not the Virgin but the angel of resurrection. Kimberly Adams insists that every feature of Dinah—hair, height, eyes, facial type, deportment—recalls Epiphanius's fourth-century description of the Virgin as quoted in Anna Jameson's *Legends of the Madonna,* a book that Eliot reviewed, *or* the *Sistine Madonna* of Raphael, upon which Eliot gazed daily in her 1858 trip to the Dresden Gallery while she was writing *Adam Bede.*[19] Adams contends, as I do, that Adam Bede becomes the new Adam, or a Feuerbach-inspired Christ more tender and forgiving and less self-

19. Adams, *Our Lady of Victorian Feminism: The Madonna in the Work of Anna Jameson, Margaret Fuller, and George Eliot,* 157.

righteous than the old Adam Bede, but I maintain that at the end of the novel Dinah's role as resurrection angel takes predominance over that as Mother of God. Like the "lily-face" description, references to the angel are echoed throughout the novel. Early in the narrative, old Lisbeth Bede, Adam and Seth's mother, who grieves over the death of her husband, is comforted by Dinah, whom she immediately describes as looking like the angel on the grave in Adam's Bible (*AB*, 141). Much later, when Adam searches for his lost Eve/Hetty, his quest takes him to Dinah at Snowfield, a hard country where, Adam supposes, "she must look as if she'd come straight from heaven, like th' angels in the desert, to strengthen them as ha' got nothing t' eat" (*AB*, 374). Near the end of the novel, when Lisbeth chastises Adam for not claiming the love of this extraordinary woman, she points to the picture "of the angel seated on the great stone that has been rolled away from the sepulchre" and tells him, "That's her—that's Dinah"—a likeness that Adam sees instantly, with the caveat that "Dinah's prettier, I think" (*AB*, 470). Dinah plays for Adam a similar role to that of Orpheus/Gilfil in *Mr. Gilfil's Love-Story* or of Consuelo to Albert—that of leading the beloved sufferer out of an underworld of suffering and into marital love. In Elizabeth Barrett Browning's *Sonnets from the Portuguese* a similar resurrection takes place and the poet, like Eliot, uses the biblical resurrection angel to exemplify the divinity of the beloved. Barrett Browning's revived female pilgrim who "yield[s] the grave for thy sake" says in reference to the lover, who has called her back from death to new life: "And I who looked for only God, Found *thee!*" In Sonnet 42, the resurrection motif is sustained:

> My ministering life-angel justified
> The word by his appealing look upcast
> To the white throne of God, I turned at last,
> And there, instead, saw thee, not unallied
> To angels in thy soul!
> . . . .
> . . . write me new my future's epigraph,
> New angel mine, unhoped for in the world![20]

Barrett Browning credits the male lover as the persona's resurrection angel who rolls the stone away from the sepulcher, leading forth the dying woman into resurrected love, life, and joy. In Eliot's novel though, the male hero, Adam, has become the suffering Christ—and a figure of the "second" Adam mentioned by the writer of the Book of Romans 5:14–19—and Dinah presides at his resurrection, representing at once both human and divine love.

20. Browning, *Sonnets from the Portuguese* 23.13, 27.8, 42.3–14, in *CWEBB*, 3:238, 240, 247.

As the tolerant Irvine teaches Arthur the Aeschylean lesson that there are repercussions from every human action, Dinah teaches that infinite love is suffering, that humans must share in the divine love of suffering for the world. Ellen Moers in *Literary Women* considers Dinah Morris a direct successor of Staël's Corinne in the category of "performing heroinism"—with Dinah's preaching on the village green being every bit as obvious a depiction of a public prophetess as is Corinne on Capitoline Hill.[21] Certainly Eliot wishes us to consider Dinah as a prophetess, although she could never accept Dinah's explicit creed. Rather, Eliot agrees with Dinah's other great prophetic message that clinging to willful sin destroys one's contentment in this present world and causes pain to others. Strictly speaking, Dinah is not an artist—although, as Moers suggests, she may be a performer. Yet as demonstrated in Chapter 1, the Staël/Sand artist is a Wisdom figure—a guide like Virgil's Cumæan Sibyl or Dante's Beatrice, and Dinah fulfills this role of divine prophetess.

Yet the preaching angel is silenced. Surprisingly, Eliot does not credit Dinah's marriage to Adam Bede as the silencer—although Adam prefers Anglican "Church" to Methodism and does not himself personally endorse the concept of women in the clergy, and although Dinah as the mother of two small Bedes by the end of the novel has plenty to occupy her life. Instead, the Methodist Conference has forbidden women to preach—an interdiction that is historically accurate. Seth believes that Dinah should have left Methodism for some other religious sect that permits a woman moved by the spirit to proclaim in a public voice. Significantly, it is Adam—not Dinah—who answers, and in so doing he suggests that the patriarchal voice will silence the matriarchal in this traditional marriage. Adam tells Seth that Dinah "thought it right to set th' example o' submitting" to the conference (*AB*, 506), and besides she is not forbidden other forms of teaching, which Dinah continues to exercise through visiting the sick and other acts of mercy and through informal lessons at gatherings in the homes and cottages of Hayslope. In this acquiescence Dinah is following the teaching of St. Paul that those who are pastors and leaders in the church have the responsibility to yield even in matters that do not violate their own conscience lest they should "cause a brother to stumble." In the conflict between Seth and Adam, Dinah—in a discreet, conciliatory, and womanly fashion—changes the subject, but Seth can see that, between Adam and Dinah, this is a "standing subject of difference rarely alluded to" (*AB*, 506). It is obvious that, although she has the compensatory gifts of a good marriage, a loving and dependable husband, and a couple of energetic children, Dinah is not quite reconciled to the silencing of her prophetic voice. Surely the reader attracted to Dinah's angelic qualities and sin-

21. Moers, *Literary Women*, 192–93.

cere, unselfish proclamations is similarly less than reconciled to the silencing of this particular "articulate, thrilling treble."

Maggie as Eliot's Corinne and Consuelo

Maggie Tulliver, the tragic heroine of the 1860 novel *The Mill on the Floss*, is an Antigone, a Medusa, the Virgin Mary, a witch, Dante's Beatrice, Sand's Consuelo, and Staël's Corinne. Eliot is explicit about the connection to Staël's artist/heroine in that Maggie identifies with Corinne. When her friend and would-be lover, Philip Wakem, gives her a copy of Staël's novel, Maggie refuses to read the conclusion because the fair-haired girl, Corinne's half-sister, Lucile, as mirrored in Maggie's cousin Lucy Deane, finds contentment in marriage to the man she loves, while the intellectual, creative, vivacious, dark-haired woman is sure to meet tragedy for having loved that same man. Maggie can sense Corinne's fate in the making, just as surely as the reader has premonitions of Maggie's death from the moment that Mrs. Tulliver says her children will probably drown, given the way they are attracted to playing near the water. Maggie is the tragic dark maiden of Eliot's rustic tragedy, a "gypsy-looking child" with a mane like a Shetland pony's; she grows into a tall, regal, and "fiery" woman, her dark hair a coronal for her head in the form of braids wrapped around like a crown. When at age nine Maggie is criticized by her tidy aunts for her disorderly dark locks, the young Medusa shears and scatters the serpents—proving that she too is untamed and disorderly. Maggie's lover Stephen senses something of a "wounded war-goddess" (*MF*, 463) in the grown-up Maggie's determination not to yield to his impertinent caress, and artistic Philip Wakem paints her as a "tall hamadryad, dark and strong and noble" (*MF*, 343).

Furthermore, Maggie is by implication the Sophoclean Antigone. In Eliot's version of the Greek trilogy, the "raskill" lawyer Wakem plays Creon, even in the detail that he was to become Maggie's father-in-law had she not left Philip in her death as Antigone did Haemon. Maggie's father is a proud, doomed Oedipus, who "had a destiny as well as Oedipus, and in this case he might plead, like Oedipus, that his deed was inflicted on him rather than committed by him" (*MF*, 143). Although Eliot's Oedipus must capitulate to his old nemesis, Maggie—who has but two "idols," in father and brother—attempts to save her father from his own vengeance and "save" her Polynices/Tom from burial by water, but ends by burying him—and herself—*in* water. In the Sophoclean allusion, Eliot suggests the tragedy of a royal and high-minded tragic heroine.

Maggie is also connected to witches—not only because her cousin Lucy sees "witchcraft" in Maggie's magic intellect that can grasp difficult notions with ease, but also because in Maggie's copy of Defoe's *History of the Devil* she reads that witches were dunked in water as a test of their guilt, a practice that the child Maggie sees as cruel because, whether innocent or guilty, the "witch" died, and Maggie feels pity for maligned and persecuted women (or doomed ones, like Corinne), as she does all wounded, crippled, and suffering beings. The child Maggie of course does not foresee that she will be drowned as a result of her own "bewitching" ways that fascinate the wrong man, Stephen Guest.[22] Her refusal vicariously to accompany Corinne to slow, dramatic death in Rome does not prevent Maggie from meeting swirling, sudden death in the flood of the Floss.

Eliot's *Bildungsroman* reveals a precocious Maggie, who is, her father fears, "over-'cute" for a woman. To her fair-haired mother, the dark Maggie is a "mulatter," and to her brother, Tom, a temperamental "Miss Spitfire" or ambitious "Miss Wisdom" (*MF,* 17, 18, 96). In addition to her impetuosity, courage, and brilliance, little Maggie exhibits another remarkable feature, her vibrant imagination. For example, she imagines characters and events from *Pilgrim's Progress* and Sir Walter Scott's romances as participating in her own narrative, of which she is the standout and star. An instance of this penchant for casting herself as heroine is her childhood plan to run away from home, join the gypsies on Dunlow Common, and become their queen. Judith Newton, noting Maggie Tulliver's fantasy life, says that in *The Mill on the Floss* George Eliot makes fantasy, like rebellion, seem dangerous. U. C. Knoepflmacher notes that Maggie, incapable of accepting the "reality principle," yields to a fantasy life like that which destroyed her father. And John P. McGowan, examining Eliot's realism, says the quixotic Maggie suffers "because she continually acts as if the world of books and of her imagination does denote *the* world, and because the fictional world 'fashioned . . . in her own thoughts' is preferable to the actual world of the Mill and of St. Ogg's."[23] It is of course this inclination to write the text of her own life that causes her to reject *Corinne,* for the determined Maggie intends not to follow *that* particular plotline. Certainly in Maggie's case the very traits that make her memorable are also those that make her vulnerable, as Newton, Knoepflmacher, and McGowan suggest. Maggie is not an artist and not in the strict sense an intellectual because deprived of access to education beyond the rudimentary and to speculative knowledge beyond the Bible, Thomas à Kempis, and Keble's *Christian Year.* She is, however, the material of which artists and intellectuals are made because she is brilliant, curious, studious, creative, and skeptical. As the narrator says, she is

22. Actually, the beginning of Maggie's tragic doom is the infatuation with Stephen. The drowning in the Floss is not brought about by some tragic *hamartia* but is more of a *deux ex machina*. This abrupt fatality is frequent criticism of Eliot's tragedy, and she herself concurred it a weakness.

23. Newton, *Women, Power, and Subversion: Social Strategies in British Fiction, 1778–1860,* 144; Knoepflmacher, *George Eliot's Early Novels: The Limits of Realism,* 212, 210; McGowan, "The Turn of George Eliot's Realism," 177.

a creature full of eager, passionate longings for all that was beautiful and glad; thirsty for all knowledge; with an ear straining after dreamy music that died away and would not come near to her; with a blind, unconscious yearning for something that would link together the wonderful impressions of this mysterious life and give her soul a sense of home in it. (*MF,* 250)

From an ugly-duckling girlhood, she emerges, briefly, into is a woman of potentially great soul. That her life is blotted out and Maggie is silenced before she reaches the status of mature Sibyl is the tragedy of *The Mill on the Floss.*

In her second novel, as in *Adam Bede,* Eliot employs the myth of Eden or the Golden Age to illustrate "we could not love the world if we had no childhood in it." Of the two "natives of one happy clime," as Eliot phrases it in her sonnet sequence "Brother and Sister" (*WGE,* 19:187), Maggie identifies with her father and the Tulliver kin, who are proud, explosive, and plagued with financial hard luck, and Tom identifies with his mother's family, the Dodsons, in that he is plodding, unimaginative, and dutiful—as well as absolutely worshipful of property and propriety. Rhadamanthine Tom's version of the sibling bond is that Maggie errs and he punishes her; Maggie's version is that Tom is cruel. Maggie is brilliant; Tom, a decidedly poor student. Having been born male, he nonetheless receives the better education, which he does his best to "forget" lest it interfere with his business acumen. The Wordsworthian Golden Age ends when the headstrong Tulliver, who once too often "goes to law," loses first Dorlcote Mill and later his job overseeing the very mill that he once owned. The two Tulliver children exit their Eden and enter "the thorny wilderness, and the golden gates of their childhood . . . forever closed behind them" (*MF,* 206).

While he is away for schooling at a clergyman's house, Tom is a classmate to Philip, the disabled son of lawyer Wakem, Mr. Tulliver's bitter enemy and more recently his employer. Philip is sensitive, artistic, talented both in drawing and in music, and an intellectual as well. He loves Maggie, and she returns his affection, although her love is inseparable from the pity she feels for all maimed and helpless creatures. Tom discovers the relationship and, predictably, puts a stop to it. When the elder Tulliver dies in bad straits and the family home is broken up, Tom works to pay the debt, buy back the mill, and care for his mother. Maggie earns her own way as a teacher, forsaking the beauty of art and literature that Philip has introduced to her for the self-renunciatory life of discipline—a choice made also by Mary Ann Evans in her Evangelical girlhood. Maggie's tragic destiny accelerates when, on holiday from school, she visits cousin Lucy. There Maggie and Stephen Guest, whom Lucy expects to marry, develop a compelling and dangerous mutual passion, and Stephen practically abducts Maggie on an outing that was to have been a boating party, not a twosome. Maggie's sense of morality—lulled by the passion that had allowed her to "drift"—is too late righted on course. As a result, in the town of St. Ogg's, Maggie is castigated as a fallen woman. On the street men leer, and the "world's wife" sees that she pays the penalty as the witch who—guilty or not—must suffer. Then in the great flood, which in local mythology is said to occur whenever Dorlcote Mill changes hands, Maggie rows to rescue Tom, but a great piece of machinery from the wharf sweeps upon their fragile craft, and "[i]n their death they were not divided" (*MF*, 547).

George Eliot's indebtedness to her "divinity" George Sand for influence on the characterization of Maggie has been noted by several critics. Similarities between the "gypsy" Maggie and *zingarelle* Consuelo were noticed by Eliot's contemporary Margaret Oliphant, by her dear friend Sara Hennell, and by Leslie Stephen.[24] Like Consuelo, and also like Dinah Morris, Maggie deliberately dresses in very simple, plain clothing—in Maggie's case, usually black. Also like Sand's heroine, Maggie is specifically referred to as a Cinderella metamorphosed from a child so homely that adults comment upon her appearance to a dazzling princess—in Eliot's novel, cousin Lucy taking particular pride as the "fairy god-mother" (*MF*, 430) who shows off her cousin's enchanting beauty. Further, Patricia Thomson notes an echo of the Anzoleto-Albert-Consuelo triangle in Maggie's attraction to both Philip and Stephen—handsome but shallow Stephen paralleling the self-centered Anzoleto, and sensitive, artistic Philip, the "noble, generous, intellectual and artistic" Count Albert. Thomson adds that the tension of certain scenes is parallel—for example, Albert intercepting Anzoleto's glances at Consuelo and Philip, merely by watching them, correctly surmising Stephen and Maggie's passion. Especially, though, Albert's idealized love for Consuelo's "grandeur d'âme" is recalled in Philip's devotion to the "great-souled" Maggie.[25] Both Consuelo and Maggie desire wisdom and goodness, not merely beauty and charm.

Comparing *Consuelo* and *The Mill on the Floss*, one notes also an ache for the freedom of lost Eden as another trait connecting the heroines of the two Georges. Like Consuelo, who throughout her adventures longs to return to her "jardin enchanté" of Eden, Maggie nostalgically longs for a return to an innocence—if not happiness—of Edenic childhood. Neither Consuelo's nor Maggie's was, in fact, a happy childhood, but Consuelo's easy, natural freedom of wandering about with Anzoleto and later Joseph Beppo is hauntingly recalled in Maggie's comparative freedom of outdoor fishing, playing, and adventuring with Tom and Bob Jakin, a familiarity with the opposite gender that proves either sexually threatening or destructive of her reputation or of family harmony when, as a young

24. Thomson quotes Hennell: ". . . *Consuelo* is the only thing to compare with it" (*George Sand and the Victorians*, 167).

25. Thomson, *George Sand and the Victorians*, 165–68.

woman, she goes alone to the Red Deeps with Philip or on the river with Stephen. Finally, both Sand's *cantatrice* and Eliot's majestic Maggie are silenced—Consuelo in losing her remarkable gift, Maggie in losing her life.

Similarities between Maggie and the sibyl Corinne are easily adumbrated. Both women are self-assured and intellectual, willful and proud; both have a passion for the intellectual and the aesthetic, and each means to be—as young Maggie says—"a clever woman." Both are perceived by the men in their lives as remarkable, regal, beautiful. As previously noted, the beauty of both is in their brunette exoticism as contrasted to fair, pleasant, conventional, blonde "sisters." Both lose a beloved father in death and consequently become more independent than other young women of their respective cultures. Corinne conducts life on her own terms in Italy, and Maggie is "strangely old for her years in everything except . . . prudence and self-command" (*MF* 290). Both lose a handsome heir to a family name, wealth, and rank to a Lucile/Lucy (or "light")—Lord Nelvil being an aristocrat in the traditional sense, Stephen Guest, the prince and heir of a mercantilism that represents the new "religion" of St. Ogg's. Nelvil's companion, d'Erfeuil, is vaguely similar to Philip, except that the former tries to instruct his male friend Nelvil, while Philip turns his efforts to enlightening not Stephen, but the woman he loves. In fact the female-male relationship of Corinne/Nelvil is reversed in *Mill,* for while Corinne is the tutor of Nelvil, introducing him to the politics and aesthetics of Italy, Philip is the mentor of Maggie, who believes that because he is lame and has suffered both physical pain and the ostracism of sturdy lads like Tom Tulliver, he can "find fault with me and teach me" to be stoic and selfless (*MF,* 433). Philip, based in large part on Eliot's friend and translator, the artist François D'Albert-Durade, *does* teach Maggie that it is not sinful to hunger for the beautiful and good and that her renunciation of learning and literature is a "narrow self-delusive fanaticism" (*MF,* 344). Philip is Maggie's instructor in aesthetics and wisdom; significantly he courts her, as Cathy Linton does Hareton Earnshaw, with books. (Interestingly Bob Jakin, the other man who has loved Maggie from his boyhood, also brings books as his offering to his adored maiden/Madonna.)

Maggie also takes on the symbolic importance to Philip that Beatrice does to Dante, and in this aspect she again recalls Corinne who, as noted in Chapter 1, serves as Nelvil's Beatrice. Stephen speculates to Lucy that his old friend Philip "must be love-sick for some unknown lady, some exalted Beatrice whom he met abroad" (*MF,* 380). In this he is only half right: Maggie *is* Philip's Beatrice, but he has not met her abroad; instead he has gone abroad because Tom Tulliver has prevented him from seeing his English Beatrice. In his own words, Philip recalls Dante's *La Vita Nuova* (his new life) in his love for Maggie. After she awakens from her mesmerized infatuation for Stephen and returns to St. Ogg's, where she is the object of calumny, Philip in a letter tells Maggie that she has been the great blessing of his life:

> . . . I write now to assure you . . . that no anguish I have had to bear on your ac-
> count has been too heavy a price to pay for the new life into which I have en-
> tered in loving you. I want you to put aside all grief because of the grief you have
> caused me. . . . [I]n loving you, I have had, and still have, what reconciles me to
> life. You have been to my affections what light, what colour is to my eyes—what
> music is to the inward ear. . . . The new life I have found in caring for your joy
> and sorrow . . . has transformed the spirit of rebellious murmuring into that will-
> ing endurance which is the birth of strong sympathy. (*MF,* 526–27)

Not only is Philip's statement an iteration of Eliot's philosophy that in suffering and sorrow, we learn to express pity and love for fellow sufferers, but also Philip twice expresses his awakened soul in terms of "new life," the Dantean term in *La Vita Nuova* in which the lady in the window—his Beatrice or Divine Wisdom—has resurrected him to spiritual hope, rescued him from the dark wood, and reconciled him to life in this present existence. That Maggie is Philip's Beatrice, as Corinne is Nelvil's, is yet another echo of Staël's text in Eliot's.

As Maggie is Philip's Beatrice, she is Bob Jakin's Madonna. Legend has it that the town of St. Ogg's was named for Ogg, a common boatman on the Floss, who accepted a ragged woman and child because "thy heart needs it" (*MF,* 128) and ferried her across a flood, whereupon she was transformed into a shimmering beauty in flowing white robes; she blessed him for his pity and prophesied "from henceforth whoso steps into thy boat shall be in no peril from the storm. . . ." After Ogg's death, visions of him in his boat were allegedly seen with the Virgin riding in his prow. Bob Jakin becomes Ogg; Maggie Tulliver, the Madonna in the prow. As previously noted, Bob, like Philip, has admired Maggie since childhood and has brought her offerings of books. Also like Philip, Bob refuses to believe that Maggie has involved herself in an illicit affair with Stephen Guest—and he generously offers to punch Stephen if Maggie were to sanction his offer. Mag-gie had already been exalted from a childhood playmate into "Bob's directing Madonna" (*MF,* 300) when she lectured him on shortchanging the wrangling customers of his packman's trade, and he chooses her name "Maggie" for his first-born child. When all of St. Ogg's ostracizes Maggie, Bob Jakin and his wife pro-vide rooms for Maggie and her mother, and when Bob asks the "fallen" Maggie to cradle her namesake, his request eloquently demonstrates that she is for him still an idealization of the Virgin Madonna. Smitten with pity, he has "relieved her heart's need." When the Floss is in flood, however, Ogg and the Madonna take separate boats—his to restore his family to high ground, hers to rescue Tom—actually to reunite the severed tie and restore the Tulliver children to an

Eden they can reclaim only in death, as they "clasped their little hands in love and roamed the daisied fields together" (*MF,* 546).

The Maggie Tulliver whose speculations about life and goodness and whose questions about suffering and pity are never completely resolved is a multifaceted woman about whom George Eliot, as she usually does with her heroines, decides one myth will not suffice. Thus Maggie is a bewitching Medusa but also a salvational Beatrice. Nina Auerbach, in *Woman and the Demon,* argues that often in Victorian fiction the angel/Madonna and the Eve/temptress are two sides of one coin, that Maggie Tulliver is "both the witch Defoe imagines . . . spreading desolation and punished for it, and her community's legendary protector, the Virgin of the Flood, who sanctifies the spot she visits."[26] Though "dark and strong and noble," Maggie Tulliver—like the dark, independent, and noble Corinne whose tragedy she refused to read—is eternally silenced.

Romola as Myth and Patriot

George Eliot's *Romola* (1863) is set in late-fifteenth-century Florence, and her protagonist, Romola di Bardi, is the consummate icon of the Virgin Mary—as well as an Antigone and Ariadne, and a tribute to Petrarch's Laura, Dante's Beatrice, and Staël's and Sand's mythic heroines. She is a pre-Raphaelite-like stunner with rippling "reddish gold colour" hair, long white hands, fair skin, and "refinement of brow and nostril" (*R,* 48). She is brilliant, gifted, and fascinating—more deity than mortal. When Eliot's friend Sara Hennell comments that Romola seems "pure idealism . . . above my own experience" and "a goddess, and not a woman," the novelist responds, "you are right in saying that Romola is ideal—I feel it acutely in the reproof my own soul is constantly getting from the image it has made." (*GEL,* 4:103–4)

Romola is a complicated novel of political and moral intrigue, complete with detailed reference to Italian history and culture. Henry James, who considered *Romola* the finest of Eliot's works, says, "A twentieth part of the erudition would have sufficed."[27] Part of the complexity of *Romola* involves three political factions: supporters of the Medici; followers of the Frate Savonarola, known as the Piagnoni; and the aristocratic and reactionary Arrabbiati. Florence is celebrated by a proud people as the city of Dante and Boccaccio, Michelangelo and Raphael, but Savonarola has chastised Florence that in the present day the arts, like everything else, are prostituted to the flattery of the powerful. Everything in Florence is political. Romola's brother, Dino, has abandoned their father's faith and poli-

26. Auerbach, *Woman and the Demon: The Life of a Victorian Myth,* 183.
27. James, "The Life of George Eliot," in James, *Partial Portraits,* 56.

tics to become Fra Luca, a Dominican and a follower of Savonarola. Her husband, the young Greek scholar Tito Melema, eventually involves himself in espionage and counterespionage with all three Florentine factions, as all the while his political star rises and his morality plummets.

The girl Romola is blessed, or perhaps cursed, with a father who rejects traditional religion, celebrates Renaissance art, worships ancient scholarship, and "crams" Romola with Greek and Latin because he requires a secretary/amanuensis/librarian. Romola marries Tito Melema after he arrives in Florence and presents himself as Bardo's assistant. Closed within the domestic space, Romola is a dutiful daughter and wife and does not emerge as a public figure until the treachery of Tito causes a sudden, wrenching change in her life. Devastated by Tito's perfidy in regard to her late father's magnificent library, Romola in disguise flees the city "free and alone" (R, 330), intending to go to the woman scholar Cassandra Fedele of Venice to learn how an "instructed woman" can support herself. Like Saul on the way to Damascus to persecute Christians, though, she is stopped on the highway by a blinding light that seems a "divine presence" (R, 329) and by the voice of Savonarola, as Saul is by the voice of Christ. Upon hearing Savonarola's recall to duty as wife and citizen, Romola is prompted by her "yearning passivity" (R, 363) to accept the confessor that Savonarola appoints to her, return to her unfaithful husband, and devote herself as an angel of mercy in her native city—which does indeed appear to be under the scourge of God that Savonarola has predicted.

Romola undertakes a second flight from Florence and is a second time silenced—this occasion after she has met Tito's "other wife," Tessa, and their children, as well as Tito's father, Baldassarre, who reveals that the traitorous Tito has ruined him, imprisoned him, and played him as false as a Judas—or as false as Sinon played Troy. As Dino had seen in his dying dream-vision, Tito's blank, or bland, face is that of Satan. Furthermore, Romola has lost all her "fathers" to death or, as she sees it, to their defection from the values they had held. And the "mothers" of the novel are of no help at all: Romola never meets the celebrated female scholar of Venice, and the two crones near at hand are a fright—the "prophetess" Camilla Recellai is a witch, and Romola's cousin, Monna Brigida, is a backsliding, would-be Piagnone who surrenders her false hair and baubles of jewelry to Savonarola's bonfire of vanities, but soon desires to reclaim them. It is after her second attempt to escape—this time in the solitude and freedom of death—that Romola finds her calling as Madonna to the greater outside world, then returns to Florence to found (with Monna Brigida, Tessa, and the children) a matriarchy similar to that which, briefly, Aurora Leigh and Marian Earle establish for themselves and Marian's son. There, Romola teaches Tito's son to eschew the lust for fame and prosperity that has destroyed his father's soul.

The statuesque "tall maiden" Romola combines the extraordinary qualities of Eliot's Dinah Morris and Maggie Tulliver—especially those qualities of being stately, natural, noble, and mythic. Like Dinah she is a "strong white lily" (*R*, 189) and a bold rhetorician. Like Maggie she hungers for learning and is majestic in appearance and bearing. Romola is frequently described as a monarch: She moves with a "queenly step" (*R*, 49), stands in "quiet majestic self-possession" (*R*, 58), and in her gold-trimmed, white silk wedding garment, she is to Tito "Regina mia!" (*R*, 197).

Romola is not only a queen, she is also a goddess. Tito says that her noble womanhood is "something like the worship paid of old to a great nature-goddess, who was not all-knowing, but whose life and power were something deeper and more primordial than knowledge" (*R*, 95). Like Staël's Corinne, she is connected symbolically to the "Great Mother" goddess and great Wisdom goddess. When Tito describes the temple of the Parthenon that alternately honored two virgin goddesses—Pallas Athena and the Virgin-Mother of God—we see aspects of both in the woman he has chosen to marry. Margaret Homans notes that, as Tiresias is stricken blind for spying upon Minerva in the text that Romola reads to her father, Bardo, in their first tableau of the novel, Romola is herself like Minerva in that she is the object of sight for the blind man and for Tito.[28] Elsewhere Romola is goddess of the dawn: Her godfather, Bernardo, says her hair is like the brightness of the morning, and her husband, Tito, calls Romola "my golden-tressed Aurora" (*R*, 177)—an allusion on his part to a goddess of light and perhaps on Eliot's part to either Aurore Dudevant or Aurora Leigh, or both.[29] Kimberly VanEsveld Adams notes that in her voyage of rebirth Romola encounters a landscape that suggests the Great Mother in the forms of Ishtar, Ceres, Eve, and Isis and that, as the Goddess in the latest form, of Virgin Mother of Christianity, she is "Eliot's ideal of woman in possession of her full powers . . . autonomous mother . . . associated with the nurturing powers and even the fertility of the great goddesses. . . ."[30] Furthermore, Dionysian Tito crowns his Romola not only as goddess and queen, but also as Ariadne. He presents as a wedding gift an elaborately painted tabernacle depicting the Bacchus and Ariadne myth, with himself as the curly haired and strikingly handsome god crowning Ariadne/Romola. The crowning by Tito proves an ersatz reign, though, and Romola as

28. Homans, *Bearing the Word: Language and Female Experience in Nineteenth-Century Women's Writing*, 207.

29. Reading Barrett Browning's *Aurora Leigh* for the third time, Eliot remarks that the book gives her a deeper sense of communion with a large and beautiful mind (*GEL*, 2:342). Later, the novel-epic became a benchmark for *The Spanish Gypsy;* Lewes gleefully reports in 1869 that the sale of Eliot's poem will likely surpass that of *Aurora Leigh*—and he has troubled himself to check Browning's total sales (*GEL*, 4:470).

30. Adams, *Our Lady of Victorian Feminism*, 177–78.

Ariadne must rescue *herself* by negotiating the labyrinth of Florence and the moral and spiritual labyrinths of conflicting factions and faiths.

Romola is also, like Maggie Tulliver, an Antigone. The painter who produces the Ariadne/Bacchus for the bridegroom also paints Romola and her blind father as Antigone and Oedipus at Colonos and calls old Bardo's precocious daughter "Madonna Antigone" (*R*, 257). Like an Antigone she attends a proud, world-weary, and blind father in his isolated old age; also like Antigone she ignores patriarchal dictate and "buries" her brother, Dino, (actually visits him in the monastery where he lies dying) after his father has disowned him for having invested his life in monastic piety. Like Antigone before the tyrant Creon, she argues justice with the arbitrary and unyielding Savonarola. In her essay "The Antigone and Its Moral," Eliot notes that the conflict of Sophocles' drama is the impulse of "sisterly piety" allied with the gods versus the "duties of citizenship" and that such conflict between family and nation has the making of tragedy inherent within it.[31] In *Romola*, more than in any other novel, Eliot has devised a symbiotic connection between heroine and political state reminiscent of *Corinne*. As Corinne is fair Italy, Romola becomes fair Florence. When the Frate Savonarola recalls her with his "arresting voice," he commissions her for a civic duty in returning to the citizens of Florence "to whom you owe the debt of a fellow-citizen" (*R*, 358). Romola debates the Frate on a public matter, although she acts on behalf of a private cause—the death sentence of her godfather. When she does so, she steps out of the private and into the public sphere; like Antigone's, hers is the conflict of family versus citizenship. And the Antigone allusion elevates her to a symbol of the state as the figure of the Cumæan Sibyl does Corinne, whose voice—like Romola's—is raised on behalf of the republic and its people.

Furthermore, Romola is the revered lady of bardic song, especially Beatrice— a connection she also shares with Staël's heroine and Eliot's Maggie Tulliver. By implication she is to the Florence of 1492 the divine muse that Beatrice had been to her fellow-citizen Dante in 1300 and Laura was to Petrarch, Bardo's favorite poet among the moderns. Various men praise Romola as "such a woman as the immortal poets had a vision of when they sang the lives of the heroes" (*R*, 128), "fair as the Florentine lily" (*R*, 39), "beyond the measure of women" (*R*, 69); men young and old visit the house in Via de' Bardi to pay homage to Romola's "womanly majesty" and grandeur, sometimes in lines from the poet Firenzuola's *Della Bellezza delle Donne* (*R*, 189n). When Romola returns from the deathbed of her brother, Dino, and Tito turns to her in fear that she will have learned of his treachery, he sees her as Dante witnesses the descent of Beatrice at the end of the *Purgatorio* and as Corinne appears to Nelvil at the crowning in Rome; her head

31. Eliot, "The Antigone and Its Moral," in *Essays of George Eliot*, 263.

is encompassed with glory that seems like a flash of lightning. Tito murmurs, "My Romola! My goddess!" and "he was in paradise: disgrace, shame, parting—there was no fear of them any longer" (*R,* 175).[32]

Romola is, however, chiefly the Madonna, and after Bardo's death, when she becomes the rescuing lady with the lamp, the citizens of plague-ridden Florence usually address her as "Madonna Romola." Tessa, the contadina with whom Tito has contracted a counterfeit marriage, encounters at the bonfire of vanities a rescuing "heavenly lady" with a "young heavenly face" and "loving hazel eyes" and addresses her "*'Addio,* Madonna" (*R,* 430, 432). The heavenly lady is of course Romola, fulfilling the duties to which that arresting voice of Savonarola has recalled her. The people await a miracle from an "Unseen Madonna," and their prayers are answered when Romola—as the "Visible Madonna," impervious to threats of the Plague—comes in the flesh to minister to the needy, sick, homeless, and dying. At the climax of the novel when Savonarola sanctions the execution of her godfather, Bernardo del Nero, Romola is utterly alone—her literal and surrogate fathers and her only sibling having died and Tito having abandoned her in his self-promotion, political intrigue, and "marriage" to the contadina Tessa—and she drifts off in a boat, intending to die. But, as if by divine intervention, the small craft is no vessel of death but a "new baptism," a "gently lulling cradle of new life" (*R,* 560, 551), resurrecting her to a new and greater service for a more desperate people than even the Florentines she has left behind in her flight.

At dawn Romola arrives in a strange place to find a hovel where a small group of Spanish or Portuguese Jews have just died of the plague. She rescues their baby boy, carries him in her arms to the village, where she upbraids the priest for having abandoned his dying people; she then sets out to feed, nurse, and comfort the sick and dying. When the town has been restored to health and normalcy and the dead have been buried, the love of Florence "come[s] back to her like hunger" (*R,* 561), and Romola decides to return to her beloved city, the scene of her "self-repressing colourless young life" (*R,* 128), and take up her work with those who need her. Recalling a familiar Madonna icon, Eliot describes Romola's departure: Cradling little Benedetto (whose name means benediction or blessing) and riding on a donkey, Romola is a mirror image of the iconography of the Virgin in flight to Egypt—minus Saint Joseph. In *Romola,* and to a lesser degree in other heroines, Eliot manipulates the impulse that Feuerbach calls the necessity of "the

---

32. For a study of *Romola* as an allegorical revisiting of Dante's descent to Hell (in Tito's moral plunge) and of Romola's ascent to the mountain of Purgatory (in her second flight from Florence), see Thompson's *George Eliot and Italy: Literary, Cultural, and Political Influences from Dante to the Risorgimento,* 88–96.

mild, gentle, forgiving, conciliating being—the womanly sentiment of God."[33]
Thus the images and allusions of *Romola* are as splendid as those Staël invoked
for Corinne, who is also repeatedly associated with symbolism of the Virgin and
a pantheon of goddesses.

As she has done in several novels, George Eliot also pays tribute to George
Sand, and several critics have noted *Romola*'s indebtedness to Sand, especially to
Consuelo. For example, a comparison between Sand's Consuelo (the "Una of
Venice") and Eliot's Romola (the "Olympian" of Florence) is noted by Margaret
Oliphant in an 1874 review of the novel. Oliphant prefers Sand's heroine as "real,
simple, natural, and true," and a loveable child of the poor; she is less enthusiastic about the "crushing loftiness and grandeur" of Eliot's Pallas Athena.[34] Not
only are the two heroines evocative of their separate cities (the grandeur of Florence and charm of Venice, Oliphant says); they also are remarkably similar in
other ways as well. The beautiful but faithless Tito Melema of the glib tongue
and beautiful voice recalls Consuelo's false love, the tenor Anzoleto, although
there is some of Hawthorne's Dionysian faun in Tito as well. Both Anzoleto and
Tito are charming and irresistible, and both are worthless. In addition, both novels depict the heart-straining pull between filial and sexual love. The solicitous
care of Consuelo for her surrogate father, Maître Porpora, as exhibited in mending his clothes, washing his linens, and locating his lost items, is recalled in Romola's attentions to her father—chiefly as his amanuensis, nurse, and companion. Consuelo longs to return to Albert but feels that the needs of her "father"
are of older origin and—honoring her father—she also hesitates to break Porpora's rule that an artist is a divinity not made for mortal love; similarly, Romola experiences relief and consequently guilt when Bardo dies and she can for the
first time devote herself entirely to the conjugal joys that await her. In fact both
Consuelo and Romola exhibit the compelling desire for freedom, not only from
the patriarchy but from multiple demands on their duty and affection, and the
desire for liberty is in both novels demonstrated in repeated flight—Consuelo's,
for example, from Anzoleto's faithlessness, Spandaw Castle, and the intrigue of
Frederik's court; Romola's from Tito's treachery, Savonarola's demands, and the
political double-dealing and danger of Florence. Both heroines are depicted as
Ariadnes imprisoned in their respective labyrinths; both *Consuelo* and *Romola* are
hymns to female freedom.[35]

33. Feuerbach, *Essence of Christianity*, 71. Feuerbach associates the Mother of God with the idea of the
Son of God, who is the feminine aspect of the deity: "the heart of the Son is the heart of the Mother"
(72).
34. Oliphant, "Two Cities, Two Books," 88, 90, 78.
35. Daniel Vitaglione notes also that in Eliot's treatment of ascetic monasticism in *Romola* (an asceti-

A question still unanswered is whether Romola is or is not silenced, and I contend that she is. In the epilogue, Romola, now without father, husband, mentor, or brother, is thirteen years older and her face has a "placidity" not evident in her youth, her eyes an "absent" gaze at distant mountains. She has been restored to a domestic space—albeit one with a trio of matriarchs and no guiding patriarch. This loggia is a reversal of the residence in Via de' Bardi; in the opening of the novel, Romola assists a father in his endless and unfinished research, and as the novel ends, she assists a "son" whose future is still a blank slate. Romola has gone from service to a dead past (dead in the sense that Bardo's work on classical scholarship is as sterile as Casaubon's "key to all mythologies") to an unknown future (unknown in that we cannot surmise whether Lillo will serve the city-state). Referring to the novel's closure with Romola as instructor to Tito's son, Lillo, but not his daughter, Ninna, Shona Elizabeth Simpson remarks, "So: silence, silent acceptance of duty and work; children, and the perpetuation of a system in which boys learn while girls do not." Deirdre David, says that—having been her father's Antigone, Tito's Ariadne, and Savonarola's Martha—Romola finds herself in a position of "shared equality of transformed power" of both male and female. David reminds us, however, that Romola "worships" the icon of a god-man Savonarola, who taught her to accept "benevolent subjugation." Margaret Homans remarks that Romola's role has always been that of "transmission" rather than of "vision" and that this trait, in fact, separates Romola from others of Eliot's magnificent women in that, while Maggie and Dorothea desire their own words "and in their early imaginativeness they appear to be artist figures," Romola has never intended to be an original, but rather a translator and transmitter. Ruby Redinger suggests that since Romola is the character into whom Eliot claims to have put "the best of myself," the chastened and humble life of the formerly mythic goddess is a "self-flagellation for her creator," who has strayed from the selfless goals she forces Romola to fulfill. Alison Booth, however, insists that Romola "unleashes her eloquence" as a mentor-guardian herself, and Dianne Sadoff says that Romola is scourged for having her own desires apart from those of the "fathers" and "brothers" who surround her and dictate to her but that she "purges fathers and brothers from the narrative and so achieves a purified, virtually female society." Finally, in Felicia Bonaparte's reading of the novel as epic, Romola is a comprehensive figure including pagan earth mother, the Virgin, and Comtean womanhood—the attainment of the quest being "salvation," which is symbolically realized in Romola's adoption of the childlike Tessa and her chil-

---

cism that Vitaglione calls "selfish," "reactionary," and "egotistic"), she recalls Sand's *Lélia* and *Spiridion* and that the novel, like Sand's, shows that "to look for God outside human emotions was to escape responsibility and suffering" (*George Eliot and George Sand,* 45–48).

dren.[36] From the foregoing litany, it is apparent that the status of Eliot's chastened Madonna is especially troubling for feminist readings.

Romola is a novel about silencing; both the dictator Savonarola and the patriot Romola are silenced. Midway through the novel Savonarola's insistent and authoritative voice has replaced for Romola the lyric, "liquid," gentle, "melting" voice of the faithless Tito. And, as Beryl Gray says, Savonarola's "movingly powerful personality is distilled as the influence of a voice—a voice that, in the course of the novel, penetrates, swells, fades and is eternally silenced."[37] The title of the novel's final chapter, "The Last Silence," refers specifically to the recanting of Bernardo del Nero, Romola's martyred godparent, who tells his brethren, "Pray for me, for God has withdrawn from me the spirit of prophecy" (*R*, 576). But Bernardo's is not the only silence.

Ironically it is because the Frate has taught Romola to listen to the voice *within* herself that she gains the courage to become, like him, a sacred rebel—even to the point that she has raised her voice against his, saying, "And therefore I must speak" (*R*, 490). She proceeds to charge him with spiritual blindness and deafness—with assuming that his party is God's party, his speech, God's voice. When the doomed prophet admits as much, Romola responds that God's kingdom is something wider than his vision, then "hastily covered her head and went out *in silence*" (*R*, 492, italics mine). When Savonarola is finally silenced in martyrdom, therefore, Romola has already been silenced by failed rhetoric. In *Romola*, silencing would seem to be the outcome for the brave and the pure—including Bernardo, Dino, Savonarola, and Romola. And although her deeds speak volumes, Romola's voice in fact is never attended as Dinah Morris's is; neither her father nor husband gives credence to her desires for scholarship, she never writes the book she intended for her father, and her Antigone-like boldness does not reverse the decree of Savonarola. Dinah pleads to the masses in a public forum, but Romola pleads to one man in private chamber—yet she does this in regard to public consequences: the execution of Bernardo and four fellow patriots, an act that will deprive Florentine citizens of an appeals process that the Frate himself had endorsed as a safeguard in the judicial system. In this action Romola has become a politician, as in her charitable works she has become a philanthropist. As Dinah is at the end restricted to acts of charity and impromptu teaching on the small scale, Romola too has scaled down her expectations in lecturing morality

36. Simpson, "Mapping *Romola*: Physical Space, Women's Place," 64; David, *Intellectual Women and Victorian Patriarchy*, 192–95; Homans, *Bearing the Word*, 217; Redinger, *George Eliot: The Emergent Self*, 454; Booth, "The Silence of Great Men: Statuesque Femininity and the Ending of *Romola*," 117; Sadoff, *Monsters of Affection: Dickens, Eliot, and Bronte on Fatherhood*, 92; Bonaparte, *The Triptych and the Cross: The Central Myths of George Eliot's Poetic Imagination*, 244.

37. Gray, "Power and Persuasion: Voices of Influence in *Romola*," 124.

to a teenage boy instead of a mighty prophet/politician. Neither woman loses any of her nobility or stateliness; in both cases it is to the credit, or blame, of the religious authorities that she is deprived of a public voice.

Romola is, after all, based in part on Eliot's close friend Barbara Bodichon, who was a landscape painter, a writer on the political and educational disadvantages of women, a cofounder of Girton College for women, and a member of the feminist group known as Langham Place Circle, which founded a journal and in the 1850s campaigned for women's education, jobs, suffrage, and property rights. Furthermore, Bodichon was not silenced. Nor, Alison Booth notes in her disappointment over the outcome for Romola, is she "transfixed as a humorless, asexual madonna exemplifying the Comtean idea of 'woman as moral providence of the species.'"[38] The political and social activism of Bodichon, as well as her associate Bessie Parkes (also an Eliot friend), and perhaps Florence Nightingale (whom Eliot praises in her correspondence), suggests the efficacy of Romola's salvific works as doctor, nurse, social worker, and educator—although one is still troubled by the question of why she teaches a son but not a daughter. Yet as a public prophetess or sibyl, she has been rendered mute.

The only reading of *Romola* that can construe the epilogue as anything other than a manifestation of the Erinna complex is that of the heroine as a symbol for Italy, and it seems to me a perfectly legitimate interpretation to read Eliot's Renaissance novel as *both/and*, rather than *either/or*. I have previously noted that Romola is Florence as Corinne is Italy; therefore she can represent, as Andrew Thompson eloquently suggests, not merely her own Florence in need of her ministrations to its illness, perfidy, intrigue, hunger, and plague but also for modern Italy of the *Risorgimento*—just as Corinne is at once the Italy of past glory and the postrevolutionary France of Staël's age. While Madonna Romola, then, is a character who has lost father, brother, husband, and voice, Italy is a suffering *mother*land that had repeatedly lost in its various attempts to oust Metternich, quell violence and assassinations, bargain with the pope, appease the French emperor, undermine espionage, unify the various provinces, and become a nation. Thompson says,

> it is Romola herself who emerges as the symbol of hope for Italy. Like the statuesque "Italia," she has endured political treachery, feuding and the influence of a corrupt Church in Florence, and been drawn to the brink of despairing self-destruction. . . . Eliot writes her own prophecy for the future of Italy which encompasses the whole of its past history, in the Petrarchan image of the heavenly Laura, Dante's Beatrice, the Madonna and "Italia" nurturing and protecting her children.[39]

38. Booth, *Greatness Engendered: George Eliot and Virginia Woolf,* 154.
39. Thompson, *George Eliot and Italy,* 82.

In this interpretation, Mother Italy, like Madonna Romola, is for the moment silenced and powerless, but nonetheless brave and hopeful.

Dorothea as Muse and Madonna

George Eliot put some of Marian Evans in each of her monumental women—and to a lesser extent her diminutive ones as well—from young Maggie's love of Sir Walter Scott to Esther Lyon's girlhood passion for Lord Byron, from Romola's care for an ailing father to Maggie's grief over an estranged brother, from Maggie's renunciation of art and beauty to Armgart's desire for glory and applause. But Dorothea Brooke, the heroine of *Middlemarch* (1872), is more like George Eliot than any of her fictional portraits, says the man who ought best to know, G. H. Lewes, who calls Dorothea the "cream of lovely womanhood" (*GEL,* 5:308). Weighing in with his own share of praise, Eliot's publisher, John Blackwood, considers Dorothea "better than any sermon that was ever preached" (*GEL,* 5:307). Putting aside for the nonce the accolades from two men who had every reason to praise and flatter a woman who apparently very much needed it, one might ask why Eliot's Dorothea is considered so remarkable when in fact she fails in almost everything she attempts, and is by her own admission "shortsighted," "blind," "dull," and "ignorant"—terms she repeatedly uses to characterize her learning, practicality, aesthetic awareness, and artistic taste.

At times Dorothea's blunders are comic: stooping to tie the unfashionable shoelaces of her pedantic husband, Casaubon, as if he were a Protestant pope; aspiring to become like Milton's miserable daughters, who could pronounce the classical languages but not understand them (in other words, wishing to be Romola); failing to recognize that Will Ladislaw is in love with her; renouncing her deceased mother's jewels only to choose the most rare and ostentatious of them, thereby prompting her naive cherub of a sister to observe, "Dorothea is not always consistent" (*M,* 17). Even her failed attempt for art appreciation serves as an apt analogy for her quest for vocation: In Rome, on her wedding journey with Casaubon, she enters a room filled with frescoes or paintings and is overcome with awe—but examining the works one by one, she finds that for her the life goes out of them. Similarly, examining Dorothea's projects one by one, the reader finds that the life goes out of them as well. She makes a bad first marriage (against the warnings of family and friends), is dissuaded from her plan to improve the cottages of the tenantry, gives up the even more grandiose project to establish a model village and school of industry, fails to attain the education she seeks, makes a colossal blunder in asking her estranged husband to become benefactor to Ladislaw—the very man whom he jealously despises. To this litany one can object that in the second half of the novel Dorothea manages to do some things right, although none of these accomplishments is singular: She marries a curly haired dilettante, Will Ladislaw, whom her friends consider a second "short-sighted" mistake in the marital department but whom she loves and helps to turn into a public man; she makes a loan to Lydgate, a desperate Middlemarch medical practitioner, thus enabling him to pay off a debt to a benefactor of more-than-questionable motives and morality; and she reunites Lydgate with his preening, shallow, manipulative wife, Rosamond. Until the second marriage materializes, however, Eliot's heroine is still very much at loose ends; if there is not enough challenge in her life—that is, if nobody needs flannel and nobody's pig has died—Dorothea wonders, What is a philanthropic woman to do with her life in a small, provincial city? Of the newly married Dorothea Ladislaw at the novel's conclusion, Dorothea Barrett says

> Dorothea is marred from the first by an innocence verging at times on stupidity and by its attendant short-sightedness. She and Lydgate are struggling from equally impure and short-sighted beginnings towards fuller awareness. Lydgate learns from his experience, but Dorothea learns regrettably little. Her obtuseness has many roots in her education, her available options, the medium in which she moves, and the psychological distortions likely to appear under such conditions.[40]

The saintliness within Dorothea is not to be measured by what Eliot's modern-day saint accomplishes.[41] Eliot in fact stresses at both beginning and end of the novel that the sum of her heroine's achievements is small for a woman who yearns to "deck herself in knowledge" and "make life beautiful—I mean everybody's life" (*M*, 86, 216). Rather it is in the monumentality of the Dorothea myth, accomplished by allusions to Saint Theresa, Saint Barbara, the Virgin Mary, Saint Clara, a Christian Antigone, Psyche, and Beatrice/Laura—in other words, making her a potential Corinne/Consuelo. Dorothea is meant to be read as great of heart, pure in intention, unselfish in aim, unaffected in demeanor, hungry for knowledge, humble in her ignorance—the ideal woman as Daniel Deronda is the ideal man. Further, she is also Eliot's attempt to combine all the best qualities of the statuesque sibyls, or would-be sibyls, of the previous novels. Like Maggie and Romola, Dorothea wants to become a learned woman. Like Dinah, Maggie, and Romola, and Sand's Consuelo and Jewsbury's Bianca as well, she shuns artifice and vanity for a nunlike simplicity. As Maggie or Romola wish, she

---

40. Barrett, *Vocation and Desire*, 152.

41. Kathleen Blake argues that love becomes vocation for women in *Middlemarch*, that Mary Garth and Dorothea Brooke succeed in making men, Fred Vincy and Will Ladislaw respectively; thus in influencing Will's support of the "far-resonant action" of the Reform Bill, Dorothea is after all a Saint Theresa (*Love and the Woman Question*, 40–46).

desires to apprentice herself to a great author or scholar, a Jeremy Taylor or John Milton—a trait that, according to Redinger, reflects Marian Evans's willingness to spend herself as an assistant to Spencer, Brabant, or Chapman, editor of the *Westminster Review*. Alexander Welsh notes, however, that among the questers of the novel Dorothea also stands out in that she alone does not also seek fame— making her lack of fame as a Saint Theresa in an unvisited tomb all the more regrettable. Alan Mintz suggests in fact that the ideal of vocation "suffuses the whole range of work-related themes in *Middlemarch* with a kind of desperate spirituality" and that vocation ultimately becomes a desire that by definition cannot be fulfilled.[42] Male characters like Casaubon, Lydgate, Ladislaw, Farebrother, and Brooke quest for scientific knowledge, political influence, or scholarly insight, but among the female characters, which include Dorothy's sister, Celia, and Mary Garth and Rosamond Vincy in the younger generation, together with a gaggle of aunts, mothers, and pastors' ladies, only Dorothy quests for knowledge. As the narrator says with obvious pity, "[S]he wished, poor child, to be wise herself" (*M*, 64). This questing trait puts her in a category outside typical womanhood and emphasizes her exceptionality. Of the ordinariness of her accomplishment at the end of an epic quest, the narrator of *Middlemarch* says, "Many who knew her thought it a pity that so substantive and rare a creature should have been absorbed into the life of another and be only known in a certain circle as a wife and mother. But no one stated exactly what else that was in her power she ought rather to have done" (*M*, 809). Like Dorothea herself, her contemporaries and her readers are at a loss to recommend a profession for such a gifted, striving woman. In marrying, mothering, and "absorbing" herself into Will's political aspirations, she seems merely to fulfill the "Angel of the House" ideal in much of Victorian literature—and Eliot has led us to expect something far more original for Dorothea.

Dorothea is different things to different characters, but like other Eliot heroines, she is usually perceived in the eyes (and ears) of men, defined and preserved in their masculine language. To Ladislaw, she is Diana and he, her worshiper; her voice is, like Corinne's, an Aeolian harp; also like Corinne, she is a Beatrice and Laura. But this would-be Dante or Petrarch who considers Dorothea herself a poem cannot get around to "writing" her, and—his talent for poetry being no higher than his genius for painting—his prosaic "conversation" has to substitute for sonnets (*M*, 352). At the Vatican she is spotted by the painter Adolf Naumann, to whom she is "the most perfect young Madonna I ever saw" and a "Christian Antigone—sensuous force controlled by spiritual passion" (*M*, 187). To Tertius

42. Redinger, *George Eliot: The Emergent Self,* 210; Welsh, *George Eliot and Blackmail,* 238–39; Mintz, *George Eliot and the Novel of Vocation,* 6–7.

Lydgate, whose neck she saves by her timely intervention in his personal and professional life, she has a "heart large enough for the Virgin Mary" (*M*, 746). And
her voice reminds good Caleb Garth of the strains of Handel's *Messiah* (*M*, 534).
Tall, dark-haired Dorothea is juxtaposed as authentic Ariadne to the blonde
"stage Ariadne," Rosamond Lydgate. As Karen Chase remarks, Rosamond invites
a hypothesis of egoism, Dorothea one of altruism; Dorothea is a current through
whom good flows, Rosamond a consuming vortex.[43] As the regal Ariadne, Dorothea is abandoned in the labyrinth of Rome by her moribund Theseus or Mino-
taur on his search for the "key" to all mythology, and her would-be rescuer Ladislaw proves a more loyal and dependable lover than Romola's Dionysian Tito is
for Romola/Ariadne. The Saint Theresa allusion suggests not only devotion and
service, but also fire and intensity (as, for example, in the famous Bernini sculpture), and the Ariadne sculpture in the Vatican, mistaken for the voluptuous
Cleopatra, leads one to conclude that at least part of Dorothea's fire is sexual intensity—the "sensuous force" that Naumann immediately sees in her.

Her erotic womanhood is also suggested in that Dorothea is, like Consuelo
and Barrett Browning's Aurora Leigh, a Psyche in search of her Cupid—her impulses for good usually characterized as "ardour," a term generally connected with
sexual love. When Casaubon on the honeymoon finally takes a rare few minutes
for Dorothea, he proposes that she might like to see Raphael's Cupid and Psyche, but he launches into such a pedantic explanation of the work's authenticity
that any beauty or possible allegory of the piece is lost upon Dorothea. To
Casaubon's query, Dorothea demonstrates indifference to their seeking out the
sculpture. This lack of curiosity on her part is significant in that she has repressed
sexual desire in order to follow her doctrine that the most appropriate husband
is a father figure and to serve as helpmate to the "embalmed" pedant Casaubon.
Thus in Rome, when she again finds Will, or rather is found by him, she gives
no conscious credence to his obvious attraction as Bacchus/Eros to her Ariadne/
Psyche. The Cupid/Psyche myth is that which George Sand uses in *La Comtesse
de Rudolstadt* to suggest Consuelo's discovery of passion for Liverani, an awakening that she has experienced with neither her childhood love, Anzoleto, nor
the esteemed and spiritual Albert, whom she has married at the conclusion of
Consuelo. Like Consuelo, whose adult sexuality emerges in the second volume of
the *Consuelo* novels, or like Aurora, who finally realizes her passionate love for
her cousin, Romney, Dorothea is not merely an anemic and asexual Madonna
but a woman of suppressed fire and passion. Such ardor may be diverted into sexual love, political or social reform, or—as in Consuelo's case—creating art. Once

43. Chase, *Eros and Psyche: The Representation of Personality in Charlotte Brontë, Charles Dickens, and
George Eliot*, 166, 173.

Casaubon is in the grave and Dorothea comes to understand that Will loves her, she throws away her inheritance and the esteem of the community in marriage to the handsome "foreigner" or "gypsy" that her friends cannot respect. Like Sand's Consuelo, she is a Psyche who has belatedly found her Cupid—and has in the process burned *herself* with the heated wax of her candle.[44] By means of the Cupid/Psyche myth, Eliot suggests a potential marriage between subjectivity and channeled activity, ardor and energy.

Dorothea is also extraordinary because of her religion—and because she becomes a religion. She has studied Taylor, Keble's *Christian Year,* and various other texts, but her faith is as natural and unpretentious as the silver-gray nunlike dress she wears. She believes that it is better to believe the best of people than to suspect the worst, that "by desiring what is perfectly good, even when we don't quite know what it is and cannot do what we would, we are part of the Divine power against evil—widening the skirts of light and making the struggle with darkness narrower" (*M,* 381). This revelation alone, together with her attempt to live her faith, makes Dorothea a modern Sophia. For Dorothea seeks a mission— a place to pour her energies, divest herself of her money, invest her power to love. The Santa Clara portrait of Naumann suggests voluntary poverty for the welfare of others, and Dorothea often considers her wealth a burden that she is glad to give away—but one allusion to suggest the depth of her self-sacrificial religion.[45] The novel is in fact a nostalgic yearning for the Golden Age, which, according to legend, was not a lockstep march through "middling" issues and reforms, but was when "ardent deeds" took shape and produced significant outcomes—for example, Theresa finding a vocation and founding an order, or Antigone burying a brother and exhibiting "heroic piety" that shook loose a tyrant. Middlemarch, though, expects and produces only "middling" accomplishments. Dorothea is silenced because she has the misfortune to be born into this diminished age, to be extraordinary in a world in which she can find neither a place for her feminine creativity and power nor a society that requires anything more of her than to be an obedient daughter, discreet widow, and behind-the-scenes wife. Adams finds the Madonna figure in *Middlemarch* more limiting than liberating, Dorothea being merely a "decorative Virgin" defined by the voyeuristic gaze of men who admire her, desire her, or hope to see their best selves reflected in her.[46] As Dinah's only message will live through her children and Romola's through Tito's

44. Rosamond is not only a stage Ariadne to Dorothea's true article; she is also a "sculpture Psyche modeled to look another way," rather than to follow Lydgate with her eyes (*M,* 622).

45. See Alan Mintz's commentary on Dorothea as Santa Clara, the thirteenth-century noblewoman of Assisi who took the vow of poverty and founded the rule of the "Poor Clares." Mintz considers Dorothea a secular Santa Clara and her commentary to Will in chapter 37 about her "kingdom" and her "rule" as reference to her benevolent order (*George Eliot and the Novel of Vocation,* 105).

46. Adams, *Our Lady of Victorian Feminism,* 185, 165, 186–90.

child, Dorothea is silenced in that her voice will not be heard, and her deeds will be felt only on the small scale in her home and immediate community.

As for Eliot's Erinna complex, it is less debilitating in the spiritual sense in those women who desire good (Dorothea, Romola, Maggie, Dinah) than among those who desire attention (Armgart, Gwendolen, the Alcharisi). But as George Eliot knew from her own experience—and as her female artists demonstrate—she who is the true artist desires both passion and performance, aesthetic creativity and accolades. Dorothea accepts her diminished life, saying, "I might have done something better if I had been better. But this is what I am going to do" (*M*, 796). She accepts the silence with more grace than do most of George Eliot's Erinna characters.

Woman as Songbird in *Mr. Gilfil's Love-Story*

Before Dinah, Maggie, Romola, and Dorothea, however, there was Caterina Sarti, George Eliot's first silenced singer. The novella *Mr. Gilfil's Love-Story* was begun Christmas Day 1856, published in 1857 in *Blackwood's*, and later was the second of three stories collected in *Scenes of Clerical Life*, the book that launched Eliot's career in the world of fiction. Gilfil is the beloved clergyman whose death at the beginning of the novella prompts the recollection of his "love-story" of the previous century, specifically the summer of 1788. The only love of Gilfil's young manhood is the "songbird" Caterina who—although she never aspires to perform on stage—is a gifted contralto with the temperament and imagination of an artist. As George Sand does in *Consuelo*, Eliot employs the Orpheus/Eurydice myth to express the art of music and supreme romantic love. Maynard Gilfil is Eliot's stalwart Orpheus who saves Caterina/Eurydice by the transcendent charms of music, only to lose her a second time when, as his young wife, she dies in childbirth. Her second death is, like Consuelo's, a silencing—but Caterina dies as artist *and* as woman, while Sand does not pursue her narrative beyond the end of *La Comtesse de Rudolstadt* to explain whether Consuelo's soul dies with her voice.

Like Staël's Corinne, Sand's Consuelo, Jewsbury's Bianca, and Barrett Browning's Aurora, and Hawthorne's Miriam of *The Marble Faun*, George Eliot's first musical heroine is Italian, a trait that by 1857 bordered on stereotype—yet a means by which Eliot, like her English predecessors, can acknowledge the influence of her French matriarchs, especially Sand.[47] Louise Hudd in fact suggests that Eliot owes much of the depiction of Caterina to *Aurora Leigh*, which Eliot had read in 1856 and again in 1857; Hudd notes not only Caterina's transplanta-

47. The artists Corinne, Bianca, Aurora, and Miriam have one English and one Italian parent.

tion from Italy to a "caged bird" life in England, but also her name as possible reference to Barrett Browning's "Catarina to Camoens," about the "abandonment of a faithless lover, a decline into early death, and the voicing of the female response to male objectification."[48] Eliot in fact reviewed *Aurora Leigh* for the *Westminster Review* and applauded it as "poetical *body*" informed by *"soul"*—a great poem displaying the powers but not the "negations" of the female sex.[49] Eliot's Caterina has great fawn-like eyes, pretty little ears and feet, striking olive skin, and a diminutiveness that caused everyone to consider her as a child or a little fairy. This timid heroine contrasts with Eliot's tall, statuesque goddesses like Maggie, Dinah, Romola, Gwendolen, and Dorothea but parallels another doll-like figure, the singer Mirah Lapidoth in *Daniel Deronda*. Thomson notes that the "passionate, artless little Italian waif, black-eyed, black-haired," is also like Consuelo, the orphaned daughter of an impoverished musician.[50] Music speaks to Caterina and through her, as it does through greater luminaries like Sand's Consuelo and Daniella. And like Corinne, as well as both of Caterina's parents, the Italian orphan is silenced by an untimely death.

Caterina is known as Tina by the Cheverels, the English family who bring her to England upon the death of her father, a primo tenore of a single season who "trod the stage in satin and feathers," then "completely lost his voice in the following winter, and had ever since been little better than a cracked fiddle, which is good for nothing but firewood" (*SCL*, 1:160–61). Already in Eliot's earliest creative works, then, is the curse of an artist deprived of a voice—in the case of Sarti, without his operatic career to earn his livelihood, he and his *bambinetta* have subsisted on his copy work until the weakened man succumbs to death. Sarti has become acquainted with the English gentry because Lady Cheverel herself is an accomplished soprano and Sarti has been engaged to copy music for her. The dying tenor believes that his grimy, undernourished child will be provided for by the kind English family, and in this hope he is not mistaken.

The Cheverels make Tina into Lady Cheverel's "protégée"; she is collected by the tourists, Jennifer Uglow says, "like an *objet d'art*." The Cheverels, as it happens, are in Italy to collect architectural ideas for Sir Christopher Cheverel's hobby of refurbishing his manor house in Italianate Gothic style; thus the dark "marmoset" that they carry home could be considered as just another of their acquisitions, another symbol of their infatuation with all things Italian. Andrew Thompson, who traces the influences of *Corinne* and *Aurora Leigh,* but not *Consuelo,* on *Mr. Gilfil's Love-Story,* notes that in fictions of Staël, Barrett Browning,

48. Hudd, "The Politics of a Feminist Poetics: 'Armgart' and George Eliot's Critical Response to *Aurora Leigh,*" 70.
49. Eliot, "Belles Lettres," 206.
50. Thomson, *George Sand and the Victorians,* 169.

and Eliot, England consistently represents rigidity, "masculine linearity," and the mind, while warm, "feminine" Italy is poetry, art, individualism, and the passions.[51] When the little Italian-prattling toddler arrives in England, she promptly wins the hearts of the servants, who were initially prejudiced against "furriners"—especially those from Papist countries where people eat too much garlic. The growth of little Tina from mischievous child to artistic woman parallels the realization of the Cheverels' other Italian project, the artistic renovation of the manor house: "While Cheverel Manor was growing from ugliness into beauty, Caterina too was growing from a little yellow bantling into a whiter maiden with . . . a voice that, in its low-toned tenderness, recalled the love-notes of the stock dove . . ." (*SCL,* 1:176).

Tina is everybody's darling, including Maynard Gilfil's. Especially, though, Tina responds to the love of her surrogate father, Sir Christopher Cheverel, her "Padroncello" to whom she is a "black-eyed monkey" and "little song bird." Caterina's position in the household is an ambiguous one—she is neither family nor servant. Lady Cheverel had intended that the dark-eyed child grow up to be an assistant to the lady's maid, to sort worsteds, keep accounts, read aloud and supply the place of spectacles "when her ladyship's eyes should wax dim" (*SCL,* 1:165). Tina is sometimes pampered like an only child, but sometimes treated like a servant by the lord and lady of the manor: told to carry Lady Cheverel's cushions, fetch the embroidery patterns, bring out the table for piquet, and play the harpsichord and sing for the entertainment of the household and their occasional guests. Naturally the musical accomplishments of a daughter would have been similarly displayed, and a daughter would certainly have been asked to make her parents comfortable in the domestic space of the home, but several aspects of the story make clear that the Cheverels do not consider Tina on a level with themselves: She is not made the Cheverel heir, Lady Cheverel's orders are issued in the somewhat imperious fashion that the lady of the manor uses when speaking to her staff, and the Cheverels are completely deaf and blind to Tina's love for Sir Christopher's nephew and heir, Captain Anthony Wybrow, simply because it has never occurred to them that she could presume to dream of someone of *their* sphere.

Caterina's remarkable musical talent is not, like Consuelo's, displayed on a stage to earn her livelihood, but in an odd way Caterina *is* a professional. Because of her remarkable voice, she has been awarded with training by an Italian music master and is intended for marriage to the country curate Maynard Gilfil, rather than being deprived of an education and relegated to the servant class. Sir

51. Uglow, *George Eliot,* 86; Thompson, *George Eliot and Italy,* 50–54. Thompson interprets the dual themes of all three works to be the repression of women "whose voices are suppressed" and of whole cultures as represented by Italy (66).

Christopher's teasing title "minstrel of the Manor" has after all a ring of truth. Not that Tina minds her role as minstrel; she is happiest when playing and singing—in part because of the beauty and passion of the music and also "because she [is] queen of the room" when she performs (*SCL*, 1:198).

Ironically, though, it is this free circulation with the family and the patriarchal indulgence of Sir Christopher that set the stage for Caterina's tragedy. For as the "little kitten" Hetty Sorrel of *Adam Bede* gives herself to Arthur Donnithorne, the "humming-bird" Caterina Sarti succumbs to the kisses, caresses, and flirtations of the Cheverels' heir, Wybrow—surrendering not her virginity as Hetty does, but only her heart, a detail that allows her to marry as Gilfil's restored Eurydice. But Wybrow, whom the aging Sir Christopher imagines as the repository of the Cheverel future once he is married and head of a family, is afflicted with heart problems in both the literal and metaphorical sense: He counts his alarmingly rapid pulse beats, is attended by a "Dr. Hart," and fails to return Tina's love because nature has endowed him with a heart capable of loving only himself—a flaw that Eliot contrasts to tender-hearted Tina, whose only talents lie in music and in loving.[52] Wybrow contracts a marriage endorsed by his uncle, brings his intended, Miss Assher, and her mother for a visit to Cheverel Manor, complains in private that the jealousy of Beatrice Assher and Caterina Sarti cause him palpitations while at the same time he perversely incites jealousy in both rivals, then dies prematurely of a heart attack before the marriage can be solemnized and, luckily for Tina, also before she can stab him with the dagger that she has concealed for that very purpose. Eliot makes obvious use of the "heart" motif with both Wybrow and Tina: In the case of the singer, her voice, when low and soft, is "whisperin' close to your heart like," she matures to passionate womanhood with a grown-up "heart that knows triumph and hate" (*SCL*, 1:135, 198), her heart "contracts" when the gardener praises the beauty of her competitor but is lifted from pain by singing, and she plans to stab her fickle love, Wybrow, in the heart. Instead, she finds his dead body at their designated point of rendezvous, suffers an emotional collapse brought on by the "madness" of her passion and realization of what she very nearly did, and she runs away.

Eliot's Orpheus and Eurydice

The faithful Gilfil, a Samson-like fellow who has adored Tina since they played and fished together as children, rescues her, lodges her with his married sister,

52. For a study of the Narcissus/Echo myth in *Mr. Gilfil's Love-Story*, see Joseph Wiesenfarth's *George Eliot's Mythmaking*, 63–67. Beautiful Wybrow falls in love with his own face in the mirror, and Tina as Echo is characterized by her voice, Wiesenfarth says, going on to note that a different myth, Orpheus/Eurydice, delineates Caterina's other love story, that with Gilfil (68–69).

and gives her a harpsichord in the hope that music will minister to a mind and heart diseased. Gilfil's prescription is effectual; Christina Sarti's soul is "born anew to music . . . born anew to love" (*SCL*, 1:295). André DeCuir comments that although Caterina has performed in her role as "private property" of the Cheverel estate, her talent could not serve as medium through which she can release her autonomous self, but that her rejuvenation finally comes through her own art, not through domestication by Gilfil.[53] While I agree with DeCuir on the power of Caterina's art, I insist that Gilfil's diagnosis includes her need for music—else he would not be, as he is in the mythic structure of the tale, her Orpheus and would not have given her the musical instrument that she plays during her recovery. But when Caterina Sarti becomes Tina Gilfil, Eliot makes no further reference to her continuing her art. Within her first year as wife, she dies in childbirth and leaves Reverend Gilfil to grieve for a lifetime, converting a room of the vicarage to a shrine in her memory.

Nobody in the novella, not even the stalwart Maynard Gilfil, who is strong, large, and dependable on the order of Eliot's Adam Bede and Hardy's Gabriel Oak, is prepared to understand the strength of Tina's adult passion nor to treat her as a morally responsible adult. She is a "kitten," "marmoset," "little grasshopper," "linnet," "little minx," "dark-eyed monkey," "little simpleton" and "fragile cyclamen" to the doting and attentive men in the novel (Sir Christopher, the Captain, Gilfil, and "Uncle" Bates, the gardener). Most often she is an "unobtrusive little singing bird" (*SCL*, 1:198) "beginning to flutter and vainly dash its soft breast against the hard iron bars of the inevitable" (*SCL*, 1:158) as Aurora Leigh does, and after Wybrow's death, she flies from Cheverel Manor like an uncaged bird, to be lost to Gilfil as Eurydice is to Orpheus. In the songbird figures, Caterina anticipates the "half-reared linnet" Mirah Lapidoth in *Daniel Deronda* (*DD*, 378), a singer whose little voice has a "cooing tenderness" and is as "spontaneous as bird-notes" (*DD*, 582). In *Mr. Gilfil's Love-Story*, even the consciously male voice of the narrator is caught up in diminutives: Tina is usually the "poor little thing" or "poor child." Eliot here makes a point that not only the characters but also the narrator have misjudged, and because they do, they deprive Tina of full, mature participation in the great human story of learning compassion by one's own suffering—for in Eliot's philosophy suffering makes anyone—artist-god or ordinary mortal—truly humane. Even Maynard hears her confession of her "wicked," murderous intent in regard to stabbing Wybrow and assures her that she is not morally culpable because not mature enough to control her passions: "You have seen the little birds . . . how all their feathers are ruffled when they are frightened or angry; they have no power over themselves. . . .

53. DeCuir, "Italy, England, and the Female Artist in George Eliot's 'Mr. Gilfil's Love-Story,'" 71–74.

You were like one of those little birds . . ." (*SCL*, 1:287). Gilfil loves Tina so much that he, as a morally mature, rescuing Orpheus, will protect her under his manly wing as one would enfold a child.[54]

On the other hand, Gilfil's pastoral lesson to Sir Christopher *does* teach pure adult humanity, which Eliot invariably insists as the great lesson of life: "We can hardly learn humility and tenderness except by suffering" (*SCL*, 1:272). Moreover, Tina's dagger, foiled murder, and guilt when the death is accomplished without her interference are recalled in Gwendolen Harleth Grandcourt's "small and sharp [knife], like a long willow leaf in a silver sheath" (*DD*, 691), her temptation to use it on Grandcourt, and her remorse when he drowns as she has wished. The significant difference, however, is that Gwendolen is considered morally an adult, not a feather-brained child; Deronda, as confessor and guardian angel, as well as a mirror to Gilfil's pastoral role to Tina, does not dismiss the murderous desire—instead, he tells Gwendolen that her desire to escape evil, rather than to embrace it, is the universal human challenge.

Although Caterina Sarti is not as fascinating as Eliot's Madonnas and goddesses, she *does* illustrate the soul and suffering of both woman and artist—and a woman whose heart finds solace in her art. While the narcissistic Wybrow copes with this love quadrangle by worshiping his cameo-like visage in the mirror, Beatrice Assher by petulance and tantrums, and Gilfil by watching over Caterina like a self-appointed guardian angel, Caterina pours her suffering into an art that is enriched by means of that suffering:

> And her singing—the one thing in which she ceased to be passive, and became prominent—lost none of its energy. She herself sometimes wondered how it was that, whether she felt sad or angry, crushed with the sense of Anthony's indifference, or burning with impatience under Miss Assher's attentions, it was always a relief to her to sing. Those full deep notes she sent forth seemed to be lifting the pain from her heart—seemed to be carrying away the madness from her brain. (*SCL*, 1:228–29)

An artist, however, cannot live perpetually in an aesthetic world, and when Tina ceases to sing, the pain, jealousy, and madness return. It remains for her Orpheus to save her from the pain of unrequited love and to resurrect her to a new life "nestled" in his home.

George Eliot knew George Sand's work and had long been an admirer and defender of Sand. References in her correspondence show that she had read *Con-*

---

54. Knoepflmacher argues that Gilfil cannot aspire to become an Orpheus because he is "bound to the material world" but that Tina "becomes a full-blown Romantic" after the order of Emily Brontë's Catherine Earnshaw (*George Eliot's Early Novels,* 72, 65–66).

suelo and a half-dozen other Sand works before 1847.[55] It may be pure coincidence that she uses the same myth for her first artist novel that Sand used for
Consuelo; in any case she does not reverse the myth as Sand does by having Eurydice become the savior/guide of Orpheus as Consuelo leads Albert through the
labyrinth of Hades and out into the world of light. In both works, however, it is
the woman, not the Orpheus character, who is singer/musician; Albert is a lesser artist than Consuelo, and Gilfil is not a musician at all but a devotee of the
music that is inseparable from his love. The Eurydice myth is made specific in
Eliot's story in that of an evening Sir Christopher likes to be entertained by his
little Christina at the harpsichord singing his favorite airs from Gluck and Pae-
siello. Of the two, the "Che farò senza Eurydice?" of Gluck's *Orfeo ed Eurydice*
recurs as motif (the operatic work, in fact, that is also the vehicle for Eliot's Armgart, who performs the role of Orpheus). Both songs, however, are yearnings
for lost love, and Caterina sings them with power and feeling because her singing
permits an outpouring of her passion for Anthony; she is rather indifferent to
Maynard Gilfil's suffering, paying no heed that the music speaks to his heart as
well.

The words that one lover sings to another prove especially important in Eliot's
novels: in *The Mill on the Floss* Philip Wakem sings for Maggie "Ah! perchè non
posso odiarti" (I love thee still) from the opera *Somnambula* in which the soprano abandons the tenor for another man—as Maggie will do (*MF*, 436); in *Daniel
Deronda* Klesmer plays for Catherine his own composition of Heine's "Ich hab
dich geliebet und liebe dich noch" (I loved thee once, I love thee still [*DD*, 244]).
Fittingly, then, it is music—to Eliot the most divine of art forms—that calls Tina
to life again when she plays Gilfil's harpsichord:

> The vibration rushed through Caterina like an electric shock: it seemed as if in
> that instant a new soul were entering into her, and filling her with a deeper,
> more significant life. . . . In a moment her fingers were wandering with their
> old sweet method among the keys, and her soul was floating in its true famil-
> iar element of delicious sound, as the water-plant that lies withered and shrunk-
> en on the ground expands into freedom and beauty when once more bathed in
> its native flood. (*SCL*, 1:294)

When Caterina is resurrected to life and love, the first work she sings is the
same air she has so often sung for Sir Christopher, Gluck's "Che farò," signifying that she as Gilfil's Eurydice has been saved. Christoph Willibald von Gluck's
work was first performed at Vienna in 1762 to celebrate the emperor's name day;

---

55. Thomson, *George Sand and the Victorians*, 154.

thus in deference to the joyous occasion the tragic ending of Eurydice's second death is modified to comic resolution or, as Gluck called it, an "azione teatrale."[56] In Raniero de' Calzabrigi's libretto, therefore, the lovers are not eternally parted, but the love god Amor hears Orpheus's anguished cry and restores Eurydice to him. George Eliot saw this version in Berlin just two years before writing *Mr. Gilfil's Love-Story* and complained:

> The scene in Elysium is immensely absurd—Ballet girls dance in the foreground and in the background are Greek shades looking like butchers in *chemises*. But the worst of it is, that instead of letting it be a tragedy, Euridice is brought to life again and we end with another Ballet girl scene before Amor's temple. (*GEL*, 2:191)

In *Mr. Gilfil's Love-Story* Eliot restores the Virgilian and Ovidian tragic element in that Eurydice finds herself in the afterlife, not in the powerful arms of Orpheus, and the novella concludes with an epilogue to Maynard Gilfil, the kindly vicar of Shepperton and the faithful Orpheus who has mourned a lifetime for his twice-lost Eurydice. In the person of the diminutive Caterina/Eurydice, however, Eliot presents an artist whose spiritual dimension has been stunted. Redinger suggests that Eliot had no choice but to kill off Tina Sarti because her jealousy and vindictiveness had grown alongside her need to love and be loved, and Eliot would have been destroyed—in her own mind, at least—by her passionate self had she not had the power, denied Tina, to "transform it into the liberating self-knowledge which brings with it self-control."[57] While Caterina does not become a Sibyl-in-training as Consuelo does, she is permitted by means of the music that saves her to overcome her near-fatal passion for a self-centered "Jackanapes" (as Blackwell, Eliot's publisher, calls Wybrow [*GEL*, 2:297]) and to invest her short future in sane, contented love for a solid, worthy, and selfless man. Caterina's voice is stilled, though, as was her father's before her, and in the loss of this particular Eurydice's second death, Eliot introduces the Erinna complex perpetually enacted through the fictional lives of her creative women artists.

Daniel Deronda as Literary Portraits of Artists

Neither Daniel Deronda nor Gwendolen Harleth, the central characters whose lives are interwoven in Eliot's final novel, *Daniel Deronda* (1876), is an artist in the sense that either earns a farthing by producing or performing original work.

56. Grout, *A Short History of Opera*, 268.
57. Redinger, *George Eliot: The Emergent Self*, 324.

Ironically, though, Daniel may well possess the talent to "take the house by storm" as the great operatic tenors do, but he hates the notion of "being dressed up to sing before all those fine people who would not care about him except as a wonderful toy" (*DD*, 170), while Gwendolen, who "want[s] to be a struggling artist herself" (*DD*, 561), has only her remarkable beauty and her melodramatic posing as exhibitionist in life's drama to inspire such preposterous and inflated notions. She must learn the devastating lesson that at twenty-one she has nothing to recommend her except her vanity and idle dreams and that "the desire and the training should have begun seven years ago—or a good deal earlier" (*DD*, 257). Gwendolen's fate, as well as the success and silencing of several artists, is a central theme of the novel.

Daniel Deronda is often recalled as "George Eliot's 'Zionism' novel," because Deronda is perceived by his friend Mordecai Cohen, as well as by the narrator, as the "new Moses" to lead a dispersed people and because Daniel, once he learns of his Jewish descent, vows to spend his life in the effort to establish a Jewish state. Thus the term "Zionist" is accurate enough, and to Eliot's gratification, Jewish rabbis from Germany, England, America, Poland, and France wrote to express their endorsement of her sympathetic portrayal of Judaism. But *Daniel Deronda* could also be called "George Eliot's artist novel" (although not *Künstlerroman*) because it is populated with fictional artists—musicians, actresses, singers, a painter, and a poet—and it is dense with allusions to and quotations of actual musicians, artists, actresses, and poets. Some characters, like Daniel Deronda and Mirah Lapidoth, the Jewess he loves, have the talent to become celebrated vocalists but lack a desire to perform, although Mirah is a successful professional until she abandons her singing career to become Daniel's wife. Others, like Gwendolen and the "mercurial" painter Hans Meyrick, have ambitious reaches that exceed their grasp. Mirah's brother, Mordecai Cohen, is a visionary and a poet. The pianist/composer Herr Klesmer lives happily with art as his "mistress"—self-assured that artists are (as Consuelo's teacher Porpora and Eliot's Armgart say) the real royalty and (as Shelley says) the true legislators of the world. Catherine Arrowpoint is a musician and composer who, after her marriage to the musical genius Julius Klesmer, becomes a patroness and sponsor of aspiring artists. Daniel's mother, the Alcharisi, is an Erinna who has abandoned a world-class career in desperation because she thought her gift had died, only to discover that she has been premature in her professional exit. Like Mirah she is one of "these great singers [who] marry themselves into silence" before their gift dies (*DD*, 437). Now a dying and embittered woman, she has never become reconciled to the loss of her career, the only thing in life that matters to her. Through Alcharisi, Mirah, and Gwendolen, Eliot depicts a varied look at women and artistry in two extremes—the terror of being on display contrasted with the greater terror of being silenced. Indeed, the Alcharisi, more than any other fictional artist with the exception of Armgart, depicts George Eliot's Erinna complex. Like Armgart, and like George Sand's Consuelo and Lucrezia Floriani, she faces the years of silence when the gift has died, the spotlight has been extinguished.

Pianist, Painter, Poet, Prophet—the Male Artists

Daniel Deronda is more concerned about the silencing of women than of men, just as it is also more concerned about the marginalization of Jews than of Christians. In fact the marginalization of "superfluous" girls and women (of whom there are many in the novel) parallels that of the Jews; both motifs are sustained throughout. Because the successes, failures, deprivations, and sacrifices of female artists and would-be artists contrast with those of male performers and painters, however, I begin with male artists of *Daniel Deronda* to illustrate the contrast. Of these, Klesmer is blessed in every way, Hans Meyrick possesses all but luck and genius, Mordecai is silenced in death, and Daniel ultimately finds his voice, not as a barrister, M.P., or singer, the professions suggested by his talents, but as the voice of his newly found people.

Herr Julius Klesmer, whose name suggests both his race and his art, exists in the novel for three purposes: to demonstrate a contented, successful artist upon whom nature and nurture have smiled, to serve as mouthpiece for the high calling of artistry and the artist, and to dash the artistic hopes of the novel's heroine, Gwendolen Harleth. Klesmer, who is tall, flamboyant, and slightly vain and arrogant, is "not yet a Liszt" (*DD*, 238) but is already celebrated in the musical world. He is supremely confident that he will one day reign in that world. With his magnificent mane of hair and his artistic affectations, not to mention his genius, intensity, and passion for music, he easily earns the love of Catherine Arrowpoint, a rich heiress who herself plays four instruments and has the discipline and sensitivity of an artist. When Catherine's parents forbid marriage on the basis that an artist is a gold digger, Klesmer quickly and deftly informs them that it is he, not they, who must put aside position and prestige and that he considers Catherine's money not as an incentive for loving her, but rather her only attribute he would change. With his confident sense of his exalted calling, he sees himself in the Romantic tradition of artist as poet/prophet/king. As for artists being hangers-on of society, as Mr. Arrowpoint implies, Klesmer tells his future father-in-law, "We are not ingenious puppets, sir, who live in a box and look out on the world only when it is gaping for amusement. We help to rule the nations and make the age as much as any other public men. We count ourselves on level benches with legislators. And a man who speaks effectively through music is compelled to something more difficult than parliamentary eloquence" (*DD*, 242).

Nor does Klesmer censor female creativity. Recognizing that Gwendolen is desperate for money and that she mistakenly believes her ravishing beauty can make her an instant success as a singer/actress, Klesmer takes the option of being cruel in order to be kind. He candidly tells her that she must unlearn all her bad habits and mistaken admirations; she must discipline voice, body, and mind; she must stop dreaming of celebrity and think only of excellence; and she must wait years for either acclaim or revenue from her art—and, if she should, despite all odds, become a success on the stage, "the indignities she will be liable to are such as I will not speak of" (*DD*, 260). After all this, he offers his fiancée as Gwendolen's patroness—an offer Gwendolen rejects as even more humiliating than accepting a position as governess. When Klesmer hears Mirah Lapidoth sing, however, the "grandiose" musician congratulates her as he would a man, saying, "Let us shake hands: you are a musician" (*DD*, 484). He immediately invites her to perform a private concert in his own home, advises her as to an instructor and on the amplitude of her voice—specifically, that it is too small for the operatic stage but right for drawing-room performances that are currently lucrative in London—and recommends his wife, Catherine, as mentor.

While Klesmer's grandiosity and artistic oddities are a frequent subject of light ridicule—for instance in Gwendolen's comment that if he were not quite sure of his own immortality, his new wife would often remind him of his godly status—he is treated by Eliot with more respect than bemusement. After all, Eliot loved music, and her Klesmer is no more full of himself than Eliot is full of praise for Liszt: "a glorious creature—one of these men whom the ancients would have imagined the son of a god or goddess, from their superiority to the common clay of humanity."[58] Indeed Klesmer is more of a stereotype than a fully developed character, yet Eliot effectively employs him as her mouthpiece for one prominent view of the artist—a view that by her own time had become a cliché—as Gwendolen cleverly notes.

Hans Meyrick, born into a family of artists and named for Holbein, is a painter with limitations, chiefly that he is not blessed with Julius Klesmer's supreme confidence and superior talent. Hans's deceased father had been a competent illustrator for the publishing trade, and his sister Kate follows the same career. Two other Meyrick daughters and their mother design and embroider fancy satin pillows for pampered men such as Daniel Deronda to sink their elbows into. Moth-

---

58. Eliot, "Liszt, Wagner, and Weimar," in *Essays of George Eliot*, 98. Gordon S. Haight, however, insists that Klesmer is based on Anton Rubinstein, whose background, childhood penury, Jewish blood, and physical appearance fit the fictional musician, adding that the "brusqueness" in Klesmer resembles both Liszt and Rubinstein (*George Eliot: A Biography*, 490).

er and daughters are devoted to art, music, books—and Hans. The three sisters are apparently not the least jealous of their sibling, who receives first a Cambridge education, then a postgraduate trip to Rome while they toil away at home. Their devotion to the male sibling who is destined to be the greatest among them reminds one of the Haworth parsonage in which Branwell Brontë was to become a painter and his sisters, governesses. To Hans's credit, though, he is far more charming than the Branwell that Brontë biographers have depicted, and in fact he has every intention of supporting Mrs. Meyrick, although—like Gwendolen, who also plans to support her widowed mother—he is rather inept at earning remuneration for his talent.

In *Aurora Leigh,* Elizabeth Barrett Browning deals with this essential difference between male and female artists: Men usually have wives or mothers to support their egos, while women artists are essentially alone—a status witnessed in both Aurora and the Alcharisi, as well as in Sand's Consuelo and Jewsbury's Bianca after the deaths of respective mothers. A jealous Aurora remarks of her fellow poets that she envies them not their "native gifts or popular applause," but rather their female support system:

> . . . that Gage comes home
> And lays his last book's prodigal review
> Upon his mother's knee, where, years ago,
> He laid his childish spelling-book and learned
> To chirp and peck the letters from her mouth,
> As young birds must. "Well done," she murmured then;
> She will not say it now more wonderingly:
> And yet the last "Well done" will touch him more,
> As catching up to-day and yesterday
> In a perfect chord of love: and so, Mark Gage,
> I envy you your mother! (*AL* 5.524–34)

In *Daniel Deronda* such a mother has Hans Meyrick, and such a wife acquires Julius Klesmer.

Like the painter Naumann in *Middlemarch,* Hans is slightly bitter about his frustrations ever to taste fame, although he attempts to diffuse his own disappointments with self-deprecating humor. After his return from Rome, he is given to painting in the heroic style, and he poses Mirah in a narrative series as Berenice—a Jewish princess who has a love affair with a Roman prince and who, like the Old Testament princess Esther, pleads for her people.[59] Deronda, who

59. Here, however, Eliot's tongue-in-cheek treatment of Hans's preoccupation with the neoclassical style is gentler than her satire of Pepin's projected romance of grandeur, decadence, passion, philosophy,

by this time is like Hans in love with Mirah, quibbles with the shape of a leg or the width of a face in Hans's series, then belatedly comes around to the real objection: He does not want Mirah displayed publicly in such a manner. Although he surmises rightly about Mirah's lack of exhibitionism (she *does* hate display), the real issue is that *Daniel* does not want her displayed. He exhibits the very same possessiveness that many a husband or lover exercises over a gifted woman— a frequent topic in Sand's artist novels and including, variously, Albert's endorsement of Consuelo's art, Jean Valreg's desire to keep Daniella from the gaze of other mortals, and Laurent's outright jealousy of the prolific Thérèse. In fact the impulse of the male lover to control not only the art, but also the image, of his beloved is also explored by Eliot in *Middlemarch,* in which Ladislaw forbids Naumann to paint Dorothea as the Virgin because, he says, English ladies do not sit as models and, furthermore, the medium is inadequate to do justice to the subject—"your painting and Plastik are poor stuff after all" (*M,* 187). By Ladislaw's behavior, though, it is obvious that his interference is prompted by jealousy, and he, like Deronda, wants to appropriate the would-be muse of the visual artist as his own muse for a different type of creativity. When Hans realizes that Deronda actually assumes the public might see his epic series, he responds, "Zounds, man! Cider-cup and conceit never gave me half such a beautiful dream. My pictures are likely to remain as private as the utmost hypersensitiveness could desire" (*DD,* 460).

When Hans realizes that fate means him to have neither Mirah nor fame, he escapes for a time into a haze of opium, then emerges from his "malady of genius" (*DD,* 782) to divulge to Daniel that he alone is the man Mirah loves, and he accepts that his neoclassical subject matter will not earn him a livelihood but that portrait painting, which he had previously eschewed, might well do so. Hans serves as Eliot's depiction of an artist who, unfortunately, does not know himself and has not discovered his own style. The final tableau of Hans is his undertaking a long-deferred painting of the three young Mallinger daughters "sitting on a bank 'in the Gainsborough style'" (*DD,* 797), which is to Hans Meyrick the ultimate in clichés. While Meyrick is too good-natured a fellow to become entirely bitter or perpetually dejected, he seems destined to have his name writ in water.

Mordecai Cohen is a poet and visionary at once more passionate and more "poetical" than other social reformers and "monomaniacs" (*DD,* 510). Eliot's characterization of Mordecai is—on the basis of realism—less than convincing, for he is more an ideal than an individual. He is a dark-eyed, emaciated con-

---

religion, rusticity, statesmen, poets, warriors, gladiators, and the "secretly working leaven of Christianity" in *Impressions of Theophrastus Such* (*WGE,* 20:190–91).

sumptive who longs for a spiritual companion to whom he can transmit his passion for the people of the diaspora. Instantly he senses he has found that person in Deronda, although at the time Mordecai first insists that Daniel is a Jew, Daniel still believes himself the illegitimate son of his guardian, Sir Hugo Mallinger. In his passionate discourse Mordecai is poetic; his mind "wrought . . . in images" (*DD*, 473); in a "strong baritone voice" he recites the Hebrew poets and speaks in the cadence of the Old Testament psalms and prophecies. As she does with the Shelleyan Klesmer, Eliot specifically connects him to the Romantic ideal of the artist. For instance he characterizes the Romantic sentiment on nature: "He yearned with a poet's yearning for the wide sky . . . the tender and fluctuating lights on [the river] which seems to breathe with a life that can shiver and mourn . . ." (*DD*, 480). Furthermore he is—like many a hero of Romanticism— a Prometheus "[b]ound not *after* but *before* he had well got the celestial fire into the νάρθηξ whereby it might be conveyed to mortals: thrust by the Kratos and Bia of instituted methods into a solitude of despised ideas"; he counts all experience "but as fuel to the divine flame" (*DD*, 471, 497). He is also, by implication, a Keats silenced by death—both in fact dying young of consumption. Eliot's headnote, which quotes the opening lines of Keats's sonnet on the Elgin marbles, makes the comparison explicit:

> My spirit is too weak; mortality
> Weights heavily on me like unwilling sleep,
> And each imagined pinnacle and steep
> Of godlike hardship tells me I must die
> Like a sick eagle looking at the sky. (*DD*, 540)

When Mordecai finds Daniel, his language of "Unity" characterizes the two male companions who study Hebrew together. Barbara Zimmerman observes, "[T]he marital paradigm in Daniel Deronda involves two men . . . who separately and together approximate a 'portrait of the artist.'"[60] Mordecai's death occurs immediately after Mirah and Daniel's wedding—and proves convenient for the newlyweds' intention to travel to the East. His final words echo the soul's passion that he expresses as sexual love: "Death is coming to me as the divine kiss which is both parting and reunion. . . . Where thou goest, Daniel, I shall go. Is it not begun? Have I not breathed my soul into you? We shall live together" (*DD*, 811).[61] And Eliot's final words in the novel are an epigraph in the form of still one more poetic quotation, Milton's "Nothing is here for tears . . ." written for the

---

60. Zimmerman, "George Eliot's Sacred Chest of Language," 162.
61. Daniel's statement also echoes that of the Old Testament heroine Ruth, who tells her mother-in-law, Naomi, "for whither thou goest, I will go . . ." (Ruth 2:16).

death of another Jewish hero, in *Samson Agonistes*. Mordecai is the only male artist in the novel who is "silenced" (as compared to *all* the women artists who are), but he dies with the distinct faith that in Daniel his voice will be heard from the grave.

Daniel Deronda is not an artist, but Eliot employs the language of artistry to characterize his talent and impulses. His precocity for "learning how human miseries are wrought" is compared to Shelley's in writing *Queen Mab* at age nineteen. As previously noted, Daniel has a fine voice and loves singing, although he would rather be a Washington or a Pericles than a performer of any type. This preference is hardly a wonder, given that Daniel has grown up as the natural son of a gentleman/statesman in a culture where Victorian drawing rooms valued the musical talent of marginal figures (females and foreigners), but where dignified and aristocratic men did not contemplate musical careers. One suspects that in her final novel Eliot attempts a hero who is as moral and noble as Adam Bede and Felix Holt, minus the hardness of the former and the moral smugness of the latter—one who is, at the same time, as beautiful as Tito, as gentle as Philip Wakem, and as passionately devoted to discovery as Tertius Lydgate.

Long before writing *Daniel Deronda*, Eliot commented that—while idle women with "flirtations and flounces" imagine themselves the heroine of any novel they read—"grave people, with opinions, like the most admirable character in a novel to be their mouth-piece" (*GEL*, 3:111). Such a "mouth-piece" she intended in her curly haired Jewish Adonis. To her chagrin, readers "cut [*Deronda*] into scraps and talk of nothing in it but Gwendolen. I meant everything in the book to be related to everything else there" (*GEL*, 6:290). In characterizing Daniel, the novelist spells out her intent: More than his memorable voice, Daniel's genius, like Dorothea Brooke's, is in his greatness of soul, or, as his guardian alliteratively says, his "passion for people who are pelted" (*DD*, 719). Among the persons whom Daniel saves are Hans Meyrick, whom he tutors at Cambridge when Hans has an eye infection (with the outcome that Hans graduates and Deronda drops out); Mirah, whom he saves from drowning, lodges in the home of Mrs. Meyrick, and reunites with her brother, Mordecai; and Gwendolen Harleth, whom he observes gambling at Leubronn in the striking first sentence of the novel, whose necklace he redeems for her gambling losses, and whose soul he redeems by becoming her spiritual confessor. Hence the basis for Eliot's frustration with a reading public more interested in the siren than the Moses. With his repeated reenactment of the rescue of maidens in distress, Deronda brings to mind Robert Browning's heroes, like Caponsacchi, who imagine themselves (as Browning himself did) as Perseus rescuing Andromeda. Deronda is also a questing hero—the quests leading him to discover his mother, his identity, and his professional calling. All quests converge in his mother, the Alcharisi, who dispels his delusion about the Mallingers, gives him documents that connect him to the Jewish patriarchy, especially the eminent Jewish grandfather who despised his daughter's art. Thus the nebulous longing for purpose and vocation and his love of Mirah and Mordecai are resolved with a love of a newly found people. The novel ends without revealing the end result of Daniel's quest, but he and Mirah are about to depart England for Palestine. Daniel Deronda abhors the self-display of an artist, but he desires to be—as Shelley says of poets and philosophers—a "legislator" of the world, and Eliot leads us to believe he will not be silenced.

Mirah as Reluctant Artist

All of the female artists and aspiring artists of *Daniel Deronda* are silenced— Mirah and Catherine because they acquiesce in their own silencing in marriage, the Alcharisi and Gwendolen in spite of their wishes. Gillian Beer notes that in *Daniel Deronda* women seek power and mastery denied them in the argument of the book—that the powers of Catherine and Mirah are executant, subdued to their instrument, and that Gwendolen achieves power only until married.[62] Also the Alcharisi achieves power only between marriages—that is, for the nine years between the death of Daniel's father and the day that she abdicates as queen of European stages to marry a Russian aristocrat, becoming the Princess Halm-Eberstein and eventually the mother of five. The Alcharisi and Mirah have in common their Jewishness and disappointing relationships with their respective fathers—Mirah running away from the father who repudiated his Jewish faith; the princess rejecting the father who tried to force her to follow hers. Both are talented singers, as well, although of the two the Alcharisi is a natural actress, while Mirah, in the words of her father's mistress, an Italian performer, "will never be an artist: she has no notion of being anybody but herself" (*DD*, 213). Alcharisi and Gwendolen, on the other hand, have in common their flair for the dramatic; they also share rebellious natures and willingness to take gambles in life, and their regal, commanding bearing. Both love power and self-display, both intend to be stars of their own dramas, and both are big-time losers in life's game of chance.

"I did not want to be an artist," is the motif of Mirah Lapidoth, who associates the divine art of music with religion, in her earliest memories of her mother singing Hebrew hymns, but associates acting with fraud—her father being an actor, stage manager, and dramatist/translator who "acted" the lie that her mother was dead and who robbed Mirah of her childhood by putting the talented child

---

62. Beer, *Darwin's Plots: Evolutionary Narrative in Darwin, George Eliot, and Nineteenth-Century Fiction*, 215.

on the stage at age nine. It is understandable, then, that Mirah loves music but despises the theater. Her father's profession is carried on among people who are constantly "strutting, quarrelling, leering" (*DD*, 219) and in a place where there is "loud laughing and disrupting, strutting, snapping of fingers, jeering faces" (*DD*, 213). As Deirdre David notes, Mirah's words for the despised theater are similar to those employed by Daniel's mother to describe the Jewish religion that she hates.[63] Mirah has suffered the "indignities" that as a gentleman Herr Klesmer cannot even bring himself to describe to Gwendolen Harleth: Insinuating men come around to talk; both men and women sneer; and the quality of the plays is decidedly inferior. As noted in previous chapters, Sand's Lucrezia Floriani also complains about these indignities, especially that of a woman selling her face and body rather than her talent, and Jewsbury's Bianca endures them. In *Armgart* the artist simply accepts sexism as part of the territory: When she appears in a chiton to sing the role of Gluck's Orfeo the women whisper "Not a pretty face!" and the men admire the "length of limb" exposed by the costume—Armgart remarking that if she were the Virgin Mother and her stage the heavens, "Gossips would peep, jog elbows, rate the price / Of such a woman in the social mart" (*A, WGE*, 19:73).

Eliot herself was interested in all forms of art and attended theatrical performances throughout Europe but was critical of debased art forms such as plays designed merely for an actress's self-exhibition. In Rome in 1869 she and Lewes went to see Ristori as Judith; Eliot writes, "[I]t is painful that one whose glory can only be in being a great artist, should show so miserable, stupid an egoism as to select a cheap company that turns the ensemble into a farce or burlesque which makes an incongruous and often fatally neutralizing background to her own figure" (*GEL*, 5:24), and Lewes criticized the same play as a group of "poses plastiques" for Ristori (*GEL*, 5:25). In Eliot's *Armgart* when the singer gives forth an uncalled-for trill for the "prurience of the full-fed mob," her teacher, Leo, sarcastically recommends that she might as well

> Jerk forth burlesque bravuras, square your arms
> Akimbo with a tavern wench's grace,
> And set the splendid compass of your voice
> To lyric jigs. Go to! I thought you meant
> to be an artist—lift your audience
> To see your vision, not trick forth a show
> To please the grossest taste of grossest numbers. (*A, WGE*, 19:71)

---

63. David, *Fictions of Resolution in Three Victorian Novels: North and South, Our Mutual Friend, Daniel Deronda*, 171.

Could she enter the profession, Gwendolen also would, Klesmer believes, play to the crowd rather than using the art to uplift the sensibilities of the audience. Of her effort he complains:

> . . . you produce your notes badly; and that music which you sing is beneath you. It is a form of melody which expresses a puerile state of culture—a dandling, canting, see-saw kind of stuff—the passion and thought of people without any breadth of horizon. There is a sort of self-satisfied folly about every phrase of such melody; no cries of deep, mysterious passion—no conflict—no sense of the universal. It makes men small as they listen to it. (*DD*, 49)

Given Eliot's repulsion of stars whose grandstanding presence supersedes their art, it is not surprising that Mirah's reserve about performance, like Daniel's, is considered refinement, as opposed to the vulgarity exhibited in Daniel's mother, the Alcharisi—as well as by the trills of Armgart and seesaw melodies of Gwendolen. Furthermore the theatrical is always suspect in George Eliot's characterizations. For instance, in *Mr. Gilfil's Love-Story,* Lady Cheverel impatiently tells Caterina to leave off her "stage-players' antics" (*SCL*, 1:153). In *Middlemarch,* Madame Laure, a Provençale, kills her husband and fellow actor on stage, then tells Lydgate when he professes his love for her, "You are a good young man. But I do not like husbands" (*M*, 152). In *Daniel Deronda* several kinds of hypocrisy and evil, in addition to that of Mirah's father, are described in theatrical terms: The cold-blooded, reptilian Grandcourt has a complexion that, in its "faded fairness," resembles an actress without cosmetics (*DD*, 111); he is an operatic "jealous baritone" of freezing glances, always singing asides (*DD*, 727); and he and his bride, Gwendolen, yachting on the Mediterranean, make a scene "as good as a theatrical representation" (*DD*, 681). Additionally, Grandcourt's mistress, the melodramatic Mrs. Glasher, stages "scenes" with Grandcourt and behaves with a "strange mixture of reality and acting" (*DD*, 351), and Grandcourt's beautiful bride, Gwendolen, positions herself as the "heroine of an admired play" (*DD*, 357) until the bridegroom imperiously commands her, "Oblige me in future by not showing whims like a mad woman in a play" (*DD*, 446). It is therefore a tribute to Mirah that she does not aspire to become an actress, a "fraud."

Blessed with a voice that is "gold, but a thread of gold dust" (*DD*, 216)—that is, not powerful enough for a large theater—Mirah has escaped the grand opera debut her father envisioned, but not before her childhood was sacrificed to the gambling addiction of Lapidoth, who exploited her talent, lived off her wages, and once tried to pimp for her—exploiting a connection between actresses and prostitutes that existed throughout the Victorian period in the popular imagination. Mirah recounts to the Meyricks how her father introduced her to a count who expected sexual favors, a situation rather like that of Marian Erle, whose mother attempts to sell the girl into sexual slavery to the landowner in Browning's *Aurora Leigh*. In fact Mirah repeatedly speaks of the theater and life with her father (the two being inseparable in her mind) as a private hell—the theater "seemed a hell to me" (*DD*, 216), no better than a "fiery furnace" (*DD*, 217), and life closes in like a "wall of fire" "scorching" her until the sun itself seems to scorch as the voice of God telling her to die (*DD*, 222). To escape her father and her despised career, Mirah has fled from Prague to seek her mother and brother in England, where Deronda saves her. Reclaimed to life, she willingly pursues singing and teaching as an honorable means of earning her living, but she repudiates the theatricality of the stage. She has no desire to be exhibited in a manner that causes people to stare and leer.

Mirah is one of Eliot's many diminutive heroines—those who are sweet, docile, and virtuous, who have small ambitions and are content with small accomplishments, and who serve as contrast to the big, bold women like Gwendolen and the Alcharisi. Such dainty and unpresumptuous women as the tiny Meyricks in their tiny house. Or that "dillicate made" "freshest blossom of youth" Eppie, who in *Silas Marner* is, even as an adult, described in diminutives—such as her hair rippling like a "brooklet" (*WGE*, 7:214, 200). Or Middlemarch's Mary Garth, of low stature, ordinary looks, and dark, unruly hair, but keen moral rectitude. Or the frivolous, Byron-loving Esther Lyon, who in *Felix Holt* becomes the "white mist-cloud" clinging to the "rock" Felix (*FH*, 417). Birdlike Mirah recalls Esther, the "white new-winged dove" (*FH*, 599), or Caterina Sarti, the "singing bird," who needs to "nestl[e] fondly under wings that are outstretched for her" (*SCL*, 1:198). Mirah is another of Eliot's singing birds; when she performs it is "like a bird's wooing for an audience near and beloved" (*DD*, 372). Of "low slim figure, with most delicate little face" (*DD*, 187), she is petite, dainty, and ladylike in demeanor—her tiny hands perpetually folded in her lap, little ankles crossed primly. When she sings "Per pietà non dirmi addio" (Have pity, do not leave me [*DD*, 564]), the reader is assured that Daniel, who has been a "rescuing angel" to many, will add her to the number of great singers who marry into silence before their voices crack. Oliver Lovesey comments: "The fragile girl woman, like the Italian singer Caterina Sarti . . . will now be an in-dwelling icon for Deronda and the remainder of her life a long, silent confession."[64] This is merely to say that Mirah has become Daniel's muse—albeit a muse for a spiritual quest rather than, as she is for Hans Meyrick, a muse to inspire a noble, beautiful face on a canvas. Nevertheless, as an artist she is silenced.

64. Lovesey, "The Other Woman in *Daniel Deronda*," 516.

Gwendolen's Artistic Ambition

In contrast to Mirah's "I did not want to be an artist" is Gwendolen's desire to "be a struggling artist herself." As previously noted, Gwendolen Harleth proves to be such a scene-stealer that she eclipses the heroic rescuing angel Deronda. Eliot's enchanted editor, Blackwood, reading the book in installments, writes that the "mermaid witch" has such a hold on him that he wants to kick Herr Klesmer for insulting her singing (*GEL*, 6:144). With her tall, stately grace and her thick coils of light brown hair, Gwendolen is stunning to behold and in fact possesses some artistic talent. She is a "moderately powerful soprano" whose voice, someone once said in flattery, is like Jenny Lind's (*DD*, 48). One of Eliot's fascinating, clever, and statuesque women, Gwendolen is also a Lamia woman, a Nereid in sea-green robes, a "witch," a "Calypso among her nymphs" (*DD*, 101), a "sylph with taper fingers," a "Diana" on the archery field, and a "goddess." Barrett notes that Gwendolen's name is that of an ancient British moon goddess; hence she is Artemis/Diana.[65]

As the "spoiled child" of the opening book, she is to *Daniel Deronda* what "Miss Brooke" is to *Middlemarch*—the initial (as well as captivating) focus of our attention. As a result of her beauty and her mother's capitulation to her rule, she is also self-centered, narcissistic (while Hetty Sorrel only gazes at her reflection in the glass, Gwendolen kisses hers), irreverent, and witty enough that she can insult Mrs. Arrowpoint, a minor would-be artist, without the older woman quite realizing that she is the brunt of Gwendolen's impertinent sallies. Bonnie Zimmerman interprets the unpleasant aspects of the spoiled Gwendolen as Eliot's endorsement of criticism by Eliza Lynn Linton, Geraldine Jewsbury, and others of the "Girl of the Period"—the emerging young woman of the 1860s and 1870s, who lived for fun, luxury, freedom, and a "fast" life—if not in fact, at least in boasts.[66] A frustrated actress, Gwendolen has a penchant for exhibiting herself in *tableaux vivants,* on the archery field, in velvet and silk evening gowns, on horseback, and—in the opening scene of the novel when Deronda first encounters her—at the gaming tables of Leubronn. She goes in for "statuesque pose[s] in . . . favourite costume" (*DD*, 58–59), for example as Shakespeare's Rosalind or Hermione, or St. Cecilia at the organ. She naively assumes that because she is

---

65. Barrett, *Vocation and Desire,* 172.

66. Zimmerman, "Gwendolen Harleth and 'The Girl of the Period,'" 196–215. As evidence Zimmerman cites that Gwendolen eschews useful work, is mercenary in husband hunting, expects freedom from traditional female values, and "[w]ith additional references to *tableaux vivants,* romps and tomboys, croquet, Wagner, natural selection, boarding-school education, and the *femme sole,*" Gwendolen is rooted in historical reality (204).

more beautiful than the Jewish actress Rachel, she can be more successful. Gail Marshall, in a cogent essay on performance and poses in *Daniel Deronda,* notes that Gwendolen, in her own "poses plastiques" (for example, her Hermione pose, which mimics that in an etching of Mrs. Siddons as Hermione), accepts and, indeed, if given the opportunity as a professional, would perpetuate "the emphasis on spectacle, conveyed through the female body, stress[ing] the visual aspect of theatre rather than its narrative impulse . . . the actress, like Galatea . . . isolated in the viewer's gaze."[67] In other words, her choices for dramatic vehicle would be as trite as the "see-saw melodies" that Klesmer denounces. Her obvious love of self-display contrasts her to the more talented Mirah and prompts Herr Klesmer to comment that it is always acceptable to "see you sing"—a compliment that she rightly interprets to mean that for a connoisseur, she looks better than she sounds.

Gwendolen is also a sexually reserved woman—delighted to have men *see* her, but repulsed by the notion of having any one of them touch her. Until now she has lived well, dashed the hopes of suitors, and flirted her way into the limelight of various scenes, but when Mrs. Davilow learns that the family inheritance has been lost, Gwendolen is practical enough to know that the commodification of women permits her, as a female of extraordinary beauty, to marry when she must, but at least to hold out for the highest bidder. And marry she must, for she is also one of the "superfluous girls" of a novel that features no less than fourteen superfluous daughters in four households (three of them headed by superfluous matriarchs). In addition, Gwendolen, like Hans Meyrick, feels the duty to support her mother, and a handsome financial arrangement for Mrs. Davilow and her fatherless daughters becomes the purchase price for the "harlotry" of Miss Harleth—a price that Mallinger Grandcourt handsomely offers. Gwendolen gambles first on a tentative engagement to Grandcourt. When she learns, though, that he has a mistress and four children, she goes for a second gamble—that of becoming an artist. Then that hope of an honest profession is dashed by the brutally honest Klesmer, who tells her that "you will hardly achieve more than mediocrity" (*DD*, 259).

Understanding that—as Eliot's Armgart bitterly remarks, a middling woman impresses the world "[w]ith high superfluousness" (*A, WGE,* 19:111)—Gwendolen next gambles at highest stakes in a marriage to Grandcourt, who proves cold-blooded, controlling, and reptilian—an "alligator," "boa constrictor," or "lizard." The new Mrs. Grandcourt at first means to rule her husband by her charm and beauty, but she is quickly brought to reality—first when her husband's longtime mistress, Mrs. Glasher, sends her the Grandcourt family jewels, which

---

67. Marshall, "Actresses, Statues, and Speculation in *Daniel Deronda,*" 122.

are "poisoned" like the robe and crown that Medea sent Creüsa, second by Grandcourt, who systematically frightens and "tames" his bride as a man breaks a horse to bridle and saddle, the man and horse portraying, in this novel, a symbolic role similar to that of Count Vronsky and Frou-Frou in Tolstoy's *Anna Karenina*. As the bitter Mrs. Transome remarks in *Felix Holt*, "Men like such captives, as they like horses that champ the bit and paw the ground: they feel more triumph in their mastery" (*FH*, 488). Both figures of speech for the marital relationship, the snake and the horse taming and riding, are of course overtly sexual.[68] Grandcourt's cool mastery is expressed both as the cold-blooded reptile in Gwendolen's boudoir and in his bringing her to "kneel down like a horse under training for the arena" (*DD*, 320), as well as in his derision of her art—both her acting and her singing.

Although during the courtship he had been enticed by her wit and vivacity, after the marriage Grandcourt repeatedly chastises Gwendolen for posing and melodrama that he no longer finds amusing, commanding that she must drop the theatrical behavior because she is making a "spectacle" of herself (*DD*, 447)— especially in her intimate conversations with Deronda. Thwarted before her marriage by Klesmer's judgment that she lacks training, talent, and discipline and after the marriage by her husband's edict that her histrionics will not do, she decides to take private voice lessons from the "exquisite singer" Mirah, but even art as a hobby is not permitted in Grandcourt's house: Amateurs who perform before others make fools of themselves, he says, and as for her singing in the privacy of their home, he does not want to hear "squalling in private" (*DD*, 588). Thus Gwendolen is convicted of mediocrity and terrified into silence.

At the climax of the novel, when she has been forced by the sadistic Grandcourt to go sailing in the Mediterranean, Gwendolen, who had wished for the death of the "dangerous serpent ornamentally coiled in her cabin without invitation" (*DD*, 672), stands frozen as a statue as her husband drowns (a mirror image of Mirah's pose before she plunges into the water to drown *herself*). Later Gwendolen repents miserably for her desire for Grandcourt's death. It is here that Daniel, in spite of himself, becomes her spiritual confessor, and he to whom she acknowledges her spiritual void. Her great gambles having served her ill, she is deprived of wealth and ease, the companionship either of the man she married or of the one she loves, and of her career as performer—either on stage or off. Her comfort is that she will rise morally; as she writes to Deronda, "[I]t shall be better with me because I have known you" (*DD*, 810). Because she has met Daniel

68. Whitney Chadwick says that the "taming" of woman in terms of breaking horses was also a preferred metaphor of both Victorian pornography and gynecological practice. In the former category women are bridled, saddled, ridden, and whipped; in the latter, strapped with their feet in the "stirrups" of examination tables that came into general use after 1860 (*Women, Art, and Society*, 186).

Deronda, then, she is spared the moral horror of metamorphosis into a Mrs. Transome, whom she resembles in several ways—especially love of power and the loss of it by means of intimidation. Of the dual protagonists whose lives are interwoven, Daniel will be transplanted into the greater world of visionary idealism and adventure, while Gwendolen will only blossom or wither back in Offendene, the family home with its "superfluity" of females.

Some critics find potential hope in Gwendolen's silencing. Phyllis Weliver argues that for the women of the novel (especially the daemonic Gwendolen), music is not chiefly about independence and performance, but about the Schopenhaueran will to understanding through music and that Gwendolen—encouraged by Daniel to sing in private—may well experience rebirth to insight as Shakespeare's Hermione is resurrected to life. But Weliver cannot with confidence assert that Gwendolen ever sings again once her "squalling" is silenced by Grandcourt. Dorothea Barrett makes a case that the character of Gwendolen represents a breakthrough for Eliot, that—because she "kills" Grandcourt and goes unpunished—"George Eliot at last flouts the establishment values that insisted that the only admirable woman was a selfless woman, a submissive woman, a woman without avowed sexual appetites and aversions."[69] On the basis that Gwendolen is now free from a miserable marriage, her situation is improved, and on the basis that she has learned the great lesson that it is wrong to profit from another's misery and she must, in Daniel's words, turn "her fear" into purposeful life, she certainly is better. But on Barrett's criteria that "love and duty, family and vocation" are in the Eliot canon essential to happiness, I would admit that Gwendolen has only the first three (if her relationship to the superfluous half-sisters to whom she has always been indifferent can be said to constitute "family," but admittedly she has a loving mother). She still lacks the fourth category, that of vocation, and there is no hint in the novel that she ever will attain it. She has merely learned that she is unfit for the vocation of teacher/governess or actress/singer. In a perceptive psychological analysis of Gwendolen, Carole Stone notes that what Gwendolen has been trying to do throughout the novel is to speak of her sexual frigidity as a result of male oppression (explored in the narrative by her complicated relationships with mother, father, stepfather, and Grandcourt), that while "she may find a voice . . . it will make no difference in the larger world" because her only hearer is Mrs. Davilow—exactly the audience she had at the beginning.[70] While Stone and I examine different aspects of Gwendolen's silencing, the point is well taken: The thwarted actress again performs, as her child-self did, before an audience of one.

69. Weliver, *Women Musicians in Victorian Fiction*, 230–38; Barrett, *Vocation and Desire*, 158.
70. Stone, "George Eliot's *Daniel Deronda*: 'The Case-History of Gwendolen H.,'" 65.

Nature has deprived Gwendolen of the talent of Mirah Lapidoth, Leonora Halm-Eberstein, or Catherine Arrowpoint, but endowed her with the desire to be what she cannot become; furthermore she is, like Maggie Tulliver, silenced before she ever learns what her destiny will be. Barbara Hardy says that—unlike the characters of Eliot's "tragedy of the little soul"—Gwendolen, Maggie, and Dorothea "rise to their tragedy, and are even nurtured by it."[71] The Lamia woman Gwendolen Harleth is one of Eliot's more memorable and fascinating sufferers of the Erinna complex.

The Silencing of the Alcharisi

The Alcharisi, as previously noted, parallels Gwendolen in several ways: Both the aging actress and the young one are tall, regal, and commanding; both were reared as spoiled daughters; and both adore being the center of attention and tend to dramatize their lives, to make the most of dramatic entrances and exits. Further, both are rebels; both covet power over men, and each is depicted as a goddess/sorceress/seductress. Both are serpentine—Gwendolen a Lamia, Leonora a Melusina. Also, both are driven by fear—Gwendolen by fear of Grandcourt and of her own spiritual decline, the Alcharisi by her fear of silencing and of death. In youth, however, the luck denied Gwendolen has favored the Alcharisi because she had the greater talent and attained the fame and universal male adulation she desired. She boasts, for instance, that Mallinger and other men throughout Europe have loved and courted her. Also unlike Gwendolen, she did enjoy power over her first husband, Daniel's father, who gave selflessly to her art. When as a dying woman she requests and receives a reunion with her son Daniel, her rhetorical defense of her decision to follow her passion at the expense of father, child, and husband is bold, iconoclastic, and memorable:

> . . . you can never imagine what it is to have a man's force of genius in you, and yet to suffer the slavery of being a girl. To have a pattern cut out—"this is the Jewish woman; this is what you must be; this is what you are wanted for; a woman's heart must be of such a size and no larger, else it must be pressed small, like Chinese feet; her happiness is to be made as cakes are, by a fixed receipt." (*DD*, 631)

Having been blessed with talent and ambition, the Alcharisi has required only freedom. Like James Joyce's Stephen Dedalus, she is impelled to fly the nets of

71. Hardy, *The Novels of George Eliot: A Study in Form*, 28. Regarding the "tragedy of little souls," Hardy has in mind characters like Amos Barton and Hetty Sorrel.

family, religion, and racial or national identity, but in her case the net of gender as well. Repeatedly she speaks of the Jewish faith, of her father's "tyrannical" rule, and of marriage and motherhood as "bonds," a "yoke," "fetters," or foot binding, from which she had to liberate herself in order to make art. The insistence on freedom to pursue the life for which "nature gave me a charter" (*DD, 664*), in the form of voice, genius, and beauty, is a distinct echo of the Staël and Sand heroine. "Vive la liberté" is a major motif of both *Corinne* and *Consuelo,* with Sand demonstrating the passion for freedom by having her heroine Consuelo locked away in various castles, fortresses, and estates and composing paeans to liberty. The Alcharisi confesses—as did George Eliot—that she never wanted to be a mother; like Sand's singer/actress Corilla in *Consuelo,* she was relieved to part with an infant who would have been a fetter for her career. And, unlike the artist Thérèse in *Elle et lui,* she does not consider the reunion with her lost son a cause of joy, but rather an unpleasant necessity.

Freedom, talent, ambition, and opportunity made the Alcharisi "queen," and her royalty gave her happiness (or so she claims) until she began to sing out of tune and was supplanted by another singer. She became terrified by the prospect of the demise of her art as she is now terrified by her impending death. Her response to fear was to be baptized a Christian and to marry and bear additional children, only to discover too late that the loss of her voice was temporary and that, had she waited, in time her queenly power over her subjects would have been restored: "If I had not been afraid of defeat and failure, I might have gone on. I miscalculated" (*DD, 666*). Lewes, who in 1875 had his "slumbering interest" in the stage reawakened by the performances of the current season and was thereby prompted to publish a book on actors and acting, comments on the actress Rachel, whose face had been "aflame with genius," but who, later in her career,

> grew careless; played her parts as if only in a hurry to get through them, flashing out now and then with tremendous power, just to show what she could do. . . . She, whose elocution had been incomparable, so delicately shaded were its various refinements and so sustained its music, came at last to gabble, and to mash up her rhythm till the verses were often unintelligible and generally ineffective.[72]

According to Lewes, then, the miscalculation of hanging on after the gift has died makes a formerly great actress appear ludicrous. No doubt Lewes and Eliot discussed the performances they attended together, as both are offended at needless theatrical excesses. In Eliot's *Daniel Deronda,* written a year after Lewes's little

72. Lewes, *On Actors and the Art of Acting,* 32.

book on acting, the Alcharisi attempts to avoid the miscalculation of Rachel by rushing precipitously into an obverse miscalculation.

George Eliot fears both errors for her own art, silencing herself either too soon or too late. For she demonstrates that Leonora Halm-Eberstein's artistic life has ended, and whatever lies ahead is only suffering and misery. Now she has, by her own confession to her son, no faith, no love, "no life left to love you with" (*DD*, 640). As Jennifer Uglow says:

> She is the woman artist as sybil and prophetess. . . . The portrait of Alcharisi burns with energy, expressing the same feelings we encounter in George Eliot's own letters—her resistance to restrictions, her sense of destiny, her defiant yet pained awareness of what she lost in cutting herself off from her family and her background and in deciding not to have children, and her fear that her gift would vanish, never to return.[73]

Indeed, there is some of George Eliot in the Alcharisi, but this particular woman/artist—for all her genius and esteem—lacks the talent for love, a talent that Eliot credits for saving herself from egotistical self-worship. And Eliot insists, in the words of both Deronda's mother and the narrator of *Mr. Gilfil's Love-Story*, that the ability to love *is* a talent. In the sense of Eliot's religion as love and compassion for other people—of being, as Dorothea says, part of the divine power against evil—the Alcharisi is an atheist.

Significantly, while Daniel vainly attempts to reach the soul of his mother, Gwendolen has witnessed the drowning of Grandcourt, and her soul cries out for someone to save her from the sin of hate and murder. Perhaps Eliot suggests that, after all, Gwendolen is more fortunate than the Alcharisi, that being a woman artist is a fearful occupation because one is tempted to worship at the altar of Self. At the end of the novel, Gwendolen has lost a voice but perhaps gained a soul; the Alcharisi has lost both voice and soul. Kathleen Leicht, who focuses on the positive aspect of women and artistry in the novel, remarks that, for Mirah and the Princess Halm-Eberstein, music provides a voice that they cannot obtain in any other way and concludes that the "privileging of the women artists in her novel reflects her own desire to be privileged."[74] Taken as a whole, though, the life of the Alcharisi does not seem "privileged"—in spite of the comparative social freedom that her professional success allows. Indeed, her genius has offered temporary liberation from the constraints of societal expectations, religious and parental authority, and female biology, but her silencing is as important to her story as is her success.

73. Uglow, *George Eliot*, 237.
74. Leicht, "The Voice of the Artist in *Daniel Deronda*," 6.

Such is the case, too, with George Eliot. Her literary successes have been pleasant, but she still dreads silencing, whether or not she is as embittered about her impending death as is her fictional singer. On December 31, 1877, in the final entry of her final journal, George Eliot writes,

> Many conceptions of works to be carried out present themselves, but confidence in my own fitness to complete them worthily is all the more wanting because it is reasonable to argue that I must have already done my best. In fact, my mind is embarrassed by the number and wide variety of subjects that attract me, and the enlarging vista that each brings with it. (*GEL*, 6:440)

Like the Alcharisi, she struggles heart and soul against the silencing, and she fears she will merely gabble rather than exhort and delight.

Armgart and the Erinna Complex

In 1870, six years before publishing *Daniel Deronda*, Eliot produced in the dramatic poem *Armgart* another portrait of a dazzling singer/actress, but also another Erinna, who, like the Alcharisi, loses her voice at the peak of her career. In fact the hubris and the reversals of the two women parallel so closely that, taken together, it almost seems that Alcharisi serves as portrait of Armgart a few years later in life, an Armgart having failed to make do without the stardom that abandons her when her voice fails. Like Alcharisi, Armgart is ambitious, passionate, and absolutely focused on her career. Also like Alcharisi, who considers herself a "born singer and actress" (*DD*, 633), Armgart pronounces "I am an artist by my birth" (*A, WGE*, 19:89). Both stars are international celebrities, and both thrive on adulation, Alcharisi repeatedly referring to herself as a "queen," Armgart announcing "Heaven made me royal" (*A, WGE*, 19:113). Indeed, in hyperbole, Armgart elevates herself above earthly thrones, considering herself as a "happy spiritual star / Such as old Dante saw, wrought in a rose / Of light in Paradise" (*A, WGE*, 19:77) and accepting gifts of "gold, incense, myrrh" as "needful signs" that her voice, instinct, and spiritual energy have stirred the crowds who have come to hear her perform as Orpheus in *Orfeo ed Euridice* (*A, WGE*, 19:78).

Like Caterina and Mirah, Armgart is a singing bird. She trills like nightingales, displays the regal demeanor of an eagle, and prompts Graf Dornberg, the man who comes courting Armgart, to misjudge her as a "[p]oor human-hearted singing-bird"—albeit one with "Caesar's ambition in her delicate breast" (*A, WGE*, 19:67). Had she not been an artist, Armgart says she would have been Mænad or murderess, because without her remarkable voice she would have had no "channel to her soul" (*WGE*, 19:68). Fortunately for Armgart, though, "Heaven

. . . [m]ade . . . every channel of my soul converge / To one high function"—that function being her voice, her charisma, her stellar performances. (*A, WGE,* 19:113). Confident of her genius and expressing that confidence in the royalty of third-person reference, she assures her admirers that they need "never tremble more / Lest Armgart's wing should fail her" (*A, WGE,* 19:70).

But according to Graf Dornberg, "Caesar's ambition" has also "unwomaned" her (in the sense that being "womanly" means to desire a nest). If, as Alcharisi says, it takes a talent to love as a woman loves, Armgart has never aspired to cultivate such talent. She has no family other than her cousin and companion, Walpurga, whom she treats like a servant, and she has no inclination for marriage. She does not intend to "miscalculate." Graf wants to marry Armgart—yet his statement that she is "unsexed" oddly echoes the same comment that Jewsbury's Conrad makes about Bianca when he has decided he does *not* want to marry her. Also it recalls a comment about the worst possible results of feminine education and success that Eliot herself states in an 1868 letter to Emily Davies, founder of Girton College:

> In the face of all wrongs, mistakes, and failures, history has demonstrated that gain [of woman's influence on morality]. And here lies just that kernel of truth in the vulgar alarm of men lest women be "unsexed." We can no more afford to part with that exquisite type of gentleness, tenderness, possible maternity suffusing a woman's being with affectionateness, which makes what we mean by the feminine character, than we can afford to part with . . . human love . . . (*GEL,* 4:467–68).

As has been noted, Eliot's disdain for the stage star is repeatedly revealed in *Daniel Deronda;* in both the novel and the poem *Armgart,* the woman who trades the "exquisite" traits of womanliness for ovations and trinkets has made a bad bargain.

Armgart has already rejected human love and the stereotypical feminine character. That she stars as Gluck's Orfeo and Beethoven's Fidelio illustrates her preference for the role of rescuer to that of rescued. She also rejects marriage to Graf on the grounds that she will renounce her art and fame for no one, that anyone who marries her must also wed her art, that Graf is as much in love with her stardom as he is with herself—that he wants, in the words of Barrett Browning's Aurora Leigh when speaking of her suitor Eglinton, "a star upon his stage" more than he wants a wife for her love and companionship. Furthermore, Armgart reasons that Graf can make his match elsewhere from the superfluous women who have no purpose, for "the type abounds." The proposal scene in *Armgart* is remarkably similar to that of Aurora's cousin, Romney, in Browning's *Aurora Leigh.* The "falcon," Aurora, intends to soar above the "caged-bird" existence of her English aunt; in refusing Romney's invitation to be his helpmate in saving the world, Aurora decrees her service to art and her own development as a poet

> . . . I go hence
> To London, to the gathering-place of souls,
> To live mine straight out, vocally, in books;
> Harmoniously for others, if indeed
> A woman's soul, like man's, be wide enough
> To carry the whole octave (*AL* 2.1181–86)

Similarly, the "eagle," Armgart, rejects Graf's invitation to "paint the future out" as the wife of a political diplomat:

> No; I will live alone and pour my pain
> With passion into music, where it turns
> To what is best within my better self.
> I will not take for husband one who deems
> The thing my soul acknowledges as good—
> The thing I hold worth striving, suffering for,
> To be a thing dispensed with easily,
> Or else the idol of a mind infirm. (*A, WGE*, 19:93)

Ego is involved in both women's choices. As Aurora fears her hands will be put to serving in the Public Baths or Ragged Schools of a man already wed to his political philosophy, Armgart suspects her voice will be subservient to Graf's and that she will be merely a muse for his political life, a performer with a much-diminished audience. She protests:

> What! Leave the opera with my part ill-sung
> While I was warbling in a drawing-room?
> Sing in the chimney-corner to inspire
> My husband reading news? Let the world hear
> My music only in his morning speech
> Less stammering than most honourable men's? (*WGE*, 19:88–89)

Romney and Graf take rejection differently: Browning's hero eventually provides Aurora another opportunity for love—this time without feeling her art compromised. Eliot's Graf, though, abandons the eagle when she loses her voice and becomes "[r]usset and songless as a missel-thrush" (*A, WGE*, 19:106). Although Eliot's talented star Armgart loses her admiring Graf as Corinne loses her Nelvil, Graf's love proves rather tepid—lasting only as long as her gift—and

Armgart, unlike Corinne, considers her would-be Nelvil of small worth. Furthermore, she is too proud to be a "pensioner in marriage" (*A, WGE,* 19:107). Having worshiped her voice and her fame, this particular Erinna turns suicidal when fate and the mistakes of a medical man who treats her throat force her early retirement from the stage. Armgart's predicament, like that of the Alcharisi, allows George Eliot to consider what happens to a gifted woman's soul after her gift has died.

In 1848 George Sand published her own version of the plight of the retired diva in the novel *Lucrezia Floriani.* Among the many references to the works of Sand in Eliot's correspondence, there is none to *Lucrezia;* therefore it is uncertain whether Eliot read the novel (although, given her admiration for Sand, it would be surprising if she had overlooked a Sand novel that seems to have ranked with *Consuelo* and *Lélia* in its fascination for British women of letters). G. H. Lewes knew the novel; in his famous essay "The Lady Novelists," Lewes not only pays Sand the supreme compliment, ". . . for eloquence and depth of feeling, no man approaches George Sand," he also mentions by name *Lucrezia Floriani* as the "most confessional" of Sand's works.[75] I do not insist that the Alcharisi and Armgart are influenced by Sand's heroine, but rather that the contrasts between Sand's actress and Eliot's operatic stars illustrate that while Sand does believe in the possibility of life after art has died, Eliot has the more serious reservations. Of the two Georges, it is Eliot who considers female silencing a most horrific nightmare. While Lucrezia has been just as successful and adored as Eliot's actresses/singers, she has chosen her retirement rather than having had it forced upon her. While they retire to a silent void with only echoes of dying applause, Lucrezia retreats to a hum of activity in a familial scene to which she seems indispensable. She possesses the talent to love that Alcharisi denies and Armgart demonstrates she cannot comprehend.

Sand's genius Lucrezia, formerly of Milan, now residing at the lake at Iseo, has been a playwright, actress, and prima donna; as a theater manager she has also been a successful businesswoman. Lucrezia, however, understands that theater is an "illusion" at best, and at worst an exploitation of women. One must be made of iron, she says, to endure the life of an actress. She has left the stage because she is exhausted, her imagination satiated. Lacking the will to perform when her heart is no longer in the enterprise, she is clever enough to call it quits before she becomes second-rate, a "torso of a soul" who "gabbles" her elocution and "mashes up" her rhythm. Lucrezia is also an earth mother, the matriarch of a clan that includes four children (by different fathers), an elderly father, and eventually the younger lover, Prince Karol de Roswald, in an *affaire de cœur* based upon Sand's

75. Lewes, "The Lady Novelists," 133, 136.

longtime liaison with the composer Frederic Chopin. Lucrezia is in Karol's view a Madonna; in the opinion of his friend Salvator, a goddess. Further, she is a virtuous woman—by her own definition that she has never had more than one lover at a time.

But complications arise from Lucrezia's emotional entanglements with men, including irrational jealousy of the part of Karol; the carping criticisms of her avaricious father, Menapace; and melodramatic posing of the second-rate actor Vandoni, who threatens that he will claim custody of their infant, now in Lucrezia's custody, should she marry Prince Karol. After the inevitable rupture with Karol, Lucrezia lives out the remainder of her life in sadness for the loss of her life's most intoxicating passion. Significant, though, is Sand's point that her despair is brought on by a failure in human love, not a failure in professional acclaim or aesthetic creativity. Like Eliot's Alcharisi, Lucrezia twice suffers silencing—in retirement and in death. But life has taught her that although youth desires to *be* happy, by a certain age a mature person knows the only happiness is that which she *gives*.

In her preface to the novel, Sand admits that as a novelist she has been given to the wild torrents of Romanticism, but that in *Lucrezia* she has instead chosen realism: "le lac uni et monotone de l'analyse"—the lucidity of a calm, monotonous lake of analysis.[76] This metaphor she has made visible in Iseo, the lake on which Lucrezia's estate has been built. Clear-headed analysis also becomes the principle on which Lucrezia bases her retirement. The aging actress realizes that she has become "mother" to her lovers and to her own father and that her maternal arms of love must stretch to encompass them all—lovers, father, children, admirers. When Sand published *Lucrezia Floriani,* she still had three decades of remaining life and no doubt hoped that she could retire to Nohant as gracefully as Lucrezia does to Iseo. But, unlike Lucrezia, she could not turn her back on the art that had brought her fame. In her "retirement" Sand played with her granddaughters, sewed puppet costumes, visited the sick, and became "the good grandmother of Nohant," but she still produced approximately two novels each year until very near the end of life. Like George Eliot, she desired to have both the happiness of an ordinary matriarch and the voice of a world-renowned novelist.[77] Nevertheless, in *Lucrezia Floriani* Sand attempts to demonstrate that life need not be life-in-death apart from the theater; Armgart knows that it is. Hence the temptation to suicide.

Armgart's down-to-earth cousin, Walpurga, indirectly inspires Armgart's sal-

---

76. Sand, "Notice," in *Lucrezia Floriani,* 2.

77. As previously noted, Eliot was relieved not to have brought children into the world; she was, however, "Mutter" to Lewes's sons, nursing one of them, Thornton Lewes, in his terminal illness and considering the children of Charles Lewes as her own grandchildren.

vation from narcissism, a second chance for life. Armgart had taken the lame cousin from the village of Freiburg and given her a "vocation" as attendant to the rising star, and for five years Walpurga has been to the singer a nonentity—uninteresting because neither talented nor beautiful. But the worm turns: When Armgart becomes suicidal because her only love has been taken from her, Walpurga informs her that she is selfish, that her haranguing on "superfluous," plain, untalented women who lead meaningless lives has all these years insulted the very woman who has uncomplainingly cared for her, tolerated her moods, and soothed her feelings. Kathleen Blake notes that Armgart's career, in which "glory saps loving-kindness," demonstrates a special danger for the woman artist whose glory is so exceptional that it exaggerates the gap between herself and her sex, that for Armgart art and love have been "destructively divided."[78] But Eliot offers at the end a chance for resurrection, and ironically the "superfluous" woman becomes the exhorting prophet when she challenges Armgart, telling her that now she is also "lame" and that she should consider the death of her voice as a "new birth from that monstrous Self" (A, WGE, 19:119).

In Eliot's religion the ability to love and to suffer for another is the highest demonstration of the god in man, the man as god. Armgart's resurrection is too abrupt to be convincing, but the poem ends on a positive note as the singer, having observed her elderly voice coach, whose own works are now seldom performed, sees that there is a graceful way to live when one's life span exceeds one's art. His manifesto is essentially that of Lucrezia with the difference that she survives for the love of her family, he for the success of his students. Armgart will become, like him, a teacher and will "pass [his] gift / to others who can use it for delight" (A, WGE, 19:123). Furthermore, she chooses to teach in Freiburg, so that Walpurga can return home. In Armgart's fall, Eliot forces her to acknowledge her overweening pride and sense of entitlement. A supranormal woman who has given birth to art instead of infants, she buries the "little corpse" of her great operatic career.

That Armgart predates the portrait of the Alcharisi, however, raises skepticism about whether an Eliot artist so long cut off from human sympathy, and living in an illusory world, can ever renounce her royalty to become an ordinary "plain brown" thrush. After all, Sand's Lucrezia Floriani claims she is satiated, while Armgart admits she is still ravenous. Lucrezia boasts that she can leave the spotlight behind her, but she remains extraordinary in ordinary circumstances; Armgart hopes she can make do without applause and accolades, but she has yet to face the test; the Alcharisi knows she cannot live without art, and she has become embittered because of her "miscalculation."

78. Blake, "Armgart—George Eliot on the Woman Artist," 79.

The Silenced Woman

Throughout her literary career George Eliot was fascinated by the lives and motivations of artists. She depicts the passion for art in the music of Caterina Sarti and Armgart; the Romanticist concept of the artist as Promethean in Mordecai and Deronda; the sensitivity of the artist in Philip Wakem; the ambivalence and insecurities of the artist in Will Ladislaw, Adolph Naumann, and Hans Meyrick; artistic dilettantism in Philip and Will; grandiosity of artistic genius in Klesmer and of artistic desire in Gwendolen; glowing purity of art in Mirah Lapidoth; and the silencing of the artist in Caterina, Armgart, and Leonora Halm-Eberstein. Silencing, however, is demonstrated by Eliot not only for her female artists but also for other monumental women—her Madonnas, Antigones, resurrection angels, and Beatrices who are more social workers than artists—whose vocation and vision are to create good in the world as the artist creates beauty. The works consistently warn the extraordinary woman that whether she is artist or reformer—or in Eliot's case both artist and moralist—her voice is hardly audible. To her fellow novelist and moralist Harriet Beecher Stowe, Eliot wrote

> I am beginning to see with new clearness, that if a book which has any sort of exquisiteness happens also to be a popular widely circulated book, its power over the social mind, for any good, is after all due to its reception by a few appreciative natures, and is the slow result of radiation from that narrow circle. I mean, that you can affect a few souls, and that each of those in turn may affect a few more, but that no exquisite book tells properly and directly on a multitude however largely it may be spread by type and paper. . . . I do not write this cynically, but in pure sadness and pity. Both travelling abroad and staying at home among our English sights and reports, one must continually feel how slowly the centuries work toward the moral good of men. (*GEL*, 5:30–31)

George Eliot wrapped herself in the mantle of Staël and Sand and placed her heroines solidly in the tradition of Corinne and Consuelo with the host of allusions that their mythology implies—Beatrice, the Madonna, Psyche, Athena, Pythian, Cumæan Sibyl, Eurydice, divine Sophia/Wisdom. She desires to "join the choir invisible"—those whose mellifluous voices teach selfless love. Like Letitia Landon's Erinna, who also considers music the highest art form and who wishes her songs to be "the young poet's first delights; / Read by dark-eyed maiden" in the moonlight, and "murmur'd by the lover" when the artist herself shall "wake no more," Eliot desires an immortality beyond the silencing.[79] As artist,

79. Landon, "Erinna," lines 340–44, 368, in *Selected Writings*, 98, 99.

sibyl, and "singer," however, she intends a higher good than Landon's Erinna, whose songs inspire passion and romantic love, for George Eliot's words shall make the small splashes from which ripples radiate outward to contribute to the moral excellence of the race:

> O may I join the choir invisible
> Of those immortal dead who live again
> In minds made better by their presence: live
> In pulses stirred to generosity,
> In deeds of daring rectitude, in scorn
> For miserable aims that end with self,
> In thoughts sublime that pierce the night like stars,
> And with their mild persistence urge man's search
> To vaster issues. So to live is heaven:
> To make undying music in the world . . .[80]

80. Eliot, "'O May I Join the Choir Invisible,'" in *WGE,* 19:271.

5

Mrs. Humphry (Mary) Ward
and the Artist as Medusa

Germaine de Staël's Corinne is an exhibitionist, spectacle, and star, perpetual object of the fascinated gaze of Oswald, Lord of Nelvil. Repeatedly in the novel Staël permits us to watch Nelvil as he observes the *improvisatrice:* Corinne reciting, Corinne reflected in the waters of the Virgin Spring, Corinne receiving the poet's laurel at the Capitol, Corinne performing as Semiramis and Juliet, Corinne dancing the tarantella—and arousing Nelvil by her tantalizing performance. These scenes in which Corinne is created by the male gaze are recreated in several female-authored texts as women novelists remark upon the mesmerizing influence of their gender on display. Another obvious instance of the gaze phenomenon is the fascinated Jean Valreg in George Sand's *La Daniella,* a novel much indebted to *Corinne* in several aspects, not the least of which is the male gaze upon the female performer. Still another instance is Jewsbury's *The Half Sisters,* which owes more to *Corinne* than to any other single source. Jewsbury's Bianca, an English Corinne, pours all her "passionate burning love" for Conrad into her own performance of Shakespeare's Juliet; Conrad is "madly in love" with the actress by the end of the first act; by the end of the drama he was "intensely jealous of every man in the theatre"—fancying that all of them wish to become Romeo to Bianca's Juliet (*HS,* 142). Even Barrett Browning's Aurora is, ever so briefly, the object of the gaze when Romney comes upon her crowning her brow with a poet's wreath and she "stood there fixed . . . arms up, like the caryatid, sole / Of some abolished temple" (*AL* 2.60–62) while her "public" of one admires the "witch, scholar, poet, dreamer, and the rest" he hopes to claim as his wife (*AL* 2.86).

In Staël's original version of the artist and the gaze, Corinne desires Nelvil's mesmerized gaze while Nelvil, jealous of the eyes of other men upon Corinne, desires to appropriate her performance for his eyes alone. In a clever and ironic play upon the effect of the gaze, Staël takes her characters to a London theatrical performance in which Corinne witnesses Nelvil's gaze shift from herself to her young half-sister, Lucile. Mrs. Siddons performs as Isabella in the tragic drama *Fatal Marriage,* and from her box Corinne watches Nelvil gaze upon Lucile, who has been reduced to tears by Mrs. Siddons's powerful acting. Thus in a circular pattern of gazes, Corinne watches Nelvil, who watches Lucile, who in turn watches a stage version of the impending tragedy of Corinne—a tragedy that Lucile will unknowingly bring about by separating Corinne from her lover. Staël understands well the effect of Nelvil's gaze. So long as the fascination endures, he is as frozen as if he had gazed upon the Medusa (the Gorgon being, after all, originally not a grotesque monstrosity but a beautiful, yet dangerous, creature.) The gaze unmans Nelvil. Lost in the throes of passion, he allows himself to be deterred from his duty as an Englishman—in this case, the duty of supporting England in the war against France. Nancy K. Miller says that Corinne has watched herself being looked at—that the female perceives herself through the male gaze. Once Nelvil leaves Italy, Miller adds, Corinne is "[c]ut off from the mobile *jouissance* of performance, through which she defies the conventional inscription of woman's body" and she "seems to enter the borderline zones of an identity in crisis. . . ."[1] Corinne enjoys power only so long as Nelvil gazes upon her, but Nelvil is incapacitated so long as his gaze is fixated upon the powerful goddess.

The Medusa myth, it would appear, is an important aspect of the woman-as-artist literary tradition, especially if the artistry involves the woman exhibited as actress, singer, dancer, or musician who performs upon a stage for the delight of her audience, but it is also operative if the female artist in question is a powerful genius whose artistic power emasculates the men who admire her, and in some cases envy her artistic power. Twice in the Sand novel *La Daniella* the "sibylle" Daniella performs, provoking in the mind of the French foreigner the same response that the sibyl Corinne inspires in the English visitor Nelvil. The "fureur sacrée" of Daniella's performance of song and dance, accompanied by tambourine, causes Jean Valreg to shiver with passion and jealousy ("frissonner d'amour et de jalousie").[2] In Sand's *Lélia* and *Elle et lui,* however, the male artist is "frozen" and emasculated because, he charges, the woman artist as muse has failed him. In *Elle et lui* the painter Laurent de Fauvel is maddened because his mistress, Thérèse, is a tranquil, wise, placid, hard-working, and amiable "sphinx" who actually produces work to support the two of them. Laurent at the same time is an idealist who cannot work without suffering, who craves love and sex—both, it seems, essential to his creative productivity—and the combined charms

1. Miller, "Performances of the Gaze: Staël's *Corinne, or Italy,*" 93–94.
2. Sand, *La Daniella,* 1:217, 2:151.

of Thérèse and various harlots cannot satisfy his boundless need. Laurent is an egoist easily bored; he needs Thérèse as mother and nurse, but he insults her art that keeps him. His is the agony of Prometheus, the frenzy of Orestes. Without her he cannot paint.[3] Similarly the poet Sténio (in *Lélia*) blames Lélia that his gift has died, for she has deprived him of love, God, and inspiration and—his muse having deserted—his pen is frozen. If Laurent's paintbrush or Sténio's pen proves sterile, then his emasculation as man and artist is complete and he must die.

Among nineteenth-century British women writers the Medusa is a recurring figure, as is the fascinating woman whose "identity" is created by the male gaze. Often the George Eliot heroine is an idealized object of a gaze that attempts to freeze and preserve a mythic perception of her: A lover paints Maggie as a tall hamadryad, another painter sees Romola as Antigone, another depicts Mirah as Berenice, and still another wants to paint Dorothea as the Madonna or Santa Clara.[4] Such Eliot heroines are not, however, castrating muses in the sense that they freeze into sterility the men who admire them. Eliot does repeatedly invoke the Medusa figure, although her Medusa is never an artist or performer who charms men, as Corinne and Daniella do. Rather, Eliot's Medusas tend toward the horrific, the nightmare vision of the conscience. In *Janet's Repentance,* the abusive husband Robert Dempster, in delirium tremens, imagines his wife with hair of hissing black serpents, arms of great white serpents to drag him into the cold water of death. In *Adam Bede,* Hetty pauses in her "journey in despair" while the narrator describes her formerly round, dimpled, childish beauty as having turned "hard and even fierce," "like that wondrous Medusa-face, with the passionate, passionless lips" (*AB,* 2:367).[5] In *Daniel Deronda,* after Gwendolen Harleth has married Grandcourt, she encounters his displaced mistress, whose Medusa-like glare paralyzes her. Eliot's Medusas, especially Janet and Mrs. Glasher, are horrifying Furies pursuing evildoers, not Medusas as mesmerizing artists.

In Elizabeth Barrett Browning's *Aurora Leigh,* the child Aurora looks upon the portrait of her deceased mother as a loving Psyche, Lamia, or "still Medusa with mild milky brows / All curdled and all clothed upon with snakes / Whose slime falls fast as sweat will" (*AL* 1.157–59)—a Medusa who has the power of paralyz-

---

3. Laurent is based in part upon Alfred de Musset, who wrote little after the end of his liaison with George Sand.

4. Kimberly VanEsveld Adams demonstrates that Dorothea Brooke of *Middlemarch* is the object of four separate "gazes": egoist, dismembering, connoisseur's, and iconizing (*Our Lady of Victorian Feminism,* 186–91).

5. Joseph Wiesenfarth shows that Eliot has in mind the Medusa Rondanini, which Eliot had seen in 1858, and had written in her Commonplace Book a summary of Adolph Stahr's commentary that this particular Medusa was antiquity's best example of the beautiful used to express the ugly (*George Eliot's Mythmaking,* 43–44).

ing the gaze of the maturing female child poet, but which, as Barbara Gelpi notes, signifies the irrational anger of the child and her deep ambivalence about becoming a woman.[6]

The late Victorian and Edwardian novelist Mrs. Humphry (Mary A.) Ward also was fascinated with the Medusa;[7] in *Eleanor,* for example, a bronze Medusa recovered from the Mediterranean seems to fix her eyes on a statue of the Virgin Mary, as if she is staring down the new religion that replaced faith in the ancient goddess. In *Robert Elsmere,* Ward's most celebrated novel, a bust of the Medusa represents intellectual sterility. Furthermore, among Ward's fictional women artists, she incorporates a range of emasculating goddesses to encode the power of female creativity—and although she does not always refer to the Gorgon by name, the Medusa serves as the overarching myth for a range of sirens, witches, and goddesses who freeze men, convert them to swine, decapitate them, or castrate them. Ward's use of the Medusa differs drastically from that of George Eliot, but the effect of the gaze upon the mesmerizing artist/goddess is very much like that of Staël's Corinne and Sand's Daniella—that is, a compelling demonstration of the frightening powers of female creativity.

Annis Pratt acknowledges the power of Medusa as source for feminine strength for Victorian women, noting that Medusa's snake locks are object of either phallic worship or are dread of castration—a point made previously, and famously, by Sigmund Freud:

> To decapitate = to castrate. The terror of Medusa is thus a terror of castration that is linked to the sight of [the female genitals] surrounded by hair . . .
>
> The sight of the Medusa's head makes the spectator stiff with terror, turns him to stone. Observe we have here once again the same origin from the castration complex and the same transformation of affect! For becoming stiff means an erection. Thus in the original situation it offers consolation to the spectator: he is still in possession of a penis, and the stiffening reassures him of the fact.[8]

---

6. Gelpi, *"Aurora Leigh,"* 37–38.

7. Ward's novels were published using her husband's name: i.e., Mrs. Humphry Ward. The prefaces and introductions to the Westmoreland edition of her works, as well as her critical works, however, are signed as Mary A. Ward. For speculation on her separate identity as creator and critic, see Bindslev, *Mrs. Humphry Ward: A Study in Late-Victorian Feminine Consciousness and Creative Expression,* 10–13. John Sutherland considers her insistence upon the name "Humphry" as "exaggeratedly old-fashioned" and absurd (*Mrs. Humphry Ward,* 59).

8. Pratt, *Dancing with Goddesses: Archetypes, Poetry, and Empowerment,* 13, 35; Freud, "The Medusa's Head," in *Sexuality and the Psychology of Love,* 212–13. Some take issue with Freud's version; Philip Slater, for example, argues that the Medusa's head symbolizes the maternal genitalia and that the fear expressed in the myth is more of impotence than of castration. Nevertheless he agrees that "ambivalent scoptophilia" is the central meaning in the Perseus myth (*The Glory of Hera: Greek Mythology and the Greek Family,* 318–32).

Although the Medusa is occasionally depicted as a horrific witch, she is also seen as beautiful and desirable, hence capable of inspiring sexual desire. It is often then the beauty of the Medusa, rather than some ghastly physical trait, that incapacitates the beholder, as Shelley notes in "On the Medusa of Leonardo da Vinci in the Florentine Gallery":

> Yet it is less the horror than the grace
>   Which turns the gazer's spirit into stone,
> Whereon the lineaments of that dead face
>   Are graven, till the characters be grown
> Into itself, and thought no more can trace;
>   'Tis the melodious hue of beauty thrown
> Athwart the darkness and the glare of pain,
> Which humanize and harmonize the strain.[9]

Pratt notes that in the eighteenth and nineteenth centuries the "Medusa rage" is directed against norms denying sensuality as a natural attribute of women. If the Medusa myth refers specifically to the artist, then the female artist affirms her sexual power but also smites her male admirer, leaving him stunned, mesmerized, and impotent.

Ward's Seductive Female Artists

In each of Mrs. Humphry Ward's first three novels (1884, 1888, 1892) she showcases a fictional woman artist whose powers are Medusa-like—in the first novel an actress, in the second a violinist, in the third a painter. The depictions of Isabel Bretherton, Rose Leyburn, and Elise Delaunay explore female artistry of terrifying power and petrifying threat. In each case the gaze of the admirer codifies the threat to his creativity or masculinity, and Ward explores the gaze phenomenon in intriguing ways, although she finally neutralizes the woman artist's power in conventional outcomes. Ward's women artists are invariably scintillating, mesmerizing, passionate, and ambitious. They also abet their creator in entertaining the most interesting questions of what price must a woman pay for art, whether love quickens art or stifles it, and whether selfish egoism is an inevitable product of genius—questions under consideration ever since the publication of *Corinne* and *Consuelo*.

But Ward's female artists are also temptresses and sirens. Irrespective of whether

---

9. Shelley, "On the Medusa of Leonardo da Vinci," lines 9–16, in *The Complete Poetical Works of Percy Bysshe Shelley*, 577–58.

they are sympathetically portrayed, they are Circe, Vivien, Undine, Salome, and Medusa, transfixing and controlling the men who desire them. This quality is rather odd, suggesting that the female artist is at once more fascinating and more dangerous than other women. Certainly they are more fascinating than other women who populate the *same* Ward novels—although in each novel Ward attempts to create at least one splendid woman. Whether the artist is by allusion and implication a Salome (the painter Elise in *David Grieve*), a Vivien (the actress Isabel in *Miss Bretherton*), or a Medusa (the violinist Rose in *Robert Elsmere*), she holds the power to turn into stone the admirer whom she holds in thrall. Gilbert and Gubar note that such "terrible sorceress-goddesses as the Sphinx, Medusa, Circe, Kali, Delilah, and Salome . . . possess duplicitous arts that allow them both to seduce and to steal male generative energy." Furthermore, Bram Dijkstra, in his study of fin-de-siècle "iconography of misogyny," points out that a familiar period icon—that of Medusa/Lilith/Eve/Lamia—represents specifically the "viragoes" or New Women, who rejected female roles and demanded male privilege. Dijkstra notes that in some fin-de-siècle paintings, the "snakes of [Medusa's] viraginity" pose a sexual threat to the male viewer.[10] In Ward's fiction this Medusa power emanates from both her sexual attractiveness and her artistry. Indeed, it is impossible to separate them.

Ward's Literary Evolution

Mary Arnold came of age a generation after Marian Evans. By the date of her marriage to Humphry Ward (1872), there were five women's colleges in England; women's struggle for franchise had been ongoing for a decade; bills for married women's property rights had been introduced; John Stuart Mill, in the recently published *The Subjection of Women,* had argued for gender equality in law, government, the professions, and education; Darwin's *Origin of Species* had for a decade influenced the world's thinking about religion and free will; the Risorgimento, which had influenced the imagination of several English writers (for example, Barrett Browning in *Casa Guidi Windows* and Eliot in *Romola*), had been resolved; the Tractarian movement was history; and contemporary novelists like Thomas Hardy were moving from realism to a naturalism much influenced by Darwinian thought and scientific determinism.

Ward was an intellectual and the daughter of a notable British family of letters. Her fraternal grandfather was "Arnold of Rugby," a friend of Wordsworth; her father was Tom Arnold, an Anglo-Saxon scholar and a friend of the poet Arthur Clough; and her fraternal "Uncle Matt," with whom she debated literary

10. Gilbert and Gubar, *The Madwoman in the Attic,* 34; Dijkstra, *Idols of Perversity,* viii, 309, 310.

ideas, was the poet Matthew Arnold. At eight Mary Arnold had tea with Harriet Martineau; at eighteen she discussed Spanish history and geography with George Eliot (who was at work on *The Spanish Gypsy*); at a Kensington dinner party, Mrs. Humphry Ward as a young wife spent an evening "tête-à-tête" with the elderly Robert Browning, who was her table partner (*WR*, 2:58–59). The Arnold family struggled financially, but measured in terms of intellectual opportunity, Ward's was an extremely privileged childhood. In her memoir she says that from childhood she lived "a life spent largely among books" (*WR*, 1:2). At the Bodleian she helped her father in his research on early English literature; at twenty she had specialized and published in the field of Spanish history and literature, her specialty the *Poema Del Cid* and Visigothic invasion. Like Barrett Browning and Eliot, she read omnivorously, and her tastes were catholic. She was fluent in German, Italian, French, Latin, early and modern Spanish, and eventually Greek. As a bride, she moved in intellectual circles in Oxford; as wife and mother, in the publishing world of London, where Humphry Ward became the art critic for the *Times*. Like George Eliot she began her literary career with the translation of an important theological-philosophical text, in Ward's case Henri Amiel's *Journal Intime*. Like both Jewsbury and Eliot, she worked as a journalist: as a young wife, she helped support the Ward household of three children by writing for *Saturday Review, Pall Mall Gazette, Macmillan's*, and the *Times*. Hers was the first serious feminist criticism of the Brontë sisters; in the prefaces to her 1899 Haworth Edition she places the Brontës in the context of French Romanticism and Russian and Continental realism, rather than dismissing them as eccentric personalities or literary curiosities.

Ward's novels—although sometimes melodramatic and, at their worst, implausible in plot and narrative, and polemic in intent—are invariably serious. Her most frequent topics are religion, politics, and art. In religion she was, like George Eliot, an Evangelical in her girlhood. Her mother, Julia Sorell Arnold, was descended from French Huguenots, and her father was a Catholic. In the Tom Arnold family, sons were educated in their father's faith, girls in their mother's—hence Mary's indoctrination into Protestantism. Arnold's Catholicism was a thorn in Julia's flesh, and Ward's 1898 novel, *Helbeck of Bannisdale,* depicts the strife of Catholic/Protestant conflict within a British family. As a young adult, Mary Ward became a Modernist who rejected the doctrine of Resurrection, holding that second-generation Christians taught the Second Coming because they could not grasp that the kingdom of God is within. The second Ward novel, *Robert Elsmere* (1888),[11] depicts an honest man's struggle to stay in the Anglican faith when he, like the author, no longer believes in biblical miracles. Elsmere in

11. Or first novel, depending upon whether one counts the children's book *Milly and Olly* (1881) and

good conscience leaves the church, a move that Ward endorsed at the time, although because of that stance the novel was a disappointment to influential Anglicans whose favor she coveted—like Browning, William Gladstone, and the Oxford idealogue Benjamin Jowett, and it possibly would have disappointed uncle Matthew Arnold, had he lived long enough to read the completed novel. In Ward's 1911 *The Case of Richard Meynell*, she is still struggling with Modernism in the established Church; in this novel the clergyman/reformer—unlike Elsmere—does not leave the fold but attempts to modernize it from within, Meynell's position being that which Ward had come to favor.

In politics a young Ward considered herself a "good Radical"; her 1894 novel, *Marcella*, treats a woman who is extremely liberal and idealistic in politics and who is—Ward's daughter says—a fictionalized Mary Arnold. Marcella is a near-socialist in philosophy, and her husband is a conservative aristocrat; in the course of the novel, they come to a meeting of minds in a commitment to help the working classes achieve economic welfare and more democratic institutions. In the sequel, *Sir George Thessady*, at issue is whether the government should protect workers from exploitation or support a laissez-faire approach to business; Marcella favors the former approach, and the Tory Sir George, the latter. Other political novels are *The Testing of Diana Mallory*, about domestic politics, electioneering, and suffrage for women, but also English colonialism in India, Afghanistan, and Nigeria (which Ward supported), and *The Marriage of William Ashe*, the story of an undersecretary in the Foreign Affairs department and his calculating mother—the characters perhaps based on Mary Ward and her own political son. Ward not only wrote on politics, she was also a social and political activist. She was one of the chief promoters behind the Edward Passmore Settlement House and Somerville Hall, founded in Oxford for the education of women.

Ward is notorious, however, for opposing women's suffrage, a stance that cost her female readers. She and the women intellectuals of Oxford did not wish, she says, to participate in a political state that stood for imperialism and sanctioned war as England did; therefore they did not seek national enfranchisement in Parliamentary elections but chose instead an approach that they hoped would influence outcomes from the local level upwards (*WR*, 1:204). Even to this reservation one might well question whether Ward had in mind a more palatable version of the "Archangels" of *William Ashe*—the wives, sisters, and mothers of important men who used their influence behind the scenes to manipulate powerful men into social contact with other powerful men. Yet to women of the time, her plan remained unpalatable because it would grant only indirect power, and that only

---

the novella *Miss Bretherton* (1884) as novels. For my purposes, *Miss Bretherton* is considered Ward's first novel because it is her first adult fiction that deals with the themes of this study.

to women of a certain social class.[12] In any case, Ward grew more conservative as she aged, and in *Delia Blanchflower* (1915) she makes her spokeswoman for the vote, Gertrude Marvell, as militant and insufferable as the feminist Isabel Fotheringham is in *Diana Mallory.*

As for her attention to artists and aesthetics, Ward frequently includes in her novels characters who are artists: playwrights, musicians, poets, actresses, and painters. In fact two of her novels *(Miss Bretherton* and *Fenwick's Career)* are *Künstlerromane* about gifted artists who begin with the disadvantages of poverty—the former about the development of an orphaned female actress, the latter about an opinionated and cheeky English painter swimming upstream against the tide of Impressionism in Paris. Furthermore her characters Rose Leyburn and Elise Delaunay—although not protagonists of their respective novels—are among the most extraordinary among Ward's fascinating women. Ward recognizes that artistic genius makes a person—whether man or woman—potentially vivacious and intriguing as a literary study, and she exploits the opportunity to illustrate the sexual power of the female artist—power that exists only so long as the artist does not come down from Olympus to marry a mortal. In her introduction to *Villette,* Ward says that in artistic fields other than fiction writing, women are amateurs, novices, and strangers "still on sufferance," but in the novel they are "masters" because—while male novelists study manners, politics, and adventures—women understand all kinds of love, but especially between men and women.[13] Therefore Ward, in employing her artistic specialty as a woman novelist, brings her female goddesses to the marriage altar, but in the Wardian conundrum when they become loving mortals—wives and mothers—they lose the powers of Medusa. Before they capitulate, they embody a fascination traceable from Staël and Sand.

Because Ward's star has dimmed, it seems implausible that she was as successful and famous as she once was. When *Robert Elsmere* was published, it sold one-half million copies within the first year, became a best-seller of the century, and sparked pirated editions and an unauthorized dramatic rendition. American acquaintances wrote to say that in their country it was the most diffused among all classes of readers and the "most effective and popular" novel since *Uncle Tom's Cabin* (*WR,* 2:91, 92). Walter Pater noted that the novel is a "*chef d'œuvre* of the kind of quiet evolution of character through circumstance, introduced into English literature by Miss Austen and carried to perfection in France by George Sand. . . ." At the end of the century, William Dean Howells wrote that "Mrs.

12. Sutherland suggests other possible reasons: political indebtedness to antisuffrage politicians who asked her support, belief that voting was "unseemly" for women, and objection to the militancy of the suffrage campaign (*Mrs. Humphry Ward,* 299, 200).

13. Ward, introduction to *The Life and Work of the Sisters Brontë,* xx, xxv.

Ward . . . alone among English writers" is worthy to be mentioned with Thomas Hardy and George Eliot. Ward's best novels are incontestably the earlier ones; the twentieth-century work is increasingly conservative, chauvinistic, and didactic. When Ward's daughter Janet Trevelyan published a biography of her famous mother in 1923, she terms the later work "autumnal," while Virginia Woolf, reviewing Trevelyan's book, remarks that only a daughter could call it autumnal, rather than call it bad. Woolf says, "None of the great Victorian reputations has sunk lower than that of Mrs. Humphry Ward." Having assigned Elizabeth Barrett Browning to bang crockery in the servants' quarters of the "mansion of literature," Woolf places Mrs. Ward's novels "in the lumber-room of letters like the mantles of our aunts" because they "produce in us the same desire that they do to smash the window and let in the air, to light the fire and pile the rubbish on top."[14] Given that the new century was to witness the demise of the triple-decker novel of complicated plot, ponderous exposition, and interconnection of characters and themes, in favor of experimentalism in streamlined style, stream-of-conscious narration, and Freudian/psychological analysis, Ward soon became dated. To writers and readers of the new century, she was decidedly too "Victorian" to be taken seriously.

Ward's Literary Matriarchs

Mary Ward's indebtedness to George Eliot is by no means a recent discovery. When *Robert Elsmere* was published, it was immediately compared to *Adam Bede*, and *David Grieve* was called the "best novel since George Eliot" (although it was also called "tedious" and "a failure"). Charles Townsend Copeland, a contemporary of Ward's, notes that comparing her to George Eliot is a frequent means of praising Ward, admitting, "And there is undoubtedly a superficial likeness. Both women are learned to the verge of pedantry, both have a far-reaching interest in life and the problems of human conduct, both get their novels under way and keep them under way by elaborate and often cumbrous means." Predictably, Copeland finds Ward to be Eliot's inferior in drama, passion, style, and humor, closing his essay with the statement that there is no excuse for "confounding

14. Pater, review of *Robert Elsmere*, in *The Guardian*, March 28, 1888 (reprinted in Pater, *Essays in Literature and Art*, 135). Howells, *Heroines of Fiction* 2:261 (Howells calls special attention to Ward's magnificent women, especially Eleanor Burgoyne and Marcella Boyce, of *Eleanor* and *Marcella*, respectively, and Lucy Purcell and Elise Delaunay, of *David Grieve*); Trevelyan, *The Life of Mrs. Humphry Ward*, 55; Woolf, "*Aurora Leigh*," and "The Compromise (Mrs. Humphry Ward)," both in Woolf, *Virginia Woolf: Women and Writing*, 134, 169. Woolf's essays were originally published in *The Common Reader: Second Series* and *The New Republic*, January, 9, 1924; Woolf refers to Trevelyan's comment about her mother's work entering a "long autumn" after *Lady Rose's Daughter* and *William Ashe* (*Life of Mrs. Humphry Ward*, 204).

ethics with genius, conscience with art, or—Mrs. Ward with George Eliot." Peter Collister notes that George Eliot was never far from Ward's consciousness and adumbrates numerous similarities in characterization. According to Collister, Ward's Marcella combines attributes of Dorothea Brooke and Gwendolen Harleth, Robert Elsmere's comparison of his wife to Dante's Beatrice recalls Ladislaw's similar musings on Dorothea, and in *Sir George Thessady* when Ward's noble Marcella intervenes, on behalf of the rising young politician/hero, with Thessady's "vulgar and naïvely ambitious wife," Letty, Ward takes her cue from Dorothea's intervention with Rosamond on behalf of Tertius Lydgate in Eliot's *Middlemarch*.[15] Collister might well have added that in *Fenwick's Career* Ward places Eugénie de Pastourelles and Phœbe Fenwick in a relationship similar to that of Dorothea and Rosamond when the young wife Phœbe has abandoned her husband, the painter John Fenwick, and Eugénie persuades her to forgive John's selfish neglect and to restore the marriage. Furthermore Eugénie is Fenwick's saint and benefactor, as Dorothea is Lydgate's; she is a Madonna-like woman, as Dorothea is; and she is also like Eliot's "foundress of nothing" in that she felt "few persons were so unprofitable as she" because she merely has used her wealth, charm, and intelligence to help the people she has encountered in life.[16] Another probable reference to George Eliot is an event in the story of Laura Fountain in *Helbeck of Bannisdale;* in establishing her headstrong likeness to Maggie Tulliver, Ward sends Laura for an outing with a suitor who presses his attention upon her and causes her to miss the train; when Laura returns home the next day, alone and unmarried, she becomes the subject for gossip and speculation, as Maggie does after her similar adventure with Stephen Guest. Also like Maggie, Laura dies by drowning. A still more striking echo of Eliot is in *David Grieve,* a novel in which the brother/sister relationship of David and Louie Grieve recalls the Tulliver children of Eliot's *The Mill on the Floss.* Whether or not the novels of George Eliot produced anxiety in Ward, they certainly produced an influence.

As for the influence of the French predecessors of the female portrait of the artist, Ward is less influenced by Staël than by Sand. She knew Germaine de Staël, but references in Ward's writing usually point to Staël as an intellectual, not to *Corinne.* One early novel, *Eleanor,* does follow the pattern of the Corinne-Nelvil-Lucy triangle that had been used successfully by several British writers, including Jewsbury, in *The Half Sisters,* and Barrett Browning, in *Aurora Leigh.* Like

15. Copeland, "George Eliot and Mrs. Humphry Ward," 503, 505; Collister, "Portraits of 'Audacious Youth': George Eliot and Mrs. Humphry Ward," 299, 309, 312; Judith Wilt also notes that Marcella's intervention "reenacts Dorothea's visit to Rosamond," in *Middlemarch* ("'Transition Time': The Political Romances of Mrs. Humphry Ward's *Marcella* and *Sir George Thessady,*" 241).

16. Ward, *Fenwick's Career,* 135, 284, 375.

Corinne, the novel is set in Italy. Eleanor Burgoyne, though no *improvisatrice,* is an accomplished musician, artist, and scholar. A regal "goddess—heathenishly divine,"[17] she assists her Nelvil, Edward Manisty, in his research of Italian history and politics and undertakes the education of the young and unsophisticated American Puritan Lucy Foster—assuming a protective, motherly position as Corinne does with Lucile. When Manisty turns his affections to Lucy, Eleanor at first tries to remove Lucy from Manisty's sight; then she repents, blesses the marriage, becomes ill, and dies young. The situation and relationships are reminiscent of Staël's masterpiece.

Although Ward is much influenced by George Eliot, it is the other George who haunts her work—or at least her novels on the nature of art and the female artist. In the preface to *David Grieve,* Ward says that although art can be propaganda (the "novel of ideas"), and art can be a refuge from problems (the creed of Scott, Austen, and George Eliot),[18] Ward herself vows to follow Rousseau, Goethe, and George Sand in a middle road of art that blends both ideas and reality with magic and imagination (*DG,* 1:xxi). Thus Sand is acknowledged as a mentor. From Ward's very first novel, in which an aspiring young actress is given a copy of *Consuelo,* the characters in Wardian fiction read and discuss Sand, or they imagine themselves reenacting scenes from Sand's biography—usually her love affairs. For example, in *Lady Rose's Daughter,* a pair of lovers read Sand, Hugo, and Musset, and are followers of Saint-Simonianism. The married Lady Rose leaves her husband to live abroad with her lover, as George Sand did with several lovers, but then—as the narrator notes—it was a generation whose ideas were shaped by reading George Sand, Emerson, and Carlyle.[19] Especially in *David Grieve,* though, is George Sand's view of art and passion used as a point of origin and of departure.

The Actress's Spell

Mary Ward's first novel, *Miss Bretherton* (1884), is the only one of the three early portraits of artists in which Ward selects the artist as protagonist and uses as its central theme "our chaotic many-headed public opinion about art and artists" (*MB,* introduction, 224). In her memoirs Ward acknowledges that *Miss Bretherton* is an immature experiment, an exercise in which she set out to study the relationship of the actress to her role and the effects of her beauty or plainness on

17. Ward, *Eleanor,* 23.
18. Ward doubts that Eliot practiced this doctrine and does not believe Eliot's works to be "an ark of refuge . . . for the common perennial passions and emotions and delights of mankind," but does not say where she encountered Eliot's alleged remark (*DG,* 1:xx).
19. Ward, *Lady Rose's Daughter,* 220.

her art. Recall that George Sand, in the *Consuelo* novels, treats the issue of an actress's accolades based upon her appearance rather than her genius, and that in *Lucrezia Floriani* her protagonist complains that an actress "sells" face and body as a prostitute does. In *Miss Bretherton* Ward wants to deliberate whether "there [is] a dramatic *art*—exacting, difficult, supreme—or is there not?" (*WR*, 2:16) and to affirm art that is "conscious, trained, deliberate" (*MB*, introduction, 225). For the romance interest of this first novel, Ward opts for a modern version of the Pygmalion myth, with the young actress Isabel Bretherton as Galatea falling under the influence of Eustace Kendal, a prematurely gray older "artist"—actually a critic of French literature—who wishes to transform her from an intellectual ugly duckling into the swan princess. As noted in previous chapters, the motif of Cinderella transformation is employed both by Sand in *Consuelo* and Eliot in *The Mill on the Floss,* but in Ward's novel the heroine is already beautiful; thus her metamorphosis is to be entirely aesthetic and intellectual. Ward says in the 1909 preface and in her memoirs that her fictional actress is based in part upon the British stage star Mary Anderson, who had played Galatea and Perdita to the acclaim of all London—including Ward, who testifies that she was "touched, captured, carried away" by Anderson's art (*WR*, 2:15; *MB*, introduction, 224). Yet in some quarters Anderson was judged brilliant because of her striking looks more than for the intelligence and subtlety of her art. And this is also the concern of both the novelist Ward and the male characters drawn to Isabel for her beauty and bearing. The novel is narrated through the sensibility of Kendal/Pygmalion, the middle-aged pedant who admits, "I have some hopes of modifying [Isabel]" (*MB*, 291); he has rather an easier task than Shaw's Henry Higgins because Isabel, already a picture of "youth and grace and loveliness" (*MB*, 258), speaks beautifully and carries herself like a countess. That the undereducated Isabel has garnered accolades for her performances is—according to Kendal—testimony to the inferiority of the British stage and British audiences in comparison to their French counterparts. Conversely, the acclaim of English philistinism is, in Kendal's view, merely further proof of Isabel's inferiority.

In *Miss Bretherton* Ward depicts several artists, among them the painter Forbes and the playwright Wallace. Forbes is so smitten by Isabel that he fails to see her lack of "finesse" that Wallace and Kendal immediately perceive. He paints and draws Isabel in several poses and attitudes, including one work that alludes to one of the many paintings of Lady Hamilton—another English beauty who, like Isabel, was admired by men for her stunning good looks but held in contempt for her ignorance. In fact, Ward first displays Isabel in an art museum, where more pairs of male eyes are fixed upon the beauty in the gallery than upon the beauties on canvas. It is as if the gaze follows the actress offstage as well as on. To the artist Forbes, Isabel is fresh as a Diana, but to Kendal she plays a more innocent Vivien to Forbes's gray-haired Merlin, who is "altogether in her toils" (*MB,* 272).[20] What Kendal initially fails to see is that he—like the painter Forbes—is falling under the spell of the actress, and it is his unconscious jealousy that prompts his depiction of the Merlin/Vivien pairing as supplanting his own Pygmalion/Galatea fantasy. The men in *Miss Bretherton* participate alternately in voyeurism and fetishism, and the Pygmalion myth is Kendal's particular fetish and fantasy. A third artist, Wallace, remains impervious to the actress's sexual charms. When Isabel aspires to land the leading female role in Wallace's new play, he—loving his art and not loving Isabel Bretherton—resolves to save the drama from the inept actress. He sends Kendal to advise Isabel as to her intellectual and artistic insufficiency and to talk her out of desiring the part. Miss Bretherton can portray no depth of character, Wallace and Kendal agree, because she has no depth of knowledge.

To her credit, Isabel's ignorance is no secret from Isabel, and she manages to become a Galatea self-created. She is much chagrined when she comes to understand why Wallace will not entrust his drama to her defective powers—an indictment that seems particularly cruel inasmuch as she is trying every resource at hand to overcome her deficiencies. Although the smitten Kendal has offered himself as mentor, he has proven stodgy and arrogant, lecturing to her as a "hair-splitting pedant" who is nonetheless "delighted" to "feel her mind yielding to his" (*MB,* 372, 295). He does, though, introduce her to appropriate mentors, in the persons of his sister, Marie, and Marie's French husband, Paul de Chateauvieux, who, like other men in the novel, is fascinated with Isabel and who sets out to become her tutor. Aside from the Frenchman, though, only the women of the novel see the promise of Isabel's talent, and one of them remarks "she will surprise us yet" (*MB,* 340). Similarly, Marie immediately perceives the blend of "ignorance and genius" in Isabel (*MB,* 361); she is the first to see that Isabel is cleverly using Kendal and his acquaintances to educate herself, saying of Isabel, "She will go find her education" (*MB,* 355). Marie becomes Isabel's fairy godmother and for her education and edification gives her a copy of George Sand's novel *Consuelo.* No doubt Marie wishes that Isabel, a poor orphan with only her talent and beauty to recommend her, will identify with Consuelo, also a penniless child with an enormous talent. And perhaps she will also take comfort in that—just as Isabel's aunt and uncle have shamelessly exploited her—Sand's artist had to deal with attempts to subvert, prostitute, and exploit her art. Finally, as Consuelo becomes goddess of the opera in Venice and Vienna, Isabel is becoming the

20. It is interesting that, in 1874, Ward's friend Edward Burne-Jones painted *himself* as the gray-haired, mesmerized Merlin and Mary Zambaco as an enticing Vivien/Nimue with Medusa-like snake locks upon her head—hence the aging Burne-Jones, like both Forbes and Kendal, is frozen and emasculated by a dangerous young seductress.

"countess" of the English stage. Thus the novel *Consuelo* illustrates for Isabel Bretherton the concept of artist as divinity—the lesson that Consuelo's Maître Porpora teaches. And as Isabel is to be granted theatrical inspiration through Consuelo, Ward no doubt seeks literary inspiration through invoking Sand.

At the novel's climax, Kendal seems about to fulfill his dream of consoling Isabel when she fails, catching her when she falls. On her return engagement in London, however, her acting demonstrates an intelligence self-attained through study, discipline, and character, and suddenly he is divided from her by "an impassable gulf" of his limitations, not hers (*MB*, 400). He is frozen and cannot make a marriage offer because he perceives his scholar's life as gray and her actress's life as brilliant. He is as helpless as the rich man gazing upon Lazarus in Abraham's bosom, while she is "Undine [who] had found her soul" (*MB*, 371). In Ward's novel the soul is not attained by loving a mortal and giving birth to his child, but by the birth of the woman's art. Thus Isabel is both a Galatea self-created and an Undine self-born.

The novelist, however, provides Kendal a family tragedy in the death of his sister, Marie, which at the denouement brings the lovely young goddess into his arms. Like Consuelo, Corinne, Bianca, Aurora, and Mirah, Isabel is a motherless child, and Marie has become a mother surrogate; therefore Marie's dying wish that Kendal protect the actress from the rigors of the stage by marrying her carries significant moral weight for both Isabel and Kendal. Ward's resolution of the novel is suspect, however, in its suggestion that the young artist should abandon her art because she lacks the stamina to continue in such a demanding career. The fragility of Isabel is a contrivance, and Ward resorts to such a ploy because it suits the conventions of the novel and plays to this particular novelist's aesthetic and personal ideology to conclude with a marriage—even though, until the very end, Isabel has never entertained the thought of Kendal as anything more personal than a teacher. Furthermore, she has known all along that he feels only sexual attraction for her, as she says "admiration for me as a woman, contempt for me as an artist!" (*MB*, 326).

Henry James's Response

Upon the publication of *Miss Bretherton*, Henry James wrote to Ward, praising her as "a woman (distinctly a woman!) Who knows how (rare bird!) to write" (*WR*, 2:18), and opening the door to a friendship that "was to ripen into one of the most precious of all Mrs. Ward's possessions."[21] James, however, did not ap-

---

21. Trevelyan, *Life of Mrs. Humphry Ward*, 46.

prove of the happy ending; he held that Ward's actress—who had "too much to spare for Kendal"—should have been carried away from her critic/lover who worships her but despises her art. James believed that the excitement and the "ferocity and egotism" that the effort to create art brings forth in Isabel would have carried this Galatea away from Pygmalion (*WR*, 2:19).

In *The Tragic Muse* (1890), James writes his own portrait of the artist as actress with "too much to spare" for a plodding and proper Englishman. The novel is a *Künstlerroman* paralleling the careers of two artists, the painter Nick Dormer and the actress Mariam Rooth. Although in the text James compares Mariam to Philina in *Wilhelm Meister*, one cannot help but think the novel was in some ways written as a response to his friend Mary Ward's *Miss Bretherton*—although it is admittedly a finer, more thoroughly developed novel with characters more psychologically compelling. Perhaps such an assumption gives too much credit to the influence of a relative unknown; by 1890 James was, after all, on intimate literary terms not only with Ward but also with a good many of the "greats" of England, America, and the Continent and would have known a number of *Künstlerromane*, in fact had written one, *Roderick Hudson*. Citing James's journal entry following a discussion with Ward while her novella was in process, D. J. Gordon and John Stokes allege, though, that *Miss Bretherton* is indeed a source for *The Tragic Muse*.[22] Whether or not James intended *The Tragic Muse* as a response to anybody's novel, the actress Mariam Rooth certainly contrasts with Isabel Bretherton and previous women artists in that she will not abandon the stage for any man. Even Corinne and Consuelo would do so for love.

Mariam is crude and uneducated; she poses and overacts. Like Isabel she is under no delusions about her ignorance and lack of training; also like Ward's actress, Mariam seeks her own mentors, assiduously courting the aging French actress Honorine Carré, petitioning her to divulge the tricks of the trade. Also like Isabel, she becomes the "project" of a sophisticated and literary man who, like a Pygmalion, falls in love with his creation. In fact, the captivated diplomat Peter Sherringham discovers that there *is* no Mariam Rooth; she is merely a woman of a hundred disguises, each being a "role" that she plays offstage. When Peter gives her Wordsworth, Shelley, Milton, and Swinburne to read, though, she does not bother, while one assumes that Isabel Bretherton *does* read the George Sand given to her by Marie. Marian is willing to work at her profession, but unwilling to become an intellectual in the process. As an actress, nevertheless, she attains the height of art, prompting the narrator's praise: "She was beauty, she was music,

22. Gordon and Stokes, "The Reference of *The Tragic Muse*," 119–20. James's notation speculates whether the dramatic gift is a "thing by itself . . . [t]he strong nature, the personal quality, vanity, etc., of the girl: her artistic being so vivid, yet so purely instinctive. Ignorant, illiterate. Rachel."

she was truth; she was passion and persuasion and tenderness. . . . [T]he whole scene glowed with the colour she communicated, and the house, as if pervaded with rosy fire, glowed back at the scene."[23]

The knowing, sophisticated man of the world becoming putty in the little hands of the woman he has shaped is potentially a delicious irony in both novels, but James enjoys his little joke more than Ward does. When Mariam's admirer learns that he is to be promoted and posted to some unnamed Central American country as his nation's ambassador, he proposes marriage. Sherringham's pitch is that Mariam's greatest talent is not as "the sibyl, the muse, the tremendous creature" but as the charming woman that makes herself pleasing to men. Further, he offers to "manage" her new career as the wife of a very important man—her stage being not merely London, but the world.[24] Essentially this is the same tack as that of the rising diplomat Graf Dornberg in George Eliot's *Armgart*, who offers with a marriage proposal the incentive: "A woman's rank / Lies in the fulness of her womanhood: / Therein alone she is royal" (*WGE*, 19:86). Mariam counters that, instead of her giving up her career to be the ambassador's wife, he should give up his in order to be the actress's husband—essentially the same challenge that Armgart issues to Dornberg.[25] Sherringham is astounded by her proposition, and when he refuses to abandon his diplomatic assignment, Marian simply marries someone who will, and does, forsake his career for hers. Finally Sherringham comes around; when he returns from America for her big opening as Shakespeare's Juliet, his fascinated gaze upon the actress recalls that of Nelvil upon Corinne's portrayal of Juliet and Conrad Percy upon Bianca's. But it is too late: Mariam has taken seriously all Sherringham's lessons on the inviolability of art. Essentially James writes the same ending he suggested to Ward.

Ward's own portrait of the artist as actress is interesting as a rehearsal for her stronger fiction to come (especially *Robert Elsmere*); its chief weakness as art is that the Galatea/Vivien artist and her Pygmalion/Merlin admirer fail to earn the empathy of Ward's reader. Ward herself castigates *Miss Bretherton* as a "trial trip" and "piece of naïveté" (*WR*, 2:20, 16), and others criticized it for a lack of passion and a "dry, theoretical air." Mandell Creighton, a scholarly friend and later Bishop of London, gently chastised Ward for being a critic within her "dainty" novel, challenging her, "Your object is really to show how criticism can affect a na-

23. James, *The Tragic Muse*, 1177.
24. Ibid., 1144, 1189.
25. James reviewed *Armgart* (along with other works in the *Jubal* collection) for the *North American Review* 119 (October 1874) and considered *Armgart* the best piece in the volume, the character herself "a very superior girl" who—though outlined in a sketchy and rigid manner by her creator—belongs to the group of "magnificently generous women—the Dinahs, the Maggies, the Romolas, the Dorotheas,— the representation of whom is our author's chief title to our gratitude" (Gordon S. Haight, ed., *A Century of George Eliot Criticism,* 91).

ture capable of receiving it. Now is this properly a subject of art? Is it not too didactic?" Others have faulted *Miss Bretherton* as being derivative; Sutherland, for
example, labels the novel's flaws as "too little story . . . too much of the Jamesian
étude."[26] Ultimately *Miss Bretherton* is a flawed work, but it is interesting nonetheless because it deals with the female artist's passion for her work, the sacrifices
she must make for art, and the demands that others make of the artist—as well
as the issue of the persona of the artist as separate from or connected to her art.
As Yeats asks, How can we tell the dancer from the dance? It also demonstrates
the persistence of artistry, a quality that most certainly resonated with Isabel
Bretherton's creator. Finally, it presents the dilemma of the female artist as object
of the male gaze and the power of the female artist to mesmerize her male critic,
an important motif dating from Staël's *Corinne* and a topic to which Ward was
to return in two subsequent novels.

The Violinist and the Medusa

The protagonist of *Robert Elsmere*, Ward's most successful novel, is an Oxford
intellectual, Anglican clergyman, and idealist who turns activist, doubter, apos-
tate, and finally founder of a religion, the New Brotherhood, which is based on
the human Jesus as opposed to the divine. Critics of Ward's day and of our own
have focused not on feminist aesthetics, but on her *"roman à thèse"* as a study of
the religious ferment of the Oxford Movement, German philosophy, post-Dar-
winian scientific skepticism, religious doubt, and secular Christianity in the form
of religious/political activism—Elsmere's spiritual quest in the novel. Indeed,
Ward says that she intended the novel as a depiction of the struggle between religious traditionalism and modernism—a struggle that takes place in Elsmere's
mind and soul. In the character of her male hero, in fact, the novelist Ward catalogs two of her own intellectual discoveries: Elsmere's exhilarating scholarship
on French history represents Ward's study of Spain, and his spiritual quest, which
culminates in denying the Resurrection except as a symbol for renewed spiritual
life on earth, mirrors Ward's own religious pilgrimage. Of the novel as an intellectual argument she notes:

> The problem, then, in intellectual poetry or fiction, is so to suggest the argu-
> ment, that both the expert and the poplar consciousness may feel its force, and
> to do this without overstepping the bounds . . . without turning either into
> mere ratiocination, and so losing the "simple, sensuous, passionate" element
> which is their true life. (*WR,* 2:69)

26. Thesing and Pulsford, *Mrs. Humphry Ward (1851–1920): A Bibliography,* 3; Trevelyan, *Life of Mrs. Humphry Ward,* 44; Sutherland, *Mrs. Humphry Ward,* 102.

In *Robert Elsmere* the hopeful Broad Church movement of the seventies has end-ed, Liberalism has been stifled, and the Church is stagnant. Elsmere is the nov-el's modern messiah and martyred hero who throws up his living in the church and "[goes] out into the wilderness, and there, amid everything that [is] poor and mean and new, he [lays] down his life."[27]

But Elsmere's young sister-in-law, the violinist Rose Leyburn, steals the scenes from the hero and from everyone else who shares the stage with her. For Rose is not only an artist of extraordinary talent, she is also vibrant and beautiful—and as single-minded in the pursuit of her art as are Isabel Bretherton, James's Miri-am Rooth, and George Eliot's Alcharisi or Armgart. Since her issues are her "di-vine right of self-development" and of "making [her] own destiny" (*RE*, 1:380, 434) as artist, it is surprising that feminist critics have paid scant attention to Rose and her struggle. The violinist is, nevertheless, one of Ward's most striking ex-amples of the artist as Medusa and at the same time one of the more vivid de-pictions of the male gaze on female art.

Following the familiar strategy of contrasting an intelligent, creative woman with her passive, traditional sister (including Staël's half sisters Corinne and Lu-cile, Jewsbury's half sisters Bianca and Alice, and Eliot's cousins Maggie and Lucy or Hetty and Dinah), Ward creates in Catherine Leyburn the kind, gentle, pious, and domesticated sister and in Rose the passionate, vivacious, gifted, mesmeric artist.[28] Catherine is the eldest sister by eight years, and she keenly feels a re-sponsibility for protecting the personal and spiritual welfare of her younger sis-ters, as her late father had admonished. For this reason she initially rejects the marriage proposal of Elsmere, the man whom she loves. Like her father, Cather-ine blends the qualities of Quakerism, Evangelicalism, and Wesleyanism and has a "Puritan distrust of joy" (*RE*, 1:285). In the Westmoreland region where the Ley-burns live, Catherine tends the ill, the poor, and the dying. She is a Deborah to whom the people come for judgment (*RE*, 1:46), she is a St. Elizabeth (*RE*, 1:20), and she has a face like that of a Madonna (*RE*, 1:22, 2:28, 230). In fashionable London, where Robert becomes a darling of the intellectuals and a prophet of an alternate religion, she "look[s] like a Quaker prophetess—like Dinah Morris in society. . . ." (*RE*, 2:389). The characterization of the eldest Leyburn sister owes much to the simple, unpretentious, and noble woman of George Eliot—a great deal of Dorothea Brooke with a bit of Dinah Morris for good measure. Cather-ine is by no means an intellectual; when Elsmere begins first to doubt and final-ly to abandon his religion and gives up his post as rector, she cannot fathom that the man she loves could be guilty of backsliding. She is "the orthodox wife of

---

27. Ward, *The Case of Richard Meynell*, 1:75.
28. Actually there is a third Leyburn sister, but Agnes is a minor figure in the novel.

a rising heretic" (*RE*, 2:337)—a situation that causes much suffering when she goes off to her Evangelical charities and returns home to pray for Robert's soul, while he exchanges ideas with Unitarians, Comtists, free-thinkers, and agnostics. Catherine is simply a lovely woman with—as Eliot would say—a "talent" for loving.

Rose Leyburn—"Miss Artistic" to her sister—is the Corinne-like sister in that she is gifted and brilliant, as well as an exhibitionist who does not mind having all eyes and ears focused upon her and her violin. No shrinking violet, she selects "startling" offbeat and flamboyant fashions and huge amber beads, her bohemian tastes similar to those of Ella Hepworth Dixon's characters in the 1894 *The Story of a Modern Woman,* in which shopkeepers' daughters attending a London painting school wear low-cut gowns beautified with strands of amber or Venetian glass beads. Rose's untamed hair resembles a wild halo with ringlets "tortured and frizzled like an aureole" (*RE*, 1:9) or—one might note as Eliot does of Maggie Tulliver's tresses—untamed serpents. A "bundle of wants" (*RE*, 1:391), Rose most wants to be a professional, to leave the Westmoreland district of her youth, to study in Berlin or London, then to perform upon the great stages of Europe. Rose is witty, irreverent, independent, talented, and calculatingly ambitious. Like Isabel Bretherton, she is willful, vowing to be an artist no matter what the cost. Also like Isabel, she is astonishingly beautiful: "dazzling" (*RE*, 2:173), "bewitching" (*RE*, 1:411), a "child of grace and genius" (*RE*, 1:431), and a "white sorceress weaving spells" (*RE*, 2:272)—Ward again, as she had done in *Miss Bretherton,* creating the artist as irresistible woman of mythic proportions. The "magic and mastery" (*RE*, 1:318) in Rose's touch refer at once to her skill as violinist and to her ability to play upon men, who cannot take their eyes from her. Watching her play the violin for the first time, her future brother-in-law, Elsmere, notes the lambent eroticism of her performance:

> She stood with her lithe figure in its old-fashioned dress thrown out against the black coats of a group of gentlemen beyond, one slim arched foot advanced. . . .
> The hand and the arm, beautifully formed, but still wanting the roundness of woman-hood, raised high for action, the lightly poised head thrown back with an air. Robert thought her a bewitching, half-grown thing, overflowing with potentialities of future brilliance and empire. (*RE*, 1:72–73)

A witness noting Elsmere's fascination says, "And as for Robert, I saw him *looking—looking* at that little minx while she was playing as if he couldn't take his eyes off her" (*RE*, 1:75). Rose's impact is even more strongly felt by Elsmere's Byronic friend, Edward Langham; when Langham hears and sees this Medusa for the first time, "his face is turned to stone" (*RE*, 1:391).

Robert Elsmere depicts various kinds of stony characters—the intellectually frozen, emotionally dead, and religiously inflexible. Because Elsmere and Rose are the novel's most dynamic and vivacious characters—both in the process of evolving as one searches for beauty, the other for truth—they contrast with the frozen, dead, and lethargic ones, especially Edward Langham, Squire Wendover, and, for a large segment of the novel, Catherine Elsmere. Catherine is so confined by the rigidity of her Protestantism that she cannot but believe that Rose's passion for the violin is an affront to God, as later she cannot function as Robert's soul mate once he has left the priesthood and the Church. Elsmere's friend Langham (his name itself a pun on *languor*) is an effete scholar bored by the Oxford life with its pedantic dons and dull scholars; he lacks energy and ambition for study, teaching, and scholarship—or even for sex. The country squire of Elsmere's parish is frozen in intellectual aloofness; he is so obdurate and indifferent about life on his estate that he allows his overseer to brutalize the people who live and die in squalor on his land. He has spent a half-century on his magnum opus and dies disheartened, not caring whether his scholarship is ever published. For him knowledge exists for its own sake, while for Robert knowledge has power only inasmuch as it can be turned to good for others. In the novel the Medusa figure recurs chiefly in connection with the dry impotence of Squire Wendover and Langham, both brilliant and both disengaged from human life, human love, and human suffering. Both, notes Laura Fasick, are "self-castrated" by "quasi-sexual failures."[29]

Elsmere encounters a bust of Medusa in the library of the squire, a brilliant scholar and, as Elsmere's mentor says, an "inhuman old cynic" (*RE*, 2:104) who has written a famous attack rationally and historically "disproving" the Bible. Ward's early readers detected in the squire a similarity to Eliot's Casaubon of *Middlemarch*, and it is certainly the case that the work of both men is plagued with a dry sterility.[30] A father/son relationship develops between the old scholar and the young clergyman, who would like to "beguile" the squire back to life. But the two men—although both skeptics—are quite opposite in their respect or derision of sacred things; to the squire, "All the religions are nothing but so many vulgar anæsthetics" (*RE*, 2:525), while to Elsmere, "Every great religion is, in truth, a concentration of great ideas" (*RE*, 2:359). Wendover's only passion is knowledge—but it is a knowledge that destroys faith rather than builds connec-

29. Fasick, "Culture, Nature, and Gender in Mary Ward's *Robert Elsmere* and *Helbeck of Bannisdale*," 27.

30. Also it was suggested that both Casaubon and Wendover are based on Mark Pattison, rector of Lincoln and friend of the G. H. Leweses, who was, like Casaubon, much older than his vivacious wife. In her introduction to the Westmoreland edition, Ward denies similarity of character, but admits superficial likenesses (*RE*, 1:xxii). It was in the Pattisons' home that the teenage Mary Arnold met George Eliot.

tions, as Elsmere attempts in drawing the support of West End intellectuals into the social programs of his East End charities. The squire is in fact unusually indifferent to people. For example, he is unimpressed with Elsmere's wife, Catherine, and he contemptuously ignores his eccentric, timid, and increasingly addled sister—yet another failed artist—a dried-up writer and an object lesson of what Rose might become if she lives for art instead of living for womanliness. Furthermore, the squire takes no interest in the property he has inherited or in the souls who live there in abominable conditions—at least until Elsmere persuades him that the fatal outbreak of diphtheria on his estate could have been avoided had he been properly engaged in health and sanitation problems. In one of the early meetings between the two men, Wendover invites Elsmere as fellow scholar to use his library, and upon a subsequent visit Elsmere makes note of a bust of Medusa in the squire's library, an image that represents to the activist Elsmere "the overgrown and absorbing life of the intellect [that] blights the heart and chills the senses" (*RE*, 1:465). Working alone in his library at Murewell estate, the squire's "frozen calm" is as still and silent as the "tortured frowning Medusa" (*RE*, 2:160). When Robert Elsmere pays his final visit to the squire's library, the old man disavows his great intellectual achievement that he has spent more than half a lifetime researching and writing. He is failing in body and mind, the hereditary mental illness of the Wendovers by this time making itself manifest in different ways in both the squire and his sister. Elsmere again notices the stoniness of the old man's intellectual hubris and stubbornness as reflected in the Medusa: ". . . the squire's face gleamed almost as whitely as the tortured marble of the Medusa just above their heads" (*RE*, 2:525).

When Elsmere first notices the squire's antique Medusa, it strikes him with extraordinary force that "to that spiritual Medusa, the man before him (the squire) was not the first victim he had known" (*RE*, 1:465). The reader at once recognizes that that first victim is Edward Langham, who shares with Squire Wendover a numb and unproductive intellectualism that has frozen him for life in the world. Langham once showed promise for original scholarship at Oxford, where he was Elsmere's tutor, but after some time his lectures have passed from brilliant to boring, his scholarship from creativity to dictionary entries. Langham has "cheated his creative faculty" (*RE*, 1:98) and is now lethargic and intellectually impotent. Suffering from a "paralysis of moral muscle," he "[writes] no more, quarrel[s] no more, meddle[s] with the passionate things of life and expression no more" (*RE*, 1:97).

Langham is perceptive, though; he finds the new wife of his former student to be "rigid" and conventional, while Rose is a "wild ambitious creature" in whom the "demon of convention has no large part" (*RE*, 1:276, 309). A talented musician himself, Langham instantly recognizes the talent and passion of Catherine

Elsmere's young sister; he soon realizes that she has the potential to be one of the leading musicians of Europe, and he is mesmerized by her playing. He falls under the spell of Rose and is entranced by the "magic and mystery," "passion and romance" of her art (*RE*, 1:318). When she returns to England after her apprenticeship in Germany, Langham is jealous of the men in Rose's chamber ensemble; he tries to protect her from the unsavory "second-rate" artists in her circle, then tries walking out on her as, in fact, he walks out on his career at Oxford. But like the moth to the flame, the "Byronic-looking creature" returns to find Rose more gifted and beautiful than ever—as well as more poised and less sartorially challenged.

Sandra Gilbert and Susan Gubar note that nineteenth-century women artists are repeatedly attracted to the Byronic/Satanic figure, who seems to be a brother or double—as Angela Leighton says, "not only a lover, but also her forbidden other self—the one who is experienced, worldly wise and, like Lélia, cynically unromantic."[31] Certainly Rose is attracted to Langham, the dark man of brooding solitude and Byronic brow, the cultured and urbane man-about-Europe. The two perform piano and violin duets, and on such occasions Langham finds that he is "more passionately alive" than he has been in years. Rose's passion and vitality are temporarily exhilarating, but Langham later decides that they are, for him, insanity. He proposes marriage (or, to be fair, passively allows Rose to assume that her love can overcome his paralyzing monotony and make him happy), then jilts Rose because her ambition scares him, and because he is a dead man who dares not let the vibrant Rose tempt him to life again. Ward makes clear, however, that Langham is just as frozen and paralyzed prior to meeting Rose as the squire is before he knows Robert Elsmere. In the introduction she refers to the "impotence and . . . paralysis of the practical will" in Amiel's *Journal Intime,* which she had translated three years earlier, noting that such spiritual paralysis precludes any type of happiness—personal or intellectual (*RE*, 1:xlii).

Thus it was not the sexual gaze that initially turned Langham to stone, although in the novel we often watch a frozen Langham watching Rose at the violin, or romping with the family pet, or flirting with men whom Langham perceives as rivals. With her wild curls or "feather boa" or fur cap framing her face, however, Rose recalls the Medusa sculpture in the squire's library. On the metaphoric and thematic level, she *becomes* Langham's Medusa. Further, Langham's stoniness persists as his key identifying factor; he stifles his romantic life as he has stifled his intellectual hopes. He stagnates, while Rose blossoms. Like Isabel Bretherton, Rose hones her talent, becoming more proficient in her art. And like Kendal, Langham finds in the female artist rather more spirit and life than

---

31. Gilbert and Gubar, *The Madwoman in the Attic,* 82; Leighton, *Victorian Women Poets,* 81.

he is capable of. Finally he imagines a "fresh gulf" opened between them, leaving Rose—like Lazarus in Abraham's bosom—"transformed on the farther side" (*RE,* 2:295). The rich man/Lazarus parable used to depict Kendal's temporary separation from Isabel in *Miss Bretherton* is used also to dramatize Langham's permanent separation from Rose. Langham is a coward, choosing to remain stony because he cannot bear to think of a little house, children, money difficulties, and Rose "spiritually starved, every illusion gone" (*RE,* 2:278). Wearing his "marble mask," he departs from Rose's life (*RE,* 2:290).

Female Artistry in *Robert Elsmere*

Rose Leyburn's creator finally murders the female's art with the weapon of matrimony. Early in the novel Elsmere notes that his sister-in-law needs a rich, dominant, masterful husband to tame her—the same observation, by the way, that is made of Ward's energetic female politician, Marcella Boyce, in the novel *Marcella.* To Elsmere's solution, Langham, while not yet in love with Rose, makes a mental note that the gifted musician should not be "cribbed, cabined, and confined" in marriage (*RE,* 1:370). Nevertheless Ward generously provides such a man as Elsmere desires for his sister-in-law in the person of Hugh Flaxman, an aristocratic widower almost twice Rose's age. Flaxman, like other men, is mesmerized by Rose; he finds the young artist a "beautiful tameless creature," and he longs to "scold her, crush her, love her" (*RE,* 2:347) and to "punish her" for having made him wait about while she lays her future at the feet of the unworthy Edward Langham. In the last one-fifth of the novel, Ward is concerned with Elsmere's settlement house, his crusading, his reconceptualization of the doctrine of the Resurrection, and his illness and death, and she abandons the issue of female artistry, failing to illustrate how Rose's art is "crushed" by love. For in that final one-fifth of the novel, we never see Rose practicing or performing, never hear her speak about the art for which she has lived. Certainly when she consents to marry an attractive and masterful older man (and a rich and titled one at that), Rose also accepts a husband who would not be content to have her perform with her "long-haired" musician friends—any more than Lord Melton of Jewsbury's *The Half Sisters,* written almost a half-century earlier, would expect his bride to continue performing in theatrical roles. In both instances there is verisimilitude in the novelists' dealing with assumptions about acceptable behavior for the wives of wealthy and substantial men. But Ward entertains neither the hard fact that Rose is making an extraordinary sacrifice nor any ambivalence about whether such a wild, passionate Medusa will be content once she is "cribbed, cabined, and confined." Given that Ward herself, as a literary artist, produced thirty-one published works while a wife and mother, it seems odd that she denies her artists any aesthetic life after marriage—but then *literary* women alone are not on "sufferance."

In Rose the novelist has created a character with too much life, too much passion for art, and Ward is incapable or unwilling to entertain her own questions of feminine aesthetics. Ward's friend Henry James wrote Ward praising the book's "great and rare beauty," but he is dissatisfied with the author's disposal of Rose:

> [I]f she is only *not* to affirm the full artistic, æsthetic . . . view of life, I don't exactly see why you gave her so much importance. I think you have made too much of her coquetry, her flippance, impertinence, etc. as if it were a necessary part of her pursuit, her ambition. I can't help wishing that you had made her serious, deeply so, in her own line, as Catherine, for instance, is serious in hers. Then, if she had been strenuous and concentrated, the opposition would have been more real and complete. And I am afraid I don't like her rich, fashionable marriage and find it too conventionally third volum-y. . . . [S]omehow I resent [Flaxman] as the solution of Rose's problem, which a sort of poetic justice in me would have craved to see fought on lines more characteristic. (*RE*, introduction, 1:xxxix)

As previously noted, James's own Mariam Rooth, unlike Isabel Bretherton or Rose Leyburn, refuses to sacrifice art for traditional domesticity. In making Mariam also a Medusa figure, James emphasizes her sexual and personal power and her magnetism as performer—just as Ward does with Rose Leyburn. James's Peter Sherringham, the lover frozen by Miriam, says to her that he would "rather see you as Medusa crowned with serpents. That's what you look like when you look best."[32] But James's sense of "poetic justice" dictates that Sherringham suffer the indignity of a refusal from his Muse/Medusa, while Ward's Flaxman succeeds in the job of taming Rose—who is, at the last, much more willing to be tamed than is James's actress.

James's criticism of the outcome of the gifted violinist of *Robert Elsmere* is sound; Ward creates in Rose a fascinating and passionate artist, then silences her violin and her voice before Rose ever proves whether a female artist can live for art alone. In examining Ward's commitment to the artistic personhood of the female artist, however, one finds her not only more conservative than her friend Henry James, but also less advanced in her thinking than her influential predecessor George Sand. In *Consuelo*, Count Rudolstadt does not object to Consuelo's life as a prima donna; indeed, he recognizes her genius as a sacred trust which—regardless of his status or his mission—he has no right to violate. On the other hand, in Sand's *La Daniella*, the artist Valreg is mesmerized by the beautiful dancer Daniella, but he wants her to perform only to delight him and arouse *his* passion. When it is discovered that she has a natural talent as a singer and that other men are fascinated by her charms as performer and believe in the possibility of her artistic success, Valreg experiences a crisis in which he must choose whether to endorse the same liberty for his wife that he as a male artist takes as a given, or whether to discourage an art form that will subject her to the male gaze. The situation is somewhat unresolved in that at the end, husband and wife are studying music together and she has yet to make her debut. At least he endorses her artistic apprenticeship. For a woman artist in a Victorian narrative, however, there is usually a presumption that—unless she is a writer—she will retire. And in the works of Ward, the presumption holds right until the end of the nineteenth century and into the twentieth.

It is a telling footnote to *Robert Elsmere* that, in Ward's 1911 sequel, *The Case of Richard Meynell*, Rose Flaxman has seemingly neither looked back nor regretted her choice. Granted, the interpretation of a text should not depend on another work produced by the same author some twenty-three years later. The insights and attitudes in a literary text, like its strengths and flaws, must stand alone. Yet Rose's position in the later novel illustrates that, in the intervening years between *Robert Elsmere* and its sequel, Ward either did not reconsider Rose's sacrifice, or considered and dismissed the possibility that abandoning her passion for music would make Rose an unhappy wife. At any rate, Rose is in *Richard Meynell* twenty years older, still slender, beautiful, and graceful, although now the mother of two nearly grown sons. She is indeed tamed, and is—by her testimony—ignorant of everything in the world but music. Rose and Hugh Flaxman are minor characters in *The Case of Richard Meynell*, but they exert considerable social and political influence in the community and they expend considerable effort in defense of Meynell, the target of slander and blackmail because he leads a revolution within Anglicanism. In *Richard Meynell*, Rose has been transformed into a professional wife and gracious, selfless woman.

If the squire and Langham are an object lesson about the selfish, stagnant egotism possible in intellectualism, then one could conclude that in providing Flaxman as a husband, Ward saves Rose from the selfish, stagnant egotism that might result also from worshiping at the altar of art. The danger seems to be that either form of egotism prohibits engagement with other people, which is offered to the male characters through stewardship, teaching, or philanthropy, and to the female characters through marriage and motherhood. By removing Rose from center stage, Ward spares her the double threat of becoming a failed artist or a successful one. In the persons of the "little weathered fairy godmother" Mrs. Darcy, who is the widowed sister of Squire Wendover, and the actress Madame Desforêts, Rose is shown two unpleasant alternatives—the former is "a little idiot," and the latter is "not a woman" but a "wild beast" (*RE*, 2:184, 252).

Lætitia Darcy, a shriveled and timid white-haired figure, is held in contempt by the squire and in gentle amusement by others for her "hobbies," which include keeping an album of signatures, practicing each day on the piano with her tiny rheumatic fingers, and writing not one, but two novels—apparently both of them abominable. She gave a copy of the first novel to Prince Albert, and when it was returned the dog-eared page indicated that he failed to read past chapter two—a failure which the old lady graciously forgives because the prince had so many responsibilities. Of the second, the squire sarcastically comments, "[T]he worst novel of the century will be out in a fortnight" (*RE*, 2:378). By the end of *Robert Elsmere*, Mrs. Darcy's eccentricities have blossomed to full-fledged senility. Hers is a pathetic life without love or companionship, success or fame, husband or children.

As for the famous actress Madame Desforêts, she is admired by Rose pretty much as the actresses Sarah Bernhardt and Mary Anderson were admired by Mary Ward. But Langham points out to Rose that her idol is selfish and unscrupulous, allowing her young sister to die rather than compromise an artistic life in order to care for her. The selfish egoism of Desforêts puts her in the tradition of Sand's Corilla, Jewsbury's Fornasari, and Eliot's Alcharisi as the artist who will never willfully surrender stardom to mitigate another's suffering or to care for her own kin. Yet one might add that the sophisticated Langham is no more capable of judging the artist apart from the woman than is the "cool young Briton," Dr. John of Brontë's *Villette*. If the squire's failed artist sister or the egomaniacal actress can be the object lesson for Rose, then Ward demonstrates that Rose is better off with the love of a controlling older man than with art. Moralizing aside, Ward does not convince her reader that the young Medusa "with Wagner and Brahms in her young blood" (*RE*, 1:161) could settle for domesticity without art. She does, however, render an interesting treatment of the mesmerizing power of woman as at once artist and object of desire.

The Gaze in *David Grieve*

Prior to the days of sound recordings and cinema, musicians and actors performed exclusively in the flesh, and a female performer thus drew attention to her physiognomy and body—chiefly arms, wrists, torso, and bosom. These parts of the female anatomy are also the focus of the male sexual gaze in Victorian novels, probably because the voluminous skirts of nineteenth-century fashions concealed other curves from view. Helena Michie speculates that in Victorian novels the parts of the female body noticed serve as synecdoche for the unseen and unmentionable parts—a "synecdochal operation [which] detaches from the heroine's body the hair and the hand and arm, inflating and fetishizing these parts." In *Miss Bretherton* and *Robert Elsmere*, respectively, Isabel and Rose are fetishized as objects of art as much as—or more than—they are valued as artists. Much is made of their hair and hands and arms. Isabel's rich, golden brown curls and Rose's tangled, reddish, pre-Raphaelite locks are repeatedly noted by their admirers. Both women are posed and sketched by male artists as they work—Isabel in costume, Rose practicing her violin. Also Rose is repeatedly complimented for her "beautifully formed" hand and arm (*RE,* 1:73); when she plays there is an "enchanting picture-like distinctness" to every curve (*RE,* 1:430), and when she concludes, her breast "heaves with excitement and exertion" (*RE,* 2:176).[33] Thus the various frozen men whom these Medusas attract are captivated by the siren's pose, whether or not her art is inspired. And mesmerized, they cannot function as objective critics of her performance. As Laura Mulvey notes in her work on film, in "scopophilia" woman is the [passive] image and man is [active] bearer of the look; she as sexual object is "*leitmotif* of erotic spectacle."[34] Thus Isabel's acting and Rose's musicianship are erotic spectacles, and their mesmerized admirers cannot separate the dancer from the dance.

On the other hand, the work of the female visual artist and that of the novelist is not performance but artifact—the painting in the gallery, the book on the shelf. Thus Ward turns, in the case of Elise Delaunay, the Parisian painter in *The History of David Grieve,* to an artist more like herself in that sexual desirability presumably counts for nothing. Her passion and power need not incapacitate men—at least not by means of the gaze. Yet this is not the case with the siren Elise, who is in allusion and iconography a dangerous sorceress, a Circe and Salome. Elise paralyzes and emasculates the susceptible David Grieve, a young bibliophile and successful bookseller from the north of England who has come to Paris to investigate international business possibilities, to discover his cultural legacy from his French mother, and—especially—to see how artists live. In Elise the romantic and imaginative English shopkeeper finds rather more than he can comprehend—even though he has prepared himself for French womanhood by having read several volumes of George Sand.

David's sojourn in Paris is the third of four books of the voluminous *David Grieve*—the first two books of which chronicle his childhood and early manhood, his discipline for scholarship and business, and his success in both endeavors; the third book, his French sojourn with Elise; the final book, his unfulfilling marriage, struggle against traditional Christianity, increasing social activism, death

---

33. Michie, *The Flesh Made Word: Female Figures and Women's Bodies,* 98. Phyllis Weliver notes that by 1870s the violin as a "lady's instrument" was gaining acceptance throughout Europe, that many British women traveled to Berlin to study with Joseph Joachim, that "beauty and grace" of the performers attracted women to the instrument (as well as men to their performances), and that even George Bernard Shaw in an 1889 review (one year after the publication of *Robert Elsmere*) remarked that the "beautiful young ladies" in violin sections of West End orchestras were an "immense improvement" (*Women Musicians in Victorian Fiction,* 48–49).

34. Mulvey, *Visual and Other Pleasures,* 19.

of his wife by cancer and of his sister by suicide, then his affirmation of faith in an unconventional religion. The novel is too long by a fourth in that Ward supplies one crisis too many for the book to sustain—and this final one clumsily narrated in part through David's journal.[35] *David Grieve* suffers in that—once David is saved from despair and restored to England—Ward should have truncated the domestic history and moral awakening of the hero. David's wife, Lucy Purcell, does indeed grow from the vain and idle child of book two into a noble wife and mother, but her transformation is neither convincing nor interesting. It is rather the egotistical artist Elise that gives the novel its sparkle and tension—mesmerizing the reader as she does David. When the novel was published, Thomas Henry Huxley wrote, "I think the account of the Parisian episode of David's life the strongest thing you have done yet. It is alive—every word of it—and without note or comment produces its ethical effect after the manner of that 'gifted authoress,' Dame Nature, who never moralizes."[36]

Following the pattern of the *Bildungsroman,* the novel begins by depicting the hero's childhood as prelude to his manhood. In the opening book of *David Grieve,* the childhood of David and Louise Grieve is painted in scenes influenced by both Wordsworth and George Eliot—along with a few brush strokes of the savagery of Heathcliff and Cathy Earnshaw. The Grieve childhood is important to Ward's theme of lost Eden, to the spiritual maturation of the hero David, and to the development of Louie Grieve from a wild and willful child into the object of another type of voyeurism, another depiction of the effects of exhibiting oneself before the male gaze. The Grieve children are reared—or rather, neglected—on a north country farm by their uncle Reuben and his greedy wife, Hannah, who appropriate the children's trust fund earnings and deprive David and Louie of the education and opportunities their dying father had intended. Because they are unsupervised and unschooled, nature is their teacher, as it is for the young adventurer of Wordsworth's *Prelude,* and because they are primitives in an Edenic existence, they perceive no shadow of what awaits when the gates of paradise clang behind them, although David as a reader of *Paradise Lost* should have an inkling of the fallen world. To David God "seem[s] more imaginatively near" when he is surrounded with the beauty of ferns, heather, and mountain ashes, and he will never again be as close to the "Kingdom of Heaven" (*DG,* 1:204, 205).

For the little Grieves, nature is refuge, schoolroom, and playground, just as it is for Eliot's little Tullivers. Knoepflmacher notes that for the two children in Eliot's *Mill on the Floss,* the "rare moments of oneness . . . come only when both children can forget their sexual differences and merge into a primordial and

---

35. Imagine *Great Expectations* with Pip's having lost Estella, Miss Havisham, and Satis House and the author trying to sustain the narrative for another three hundred pages.
36. Trevelyan, *Life of Mrs. Humphry Ward,* 100.

undifferentiated natural world such as the quasi-magical Round Pool."[37] Similarly David and Louie have their own version of the "Round Pool" in the "Witch's Pool"—also known as the "Mermaid's Pool" or "Hamadryad's Pool." It is round as an open eye lying on the landscape and supposedly haunted by a witch who was drowned there. David as the older, more balanced, and more practical of the two Grieve children with, as it later turns out, a head for business as effectual as Tom Tulliver's, scolds and punishes Louie in pretty much the same way Tom does Maggie. Unlike the pragmatic and intellectually narrow Tom Tulliver, though, David Grieve values the intuitive, the emotional, and the intellectual.

Louie, a hater of books, is also no Maggie, although Ward carefully builds upon similarities to dramatize the differences. Like Maggie, Louie is both a witch and a Hamadryad (*DG*, 1:35). Although she is headstrong and high-tempered, Louise is cursed with the hereditary inclination for self-destruction inherited from her French mother, who committed suicide during Louie's babyhood, and also with the proclivity for destructive "wildness" or "madness" that destroys numerous Ward women. Louie is associated with drowned witches when—to terrify the superstitious country people—she impersonates the legendary witch Jenny Crum at the Witch's Pool. Here Louie's behavior is connected with Maggie's fascination with drowned witches in Defoe's book. Also like the witch Maggie, the beautiful Louie is destined to die young: her disastrous life foreshadowed in that "[i]t was the tragedy of Louie Grieve's fate—whether as child or woman—that she was not made to be loved" (*DG*, 1:120). The "grieving" of the name and of the novel, however, is primarily David's in a tragedy that by the end of the fourth book deprives the hero of virtually everything a Greek drama would demand, with the exception of his child.

David Grieve is a romantic—not only in his Wordsworthian childhood but also in his imagination. In his Romantic reading tastes, the fictional young Grieve follows, in fact, the literary inclinations of Tom Arnold, who, according to his daughter Mary, formed his sensibilities by reading Emerson, Carlyle, and George Sand at a time when young Oxfordians had a "passion" for Sand's *Consuelo* (*WR*, 1:16). Having read *Consuelo, Valentine, Mauprat, Lélia,* and *Jacques,* David has opened his heart to the possibility of a great romantic passion, has prepared himself to fall in love with the first fascinating woman he meets in Paris. As he pre-

37. Knoepflmacher, "Mutations of the Wordsworthian Child of Nature," 419. In this essay Knoepflmacher refers to Ward's *Milly and Olly* (her children's book written for the little Wards) as an example of her use of the Wordsworthian childhood motif but does not make reference to *David Grieve*. Peter Collister notes that the novel's "strengths of rural life are consolidated in a Wordsworthian set of customs and characters"—for example, Sandy Grieve (father of David and Louie) as mirroring Luke in "Michael." Collister compares and contrasts David himself to Hardy's Jude Fawley and Kingsley's Alton Locke, rather than to a Wordsworthian figure. ("Some Literary and Popular Sources for Mrs. Humphry Ward's *The History of David Grieve*," 223, 219–26.)

pares for travel, he imagines "George Sand at Fontainebleau roaming the mid-night forest with Alfred de Musset" (*DG*, 1:456) and the grand passion of "dying for love like George Sand's Sténio" (*DG*, 1:457), and he does not foresee that his pathetic adventures in France will be a cheap parody of Sandian fiction. But in the section of *David Grieve* romantically titled "Storm and Stress" David meets and loves Elise Delaunay, who mocks David and his Sandian fixation: "You are really too amusing . . . but I cannot ask Consuelos and Teverinos to meet you" (*DG*, 2:23). Indeed Elise herself proves to be no Consuelo but a Parisian Circe with whom the handsome Englishman forms a liaison which very nearly destroys him and does, indirectly, contribute to the death of his sister, Louie.

The French Salome

That Elise Delaunay is "a Bohemian" and "a déclassée" (*DG*, 2:57) and that she lives without a chaperone in a flat of Algerian-inspired décor in Europe's most cosmopolitan city sets her apart from the two Manchester maidens, Lucy Purcell and Dora Lomax, who have loved the *"bourgeois"* Englishman. Elise is at once androgynous and captivating. She is a free spirit who vows never to be tamed, a wild bird never to be caged. She proclaims, "That woman that has art is free and she alone" (*DG*, 2:116) and that only the female artist has scaled the man's heav-en and, like Prometheus, stolen the sacred fire—Prometheus's theft serving as ref-erence for women's art dating at least from Madame de Staël's *Corinne*. Elise's cre-do is simple: "Its first article is art—and its second is art—and its third is art!" (*DG*, 2:28). With her masculine voice and mannish airs of smoking cigarettes, she reminds Grieve of George Sand. And with her *"hauteur,"* her petite beauty, and her fierce independence, she embodies all the romantic longings that David has been imaginatively creating from his forays into French literature. That Ward makes Grieve's seductress a Parisian is not surprising; after all, many British nov-els of the century depict dangerous French sirens who happen to be artists—among them the dancer Annette in *Jane Eyre* and actress Laure in *Middlemarch*. By taking her hero from England to France, Ward also puts him in a location where several women artists studied, exhibited, and competed; from the 1850s there were in Paris a large number of *"ateliers féminins,"* and after 1877 there were five or six exhibitions in which women artists could compete against their male counterparts.[38] Further, these women artists of the latter half of the century lived,

---

38. Yeldham, *Women Artists in Nineteenth-Century France and England*, 1:51, 53. Among them Berthe Morisot, Rosa Bonheur, Eva Gonzàles, Henriette Browne, Louise Breslau, Virginia Breton, Marie Bash-kirtseff, and the American Mary Cassatt (the model for Miss Cassal in Alcott's artist novel *Diana and Persis*).

as the fictional Elise does, with considerably fewer restraints than their English counterparts, and more of them achieved international acclaim. Female artists of Paris were not admitted into the café society where their male counterparts met to discuss art, however, and neither does Elise frequent "Les Trois Rats" with the men in her circle. Even in Paris influential voices opposed their acceptance—for example, Renoir commented, "I consider women writers, lawyers, and politicians (such as George Sand, Mme Adam and other bores) as monsters. . . . The woman artist is merely ridiculous," but he adds "I am in favor of the female singer and dancer."[39] Possibly because unlike writers, lawyers, and politicians, she is pleasant to gaze upon.

The characterization of Elise may have been influenced in part by Henry James's Noémie Nioche of the important 1877 novel *The American*. Newman, James's American of the title, is like Grieve a self-made, rich and handsome young barbarian; in Paris both young men, seeking culture and "pictures," find attractive young women artists painting studies and reproductions of works in the Louvre. Elise calls to mind Noémie, who is also androgynous ("boyish"), flamboyant, and absolutely remorseless in self-promotion—her "one perfect gift" being her "perfect heartlessness." Elise, however, has genuine talent for art; Noémie's "crooked little daubs" are "absolutely execrable"—and Newman, though he dallies, does not fall for Noémie as David does for Elise. Also, the name Delaunay may have been chosen as reference to Marie-Thomase-Amélie Delauney, the French actress known as Marie Dorval, who was at the very least a good friend of George Sand and has been rumored to have been Sand's lover.[40]

The most obvious source for Elise, however, is the Russian artist Marie Bashkirtseff, who lived and worked in Paris—Ward admitting in the introduction that some of the traits from Bashkirtseff's *Journal* had gone into the creation of Elise (*DG*, 1:xxxv). Peter Collister lists the similarities: In physical appearance, both women are petite and have exquisitely small feet and light gold hair; both enjoy the freedom of association with men and know how to create mystery and sustain interest by making timely exits; both love Velasquez; both work indefatigably and receive honorable mention from the salon; both are obsessively jealous of female rivals in art—Bashkirtseff's rival being Louise Breslau and Elise's the fictional painter Bréal; both are interested in the exoticism of Moorish or Arabic culture; both "embod[y] a temperament which mixed, in a volatile way, creative ideals with a crude ambitiousness." Bashkirtseff had a talent for self-dramatization, as does Elise, and the dialogues of her brief flirtation with "A____" (the pattern for Elise's with David) take on the flavor of a love scene from Staël or Sand—

39. Chadwick, *Women, Art, and Society*, 215.
40. James, *The American*, 517, 657, 562, 657. The possibility of a lesbian relationship between Sand and Dorval had been rumored for years (Jack, *George Sand: A Woman's Life Writ Large*, 204–14).

both of whom, naturally, Bashkirtseff read. In the *Journal* she remarks that her life is like a novel, then she proceeds to characterize her life and death in novelistic terms—most notably prophesying and visualizing her own death, as Corinne does.[41]

Ward's Elise—also echoing Marie Bashkirtseff—candidly acknowledges that she is egocentric and selfish, saying, "I am incorrigible. I am an artist. I mean to live by myself and work for myself" (*DG*, 2:26). She warns David that a romance with her will destroy him, but that she on the other hand does not intend for an *affaire de cœur* to spoil her career. She is brutally honest; of her self-centered egotism, she says, "I am as vain as a peacock . . . I am jealous and proud and absurd" (*DG*, 2:25). Like the mesmerizing Rose Leyburn, Elise has a fetish for exotic clothing, especially shoes for her pretty feet. When Grieve encounters Elise, she is also what Rose would have become had she continued to polish a cosmopolitan sophistication, continued to frequent the salons, rehearsal spaces, and music halls of male musicians as Elise frequents the ateliers, galleries, and restaurants of artistic Paris. In removing Rose into the domestic space of marriage, then, one might conclude that Ward saves her from independence and androgyny, as well as from ego and temptation. Elise is in fact one of the depictions of womanhood that detractors of the New Woman lifestyle liked to cite as an example of what was wrong with the modern woman of the fin de siècle. According to Linda Dowling, the "decadent and the New Woman were twin apostles of social apocalypse"—allegedly advocating Socialism, Nihilism, and Egoism.[42] Their androgyny, acceptance of free love, advocacy of classlessness, and rejection of procreative sex and traditional marriage had the potential to undermine race, class, and gender. Among Ward's three female artists of this study, only Elise—with her rejection of marriage, motherhood, and class and gender restrictions—comes close to the mannish androgyne that had become society's stereotype of the New Woman. Elise angrily rebels against the traditional woman's destiny that would kill both her youth and her art; she hates God, man, and nature and charges that woman's biology makes her man's victim (in a tirade she pours on Grieve when at Saint-Germain they witness a young mother burdened with children and the remnants of a too-quickly-faded youth and beauty).

In addition to her flamboyant style, her single-minded passion for art, and her rejection of traditional womanhood, Elise is also a "very siren of provocation and

41. Collister, "Marie Bashkirtseff in Fiction: Edmond de Goncourt and Mrs. Humphry Ward," 58–66, 63; Bashkirtseff, *The Journal of a Young Artist, 1860–1884*, 134, 141, 210, 219. These references name or quote Staël and Sand, but I do not here list all the references that *recall* Corinne—at the Capitol, as Venus and Beatrice, as performer and object of the gaze (Bashkirtseff was a mezzo-soprano as well as a painter), as sick and dying. Bashkirtseff is decidedly not a Consuelo; she is critical of Sand, especially on the basis of Sand's "ignoble" theme of sexual transgressions across class lines.

42. Dowling, "The Decadent and the New Woman in the 1890's," 447, 440. Dowling mentions Ward's Marcella, but not Elise, as a fictional "New Woman" attacked for her modern ideas, 441–43.

wild charm" (*DG*, 2:111), a Medusa who freezes the man who loves her, and a Salome who decapitates him. Ward chooses the biblical Salome as the particular version of the siren because of the appropriate timing of a famous French painting of Herodian's daughter. Early in the novel, Grieve meets the celebrated painter Henri Regnault and views Regnault's sizzling painting *Salome,* which is the toast of the artistic season in Paris. Regnault's is the painting that Oscar Wilde, who created his own version of Salome for the stage, considered a bold gypsy girl. David is fascinated by the painting, "its extraordinary brilliance and energy, combined with its total lack of all emotion, all pity, t[ake] indelible hold of the English lad's untrained provincial sense" (*DG*, 2:61). David has nightmares about the painting—although Regnault's Salome is a strong brunette, he notes, and Elise a delicate blonde. Given that in Freudian theory the power to decapitate is also the power to castrate, the terror of Salome, like that of Medusa, is a terror of castration. Furthermore, according to Dijkstra, "In the turn-of-the-century imagination, the figure of Salome epitomized the inherent perversity of women: their eternal circularity and their ability to destroy the male's soul. . . ."[43] Thus David unconsciously fears the decapitating, emasculating Elise. Nevertheless he is "dazzled" (*DG*, 2:41) by her voice and by her "siren's face" (*DG*, 2:57), her "ravishing" foot modeled for Dalon's Siren (*DG*, 2:16), her profusion of blonde curls. He is determined to love her, serve her, marry her, even immigrate to live with her. Grieve has been metamorphosed into stone; he has eaten the Lotus fruit; he is "paralyzed" (*DG*, 2:112), "tongue-tied" (*DG*, 2:19), and—we are repeatedly told—"intoxicated" (*DG*, 2:21, 2:114, 2:146, 2:154). Elise's effect on David Grieve parallels that of Rose on Edward Langham, with the notable exception that Rose would marry Langham, while Elise accepts only "*l'union libre.*" She consents to a temporary liaison with David. Then when her rival, Bréal, rates a favorable notice in the press, Elise—terrified that she is losing ground in the cutthroat artistic competition in Paris—decides that sexual passion is poisoning her art. Her credo being art first, second, and third, she flees their cottage near Fontainebleau, and David's happiness is sacrificed for her ambition.

Not only is Elise a deadly Salome, she is also David's Bathsheba, and the reference to Old Testament voyeurism cements Ward's insistence upon the power of female beauty, the susceptibility of the male gaze. The child David Grieve is, like the David of II Samuel, an inordinately handsome shepherd boy. Elise in fact thinks David Grieve looks like Donatello's David, only broader and handsomer. Also like the Old Testament David, Grieve is beloved by several women once he has become a conqueror, Grieve's empire being that of a successful entrepreneur

---

43. Dijkstra, *Idols of Perversity,* 384. Dijkstra's litany of Salome depictions of 1870–1900 includes works not only by Wilde, but also by Moreau, Flaubert, Mallarmé, Toudouze, Symons, Slevogt, von Habermann, Romani, Pell, Klimt, and Corinth, among others (379–401).

instead of a military hero and giant-slayer. And like the Israelite king, who forgets his wives, Michal and Abigail, when he comes under the sway of Bathsheba, David forgets Lucy Purcell and Dora Lomax, the two English maidens who adore him. In Ward's version of the David story, it is not Uriah, the husband of Bathsheba, who is slain in order for the affair to flower, but rather it is the sister of David who becomes a casualty to David's fascination. In his dalliance with his French Circe/Salome/Bathsheba, David loses moral authority with Louie and abandons her to seduction by an accomplished rake.

Both Grieves are astonishingly beautiful, and from the time they arrive in the artist quarter of Paris, several persons request that they sit for portraits. Headstrong Louie immediately begins posing as a model for the Maenad that is predicted to make a name for the libertine sculptor Jules Montjoie, and David is shocked by the "pack of brutes" (*DG*, 2:67) who, as observers in Montjoie's studio, stand around making comments on various points of the model's attractions beneath the flow of her chiton. Seeing his sister the object of what he considers an improper male gaze, the provincial David explodes, but to no avail. Louie, like others among Ward's female exhibitionists, is doomed.[44] Maddened not by wine as a Maenad but by her own volatile and vengeful personality, she revenges herself by ruining herself. When David goes away to spend a month with Elise at Fontainebleau, Louie, in retaliation, offers herself to the Frenchman Montjoie, who makes of her a "fallen" woman and systematically destroys her happiness over the next decade by his gambling, womanizing, drunkenness, debts, and deceit. The fate of Louie as muse, model, and victim of a French artist in fact exactly parallels David's—except that he has the moral resilience to survive. In the final book of *David Grieve,* Louie reappears in David's life as a witch who badgers him about money, abuses her only child in the presence of David's wife and son, and commits suicide when her daughter dies. Louie's moral death is a by-product of David's passion for Elise; her literal death is merely a relief.

George Sandism and *David Grieve*

As a believer in *l'union libre,* Elise will not marry David but consents to take a vacation from painting to spend a month with him at Fontainebleau. Just as David had been inept at interpreting Lucifer's fall in connection with his own, he is equally incapable of realizing that he and Elise are about to reenact the Fontainebleau scene between George Sand and Alfred de Musset that he has imagined and that afterwards he will attempt suicide as Sand's Sténio kills him-

---

44. Ward's other performers include a singer in *The Testing of Diana Mallory,* a singer/actress and a thespian/dancer in *The Marriage of William Ashe,* and of course the actress Desforêts in *Robert Elsmere.*

self over Lélia. First, though, the Siren completes the emasculation of her lover, metamorphosing him into female. Already Elise has been reshaping David's artistic tastes—a reversal of the Galatea/Pygmalion myth seen in so many Victorian novels, including *Miss Bretherton*. Furthermore, he becomes her muse: She spends several blissful days of their liaison posing and painting him *en plein air* and several nights working on the painting that will be her masterpiece. When she frets, then despairs about the painting, which she says lacks unity, truth, and repose, she wants to drive her palette knife though it—a fickle change of heart that the model/muse should read as a prediction of what Elise will do to him as well. In the forest Elise suffers a twisted ankle, and David, like a mother, tenderly nurses her injury, and his "womanish consideration and sweetness amaz[e] her" (*DG*, 2:154)—David's feminine instincts recalling those of Eliot's Deronda or Ladislaw.

The ironic gender reversal developed by means of David as his mistress's student, model, muse, mother, nurse, and angel seems even more brilliant when one considers that Ward is upending a similar scene from Sand's *Elle et lui*, based upon the love affair of the artists Sand and Musset and published in 1858, after Musset's death. In that novel the artists Thérèse Jacques, the mother/muse/nurse and "angel," and Laurent de Fauvel, a petulant, passionate, and fiery artist and prodigal, have gone into the country to walk in a forest in the moonlight. There Laurent unaccountably and perversely confesses to Thérèse that he has previously brought another woman to this same place, where the lovers have just enjoyed the splendid night sky and a ramble on the rocks. The account is based upon a similar evening in the Franchard woods when Musset told Sand that he had brought another young woman to this same location and then, near a cemetery, was terrified by an apparition of his own ghost. In *Elle et lui* the events unfold pretty much as they had in Sand's memory, except that she adds Laurent's fall over a precipice and Thérèse's rescue of the terrified Laurent who, having seen the apparition, is trembling convulsively and behaves "comme don Juan après la réponse de la statue."[45] Thérèse comforts Laurent, holds him in her arms, then humors him as if he were a spoiled child.

Ward's revision of Sand's novel proves fruitful, for in *David Grieve* it is the *man* who, as muse/mother/nurse, comforts the petulant, fiery, and passionate artist when *she* is injured, temperamental, or depressed, and it is the *woman*—not the man—who abruptly asks him, "Do you imagine you are the first?" (*DG*, 2:149). Then she laughs and tells David of the "cousin" who has preceded him and who has offered to marry her. Appropriately, David reads Musset's "La nuit de Mai" (a poetic dialogue between a poet and his muse) to Elise after the moonlit night

45. Barry, *Infamous Woman*, 168–69; Sand, *Elle et lui*, 89.

of her confession, and she agrees with Musset that the miseries of an artist's petty life are dwarfed by his lordship of life and nature. Further, the callous an-
nouncement to David by Elise and to Thérèse by Laurent is identical—the "lordship" of the artist justifying such treatment of "petty" mortal lovers. Learning of
Bréal's success, hearing rumors that she herself has thrown over her painting for
an intrigue with the foreigner, and fearing her art is being destroyed by love, Elise
then simply walks out on the concubine, who has become a "beggar, living upon
her alms" (*DG*, 2:162). Grieve is bereft; he attempts suicide, curses Elise's art, and
returns to England where—his French Romantic phase transcended—he is renewed to his shopkeeping English self and to Lucy, who is not imaginative, independent, or artistic but who loves David and is willing to undergo difficulty
for his well-being. Hence David settles down with a wife who is the very opposite of Elise.

In the case of Elise Delaunay, Ward seems to have followed James's recommen-
dation to avoid disposing of a fascinating female artist in a conventional marriage.
Neither a rich older man (like Flaxman) nor a learned older man (like Kendal)
could tame, "scold," or "crush" Elise. While both these men are more sophisticated, worldly, and masterful than their respective female artists, Rose and Isabel,
Grieve is considerably less so. And Elise is more determined to live for art, yet at
great expense. Her "insatiable vanity" and "reckless ambition" (*DG*, 2:112), as well
as her vulgarity and selfishness, exact a heavy toll. As Salome/Medusa she not
only mesmerizes and castrates Grieve, but also mutilates her spiritual self. Elise
understands her womanly nature and female desires, but she sacrifices her womanliness for artistic freedom, and unless she changes course, Ward intimates that
she will become like the "animal" Desforêts. Years later, though, when an older
Grieve, searching for his disappeared and doomed Louie, meets Elise in Paris, she
is wife to the "cousin" Pimodan, who had liberated her from her passionate in-
terlude with David. She agreed to the marriage only because Guillame Pimodan,
a medical man, gallantly promised to protect her when, in the Franco-Prussian
War, the Germans took Paris and Elise refused to flee the city. As a result of an
accident in surgery, he has become her dependent and now Elise supports her
"crippled" husband—a situation that recalls Aurora Leigh in Browning's poem
or Jane Eyre in Charlotte Brontë's novel. Elise tells David that she paints anything that will sell for a trifle in order to insure there will be soup in the pot, but
she "ha[s] not painted a *picture* for years" and is "no longer an artist but an artisan" (*DG*, 2:566). She admits, however, that because she loves, she is not unhappy, "if he will only live. He depends on me for everything. It is like a child, but
it consoles" (*DG*, 2:566). Nevertheless, Elise's dream has died, and her art has
died.

The decade of the 1890s appears to be that of the female *Künstlerroman* as defeated artist—for instance Ella Hepworth Dixon's painter Mary in *The Story of a Modern Woman,* Mona Caird's pianist, Hadria, in *The Daughters of Danaus,* and Mary Cholmondeley's novelist, Hester, in *Red Pottage.* Elise Delaunay is never to have the success and fame for which she has lusted, but offstage she becomes a caring mortal, rather than a castrating bitch. As she has done with Rose, Ward writes Elise out of the text. We are not permitted to witness the strangulation of Elise's art; we only learn that it has died. Yet Elise as siren, Salome, artist, and rebel—and perhaps as figure for the disappointed female artist of the late Victorian era—proves a powerful and compelling myth. Her power, like Louie's, is encapsulated in the gaze. But once Montjoie possesses his model, he loses interest, and consequently Louie loses power. Conversely, David never has power over Elise; thus he retains only the memory of what his gaze temporarily promised. When Elise yields to Pimodan, though, she relinquishes the power of Circe or Salome, Bathsheba or Medusa, and gains a soul.

Of Ward's fiction Anne M. Bindslev says, "if the heroine lacks authenticity when abiding by the Ruskinian female ideal, and if she assumes a tragic dimension when rebelling against it, it is a sign that this ideal on the one hand was seriously questioned and, on the other, impossible to transcend."[46] Elise—as a George Sand–like iconoclast—questions the ideal but cannot transcend. Given Ward's notion that rendering justice translates into either reforming the rebel or punishing her, it is little wonder that Elise is saved from herself by marriage. Marie Bashkirtseff, Ward's major source for Elise Delaunay, died at age twenty-three. Had Ward desired Elise's outcome to have the "poetic justice" of punishment for the pain she has caused David Grieve, Ward could as easily have killed off Elise with her pen as Bashkirtseff was slain by tuberculosis. Significantly, however, Ward finds something worth redeeming in each of her three women artists, and she saves all three from the potential selfishness of their careers by offering them romantic love. Isabel Bretherton and Rose Leyburn are saved from becoming "animals" like Desforêts or Rossi (the star of La Scala who has her lover murdered in *The Marriage of William Ashe*). Similarly, Elise is saved from dying like Bashkirtseff because she eventually serves love and another human being, rather than serving her own ego. Ann L. Ardis coins a term, the "boomerang book," for the New Woman novel that launches a talented, ambitious, political or artistic woman, only to cure her from her "New Womanly 'spasms'" in a conventional marriage. Marriage is therefore a moral salvation, and the gifted woman of genius is "tamed" for love and domesticity. In Ward's fiction her men are "masterful," and her women characters like to be mastered. And in the Ward canon,

46. Bindslev, *Mrs. Humphry Ward: A Study in Late-Victorian Feminine Consciousness and Creative Expression,* 143.

any woman who deems it her inherent right to hold center stage—whether or not that woman is a professional artist—is either discreetly removed from the limelight or she is doomed.[47]

Ward's Male Artists

Not every reader is critical of the mandatory silencing of Ward's artists into traditional roles. Of the marriage of Isabel and Rose, Peter Collister says

> [T]hese weddings offer more than consolation for the young, ardent lady. In its capacity for fulfillment and its liberating of the spirit through the partial abnegation of the self, marriage assumes an almost mystical function in Wardian fiction. Two of her male artists, the writer Edward Manisty in *Eleanor* and the painter John Fenwick in *Fenwick's Career,* are in some sense restored and re-find their creative balance through marriage. Elise Delaunay also has her place in this pattern that sets off love and self-sacrifice against a single-minded pursuit of artistic excellence.[48]

Collister is correct in his comment that Ward endorses marriage, but he would be wrong in any implication that the "creative balance through marriage" means balanced treatment for artists of both genders. As for his first example, Manisty is not an artist, but a politician; his "tragi-comedy" of a failed book is not a novel or volume of verse, but an indictment of liberalism in modern Italian politics—from Cavour to the Crispi government—and a support of papal power in the future Italian state. Admittedly, he certainly seems delighted with his child-bride, Lucy Foster, who, as previously noted, is Lucile to the dying Eleanor's Corinne. And when he vows to return to England's "fresh woods and pastures new," the quotation from *Lycidas* suggests that this "intellectual soldier of fortune" intends to go right on fighting political wars, only now he will have a lovely nurse to bind up his battle wounds.[49]

As for John Fenwick, his reconciliation with his wife and daughter, from whom he has been separated for twelve years, restores his muse/model; lifts him out of depression, self-pity, and serious illness; and reverses the downward spiral in his career. But unlike Isabel, Rose, and Elise, Fenwick does not lose his gift

47. Ardis, *New Women, New Novels: Feminism and Early Modernism,* 140. A case in point is Marcella Boyce; in *Sir George Thessady* Marcella presents a public address in support of the reform bill her husband has proposed in Parliament. Attacked by hecklers and pelted with stones, she learns never again to bear witness in public to her political ideology. (Although not an artist, Marcella resembles Rose Leyburn and other artists because she is a visible, public, *performing* woman.)

48. Collister, "Marie Bashkirtseff in Fiction," 62.

49. Ward, *Eleanor,* 503, 55.

permanently, nor is he silenced, nor is he expected to resign his artistic aspirations. And this is the point that Collister ignores in his commentary on the "mystical function" of marriage. The "self-abnegation" of which he speaks implies, for either gender, repentance and, insofar as possible, restitution, but it does not imply sacrificing the passion for art—unless the artist is a woman.

Based loosely on the Westmoreland painter George Romney, who left his young wife and became fascinated with Lady Hamilton, *Fenwick's Career* takes the struggling painter from Westmoreland to Paris, and from his wife, Phœbe, to Eugénie de Pastourelles, the beautiful art patron who becomes his feminine ideal. The prodigal Fenwick abandons his family, squanders money, quarrels, and angles for attention. Years elapse and when Fenwick finds Phœbe and the child, he is a broken man—his talent apparently dead and Fenwick himself apparently dying. When both marital partners have repented and begged forgiveness for different types of abandonment, Fenwick begins to heal. He undertakes a painting of his wife and daughter, and imagines "the doors [are] opening upon a new room in the House of Life."[50] At the end, the sadder but wiser couple leaves for Italy, where Fenwick will pursue his art. Elise and Pimodan will never go to Italy for Elise's career. At the close of *Fenwick's Career,* the tone suggests a resurrection for the artist's soul, but in *David Grieve* art is permanently dead.

Ward returned again to the life and struggles of an artist in *Lady Connie,* a novel published in 1916 but set in the 1880s. In that novel, Otto Radowitz, a Polish patriot and pianist with a halo of sun-gold hair, is a promising young Chopin of the new generation. In a cruel and senseless beating by young men jealous of his accomplishments and annoyed by his affectations, Radowitz is severely injured and must give up a concert career. His former enemy, Douglas Falloden, saves his own soul by devoting himself to nursing the doomed musician, now maimed, depressed, and terminally ill with consumption. And Lady Connie encourages Radowitz, "You are not to despair. Your music is in your soul—your brain. Other people shall play it for you."[51] Radowitz believes he can never compose without improvising at the piano, cannot work with musical notes as he says George Sand did with dots and scratches on the page to sketch out her plots. Falloden and Connie go to great lengths to make the literal sounds available to Radowitz, even persuading Radowitz's countryman Paderewski to record Polish melodies on the new technology of sound recordings so that Radowitz can hear the music he can never again play. At the end of the novel, Radowitz experiences his first triumph as composer when the Royal College of Music performs his symphony. Like Fenwick, Radowitz must change his art to accommodate horrible reversals

50. Ward, *Fenwick's Career,* 364.
51. Ward, *Lady Connie,* 388.

in his life, and like Chopin and Keats, he will be silenced by death when his brain is still teeming with compositions. While Radowitz's fate is, then, an account of the silencing of a *male* artist, there is never an assumption that he should give up his great gift. Quite the opposite, every attempt is made to accommodate him and to permit his genius to flourish in whatever time he has left. Ward's female artists are not similarly nursed and nurtured, because in her culture the death of female art was not considered a great tragedy like the "murder" of Radowitz's career.

In Mary Ward's fiction, if a woman is cursed with genius other than the penchant for writing novels, she is in a double bind. She cannot have art and domesticity, cannot cultivate her genius and her humanity. If she goes against her womanly nature by remaining in her profession, she has no objective measures of her work because male critics, the arbiters of taste, are incapable of objective judgment when they are frozen by the Medusa power of feminine art. For example, the British theater critics in *Miss Bretherton* and the German musicians in *Robert Elsmere* admit that they cannot take seriously as an artist a woman who is also beautiful. At the same time, they are captivated by her and desire to possess her. Further, female artists who, like Mrs. Darcy, dabble at art are fools, and those who, like Madame Desforêts, live for art alone are monsters. And seductresses like Isabel, Rose, and Elise—so long as they are the darlings of stage, music halls, ateliers, and exhibition galleries—emasculate men to the damage of their own souls.

6

The New Woman *Künstlerroman*

WHEN IT CAME TO creating fictional woman artists, not every Victorian novelist wanted into the act. Elizabeth Gaskell, one of the better novelists of the period, depicted no woman artists. Her Mary Barton and Ruth Hilton are assistants to dressmakers, and her Margaret Hale and Molly Gibson are professional daughters to a clergyman and a doctor, respectively. Charlotte Brontë's Jane Eyre certainly takes meticulous pains and defensive pride in her watercolors, but she earns her living not as a painter but as a governess. Brontë's Shirley Keeldar is a businesswoman and heiress, Caroline Helstone becomes an unofficial social worker and a wife as well, and the diligent educator Lucy Snowe, of *Villette,* says, "Of an artistic temperament, I deny that I am. . . ."[1] Yet the preoccupation with female artistry, together with the influence of Germaine de Staël and George Sand on the consciousness of English novelists, did produce numerous English Corinnes and Consuelos in addition to those of Jewsbury, Barrett Browning, Ward, and Eliot. Among the vivacious and successful artists of Victorian fiction, Anne Brontë's painter, Helen Huntingdon, in *The Tenant of Wildfell Hall,* earns independence from an abusive husband by selling her works, and Dinah Craik's painter Olive Rothesay, in *Olive,* supports herself and her weak mother just as Jewsbury's Bianca does—by means of her phenomenal gift. After midcentury, however, the influence of Staël waned in the British *Künstlerroman,* while that of Sand lasted until nearly the end of the century—especially in the works of Mrs. Humphry Ward, the best-selling novelist of her era. In the final decade of the Victorian era, however, female writers began to look upon the Romantic quests of a Consuelo-like artist as rather archaic and inaccurate depictions of a woman artist's endeavors. By the end of the century, the would-be Corinnes and Consuelos of the New Woman novel were failing to create great art and at the same time failing to create fulfilling alternative roles. The ache of modernism had begun.

---

1. Brontë, *Villette,* 1:71.

The Status of *Fin-de-Siècle* Woman

The final two decades of the nineteenth century, especially the 1890s, were the era of the New Woman, both in English life and English fiction. In the fresh wave of feminism that succeeded the asking of the "Woman Question," the New Woman—occasionally known also as the "Wild" Woman—advocated gender equality, the availability of birth control information, and the right to receive an education and enter the professions. In the 1880s the Married Woman's Property Act gave women a right to retain property after marriage; also, more women were entering colleges and finding employment in businesses (although usually in lower ranks as clerks). In 1889 the Women's Trade Union was formed, and that same year some women were elected to the London County Council. By 1895 half of the new Parliament theoretically favored suffrage, although it could not have been a high priority, considering how long women had to wait for the vote. Liberation from stays and tight laces signaled the New Woman's interest in her own health and comfort—as well as her demand for increased freedom of movement. She insisted also upon the right to go out without a male escort and often preferred bicycle-riding—a practice scandalous in part because it permitted her to dash about the streets without a chaperon. She lobbied for the vote, for jobs, and for dignity for her sex, and against the Contagious Diseases Acts, which until repeal in 1886 permitted the forced vaginal examination of any woman suspected to be a prostitute on the grounds of "protecting" Englishmen from venereal disease, but at the same time did nothing to protect women—whether wives, mistresses, or sex workers—from infection by their male sexual partners. A. R. Cunningham suggests that, in addition to the fresh round of feminist agitation, the first English production of Henrik Ibsen's *A Doll's House* in 1889 and *Hedda Gabler* in 1891 accelerated the emphasis on the liberated woman of British literature. The final decade of Victoria's reign was also the first decade of this more insistent woman's movement—a movement with which the Queen was not in sympathy—but it lost some momentum, or at least public attention, during the Diamond Jubilee and the crises of the Boer War and the Great War. Bram Dijkstra posits that one response to the New Woman was a backlash that could be called "a war on woman . . . a war largely fought on the battlefield of words and images, where the dead and wounded fell without notice into the mass grave of lost human creativity. . . ."[2]

According to Gail Cunningham the New Woman of the nineties was "New" only if her conflict with social convention was based on principle, rather than on

2. Cunningham, "The 'New Woman Fiction' of the 1890s," 178; Dijkstra, *Idols of Perversity*, vii.

mere eccentricity or flamboyance, and if her radical stance was a matter of personal choice. Ann L. Ardis, noting that over a hundred New Woman novels were written between 1883 and 1900, says the novels are based upon distinctive traits: the focus on women's relationships with other women as opposed to the traditional marriage plot, a demystification of the ideology of "womanliness," an interest in legitimizing nondomestic responsibilities for women, and the replacing of a rigidly developed model of character with a more fluid concept of identity apart from "bourgeois patriarchy in which unmarried women are deemed odd and superfluous. . . ."[3] Several of the New Woman novels of the decade are also artist novels, a natural choice because an artist requires independence, freedom, and acknowledgment of her creativity—just as the New Woman did. In fact the most famous of this new breed, Sue Bridehead of Hardy's *Jude the Obscure,* is an artist of sorts, or at least a skilled artisan who earns her livelihood by crafting religious script.

Some of the New Woman novels also deal with the literary influences of the two Georges—Sand and Eliot—to pay homage to the great precursors and to question whether women writers of the 1890s have greater opportunities than Sand and Eliot—or whether in fact may be more constrained by class, society, and sex stereotypes than the Georges who broke free in their lives and their fiction. Ardis notes, for example, that the 1894 *George Mandeville's Husband,* by C. E. Raimond (Elizabeth Robins), is "quite ruthless" in characterizing a woman who, imagining herself the successor of the "other Georges," capitalizes upon the pain of her family in order that she might convert it into fiction. Furthermore, as Elaine Showalter notes, the period after George Eliot's death in 1880 was a period of "textual anarchy," in which—the queen of the English novel having departed—the heirs fought over her crown by confronting the powerful literary precursor, who was at once their "madonna" and monarch. The influence of Eliot is still obvious in the *Künstlerroman* of the 1890s, but the would-be artist-as-deity of the New Woman novel rarely attains a success to match that of Armgart and Leonora Halm-Eberstein. Rather the decade is that of a woman whose wings are clipped before she soars, who—like Kate Chopin's American painter Edna Pontellier—is the "sad spectacle" of a weakling bird, "bruised, exhausted, fluttering back to earth."[4]

---

3. Cunningham, *The New Woman and the Victorian Novel,* 4–5; Ardis, *New Women, New Novels,* 4, 3. Ardis says she was called not only the New Woman, but also the Odd Woman, the Wild Woman, and the Superfluous Woman (1).

4. Ardis, *New Women, New Novels,* 148–49; Showalter, *Sexual Anarchy: Gender and Culture at the Fin de Siècle,* 60–61; Chopin, *"The Awakening" and Selected Short Stories,* 110.

The New Woman as Artist

A sampling of New Woman novels illustrates that failed promise is often the outcome of a promising talent. In Mona Caird's 1894 novel, *The Daughters of Danaus,* for example, one woman artist tells another, the aspiring pianist Hadria Fullerton Temperly, that to be an Aeolian harp means to suffer, but that suffering guarantees neither brilliance nor success: ". . . often the harp rings false. Its strings get loosened; one hangs slack and jars, and where then is your harmony?" Weary of tea and tennis, of domesticity and social vacuities, Hadria imitates Ibsen's Nora in walking out on her husband and children. In Paris she studies piano and composes music inspired by haunting Celtic melodies. Hoping to succeed *in spite of* her gender, though, she fails *because of it* when she is summoned home to nurse an ailing parent. With the myth that James Joyce was to use for Stephen Dedalus's flight from the nets of country, religion, and language, Caird illustrates her artist as Icarus—but an Icarus who drowns "in the blue depths," her wings "closing over-head, wet and crippled."[5]

Ella Hepworth Dixon's only novel, *The Story of a Modern Woman,* was published the same year as Caird's novel, and it also features a failed artist. In Mary Erle's case twice failed—first as painter, second as novelist. Like Jewsbury's Bianca, Barrett Browning's Aurora, Anne Brontë's Helen, George Eliot's Mirah, and most other female artists in nineteenth-century fiction, Dixon's protagonist, Mary, chooses an artistic career because of financial desperation. Her friend, the novel's most ardent feminist, warns her, "No woman ever made a great artist yet . . . but, if you don't mind being third-rate, of course go in and try." Mary inadvertently proves her right. Beginning her career as a third-rate artist in a third-rate art academy, she eventually becomes a writer, producing works very much like "hundreds of third-rate authors of fiction whom she had read." She bitterly observes, "It is because they suffer so that women have written supremely good fiction."[6] It does not follow, though, that all would-be artists have mastered the alchemy that turns suffering into art.

The year 1894 was a bonanza year for women novelists, and in addition to the *Künstlerromane* of Caird and Dixon, artist novels were published by Edith Johnstone, Mrs. Everard Cotes, and George Paston. Like Caird and Dixon, these novelists created artists who failed to prosper. In Johnstone's *A Sunless Heart,* a female artist, Gaspardine O'Neill, is belatedly recognized for her painting decades after she has abandoned it; in Cotes's *A Daughter of Today,* the heroine, Elfride, studies art in Paris but becomes only an art critic; in Paston's *A Modern Amazon,*

5. Caird, *The Daughters of Danaus,* 61, 388.
6. Dixon, *The Story of a Modern Woman,* 42, 106, 122.

a woman tries an independent literary career but "end[s] up in [her] husband's arms, acknowledging that this is [her] rightful place."[7]

In the 1898 *A Writer of Books*, by George Paston (Emily Morse Symonds), a novelist, Cosima Chudleigh, is forced by the publisher to strike from her manuscript the "moralisings and digressions" and to provide a happy ending. As Mary Erle is advised to write "a thoroughly breezy book with a wedding at the end," Cosima is instructed that "a wedding's every bit as natural as a funeral, and a lot more cheerful." So she "slash[es] and mutilate[s] the offspring of her brain, and soon beg[ins] to feel as if she were up to her elbows in gore." Cosima is in some ways more fortunate than most New Woman artists because an open-minded "New Man" advises her to stop trying, "like George Eliot and her followers, to write like a man, and to think like a man," but rather to give the world a woman's view of her age. Cosima decides to become at last an independent woman and novelist, to depict her age rather than to reform it; she walks out of an unhappy marriage and into the novel that is to be her masterpiece. At last she has learned that she need not settle for what Madame de Staël calls existing "comme suffrance."[8] Her triumph is an exception among New Women artists.

Mary Cholmondeley's *Red Pottage* (1899) features the doomed art of another fictional novelist, Hester Gresley. Art is Hester's passion; it combines the sentiments of religious fervor, sexual love, and maternal nurture; when she speaks of her writing, she blushes and goes pale, and "she is transfigured." Such passion for her art as Sand depicts as residing in Consuelo or Jewsbury in Bianca, Cholmondeley claims also for Hester. When in Hester's absence the galleys for her new novel arrive at the home of her brother, the vicar, he burns the manuscript because it is an embarrassment and an abomination. Of the climax Elaine Showalter says, "Thus the century ends with an image of English women's fiction going up in flames and reduced to ashes—another apocalyptic conflagration." And Ann L. Ardis agrees that the book burning is no mere conflict between siblings but "an instance of the general critical response toward New Woman novels at the end of the century"—in other words, the violence and "war" against women that Dijkstra notes. Hester cries out that her brother has murdered her progeny:

> If I had a child . . . and it died, I might have ten more, beautiful and clever and affectionate, but they would not replace the one I had lost. Only if it were a child . . . I should meet it again in heaven. There is the resurrection of the body

7. For commentary on these out-of-print novels, see Ann L. Ardis's *New Women, New Novels*, 135–38, and Kate Flint's introduction to *The Story of a Modern Woman*, xv.

8. Paston, *A Writer of Books*, 78–79; Dixon, *Story of a Modern Woman*, 183; Paston, *Writer of Books*, 81, 174, 144.

for children of the body, but there is no resurrection that I ever heard of for children of the brain.[9]

Sarah Grand (the pen name for Frances Elizabeth McFall), who coined the term "New Woman" in 1894, traces her literary lineage from George Sand and George Eliot, but her "woman of genius" in the 1897 *The Beth Book* attains the success of neither George, although Beth finds elements of herself in Sand's autobiography, *Histoire de ma vie*. A frustrated artist and would-be seducer in fact flatters Beth by comparing her to the French George: "[Y]ou promise to be to England what George Sand was to France . . . a new light on the literary horizon." He suggests that Sand would never have become a great novelist without her liaison with Alfred de Musset, and his proposition, which follows, becomes one of the more unusual (and laughable) in late Victorian literature: "Will you— will you let me be to you—De Musset?" Beth responds with the derision the invitation merits and says that if, as he suggests, passion is what made George Sand, she herself prefers the "serene spirit" of George Eliot—both for her life and for her art.[10]

The Beth Book is a novel about the development of a child of genius—Grand defining *genius* as "an irresistible impulse, a craving to express something for its own sake and the pleasure of expressing it" and "sympathetic insight made perfect."[11] To Grand, genius has nothing to do with ego and fame; it has everything to do with sensibility—love for the creative medium and for the human subjects it treats and to whom it appeals. Grand's Beth is a skilled pianist, an inventive songwriter and poet, and eventually a published novelist. The education of Beth moves her from self to selflessness, from passion to contemplation, from self-pity to compassion for prostitutes, hungry children, and animals that fall under the vivisector's knife. In the course of the novel, Beth evolves from the impulsive and emotional little Beth Caldwell, with a proclivity for music, poetry, and preposterous narrative fabrications, into Beth Maclure, an unhappy wife who preserves her sanity and begins writing her first book in a hidden room that parallels Edna Pontellier's studio. After five hundred pages of struggle, Beth befriends and marries an American artist who is also one of the few men in her experience who has not preached women's inferiority. Finally she turns her public fame into a higher good, her "vocation" as eloquent speaker for the dignity of womanhood—a

9. Cholmondeley, *Red Pottage*, 67; Showalter, introduction to *Red Pottage*, viii; Ardis, "'Retreat with Honour': Mary Cholmondeley's Presentation of the New Woman Artist in *Red Pottage*," 335; Cholmondeley, *Red Pottage*, 334.

10. Sally Mitchell credits Grand with naming the period "New Woman" in an 1894 essay (introduction to *The Beth Book*, vi); Grand, *The Beth Book: Being a Study from the Life of Elizabeth Caldwell Maclure, a Woman of Genius*, 524, 469.

11. Grand, *Beth Book*, 233, 80.

profession that Grand, who followed the same trajectory in her own life, affirms to be more creative and more worthwhile than that of the second-rate novelist, poet, or literary critic.

Prior to the New Woman era, the *Künstlerroman* written by a female novelist usually featured an actress or singer—that is, a public performer (although sometimes a painter, rarely a poet or musician/composer). But Dixon's Mary, Grand's Beth, Caird's Valeria du Prel in *The Daughters of Danaus,* Cholmondeley's Hester, and Paston's Cosima are—like their creators—writers of fiction. Hence at the end of the century more authors were projecting their creative struggles into artists whose work was more nearly like their own. In most cases the fictional novelists are, like the New Woman novelists, writing New Woman novels. Compared to English poets and novelists earlier in the century, the New Women were less inclined to worship at the shrine of Staël or Sand, probably because these great matriarchs seemed voices of the past that New Women were willing to dismiss as they prepared to turn the page of the century.

Victorian England and the Woman Artist

Throughout the nineteenth century, and especially during the reign of Queen Victoria, a large number of women novelists and poets asked the very questions that feminism in the academy revised at the end of the twentieth century. The second time around, the questions have been asked primarily by literary critics; the first time, the queries were presented in depictions of fictional poets and painters, actresses and singers. Employing the *Künstlerroman* as vehicle, gifted women speculated upon whether one's gender contributes to or detracts from art, and whether genius is sexed. They asked whether the woman artist is guilty of narcissism, and, if she is, whether that quality is admissible in her work (as it apparently is in the artistic creations of her male counterpart), and whether she may evolve out of narcissism as her art evolves. They speculated, as Staël and Sand had done in French belles lettres, whether a woman's sexuality informs and enhances her art, or whether it smothers and slays it. They wondered about the female artist's mesmerizing power over her male audience and whether her artistry should—or could—be judged apart from her sexual charms. They complained that they were admitted to art only "on sufferance" and that they were criticized harshly because they were female. They worried, as George Eliot did, about the silencing of female genius, and they speculated about the risks an artist assumes when she puts her faith in her gift rather than in typical female roles and relationships. They questioned whether female art is of necessity always inferior to male art, or whether, as Barrett Browning's poet Aurora Leigh says, "A woman's soul, like man's, be wide enough / To carry the whole octave" (*AL* 2.1185–86).

And they explored a mythology to embody the female artist—the artist as sibyl, pythoness, goddess, Athena/Sophia, seductress, and as an English version of Corinne and Consuelo.

Their fictional women artists reach phenomenal heights. Geraldine Jewsbury's actress Bianca Pazzi, the "woman for whom the stage has long waited," receives adulation, applause, "bouquets, bracelets, wreaths, every possible missile of admiration . . . flung at her in profusion" (*HS,* 171). Elizabeth Barrett Browning's poet Aurora Leigh pens verse that ignites the imagination of young romantics, touches the intellect of aging aristocrats, and prompts the love of a worthy critic, who tells her, "the book is in my heart, / Lives in me, wakes in me, and dreams in me" (*AL* 8.265–66). George Eliot's statuesque singers Armgart and Alcharisi understand the power of having "a man's force of genius in you" and realize that "[a] great singer and actress is a queen" (*DD,* 631, 634). Mrs. Humphry Ward's painter and performers mesmerize their audience—Isabel Bretherton as empress of the stage, free-spirited Rose Leyburn as a sorceress with a violin, Elise Delaunay as a provoking siren but also a skilled painter whose talent is recognized by both instructors and competitors. Admittedly, happiness for these gifted women is not guaranteed, nor is success perpetual. Bianca retires from the stage upon her marriage to an English aristocrat. Aurora, still dissatisfied with her work, will aspire to greater heights. Alcharisi and Armgart abdicate their respective reigns when their voices fail them; Eliot's Caterina is silenced in death, and her Mirah places her lover's dream of Zionism above her music. Ward's heroines voluntarily abandon their careers for love and conventional marriage, just as Jewsbury's heroine had done four decades earlier. For a time, however, these artists' respective stars were ascendant, and because they were, their creators were able to raise the aforementioned questions about female art—whether or not they bring their heroines to a near-apotheosis on a par with that in *Aurora Leigh.*

Among end-of-century works, however, there is less optimism. Whether painter, musician, novelist, or poet, the fin-de-siècle artist is more dispirited, less triumphant, and less successful than Corinne, Consuelo, Bianca Pazzi, Aurora Leigh, Alcharisi, and Armgart in their prime. For that matter, they are less successful than the artists Isabel, Elise, and Rose created by the New Woman's more conservative contemporary Mrs. Humphry Ward. If fictional New Women artists do publish or perform, they usually have to settle for scaled-down versions of greatness. Protecting them from becoming "unsexed" or "unwomaned," their husbands, brothers, fathers, and lovers stifle their creativity and burn their books. Because they are isolated from one another, they even find it difficult to form a community of women artists. Besides, they are initiated into a competitive system in which success too often requires stepping over the bodies of their fallen sisters. Even Ward's 1900 novel, *Eleanor,* features a woman who, instead of writing her own book, assists in the stillbirth of a book written by the man she loves. Like Chopin's striving would-be artist Edna Pontellier, Eleanor dies. Indeed, the enduring image of the fin-de-siècle's female *Künstlerroman* is that of a drowning woman—Hadria Fullerton going down in the indifferent blue ocean with her "wings closing over-head, wet and crippled," and Edna Pontellier as a "bird with a broken wing . . . beating the air above, reeling, fluttering, circling disabled down, down to the water."[12] Midway through the century, however, the novelists George Eliot and Geraldine Jewsbury and the poet Elizabeth Barrett Browning—inspired by the French matriarchs Germaine de Staël and George Sand—believed in the possibility that a female artist might soar.

12. Chopin, *"The Awakening" and Selected Short Stories,* 152.

WORKS CITED

Primary Sources

The Actress of the Present Day. 3 vols. London: James Harper, 1817.

Alcott, Louisa May. *Diana and Persis.* Ed. Sarah Elbert. New York: Arno Press, 1978.

Apuleius. *Metamorphoses.* Ed. and trans. J. Arthur Hanson. 2 vols. Cambridge: Harvard University Press, 1989.

Augustine, Saint. *City of God against the Pagans.* Trans. William M. Green. 7 vols. London: William Heinemann; Cambridge: Harvard University Press, 1957–1972.

Bashkirtseff, Marie. *The Journal of a Young Artist, 1860–1884.* Trans. Mary J. Serrano. New York: Cassell & Company, 1889.

Baudelaire, Charles. "The Painter of Modern Life." In *Baudelaire: Selected Writings on Art and Literature,* trans. P. E. Charvet. Harmondsworth, Middlesex, England: Penguin Books, 1972.

Boccaccio, Giovanni. *The Decameron of Giovanni Boccaccio.* Trans. John Payne. New York: Modern Library, n.d.

Brontë, Charlotte. *Villette.* 2 vols. The Shakespeare Head Brontë. Boston: Houghton Mifflin, 1931.

Browning, Elizabeth Barrett. *Aurora Leigh.* Ed. Margaret Reynolds. Athens: Ohio University Press, 1992.

———. *"Aurora Leigh" and Other Poems.* Ed. Cora Kaplan. London: Women's Press, 1978.

———. *The Brownings' Correspondence.* Vols. 1–8, ed. Philip Kelley and Ronald Hudson; vols. 9–14, ed. Philip Kelley and Scott Lewis. Winfield, Kans.: Wedgestone Press, 1984–1998.

———. *The Complete Works of Elizabeth Barrett Browning.* Ed. Charlotte Porter and Helen A. Clarke. 6 vols. New York: Thomas Y. Crowell, 1900.

———. *The Letters of Elizabeth Barrett Browning.* Ed. Frederic G. Kenyon. 2 vols. New York: Macmillan, 1898.

————. *The Letters of Elizabeth Barrett Browning to Mary Russell Mitford, 1836–1854.* Ed. Meredith B. Raymond and Mary Rose Sullivan. 3 vols. Waco: Armstrong Browning Library of Baylor University, 1983.

Caird, Mona. *The Daughters of Danaus.* New York: Feminist Press at City University of New York, 1989.

Carlyle, Thomas. *The Works of Thomas Carlyle in Thirty Volumes.* Centenary Edition. New York: AMS Press, 1969.

Cholmondeley, Mary. *Red Pottage.* London: Virago Press, 1985.

Chopin, Kate. *"The Awakening" and Selected Short Stories by Kate Chopin.* New York: Bantam Books, 1992.

Craik, Dinah Mulock. *The Head of the Family.* London: Ward, Lock and Co., n.d.

————. *"Olive" and "The Half-Caste."* Oxford: Oxford University Press, 1996.

Dante Alghieri. *The Divine Comedy.* Trans. Charles S. Singleton. Princeton: Princeton University Press, 1973.

Dixon, Ella Hepworth. *The Story of a Modern Woman.* London: Merlin Press, 1990.

Eliot, George. *Adam Bede.* New York: New American Library, 1961.

————. "Belles Lettres." *The Westminster Review* 11 (1857): 306–26.

————. *Daniel Deronda.* Ed. Terence Cave. Harmondsworth, Middlesex, England: Penguin, 1995.

————. *Essays of George Eliot.* Ed. Thomas Pinney. New York: Columbia University Press, 1963.

————. *Felix Holt, the Radical.* Harmondsworth, Middlesex, England: Penguin, 1972.

————. *Middlemarch: A Study of Provincial Life.* Harmondsworth, Middlesex, England: Penguin, 1964.

————. *The Mill on the Floss.* Harmondsworth, Middlesex, England: Penguin, 1981.

————. *Romola.* Ed. Dorothea Barrett. Harmondsworth, Middlesex, England: Penguin, 1996.

————. *The Writings of George Eliot Together with the Life by J. W. Cross.* Warwickshire Edition. 25 vols. Boston: Houghton Mifflin; Cambridge: Riverside Press, 1907–1909.

————. *The Yale Edition of the George Eliot Letters.* Ed. Gordon S. Haight. 7 vols. New Haven: Yale University Press, 1954.

Feuerbach, Ludwig. *The Essence of Christianity.* Trans. George Eliot. Buffalo, N.Y.: Prometheus Books, 1989.

Freud, Sigmund. *Sexuality and the Psychology of Love.* Ed. Philip Rieff. New York: Macmillan, 1963.

Fulgentius, Fabius Planciades. *Fulgentius the Mythographer.* Trans. Leslie George Whitbread. Columbus: Ohio State University Press, 1971.

Fuller, Margaret. *Woman in the Nineteenth Century and Kindred Papers Relating to the Sphere, Condition and Duties, of Woman.* Boston: John P. Jewett, 1855.

Grand, Sarah. *The Beth Book: Being a Study from the Life of Elizabeth Caldwell Maclure, a Woman of Genius.* 1898. Reprint, Bristol, England: Thoemmes Press, 1994.

Hawthorne, Nathaniel. *The Marble Faun; or, The Romance of Monte Beni.* Centenary Edition. Vol. 4. Ohio State University Press, 1968.

Hemans, Felicia. *Mrs. Felicia Hemans.* Chicago: M. A. Donohue, n.d.

Herodotus. *The History of Herodotus.* Trans. George Rawlinson. 2 vols. London: J. M. Dent and Son, 1910.

Hesiod. *Theogony, Works and Days, Shield.* Trans. Apostolos N. Athanassakis. Baltimore: Johns Hopkins University Press, 1983.

Hopkins, Gerard Manley, and Richard Watson Dixon. *The Correspondence of Gerard Manley Hopkins and Richard Watson Dixon.* Ed. Claude Colleer Abbott. London: Oxford University Press, 1935.

James, Henry. *The American.* In *Henry James: Novels, 1871–1880,* ed. William T. Stafford. Literary Classics of the United States. New York: Viking Press, 1983.

———. *The Tragic Muse.* In *Henry James: Novels, 1886–1890,* ed. Daniel Mark Fogel. New York: Library of America, 1989.

Jewsbury, Geraldine E. "The Civilisation of 'The Lower Orders.'" *Douglas Jerrold's Shilling Magazine* 6 (1847): 443–52.

———. *Constance Herbert.* 3 vols. London: Hurst and Blackett, 1855.

———. *The Half Sisters.* Ed. Joanne Wilkes. Oxford: Oxford University Press, 1994.

———. *The History of an Adopted Child.* New York: Harper & Brothers, 1853.

———. *Marian Withers.* 3 vols. London: Colburn and Company, 1851.

———. *Right or Wrong.* 2 vols. London: Hurst and Blackett, 1859.

———. *Selections from the Letters of Geraldine Endsor Jewsbury to Jane Welsh Carlyle.* Ed. Mrs. Alexander Ireland. London: Longmans, Green, and Company, 1892.

———. *The Sorrows of Gentility.* 2d ed. London: Chapman and Hall, 1864.

———. *Zoe: The History of Two Lives.* 3 vols. 1845. Reprint, New York: Garland Publishing, 1976.

Jewsbury, Maria Jane. *The Three Histories: The History of an Enthusiast, The History of a Nonchalant, The History of a Realist.* Boston: Perkins & Marvin, 1831.

Landon, Letitia Elizabeth. *Selected Writings.* Ed. Jerome J. McGann and Daniel Riess. Peterborough, Ont.: Broadview Press, 1997.

Nightingale, Florence. *"Cassandra" and Other Selections from "Suggestions for Thought."* Ed. Mary Poovey. New York: New York University Press, 1992.

Paston, George [Emily Morse Symonds]. *A Writer of Books*. Chicago: Academy Chicago Publishers, 1999.

Pausanias. *Guide to Greece*. Trans. Peter Levi. 2 vols. Harmondsworth, Middlesex, England: Penguin, 1971.

Ruskin, John. *The Queen of the Air, Being a Study of the Greek Myths of Cloud and Storm*. London: Smith, Elder, 1869.

————. *Sesame and Lilies*. Philadelphia: Henry Altemus, 1892.

Sand, George [Aurore Dudevant]. *Adriani*. Paris: Calmann-Lévy, Éditeurs, n.d.

————. *Consuelo* and *La Comtesse de Rudolstadt*. Ed. Simone Vierne and René Bourgeois. 3 vols. Les Éditions de l'Aurore, 1983–1991.

————. *Contes d'une grand-mère*. Ed. Philippe Berthier. 2 vols. Les Éditions de l'Aurore, 1982–1983.

————. *Elle et lui*. Ed. Thierry Bodin. Paris: Les Éditions de l'Aurore, 1986.

————. *Jeanne*. Ed. Simone Vierne. Paris: Les Éditions de l'Aurore, 1986.

————. *La Daniella*. Ed. Annarosa Poli. 2 vols. Paris: Éditions de l'Aurore, 1992.

————. *La petite Fadette*. Ed. Pierre Salomon and Jean Mallion. 2 vols. Paris: Éditions Garnier Frères, 1958.

————. *Lélia*. Ed. Béatrice Didier. 2 vols. Paris: Les Éditions de l'Aurore, 1987–1988.

————. *Les maîtres sonneurs*. Ed. Marie-Claire Bancquart. Paris: Éditions Gallimard, 1979.

————. *Letters of George Sand*. Trans. and ed. Raphaël Ledos de Beaufort. 3 vols. London: Ward and Downey, 1886.

————. *Lucrezia Floriani*. Ed. Georges Lubin. 1855. Reprint, Editions d'aujourd'hui, n.d.

————. *My Life*. Trans. and adapted by Dan Hofstadter. New York: Harper and Row, 1979.

————. *Théatre complet de George Sand*. 2 vols. Paris: Michel Levy Frères, 1866.

Sand, George, and Gustave Flaubert. *The George Sand–Gustave Flaubert Letters*. Trans. Aimee L. McKenzie. 1921. Reprint, Chicago: Academy Chicago, 1949.

Shelley, Percy Bysshe. *The Complete Poetical Works of Percy Bysshe Shelley*. Ed. Thomas Hutchinson. London: Oxford University Press, 1935.

————. *The Complete Works of Percy Bysshe Shelley*. Ed. Roger Ingpen and Walter E. Peck. 10 vols. New York: Gordian Press, 1965.

Staël, Mme Germaine de. *Corinne; or, Italy*. Trans. Isabel Hill. New York: A. L. Burt, n.d.

————. *Corinne, ou, l'Italie*. Ed. Simone Balayé. France: Éditions Gallimard, 1985.

————. *An Extraordinary Woman: Selected Writings of Germaine de Staël*. Trans. and ed. Vivian Folkenflik. New York: Columbia University Press, 1987.

————. *Madame de Staël on Politics, Literature, and National Character*. Trans. and ed. Morroe Berger. Garden City, N.Y.: Doubleday, 1964.

———. *Œuvres complètes de Madame la Baronne de Staël-Holstein.* 2 vols. Genève: Slatkine Reprints, 1967.

———. *Œuvres posthumes de Madame la Baronne de Staël-Holstein.* Genève: Slatkine Reprints, 1967.

Swedenborg, Emanuel. *The Delights of Wisdom Pertaining to Conjugial Love.* New York: American Swedenborg Society Printing and Publishing, 1909.

Tristan, Flora. *The London Journal of Flora Tristan, 1842; or, The Aristocracy and the Working Class of England.* [Trans. of *Promenades dans Londres.*] Trans. Jean Hawkes. London: Virago Press, 1982.

Virgil. *The Works of Virgil.* Trans. John Dryden. Oxford: Oxford University Press, 1932.

Ward, Mary Augusta. *The Case of Richard Meynell.* Vol. 16 of *The Writings of Mrs. Humphry Ward.* Westmoreland Edition. Boston: Riverside, 1911.

———. *Eleanor.* Vol. 10 of *The Writings of Mrs. Humphry Ward.* Westmoreland Edition. Boston: Riverside, 1911.

———. *Fenwick's Career.* Vol. 13 of *The Writings of Mrs. Humphry Ward.* Westmoreland Edition. Boston: Riverside, 1911.

———. *Helbeck of Bannisdale.* Vol. 9 of *The Writings of Mrs. Humphry Ward.* Westmoreland Edition. Boston: Riverside, 1911.

———. *The History of David Grieve.* Vols. 3 and 4 of *The Writings of Mrs. Humphry Ward.* Westmoreland Edition. Boston: Riverside, 1911.

———. *Lady Connie.* New York: Hearst's International Library Company, 1916.

———. *Lady Rose's Daughter.* Vol. 11 of *The Writings of Mrs. Humphry Ward.* Westmoreland Edition. Boston: Riverside, 1911.

———. *Miss Bretherton.* Vol. 8 of *The Writings of Mrs. Humphry Ward.* Westmoreland Edition. Boston: Riverside, 1911.

———. *Robert Elsmere.* Vols. 1 and 2 of *The Writings of Mrs. Humphry Ward.* Westmoreland Edition. Boston: Riverside, 1911.

———. *A Writer's Recollections.* 2 vols. New York: Harper, 1918.

Ward, Mary Augusta, ed. *The Life and Work of the Sisters Brontë.* 7 vols. New York: Harper, 1899–1900.

Wollstonecraft, Mary. *A Vindication of the Rights of Woman with Strictures on Political and Moral Subjects.* 1792. Facsimile reprint, New York: Garland Publishing, 1974.

Secondary Sources

Abel, Elizabeth, Marianne Hirsch, and Elizabeth Langland, eds. *The Voyage In: Fictions of Female Development.* Hanover: University Press of New England for Dartmouth College, 1983.

Adams, Kimberly VanEsveld. *Our Lady of Victorian Feminism: The Madonna in the Work of Anna Jameson, Margaret Fuller, and George Eliot.* Athens: Ohio University Press, 2000.

Ardis, Ann L. *New Women, New Novels: Feminism and Early Modernism.* New Brunswick, N.J.: Rutgers University Press, 1990.

————. "'Retreat with Honour': Mary Cholmondeley's Presentation of the New Woman Artist in *Red Pottage.*" In *Writing the Woman Artist: Essays on Poetics, Politics, and Portraiture,* ed. Suzanne W. Jones. Philadelphia: University of Pennsylvania Press, 1991.

Auerbach, Nina. *Woman and the Demon: The Life of a Victorian Myth.* Cambridge: Harvard University Press, 1982.

Barrett, Dorothea. *Vocation and Desire: George Eliot's Heroines.* London: Routledge, 1989.

Barry, Joseph. *Infamous Woman: The Life of George Sand.* Garden City, N.Y.: Doubleday, 1977.

Barthes, Roland. *Mythologies.* Trans. Annette Lavers. New York: Hill and Wang, 1972.

Baym, Nina. *Woman's Fiction: A Guide to Novels by and about Women in America, 1820–1870.* Ithaca, N.Y.: Cornell University Press, 1980.

Beauvoir, Simone de. *The Second Sex.* Trans. and ed. H. M. Parshley. New York: Random House, 1974.

Beebe, Maurice. *Ivory Towers and Sacred Founts: The Artist Hero in Fiction from Goethe to Joyce.* New York: New York State University Press, 1964.

Beer, Gillian. *Darwin's Plots: Evolutionary Narrative in Darwin, George Eliot, and Nineteenth-Century Fiction.* Cambridge: Cambridge University Press, 1983.

————. *George Eliot.* Brighton, Sussex: Harvester Press, 1986.

Bindslev, Anne M. *Mrs. Humphry Ward: A Study in Late-Victorian Feminine Consciousness and Creative Expression.* Stockholm: Almqvist and Wiksell International, 1985.

Blainey, Ann. *The Farthing Poet: A Biography of Richard Hengist Horne, 1802–84, a Lesser Literary Lion.* London: Longmans, 1968.

Blake, Kathleen. "*Armgart*—George Eliot on the Woman Artist." *Victorian Poetry* 18, no. 1 (1980): 75–79.

————. *Love and the Woman Question in Victorian Literature.* Totowa, N.J.: Barnes and Noble, 1983.

Blind, Mathilde. *George Eliot.* Boston: Little, Brown, 1910.

Bloom, Harold. *The Anxiety of Influence: A Theory of Poetry.* New York: Oxford University Press, 1973.

Blount, Paul G. *George Sand and the Victorian World.* Athens: University of Georgia Press, 1979.

Bonaparte, Felicia. *The Triptych and the Cross: The Central Myths of George Eliot's Poetic Imagination*. New York: New York University Press, 1979.

Booth, Alison. *Greatness Engendered: George Eliot and Virginia Woolf.* Ithaca, N.Y.: Cornell University Press, 1992.

——. "The Silence of Great Men: Statuesque Femininity and the Ending of *Romola*." In *Famous Last Words: Changes in Gender and Narrative Closure*, ed. Alison Booth. Charlottesville: University Press of Virginia, 1993.

Browning, Oscar. *Life of George Eliot*. London: Walter Scott, Limited, 1892.

Brownstein, Rachel M. *Becoming a Heroine: Reading about Women in Novels*. New York: Columbia University Press, 1994.

Calder, Jenni. *Women and Marriage in Victorian Fiction*. New York: Oxford University Press, 1976.

Chadwick, Whitney. *Women, Art, and Society*. London: Thames and Hudson, 1990.

Chase, Karen. *Eros and Psyche: The Representation of Personality in Charlotte Brontë, Charles Dickens, and George Eliot*. New York: Methuen, 1984.

Chodorow, Nancy. *The Reproduction of Mothering: Psychoanalysis and the Sociology of Gender*. Berkeley: University of California Press, 1978.

Cixous, Hélène. "The Laugh of the Medusa." In *New French Feminisms: An Anthology*, ed. Elaine Marks and Isabelle de Courtivron. New York: Schocken Books, 1981.

Clarke, Norma. *Ambitious Heights: Writing, Friendship, Love: The Jewsbury Sisters, Felicia Hemans, and Jane Welsh Carlyle*. London: Routledge, 1990.

Collister, Peter. "Marie Bashkirtseff in Fiction: Edmond de Goncourt and Mrs. Humphry Ward." *Modern Philology* 82 (1984): 53–69.

——. "Portraits of 'Audacious Youth': George Eliot and Mrs. Humphry Ward." *English Studies* 64 (1983): 296–317.

——. "Some Literary and Popular Sources for Mrs. Humphry Ward's *The History of David Grieve*." *Review of English Studies* 40, no. 158 (1989): 215–31.

Cooper, Helen. *Elizabeth Barrett Browning, Woman and Artist*. Chapel Hill: University of North Carolina Press, 1988.

Copeland, C. T. "George Eliot and Mrs. Humphry Ward." *North American Review* 154 (1892): 503–5.

Cunningham, Gail. *The New Woman and the Victorian Novel*. London: Macmillan Press, 1978.

Cunningham, A. R. "The 'New Woman Fiction' of the 1890's." *Victorian Studies* 17 (1973): 177–86.

David, Deirdre. "'Art's a Service': Social Wound, Sexual Politics, and *Aurora Leigh*." In *Critical Essays on Elizabeth Barrett Browning*, ed. Sandra Donaldson. New York: G. K. Hall, 1999.

————. *Fictions of Resolution in Three Victorian Novels:* North and South, Our Mutual Friend, Daniel Deronda. New York: Columbia University Press, 1981.

————. *Intellectual Women and Victorian Patriarchy: Harriet Martineau, Elizabeth Browning, George Eliot.* Ithaca, N.Y.: Cornell University Press, 1987.

Davis, Tracy C. *Actresses as Working Women: Their Social Identity in Victorian Culture.* London: Routledge, 1991.

DeCuir, André L. "Italy, England, and the Female Artist in George Eliot's 'Mr. Gilfil's Love Story.'" *Studies in Short Fiction* 29, no. 1 (1992): 67–76.

Dehon, Claire L. "*Corinne:* Une artiste heroine de Roman." *Nineteenth-Century French Studies* 6 (1980): 1–9.

DeJean, Jean. "Portrait of the Artist as Sappho." In *Germaine de Staël: Crossing the Borders,* ed. Madelyn Gutwirth, Avriel H. Goldberger, and Karyna Szmurlo. New Brunswick, N.J.: Rutledge, 1991.

Dennis, Barbara. *Elizabeth Barrett Browning: The Hope End Years.* Bridgend, Mid Glamorgan, Wales: Poetry Wales Press, 1996.

Dijkstra, Bram. *Idols of Perversity: Fantasies of Feminine Evil in Fin-de-Siècle Culture.* New York: Oxford University Press, 1986.

Donaldson, Sandra. "Elizabeth Barrett's Two Sonnets to George Sand." In *Critical Essays on Elizabeth Barrett Browning,* ed. Sandra Donaldson. New York: G. K. Hall, 1999.

Dowling, Linda. "The Decadent and the New Woman in the 1890's." *Nineteenth-Century Fiction* 33 (1979): 434–53.

Fasick, Laura. "Culture, Nature, and Gender in Mary Ward's *Robert Elsmere* and *Helbeck of Bannisdale.*" *The Victorian Newsletter* 83 (1993): 25–31.

Forster, Margaret. *Elizabeth Barrett Browning: The Life and Loves of a Poet.* New York: St. Martin's, 1988.

Foster, Shirley. *Victorian Women's Fiction: Marriage, Freedom, and the Individual.* Totowa, N.J.: Barnes and Noble, 1985.

Friedman, Susan Stanford. "Gender and Genre Anxiety: Elizabeth Barrett Browning and H. D. as Epic Poets." *Tulsa Studies in Women's Literature* 5, no. 2 (1986): 203–28.

Fryckstedt, Monica Correa. "Geraldine Jewsbury and *Douglas Jerrold's Shilling Magazine.*" *English Studies* 66 (1985): 326–37.

Frye, Northrop. *Anatomy of Criticism: Four Essays.* Princeton: Princeton University Press, 1957.

Gelpi, Barbara Charlesworth. "*Aurora Leigh:* The Vocation of the Woman Poet." *Victorian Poetry* 19, no. 1 (1981): 35–48.

Gilbert, Sandra M., and Susan Gubar. *The Madwoman in the Attic: The Woman Writer and the Nineteenth-Century Literary Imagination.* New Haven: Yale University Press, 1979.

Glover, Edward. "Victorian Ideas of Sex." In *Ideas and Beliefs of the Victorians: An Historic Revaluation of the Victorian Age,* ed. Harman Grisewood. New York: E. P. Dutton, 1966.

Godwin-Jones, Robert. "Consuelo's Travels: The German Connection." In *The Traveler in the Life and Works of George Sand,* ed. Tamara Alvarez-Detrell and Michael G. Paulson. Troy, N.Y.: Whitson, 1994.

Gordon, D. J., and John Stokes. "The Reference of *The Tragic Muse.*" In *The Air of Reality: New Essays on Henry James,* ed. John Goode. London: Methuen, 1972.

Gorham, Deborah. *The Victorian Girl and the Feminine Ideal.* Bloomington: Indiana University Press, 1982.

Gray, Beryl. "Power and Persuasion: Voices of Influence in *Romola.*" In *From Author to Text: Re-reading George Eliot's* Romola, ed. Caroline Levine and Mark W. Turner. Aldershot, Hants, England: Ashgate, 1998.

Grout, Donald Jay, and Hermine Weigel Williams. *A Short History of Opera.* 3d ed. New York: Columbia University Press, 1988.

Gutwirth, Madelyn. "*Corinne* and *Consuelo* as Fantasies of Immanence." *George Sand Studies* 8 (1986–1987): 21–27.

———. *Madame de Staël, Novelist: The Emergence of the Artist as Woman.* Urbana: University of Illinois Press, 1978.

———. "Mme de Staël's Debt to *Phèdre: Corinne.*" *Studies in Romanticism* 3 (1964): 161–76.

———. "Seeing *Corinne* Afresh." In *The Novel's Seductions: Staël's* Corinne *in Critical Inquiry,* ed. Karyna Szmurlo. Lewisburg, Pa.: Bucknell University Press, 1999.

———. *The Twilight of the Goddesses: Women and Representation in the French Revolutionary Era.* New Brunswick, N.J.: Rutgers University Press, 1992.

Haight, Gordon S. *George Eliot: A Biography,* New York: Oxford University Press, 1968.

Haight, Gordon S., ed. *A Century of George Eliot Criticism.* Boston: Houghton Mifflin, 1965.

"The Half Sisters: A Tale." Review of *The Half Sisters,* by Geraldine Jewsbury. *Douglas Jerrold's Shilling Magazine* 7 (1848): 367–74.

Hardy, Barbara. *The Novels of George Eliot: A Study in Form.* London: Athlone Press, 1959.

Hartley, J. M. "Geraldine Jewsbury and the Problems of the Woman Novelist." *Women's Studies International Quarterly* 2 (1979): 137–53.

Hayter, Alethea. *Mrs. Browning: A Poet's Work and Its Setting.* London: Faber and Faber, 1962.

Heilbrun, Carolyn G. *Reinventing Womanhood.* New York: W. W. Norton, 1979.

Hickok, Kathleen. "'New yet Orthodox': The Female Characters in *Aurora Leigh.*"

In *Critical Essays on Elizabeth Barrett Browning*, ed. Sandra Donaldson. New York: G. K. Hall, 1999.

Himmelfarb, Gertrude. *The De-moralization of Society: From Victorian Virtues to Modern Values.* New York: Alfred A. Knopf, 1995.

―――. *Victorian Minds.* New York: Harper and Row, 1970.

Hirsch, Marianne. "Spiritual Bildung: The Beautiful Soul as Paradigm." In *The Voyage In: Fictions of Female Development,* ed. Elizabeth Abel, Marianne Hirsch, and Elizabeth Langland. Hanover: University Press of New England, 1983.

Holloway, John. *The Victorian Sage: Studies in Argument.* New York: W. W. Norton, 1965.

Holmes, Alicia E. "Elizabeth Barrett Browning: Construction of Authority in *Aurora Leigh* by Rewriting Mother, Muse, and Miriam." *The Centennial Review* 36, no. 3 (1992): 593–606.

Homans, Margaret. *Bearing the Word: Language and Female Experience in Nineteenth-Century Women's Writing.* Chicago: University of Chicago Press, 1986.

Hoog, Marie-Jacques. "George Sand and the Romantic Sibyl." In *The World of George Sand,* ed. Natalie Datlof, Jeanne Fuchs, and David A. Powell. Hofstra University Contributions in Women's Studies no. 122. New York: Greenwood, 1991.

Houston, Gail Turley. "Gender Construction and the *Kunstlerroman: David Copperfield* and *Aurora Leigh.*" *Philological Quarterly* 72, no. 2 (1993): 213–36.

Howe, Susanne. *Geraldine Jewsbury: Her Life and Errors.* London: G. Allen and Unwin, 1935.

Howells, William Dean. *Heroines of Fiction.* 2 vols. New York: Harper and Brothers Publishers, 1901.

Hudd, Louise. "The Politics of a Feminist Poetics: 'Armgart' and George Eliot's Critical Response to *Aurora Leigh.*" In *Poetry and Politics: Essays and Studies, 1996,* ed. Kate Flint. Cambridge, England: D. S. Brewer, 1996.

Huf, Linda. *A Portrait of the Artist as a Young Woman: The Writer as Heroine in American Literature.* New York: Ungar, 1983.

Ingram, Angela, and Daphne Patai, eds. *Rediscovering Forgotten Radicals: British Women Writers, 1889–1939.* Chapel Hill: University of North Carolina Press, 1993.

Jack, Belinda. *George Sand: A Woman's Life Writ Large.* New York: Alfred A. Knopf, 2000.

James, Henry. *Partial Portraits.* London: Macmillan, 1911.

James, Lawrence. *The Rise and Fall of the British Empire.* New York: St. Martin's Press, 1994.

Jameson, Anna. *Legends of the Madonna as Represented in the Fine Arts.* Boston: Ticknor and Fields, 1864.

Kadish, Doris Y. "Narrating the French Revolution: The Example of *Corinne.*" In *Germaine de Staël: Crossing the Borders,* ed. Madelyn Gutwirth, Avriel Goldberger, and Karyna Szmurlo. New Brunswick, N.J.: Rutgers University Press, 1991.

Kaplan, Cora. Introduction to *"Aurora Leigh" and Other Poems,* by Elizabeth Barrett Browning. London: Women's Press, 1978.

Knoepflmacher, U. C. *George Eliot's Early Novels: The Limits of Realism.* Berkeley: University of California Press, 1968.

———. "Mutations of the Wordsworthian Child of Nature." In *Nature and the Victorian Imagination,* ed. U. C. Knoepflmacher and G. B. Tennyson. Berkeley: University of California Press, 1977.

Leicht, Kathleen. "The Voice of the Artist in *Daniel Deronda.*" *Publications of the Missouri Philological Association* 22 (1997): 1–7.

Leighton, Angela. *Elizabeth Barrett Browning.* Bloomington: Indiana University Press, 1986.

———. *Victorian Women Poets: Writing against the Heart.* Charlottesville: University Press of Virginia, 1992.

Levine, George. "George Eliot's Hypothesis of Reality." *Nineteenth-Century Fiction* 35, no. 1 (1980): 1–28.

Lewes, George Henry. "The Lady Novelists." *The Westminster Review* 58 (1852): 129–41.

———. *On Actors and the Art of Acting.* New York: Grove Press, 1957.

Lewis, Linda M. *Elizabeth Barrett Browning's Spiritual Progress: Face to Face with God.* Columbia: University of Missouri Press, 1998.

Loeffelholz, Mary. "'In Place of Strength': Elizabeth Barrett Browning's Psyche Translations." *Studies in Browning and His Circle* 19 (1991): 66–75.

Lovesey, Oliver. "The Other Woman in *Daniel Deronda.*" *Studies in the Novel* 30, no. 4 (1998): 505–20.

Lukacher, Maryline. "Consuelo ou la défaite politique de la femme." *George Sand Studies* 12, no. 1–2 (1993): 36–45.

Manuel, Frank E. *The Prophets of Paris: Turgot, Condorcet, Saint-Simon, Fourier, and Comte.* New York: Harper and Row, 1962.

Markus, Julia. *Dared and Done: The Marriage of Elizabeth Barrett and Robert Browning.* New York: Alfred A. Knopf, 1995.

Marshall, Gail. "Actresses, Statues, and Speculation in *Daniel Deronda.*" *Essays in Criticism* 44, no. 2 (1994): 117–39.

McGowan, John P. "The Turn of George Eliot's Realism." *Nineteenth-Century Fiction* 35, no. 2 (1980): 171–92.

Merchant, Carolyn. *The Death of Nature: Women, Ecology, and the Scientific Revolution.* New York: Harper and Row, 1980.

Michie, Helena. *The Flesh Made Word: Female Figures and Women's Bodies.* New York: Oxford University Press, 1987.

Miller, Nancy K. "Performances of the Gaze: Staël's *Corinne, or Italy.*" In *The Novel's Seductions: Staël's* Corinne *in Critical Inquiry,* ed. Karyna Szmurlo. Lewisburg, Pa.: Bucknell University Press, 1999.

Mintz, Alan. *George Eliot and the Novel of Vocation.* Cambridge: Harvard University Press, 1978.

Moers, Ellen. *Literary Women.* Garden City, N.Y.: Doubleday, 1976.

Mulvey, Laura. *Visual and Other Pleasures.* Bloomington: Indiana University Press, 1989.

Murphy, Patricia. "Reconceiving the Mother: Deconstructing the Madonna in *Aurora Leigh.*" *The Victorian Newsletter* 91 (1997): 21–27.

Naginski, Isabelle Hoog. *George Sand: Writing for Her Life.* New Brunswick, N.J.: Rutgers University Press, 1991.

———. "Germaine de Staël among the Romantics." In *Germaine de Staël: Crossing the Borders,* ed. Madelyn Gutwirth, Avriel Goldberger, Karyna Szmurlo. New Brunswick, N.J.: Rutgers University Press, 1991.

Neumann, Erich. *Amor and Psyche: The Psychic Development of the Feminine. A Commentary on the Tale by Apuleius.* 1956. Reprint, London: Routledge, 1999.

Newton, Judith Lowder. *Women, Power, and Subversion: Social Strategies in British Fiction, 1778–1860.* New York: Methuen, 1981.

Oliphant, Margaret. "Two Cities, Two Books." *Blackwood's Edinburgh Magazine* 116 (1874): 72–91.

Olson, Paul A. *The Journey to Wisdom: Self-Education in Patristic and Medieval Literature.* Lincoln: University of Nebraska, 1995.

Pater, Walter. *Essays on Literature and Art.* Ed. Jennifer Uglow. London: J. M. Dent and Sons, 1973.

Peel, Ellen, and Nanora Sweet. "*Corinne* and the Woman as Poet in England: Hemans, Jewsbury, and Barrett Browning." In *The Novel's Seductions: Staël's* Corinne *in Critical Inquiry,* ed. Karyna Szmurlo. Lewisburg, Pa.: Bucknell University Press, 1999: 204–20.

Pratt, Annis. *Dancing with Goddesses: Archetypes, Poetry, and Empowerment.* Bloomington: Indiana University Press, 1994.

Prévost, Maxime. "Portrait de la femme auteur en cantatrice: George Sand et Marceline Desbordes-Valmore." In *Masculin/féminin: Le XIXe siècle à l'épreuve du genre,* ed. Chantal Bertrand-Jennings. Toronto: Centre d'études du XIXe siècle Joseph Sablé, St. Michael's College, 1999.

Redinger, Ruby V. *George Eliot: The Emergent Self.* London: Bodley Head, 1975.

Rich, Adrienne. *Of Woman Born: Motherhood as Experience and Institution.* New York: W. W. Norton, 1986.

Rosen, Judith. "At Home upon a Stage: Domesticity and Genius in Geraldine Jewsbury's *The Half Sisters* (1848)." In *The New Nineteenth Century: Feminist Readings of Underread Victorian Fiction*, ed. Barbara Leah Harman and Susan Meyer. New York: Garland Publishing, 1996.

Rosenblum, Dolores. "Face to Face: Elizabeth Barrett Browning's *Aurora Leigh* and Nineteenth-Century Poetry." *Victorian Studies* 26, no. 3 (1983): 321–38.

Rosowski, Susan J. "The Novel of Awakening." *Genre* 12 (1983): 379–402.

Sadoff, Dianne F. *Monsters of Affection: Dickens, Eliot, and Bronte on Fatherhood*. Baltimore: Johns Hopkins University Press, 1982.

Scheinberg, Cynthia. "Elizabeth Barrett Browning's Hebraic Conversions: Feminism and Christian Typology in *Aurora Leigh*." In *Critical Essays on Elizabeth Barrett Browning*, ed. Sandra Donaldson. New York: G. K. Hall, 1999.

Schor, Naomi. *George Sand and Idealism*. New York: Columbia University Press, 1993.

Seybert, Gislinde. "George Sand, *Consuelo, La Comtesse de Rudolstadt*: A Woman on the Road between Violence and Desire." In *The Traveler in the Life and Works of George Sand*, ed. Tamara Alvarez-Detrell and Michael G. Paulson. Troy, N.Y.: Whitston, 1994.

Showalter, Elaine. "The Greening of Sister George." *Nineteenth-Century Fiction* 35, no. 2 (1980): 292–311.

———. *A Literature of Their Own: British Women Novelists from Brontë to Lessing*. Expanded ed. Princeton: Princeton University Press, 1999.

———. *Sexual Anarchy: Gender and Culture at the Fin de Siècle*. New York: Viking Penguin, 1990.

Simon, Henry W., ed. *The Victor Book of the Opera*. 13th ed. New York: Simon and Schuster, 1968.

Simpson, Shona Elizabeth. "Mapping *Romola*: Physical Space, Women's Place." In *From Author to Text: Re-reading George Eliot's* Romola, ed. Caroline Levine and Mark W. Turner. Aldershot, Hants, England: Ashgate, 1998.

Slater, Philip E. *The Glory of Hera: Greek Mythology and the Greek Family*. Boston: Beacon Press, 1968.

Sourian, Eve. "Madame de Staël and George Sand." In *George Sand Papers: Conference Proceedings, 1978* (Hofstra University), ed. Natalie Datlof et al. New York: AMS Press, 1978.

Spacks, Patricia Meyer. *The Female Imagination*. New York: Alfred A. Knopf, 1975.

Srebrnik, Patricia Thomas. "The Central Truth": Phallogocentrism in *Aurora Leigh*." *The Victorian Newsletter* 84 (1993): 9–11.

Stephenson, Glennis. "'Bertha in the Lane': Elizabeth Barrett Browning and the Dramatic Monologue." *Browning Society Notes* 16 (1986–1987): 3–9.

———. *Elizabeth Barrett Browning and the Poetry of Love*. Ann Arbor: UMI Research Press, 1989.

Stewart, Grace. *A New Mythos: The Novel of the Artist as Heroine, 1877–1977*. St. Albans, Vt.: Eden Press, 1979.

Stone, Carole. "George Eliot's *Daniel Deronda:* 'The Case-History of Gwendolen H.'" *Nineteenth Century Studies* 7 (1993): 57–67.

Stone, Marjorie. *Elizabeth Barrett Browning*. New York: St. Martin's Press, 1995.

Surridge, Lisa. "Madame de Staël Meets Mrs. Ellis: Geraldine Jewsbury's *The Half Sisters*." *Carlyle Studies Annual* 15 (1995): 81–95.

Sutherland, John. "The Underread." Foreword to *The New Nineteenth Century: Feminist Readings of Underread Victorian Fiction*, ed. Barbara Leah Harman and Susan Meyer. New York: Garland Publishing, 1996.

———. *Mrs. Humphry Ward: Eminent Victorian, Pre-eminent Edwardian*. New York: Oxford University Press, 1990.

———. *The Stanford Companion to Victorian Fiction*. Stanford, Calif.: Stanford University Press, 1989.

Taylor, Barbara. *Eve and the New Jerusalem: Socialism and Feminism in the Nineteenth Century*. New York: Pantheon Books, 1983.

Thesing, William R., and Stephen Pulsford. *Mrs. Humphry Ward (1851–1920): A Bibliography*. Victorian Fiction Research Guides no. 13. St. Lucia, Australia: University of Queensland, 1987.

Thompson, Andrew. *George Eliot and Italy: Literary, Cultural, and Political Influences from Dante to the Risorgimento*. London: Macmillan Press, 1998.

Thomson, Patricia. *George Sand and the Victorians: Her Influence and Reputation in Nineteenth-Century England*. New York: Columbia University Press, 1977.

Trevelyan, Janet Penrose. *The Life of Mrs. Humphry Ward*. London: Constable, 1923.

Uglow, Jennifer. *George Eliot*. New York: Virago/Pantheon, 1987.

Vallois, Marie-Claire. *Fictions féminines: Mme de Staël et les voix de la Sibylle*. Saratoga, Calif.: Anma Libri, 1987.

Vitaglione, Daniel. *George Eliot and George Sand*. New York: Peter Lang, 1993.

Walsh, Susan. "'Doing the Afra Behn': Barrett Browning's Portrait of the Artist." *Victorian Poetry* 36, no. 2 (1998): 163–86.

Warner, Marina. *From the Beast to the Blonde: On Fairy Tales and Their Tellers*. New York: Noonday Press, 1994.

———. *Monuments and Maidens: The Allegory of the Female Form*. London: Weidenfeld and Nicholson, 1985.

Weliver, Phyllis. *Women Musicians in Victorian Fiction, 1860–1900: Representations of Music, Science, and Gender in the Leisured Home*. Aldershot, England: Ashgate, 2000.

Welsh, Alexander. *George Eliot and Blackmail.* Cambridge: Harvard University Press, 1985.

Wiesenfarth, Joseph. *George Eliot's Mythmaking.* Heidelberg: Carl Winter, 1977.

Wilkes, Joanne. *Lord Byron and Madame de Staël: Born for Opposition.* Aldershot, England: Ashgate, 1999.

Wilt, Judith. "'Transition Time': The Political Romances of Mrs. Humphry Ward's *Marcella* and *Sir George Thessady.*" In *The New Nineteenth Century: Feminist Readings of Underread Victorian Fiction,* ed. Barbara Leah Harman and Susan Meyer. New York: Garland Publishing, 1996.

Woolf, Virginia. "George Eliot." *Times Literary Supplement,* November 20, 1919: 657–58.

———. "Geraldine and Jane." *Times Literary Supplement,* February 28, 1929: 1–2.

———. *Virginia Woolf: Women and Writing.* Ed. Michèle Barrett. New York: Harcourt Brace Jovanovich, 1979.

Yeldham, Charlotte. *Women Artists in Nineteenth-Century France and England.* 2 vols. New York: Garland Publishing, 1984.

Young, G. M. *Victorian England: Portrait of an Age.* 2d ed. London: Oxford University Press, 1960.

Zimmerman, Bonnie. "George Eliot's Sacred Chest of Language." In *Famous Last Words: Changes in Gender and Narrative Closure,* ed. Alison Booth. Charlottesville: University Press of Virginia, 1993.

———. "Gwendolen Harleth and 'The Girl of the Period.'" In *George Eliot: Centenary Essays and an Unpublished Fragment,* ed. Anne Smith. Shepperton, Middlesex, England: Vision Press, 1980.

Zonana, Joyce. "The Embodied Muse: Elizabeth Barrett Browning's *Aurora Leigh* and Feminist Poetics." *Tulsa Studies in Women's Literature* 8, no. 2 (1989): 241–62.

INDEX